POLITICIANS AT WAR

POLITICIANS AT WAR
July 1914 to May 1915

*A prologue to the triumph of
Lloyd George*

CAMERON HAZLEHURST

Jonathan Cape Thirty Bedford Square London

FIRST PUBLISHED 1971
© 1971 BY CAMERON HAZLEHURST

JONATHAN CAPE LTD, 30 BEDFORD SQUARE, LONDON WC1

ISBN 0 224 61863 6

PRINTED IN GREAT BRITAIN
BY BUTLER & TANNER LTD, LONDON AND FROME

Contents

214793

6 CONTENTS

Acknowledgments

During the eight years since I began to study the history of the Asquith premiership, I have been guided and sustained by many people. My research could not have been completed without the support of Monash University, which awarded me a Travelling Scholarship in 1965, and of Nuffield College, Oxford, whose Warden and Fellows elected me to a Studentship in 1966 and a Research Fellowship in 1968.

I am indebted to Frances, Countess Lloyd-George of Dwyfor who has read several drafts of this work and answered many questions about the men and events of the first world war; and to Mrs Judy Gendel and the Hon. Mark Bonham Carter for allowing me to consult and quote from transcripts of the letters of H. H. Asquith to Venetia Stanley. I have also been privileged to receive information and reminiscences from Sir Richard Acland Bt, the late Sir Alan Barlow Bt, Sir Felix Brunner Bt, Lady Burke, the Baron Cawley, the late Hon. Randolph S. Churchill, Dame Margery Corbett Ashby, Mr R. H. Davies, the late Hon. Mrs Cecilia Dawson, Lady Duff, Mr Douglas Duff, Sir John Elliot, Miss M. Glyn-Jones, Sir Horace Hamilton, Miss Anne Holt, Professor J. H. Jones, Mrs Lucy Masterman, the Hon. Joseph Pease, the Baron Rea, the Hon. Sir Steven Runciman, Margaret, Viscountess Stansgate, Mrs Hugh McKinnon Wood, Sir Philip Magnus Bt, and Sir Harry Verney Bt.

Although every effort has been made to trace the holders of the copyright in the letters and other documents which are quoted in this book, the search has in some cases been unsuccessful. I trust that anyone whose copyright has been unwittingly infringed will accept sincere apologies. For permission to quote from documents whose copyright they control, I am grateful to Her Majesty the Queen; Sir Richard Acland Bt; the Earl of Balfour; Beaverbrook

Newspapers Ltd and the Beaverbrook Foundations; the Earl of Birkenhead; the Librarian, the University of Birmingham; C. & T. Publications Ltd; the Curators of the Bodleian Library; the Hon. Mark Bonham Carter; the Trustees of the British Museum; Churchill College, Cambridge; Mrs Elizabeth Clay; Mrs Pauline Dower; Lady Duff; Mr Douglas Duff; Mrs Judy Gendel; the Earl Haig; the Viscount Harcourt; Sir Geoffrey Harmsworth Bt; the Controller of Her Majesty's Stationery Office; Miss Anne Holt; Mr Henry Illingworth; the Marquess of Lansdowne; the Viscount Long of Wraxall; Mr J. H. MacCallum Scott; Mr David McKenna; Mrs H. McKinnon Wood; Mr J. C. Medley; Mr Edward Milligan; the National Library of Scotland; the National Library of Wales; Mr J. G. Osborne; the Hon. Joseph Pease; the Baron Ponsonby of Shulbrede; the Viscount Runciman of Doxford and the Hon. Sir Steven Runciman; the Hon. Godfrey Samuel; the Viscount Scarsdale; Mr Laurence Scott; Mrs Joan Simon; the Viscount Simon; the Viscountess Stansgate; Mr H. A. Taylor; Mr A. F. Thompson; the West Sussex Record Office; and Major Cyril Wilson.

The unpublished theses of Dr Michael Dockrill, Dr Nicholas d'Ombrain, Dr A. J. Dorey, Dr Michael Ekstein, Dr James Lindsay, Dr Howard Moon, Dr Keith Robbins, Dr Neil Summerton, and Professor Trevor Wilson have kindly been lent to me by their authors; and I have learnt much from Mr Martin Gilbert's forthcoming volume of the biography of Sir Winston Churchill covering the period July 1914 to December 1916 which Mr Gilbert has shown me in typescript.

Many professional colleagues and friends have read the various drafts through which this book has passed. Mr A. J. P. Taylor, Mr Robert Blake, and Mr Martin Gilbert have scrutinized the text several times, and have often discussed the problems of the period with me. My debt to them extends far beyond the improvements they have helped me to make in this book. I have also received many valuable criticisms and suggestions from Miss Rosemary Brooks, Dr David Cuthbert, Mr Bill Kent, Mrs Dale Kent, Mr David Machin, Mr Ross McKibbin, Dr Austin Mitchell, Dr Kenneth Morgan, Mr Maurice Shock, Dr Zara Steiner, Mr Ed. Victor, Mr Philip Williams and Mr Keith Wilson. Dr Peter Corris and Mrs Christine Woodland have generously brought fresh, keen eyes to the reading of the proofs. The book was typed, and patiently re-typed, by my former secretary, Mrs Sue Lloyd.

My wisest counsellor throughout the years in which we have worked together has been my wife. What I owe to her as the bearer of the real burdens created by the writing of this book I cannot begin to adequately acknowledge.

I dedicate the book to my parents with affection and respect.

Nuffield College, Oxford   CAMERON HAZLEHURST
17 *April* 1970

TO MY PARENTS

Politicians at War is the first of three volumes on British politics from July 1914 to December 1916. In the subsequent volumes – *The Crisis of Liberalism* and *The Triumph of Lloyd George* – the great controversies and conflicts of the second half of 1915 and the whole of 1916 will be chronicled. This book deals with the first nine months of war. It examines in detail how and why Britain declared war on Germany. It illustrates some of the political developments of the autumn and winter of 1914–15, and investigates the coming of coalition in May 1915.

Introduction

'A vast fog of information envelops the fatal steps to Armageddon,'
Winston Churchill wrote nearly forty years ago. 'But in this cloud
of testimony the few gleaming points of truth are often successfully obscured.' In the first part of this book an attempt is made to
penetrate the fog and explain the making of Britain's decision for
war in August 1914.

I have not focused attention on the stream of telegrams and
dispatches accumulated in the Foreign Office. Generations of
diplomatic historians have ransacked the *British Documents on the
Origins of the War*. Scholars currently at work are exploring the
unpublished Foreign Office papers. But, in spite of the many
biographies and monographs that are now available, there has
never been a systematic and comprehensive inquiry into the arena
of political decision-making in July and August 1914.

This study is based on the 'vast fog of information' to which
Churchill referred, and on the immense quantities of printed
material which have subsequently appeared. In addition, I have
consulted the available private papers of all the principal participants in the crisis. Among the sources used are several collections
of ministers' papers that have not previously been accessible to
students of the outbreak of war: the diaries and correspondence of
J. A. Pease; the papers of Sir Winston Churchill; the Lloyd George
papers; the Edwin Montagu papers; the papers of Walter Runciman; of Herbert Samuel; and of Sir Charles Trevelyan and Sir
Francis Acland.

The Pease diary contains the only detailed contemporary account
of cabinet proceedings in 1914 and 1915 which has yet come to
light. Together with Herbert Samuel's letters to his wife, and H.
H. Asquith's letters to Venetia Stanley, it is an invaluable supplement and corrective to Lord Morley's *Memorandum on Resignation*,

and the memoirs of the leading personalities. In examining the activities and opinions of the government's supporters in the House of Commons, the diaries of Richard Holt and Alexander MacCallum Scott, and the correspondence of T. E. Harvey, have greatly enriched the store of information already accessible.

Collation of the new evidence with the old has suggested a number of revisions in the accepted notions of how the cabinet came to take its decisions for war. The cherished belief that an unexpected attack on neutral and helpless Belgium alone persuaded the majority of the cabinet to take the field against Germany can be shown to be inconsistent with the evidence of discussions in private and in cabinet. Most ministers, including Lloyd George, were more realistic but less candid than they allowed themselves to appear. In addition, the picture of a cabinet divided into a doggedly pacific bloc and a patient, honourable minority which wished to uphold treaty obligations and preserve British interests does not withstand close scrutiny. There were many waverers; and, by investigating the various causes of their indecision and the way in which Asquith brought most of them to the point of resolution, it is possible to construct a more credible version of Britain's drift to commitment.

A better understanding of the behaviour of Asquith and his colleagues in July and August 1914 provides a basis for exploring the peculiar and testing conditions of war politics, and for demonstrating how mistaken is the view that the outbreak of war 'abolished in an instant the inter-party hatreds which had preceded it'. Pre-war animosities were not quickly forgotten. And the frustration of patriotic opposition added fresh strains to the suppressed Irish, Welsh, and other issues that formerly had aroused passionate controversy. But, with the exception of Dr Robbins's excellent unpublished study of the radicals and pacifists, and of Dr Wilson's sparsely documented survey of the wartime history of the Liberal Party, there has been little recent scholarly investigation of British politics in the first months of the war.

In broad outline, as well as in fine detail, the military history of the war is well known. Strategy — the development of deadlock in the west and the origins of the Dardanelles campaign, especially — has not lacked its historians. And Lord Hankey's massive volumes have told us much about the formal organization of *The*

Supreme Command, military and political. But, beneath the surface of events, unpredictable alignments and upheavals were germinating.

Lord Beaverbrook's enthralling tales of olympian intrigue and ambition have never been surpassed as authentic chronicles of high politics. But much remained obscured from Beaverbrook's alert eye; and even his assiduous accumulation of documents left much to be discovered by later investigators. Moreover, Beaverbrook's *Politicians and the War* is not a dispassionate analysis. Nor does it attempt to set the problems of Lloyd George and Asquith, Bonar Law and Lansdowne, in the context of parliamentary opinion and loyalties.

The politicians at war were constrained, and sometimes inspired, by the moods of the House of Commons. New political combinations could not come until the House was reconciled both to prolonged European conflict and the need, while the conflict lasted, to set aside the customary habits of opposition.

War changed the aims and prospects of many men. To David Lloyd George, it meant turning from the task of social amelioration, to which all his energies had been harnessed for eight years, and applying his mind to financing the allied cause. But his curiosity and concern quickly took him into fields far removed from traditional Treasury preserves.

Recruiting, strategy, the supply of munitions, industrial relations, the health and efficiency of the labour force, all fell within the range of the Chancellor of the Exchequer's restless intervention in the higher direction of the war. Why did Lloyd George involve himself so deeply in the effort to mobilize the nation for war? Referring to the Chancellor's plan for the state purchase of the liquor trade, Mr A. J. P. Taylor has written that this was 'the first of his many attempts to find an inspiring cause that would sweep him to national leadership'.

Accusations of consuming ambition have long lingered around Lloyd George's reputation. But evidence to substantiate the charges has been in short supply. In fact, there is no reason to suppose that Lloyd George was more interested in displacing Asquith than any of the Prime Minister's other colleagues. He wished to stimulate but not to oust his leader. It is also evident, when the documents are studied, that up to May 1915, Lloyd George the intriguer, coalitionist, and compulsionist exists only in gossip and fable.

Churchill, like Lloyd George, suffered from malicious rumour; and Haldane also found himself sacrificed to the Tory scandal-mongers who were too powerful to be bridled by their leaders. Yet, notwithstanding some contemporary suspicions that the fall of the Liberal government was engineered by conspirators led by Churchill and Lloyd George, the sudden creation of coalition in May 1915 was a product of forces over which neither of the supposed cabinet intriguers had control.

Coalition had been considered and rejected in August 1914. It was never out of mind as a possible means of eliminating the threat of a Conservative eruption. But coming secretly, and seemingly at the demand of the opposition, it angered Liberals. At the same time, Asquith's defiant endorsement of the principles which had hitherto governed the Liberal direction of the war only antagonized his prospective Conservative partners. The coalition settled little that was relevant except to destroy organized opposition. There remained to be decided what balance the nation would strike between its vaunted freedoms and the systematic, even compulsory, allocation of men and resources which the war demanded.

As the lines of political conflict emerged, so too would person-alities diverge. Tension long predicted between Lloyd George and his leader would at last precipitate a crisis of leadership. But by May 1915 only hints of such developments can be perceived. Lloyd George sought first to win the war, and for that purpose, if for no other, he was loyal to his chief. Unsuspected by most of his contemporaries and historians, timidity joined with patriotism in limiting his ambition.

Sixty years ago, propagandists for Britain's Liberal cabinet proclaimed that no finer body of men had ever governed the nation. In the generation after Gladstone and Salisbury, it was a bold claim. Yet, even the government's bitterest opponents admitted that H. H. Asquith and his colleagues were a formidable combination. And historians of later generations have not chal-lenged the almost unanimous judgment of contemporaries.

In 1914, the Prime Minister himself, aged sixty-two, was at the height of his powers. Sir Edward Grey, the Foreign Secretary,

enjoyed massive prestige and authority at home and abroad. At
the Treasury, David Lloyd George's social and financial reforms
had made him the most controversial figure in British politics.
Winston Churchill, as First Lord of the Admiralty, combined
executive and oratorical talents of the highest calibre.

After eight years of Liberal rule, some prominent members of
the Asquith cabinet were declining in influence and effectiveness
— Lord Haldane, Lord Morley, and John Burns, for example.
Others, like Lord Crewe, and Lewis ('Loulou') Harcourt, retained
reputations for sagacity for which their records in office provided
scant justification. But among the Prime Minister's colleagues, in
addition to the dominant personalities of Lloyd George, Grey,
and Churchill, there were a number of other men of outstanding
ability and promise. Reginald McKenna, though barely fifty years
old, had long established himself in the front rank of the government; after serving as President of the Board of Education, and
First Lord of the Admiralty, he was appointed Home Secretary in
1911. McKenna's closest ally in the cabinet was Walter Runciman,
the only one of Asquith's senior ministers with a background in
business. President of the Board of Agriculture from 1911,
Runciman moved to the Board of Trade in August 1914, where
his knowledge of the shipping industry was to prove a special
asset.

The rest of Asquith's ministers displayed diverse qualities and
aptitudes: Jack Pease's diligence and honesty, Augustine Birrell's
wit, Herbert Samuel's quiet mastery of the details as well as the
philosophy of Liberalism, all fitted them in different ways for
emollient or inspiriting roles in the Liberal team.

In so powerful a company, with Charles Masterman, Edwin
Montagu, Charles Trevelyan, Francis Acland, and Lord Beauchamp, still largely untested by any major administrative responsibility, no single figure among the younger ministers was clearly
marked as the man of the future. One man, perhaps more than
most, did seem to bask in the Premier's favour: the enigmatic and
ambitious Attorney-General, John Simon. In temperament and
ability, Simon was cast in an unmistakably Asquithian mould.

But, in the public eye, Lloyd George was the Prime Minister's
principal lieutenant, the most likely successor to the premiership
in the event of Asquith's sudden death or departure from politics.

In eight years of office, Lloyd George had left behind the local heroics of Welsh nationalism to become the champion of English radicalism, and the dominating practical expositor of the new Liberalism. Old friends, inevitably, were left along the way. Each personal advance or ameliorative social proposal created for the Chancellor fresh antagonisms and jealousies. The Liberal journalist Alfred Gardiner wrote in 1913 that in Conservative 'Society' hatred of Lloyd George had become 'a frame of mind, a free-masonry, a kind of eleventh commandment – unlike most commandments in the constancy with which it is observed'. Gardiner went on to say:

> To put him out of the firing line has become the first article of Conservative policy. Hence the extreme virulence of the Marconi campaign. His rather casual habit in his own affairs had laid him open to attack on a matter of judgment rather than of morals, and, owing to the fury of the storm that broke over him, he came perilously near disaster. He learned then how little mercy he has to expect if ever the battle goes against him.

Undogmatic, volatile, pugnacious on the platform, rejecting the embrace of London society, yet bewitching in private encounters, Lloyd George had a disturbing effect on his colleagues as well as on his adversaries. His dazzling successes – based so obviously on his own unaided talents – left an impression of boundless energy and vaulting ambition. It seemed somehow inconceivable that a man who, without family connection or educational privilege, had risen so far, should be satisfied with anything but the first place.

How could his bold impulses and visionary policies find full expression as long as he remained a subordinate? The premiership it seemed to many observers, must be his goal. 'Of course,' Margot Asquith assured a friend, 'you must never think I think LG disloyal to Henry. I think the very reverse, but I think he is at times a little too hasty in pushing things.'

In a long letter, written for the eyes of the Prime Minister alone, Edwin Montagu wrote a frank appraisal of Lloyd George at the end of May 1914. Montagu had served Asquith faithfully as parliamentary private secretary for several years. He had become a member of the Premier's intimate circle. Then, as Financial Secretary to the Treasury, he had become for a time Lloyd George's closest ministerial associate. Consumed by melancholy and introspection, Montagu strove to remain loyal to both his masters. He recognized their faults, but respected them for their virtues. Like Lord Reading, and Lord Murray of Elibank, he made his principal task in politics the strengthening of the vital partnership between the Prime Minister and the Chancellor. In the complementary abilities and aspirations of these two men, Montagu believed, lay the future of Liberalism. Of Lloyd George, Montagu wrote to Asquith:

> I believe him to be perfectly honest when he says, as he frequently does, that he never wishes to be Prime Minister. He wants to control the machine, and the policy of the machine, but he recognizes his own limitations. He has a reverence and a loyalty for you, and if the Party would let him, I think they would find genuinely that he would rather serve under almost anybody, provided he could be secured in the second place. He has never made any disguise of the fact to me that the Treasury is the wrong place for him. He feels, as every critic must feel, that his genius is not for departmental work, or for the details of complicated Acts of Parliament. He recognizes that the position of the Chancellor of the Exchequer is such that he could not get his way if another man was Chancellor, nor could he claim his coveted second place; but he hates the routine work, he loves big splashes of colour and particular principles ...

No two contemporary politicians of comparable prominence were more different in character, yet more dependent on each other, than Lloyd George and his chief. Where the impulsive Welshman seemed at times to make a profession of charming his most implacable foes, Asquith sought not the approbation of others but the certitude of keeping to his own course. Asquith's rise to the premiership had appeared inevitable for twenty years before he succeeded Campbell-Bannerman. Lucid, fluent, dexterous but powerful in debate, he was marked out from his earliest days at Westminster as the predestined favourite of the House of Commons. Alfred Spender, the Liberal editor and biographer of both Campbell-Bannerman and Asquith, wrote of Asquith's years in opposition: 'The one criticism of him was that with these remarkable gifts he suffered from a certain lethargy of temperament.'

Nevertheless, overcoming the initial suspicion of his more radical followers that he was an incorrigible Liberal imperialist, Asquith led the Liberal Party through a period of unprecedented legislative activity and constitutional upheaval. Old age pensions, national insurance, town planning, rural development, taxation of land values – advance was swift in social and economic policy. But to these reforms, and still more to Welsh Disestablishment, Home Rule for Ireland, and the abolition of plural voting, the Tories offered fierce resistance. It was a measure of Asquith's achievement that, after a series of cabinet wrangles and unyielding confrontations with the Unionist opposition, he had survived as premier for six years. But survival had its cost. He mastered the political scene; he could not win affection. Distant and abrupt of manner, except in the intimate company in which his mask of shyness dropped, he offended allies and infuriated enemies. He was, wrote a friendly journalist, 'neither an adventurer, nor a political gambler, nor an idealist … He has himself expressed his agreement with Pitt that the highest virtue of statesmanship is patience, and few men have shown a more abundant supply of that virtue in trying situations.'

In July 1914, an angry Tory critic presented a more savage view. Despairing that the nation was drifting into civil war over Ireland, L. S. Amery wrote anonymously in the *Quarterly Review*:

If we stand today on the brink of an appalling catastrophe it is due in no small measure to the fact that in a critical period the supreme power in the State has fallen into the hands of a man who combines unrivalled gifts of parliamentary leadership with a complete incapacity to face facts or to come to any decision upon them.

… There is a Mr Asquith of current legend – austere, unflinching, logical and lucid. Whatever substratum of fact may once have existed for these epithets, they have little application to the real Mr Asquith of the present day. His famed lucidity, it is true, still survives, in a sense, and still receives from his opponents in debate the customary homage of a banal compliment. But it is a lucidity of phrase alone, and not of thought, a lucidity which explains but never enlightens … For twenty years he has held a season ticket on the line of least resistance and has gone wherever the train of events has carried him, lucidly justifying his position at whatever point he has happened to find himself … And if Civil War should break out, as it well may, next month or the month after, he will still be found letting things take their course, and justifying himself with dignity, conciseness and lucidity till some impatient man of action among his colleagues decides to lock him up.

Part I Decision for War

1 Ireland and Armageddon

In the seventh year of his premiership, in the eighth month of the Great War, and a few weeks before his Liberal ministry was toppled, H. H. Asquith wrote a little play. The scene of the play was 'The Infernal Tribunal'; the characters, Rhadamanthus, and the self-released shade of the Prime Minister. Asquith addressed himself in the words of Rhadamanthus, like this:

> You were, in the world above, almost a classical example of *Luck* ... *Luck* helped you in external things—in unforeseen opportunities, in the disappearance of possible competitors, in the special political conditions of your time: above all (at a most critical and fateful moment in your career) in the sudden outbreak of the Great War.[1]

Few people greeted the first world war as a stroke of luck. Very few people needed as much luck as Asquith seemed to need in July 1914. The by-election record of the Liberal government was depressing. Its senior members had, at the beginning of the year, fought each other to the brink of resignation over naval estimates. Many of its parliamentary followers were restless for further instalments of social and political reform. Others resisted the rising spiral of naval expenditure; and a small number remonstrated against 'the ill-considered & socialistic tendencies of the Government finance'.[2] However great the achievements of the Asquith government, they were bought at heavy cost. The years of struggle for the People's Budget, the Parliament Act, and national insurance had been exhausting. Welsh Disestablishment and plural voting (not to speak of female suffrage which was a 'non-party' question) had done nothing to lower the political temperature;

[1] Roy Jenkins, *Asquith* (London, 1964), pp. 334-5.
[2] Richard Holt's Diary, 19 July 1914, Holt MSS.

and Irish Home Rule provoked opposition of unprecedented ferocity.

Over the government's Home Rule Bill, the Irish Nationalist leader, John Redmond, warned the Prime Minister that:

> ... if concessions were announced by the Government which I did not agree to, it would in my opinion, be my duty to vote against the second reading of the Bill, and I had reason to believe that, in that event, the great bulk of the Liberal Party and the whole of the Labour Party would vote with me.[1]

The King, at Asquith's request, summoned a conference at Buckingham Palace, at which representatives of the government and opposition, as well as Irish Nationalists and Unionists, might strive to reach agreement. The area of Ulster which might be excluded from the Bill and the period during which exclusion would last were scheduled for negotiation. A settlement of these points would enable an Amending Bill to be passed at the same time as the Home Rule Bill, excluding 'Ulster' from its area of operation, either permanently or temporarily. But the discussions were in vain. On July 24, after four fruitless days, they were abandoned.

Within the Liberal Party, Asquith's handling of the Irish problem encountered growing impatience and dissatisfaction. In the last weeks of peace, as Walter Runciman learnt from Charles Trevelyan, the government's stocks were slumping catastrophically:

> I have just been down to a gathering of Liberals from Halifax, Elland and Sowerby Bridge. I feel bound to tell you what I found. They were entirely faithful men. They did not use violent language. But they say that the whole of the Liberal working-class is on the point of revolt, that the prestige of the government is gone, and that the great mass of working-men think that the government is funking. They have never approved of leaving Carson alone, they were more angry about the gunrunning, and they are quite furious about the Conference.
>
> There is *no one at all* in favour of it. I have never seen such

[1] Memorandum by Redmond, 16 July 1914. Denis Gwynn, *The Life of John Redmond* (London, 1932), p. 335.

unanimity. Now the point is this. Half are wretched. Half think they are being tricked.

1.) Any further delay will mean a violent explosion of Liberal feeling which will be immediately reflected in the House. You ought not even to give two days for the second reading of the Amending Bill.

2.) So low has government stock fallen that the mere passing of the Bills under the Parliament Act won't at once revive Liberal feeling. The whole programme must be carried through or our people won't work at all. You must suppress Carson, if it becomes necessary, *without an election*. If you appeal to the country on Carson's rebellion without having taken the most drastic steps to suppress it, you won't have the support of the mass of working-men. They won't trust you to be strong if they gave you new power. They say you have it now if you choose to use it.

The long and the short of it is the government has got to show itself top dog *now*, or the Liberal Party will disintegrate, even in the West Riding. I know what I am talking about, and by this time I am not afraid of misjudging these people here.

You have got to go on till you are driven out by the King or by a complete and hopeless revolt in the army. If you don't you haven't a dog's chance of getting back to power.[1]

According to Cecil Beck, one of the party's abler young organizers and parliamentary private secretary to the Chief Whip, there was no disguising the fact that 'just now there is a slight rot in the party, & considerable distrust as to the intention of you folk who lead it'.[2] *The Manchester Guardian*'s lobby correspondent reported to his editor towards the end of July that 'The Liberal Party in the House with one or two honourable exceptions is at present engaged in trying to save its own skin.'[3] Ireland, defying solution, threatened to tear apart the Liberal Party, or the nation, or both. Meanwhile, organized labour was, in the words of Sidney and Beatrice Webb, 'working up for an almost revolutionary outburst

---

[1] Trevelyan to Runciman, 25 July 1914, Runciman MSS.
[2] Beck to Charles Masterman, 26 May 1914, Lloyd George MSS, C/5/15/5.
[3] G. H. Mair to C. P. Scott, 22 July 1914, *Manchester Guardian* MSS.

of gigantic industrial disputes'. An infectious spirit of working-class revolt found expression not only in the articulation of grievances against employers but in the rejection of the normal channels of redress. From midsummer, the miners, railwaymen, and transport workers gave notice of a united strike. The railwaymen wanted full union recognition, a 48-hour week, and a five-shilling wage increase; and the whole weight of the newly created 'Triple Alliance' backed their claim. To the menacing prospect of simultaneous strikes in the nation's vital industries there was no obvious political remedy. Legislation provided no solution. Conciliation and compromise were essential. Addressing an audience of City financiers and merchants at the Lord Mayor's annual Mansion House banquet on 17 July 1914, the Chancellor of the Exchequer, David Lloyd George, uttered words of solemn warning. If mass industrial action should coincide with civil strife over the fate of Ulster, 'the situation will be the gravest with which any Government in this country has had to deal for centuries'.

Earlier in the speech, referring to the clouds in the international sky, Lloyd George said, ' ... having got out of greater difficulties last year, we feel confident that the common sense, the patience, the goodwill, the forbearance which enabled us to solve greater and more difficult and more urgent problems last year, will enable us to pull through these difficulties at the present moment'.

Perhaps Lloyd George was too apprehensive about the domestic troubles. But there was a good reason for disquiet. The military members of the army council had warned the Prime Minister less than a fortnight earlier that the military strength of the nation was dangerously stretched. India, Egypt, and Europe were unsettled; and two to three hundred thousand men—Nationalist and Ulster volunteers—were under arms in Ireland. Simultaneous conflagrations in several places might at any moment place burdens upon the army which the military members were afraid it would be incapable of bearing.

The army council's paper had been prepared by Major-General Henry Wilson, the Director of Military Operations. As a dedicated Unionist and implacable enemy of Asquith and his 'pestilent Govt', Wilson was quite capable of exaggerating the danger of the situation in the hope of scaring the Prime Minister into concessions over Home Rule. Asquith was angered by the military members' presumption in submitting an unsolicited opinion on the military aspect of civil war.[1] But it was hardly surprising that the generals should have taken such a step. They addressed Asquith both as Prime Minister and as Secretary of State for War. Asquith had taken over the War Office at the end of March after the Curragh incident had raised the spectre of disloyalty among the English officers in Ulster. Although he was displeased by the army council's intrusion into affairs outside what he considered to be their legitimate province, Asquith does not seem to have been alarmed by their tone of foreboding. Indeed, he gave the impression at this time of confidently expecting a settlement of the Irish problem.

Asquith's handling of Irish affairs, seeming at times to be almost culpably nonchalant, was perhaps partly justified by the indifference of a large segment of the English electorate to Home Rule. In contrast to Charles Trevelyan's alarming tale of Liberal disaffection in the West Riding, Conservative leaders were receiving a very different picture. Arthur Steel-Maitland, the Conservative Party chairman, was convinced that:

> aversion to Home Rule will have an effect on a few leading individuals, but upon the mass of voters in England, this will be confined to very few strongly Protestant districts. As a general rule, however, there is no enthusiasm for it; very little more against it, and in some cases a tendency to tired acquiescence. Public opinion will need a great deal of rousing by ordinary methods.

Steel-Maitland's memorandum dealing with the 'Need for an Autumn Campaign' did concede that 'if the Bill is once passed and Ulster really does fight, the whole state of affairs will be greatly changed ... But until the national attention and conscience is so struck, or by some fact equally spectacular and convincing,' Steel-Maitland concluded, 'Home Rule is of little use as an electioneering Asset.'[2]

Nevertheless, the government took steps to ensure that neither fatigue nor indifference in the ranks of their supporters endangered the passage of the Home Rule Bill and the Amending Bill. The

[1] Henry Wilson's Diary, 30 June, 1, 4, and 10 July 1914, Wilson MSS.
[2] Steel-Maitland's Untitled Memorandum, (? June) 1914, Steel-Maitland MSS, GD 193/80/5.

Chief Whip, Percy Illingworth, circulated all Liberal M.P.s on July 13 with an appeal for a sustained effort and 'constant attendance and support for the remainder of the Session'.[1] Paradoxically, it was not parliamentary defeat which held most danger for the ministry. It was success itself, with all its anathemic implications for the Unionists, which was most likely to bring disaster.

Yet even if civil war or electoral disaster had been averted, Asquith and the Liberal government could scarcely have extricated themselves from the Irish situation without discredit. The danger of Asquith's doctrine of 'wait and see' was that those who waited sometimes saw; and what they saw they did not like.

There were times when what Mr A. P. Ryan has called Asquith's 'massive common sense and refusal to be stampeded into the excitement of the moment', were an undisputed asset. But there were other, and increasingly more frequent, occasions when imperturbability seemed only to veil poverty of inspiration or sheer paralysis of will. To an admiring colleague like Walter Runciman, the verdict of late June 1914 was that 'the P.M. is at the top of his fame and popularity.'[2] This, as we have seen, was a view which would not have passed unchallenged in some of the strongholds of local Liberalism. And, among men of decided Unionist persuasion, few politicians then or since have aroused more deeply felt antagonism than Asquith had cumulatively provoked after 1912. Professor A. V. Dicey, for example, wrote to Lord Milner on 9 May 1914:

> Asquith as a political leader is thoroughly untrustworthy. I know nothing of him personally ... but I have observed his public career with great care and I am certain that politics is to him a game on which his own reputation is staked, and which he plays with no great scrupulosity ... Asquith ... will not probably tell a direct lie, or escape from the effect of a promise unless he has already expressed it in language so ambiguous that he cannot be charged with indubitable breach of faith ... Hence the extreme danger of entering into private negotiations with him ... [3]

[1] Illingworth to Liberal M.P.s, 13 July 1914 ('Strictly Personal and Confidential' duplicated letter), Norman MSS.
[2] Runciman to Sir Robert Chalmers, 24 June 1914, Runciman MSS.
[3] A. M. Gollin, *Proconsul in Politics* (London, 1964), p. 221.

General Wilson, in language of uncharacteristic restraint, wrote despairingly a few weeks later: 'He doesn't understand anything about either the Army or Ulster.'[1] And on July 14, Wilson recorded in his diary: 'C.I.D. meeting today. I hope the last with Squiff & his filthy Cabinet present.'

It is clear that the bitter constitutional struggles of 1909 to 1914 had left a legacy of distrust for the Prime Minister in the minds of several men whose attitude to him was to be important in the months that followed.

Asquith seemed unruffled by the eruption of Europe. 'The marvellous calmness of the P.M. is our only natural asset,' Edwin Montagu informed his mother. 'Would that I could say the same of the Chancellor.'[2] Imminent civil conflict and industrial turmoil at home made a brisk little continental war tantalizingly convenient. As his confessional playlet hints, the intractability of the Irish problem rendered Asquith susceptible to an adventurous diversion across the Channel. There can be no doubting that his decision to stand by France and Belgium was consciously grounded on obligations of honour and calculations of national interest. But no account of the decision for war can be anything but incomplete if the looming presence of Ireland is forgotten.

There was scarcely an hour during the last weeks of peace when Ireland was totally excluded from the minds of Asquith and his colleagues. In a temporarily hopeful moment on July 25, for example, Asquith was asked by Lady Ottoline Morrell what would happen about Austria and Serbia. There was something more in the reply than the studied jocularity which Asquith often affected in feminine company: 'This will take the attention away from Ulster, which is a good thing.'[3] The Prime Minister laughed. Though he had admitted in his cabinet letter to the King a few hours earlier that the Austrian ultimatum to Serbia was the gravest event in European politics for many years, he seemed unperturbed.[4] News had been received in London that the Austrian ultimatum was not to be considered as an ultimatum but

[1] Wilson's Diary, 23 May 1914, Wilson MSS.
[2] Montagu to Lady Swaythling, 2 August 1914, Montagu MSS.
[3] Lady Ottoline Morrell's Journal, 25 July 1914. Robert Gathorne-Hardy (ed.), *Ottoline* (London, 1963), p. 258.
[4] J. A. Spender and Cyril Asquith, *Life of Herbert Henry Asquith, Lord Oxford and Asquith* 2 vols (London, 1932), vol. II, p. 80.

as 'a *démarche* with a time limit'.[1] And it is possible, but unlikely, that advance notice of Serbia's conciliatory reply had reached the Prime Minister at the Wharf, the Asquiths' Berkshire house. But when news of the Serbian capitulation was definite the next morning, Asquith was doubtful if Austria would be satisfied: ' ... it is the most dangerous situation of the last forty years. It may incidentally have the effect of throwing into the background the lurid pictures of civil war in Ulster.'[2] On July 29, Asquith again noted that the Amending Bill to the Home Rule Act and 'the whole Irish business' had been put into the shade by what he fatalistically described as 'the coming war'. Not until the 30th, after Bonar Law and Carson had taken the initiative, did Asquith put aside his map of Ulster, his files of population and religious statistics, and postpone the second reading of the Home Rule Amending Bill.[3] Cynical detachment gave way to concern. New priorities prevailed. But, even as the prospects of peace dwindled away, Asquith returned to the Irish theme. After dinner, and the inevitable rubber of bridge, on August 3, he remarked to J. A. Pease, his former Chief Whip and present President of the Board of Education, that 'the one bright spot in this hateful war, upon which we were about to enter, was the settlement of Irish strife and the cordial union of forces in Ireland in aiding the Government to maintain our supreme National interests'. There seemed to Asquith something providential about it. 'God moves in a mysterious way', he added, 'His wonders to perform.'[4]

[1] Communication from the Austrian Ambassador to Sir Edward Grey, 24 July 1914, printed as item No. 104 in G. P. Gooch and Harold Temperley (eds), *British Documents on the Origins of the War, 1898-1914* (London, 1926), pp. 83-4. This volume will be cited hereafter as *BDXI*.

[2] Asquith to Venetia Stanley, 26 July 1914, Montagu MSS, cited as a 'Contemporary Note' in the Earl of Oxford and Asquith, *Memories and Reflections, 1857-1927*, 2 Vols (London, 1928), vol. II, p. 6. The documents described in this volume and elsewhere as 'Contemporary Notes' were actually letters to Miss Stanley, as may be seen by comparing the slightly different text of a letter quoted in Roy Jeknins, op. cit., p. 352, with the 'Contemporary Note' of the same date quoted in *Memories and Reflections*, vol. II, p. 59.

[3] Asquith to Venetia Stanley, 27, 28 July 1914, Montagu MSS.

[4] Pease's Diary, 3 August 1914, Gainford MSS.

2 Dissent Disarmed

It would go beyond any permissible inference to suggest that as far as Asquith, or any of his colleagues, were concerned, the decision for war depended on domestic political calculations. At the same time, it must be said that Irish considerations, so precipitately interrupted, could not have been thrust below the threshold of consciousness. That the grave Irish situation should remain in the Prime Minister's mind was not only natural, but entirely proper. Nor is it surprising that Asquith should perceive domestic salvation in a war whose prospects were otherwise unrelievedly grim. But, if European war might avert civil war, and divert one militant section of the government's supporters, it could only exchange new problems for old. 'I suppose', Asquith wrote to Miss Stanley on August 2, 'a good ¾ of our own party in the House of Commons are for absolute non interference at any price. It will be a shocking thing if at such a moment we break up —with no one to take our place.'[1] Although he noted the danger, Asquith did little to deal with it directly. He had few contacts with the back benches, and this was not the time to try to repair the neglect of a decade. His strategy was, as always, to corral the cabinet. If the ministry held together, it would be both a proof and a guarantee that no wider rift would open.[2]

While Asquith fixed his attention on the problem of holding the cabinet together, there were powerful disruptive forces at work outside. For a week after the Austrian ultimatum to Serbia the radicals in Parliament were silent. Partly out of sheer bewilderment, and partly because they chose to allow the government an

[1] Asquith to Venetia Stanley, 2 August 1914, Montagu MSS. The 'Contemporary Note', 2 August 1914 (Earl of Oxford and Asquith, op. cit., vol. II, p. 9) omits the phrases 'at any price' and 'with no one to take our place', and includes the vague phrase 'a good number' instead of the more precise original 'a good ¾'.

[2] Spender and Asquith, op. cit., vol. II, p. 95.

unhampered area of manœuvre, they confined themselves to private discussions and representations. However, the Liberal press was under no restraint. J. A. Spender's *Westminster Gazette* and Robert Donald's *Daily Chronicle* were cautious. But C. P. Scott, A. G. Gardiner, and H. W. Massingham through *The Manchester Guardian*, *The Daily News*, and *The Nation*, insisted on British neutrality. Many leader-writers employed the characteristic device of contending that their own view represented not only the best interests of the country but the actual opinions of the majority of their fellow-countrymen. Thus on August 1, *The Nation* stated: 'There has been no crisis in which the public opinion of the English people has been so definitely opposed to war as it is at this present moment.' In the absence of positive evidence to the contrary, assessments of this kind could not lightly be dismissed by ministers eager for some guide to public feelings. *The Nation's* report, for example, was probably true when it was written. The war to which *The Nation* primarily addressed itself, and which Liberals would be expected to loathe, was war for the sake of Russia.

But by Sunday, August 2, it was impossible any longer to evade the fact that the real issue was Britain's role in a Franco-German conflict. *The Times* found in the Sunday papers 'an almost unanimous demand ... that England should fulfil the obligations which accompany our friendship with France'.[1] Still, however, there was hope and anxious searching for avenues to peace. As Richard Holt, Liberal M.P. for Hexham, wrote, expressing a common backbench opinion: ' ... it is almost impossible to believe that a Liberal Government can be guilty of the crime of dragging us into this conflict in which we are in no way interested.'[2] With such views widely held, and a tide of neutrality agitation already rising across the country, it might have seemed that all the conditions were ripe for a great anti-war crusade. Mr A. J. P. Taylor has spoken of a 'ready-made opposition' of two hundred M.P.s.[3] Who would be the members of this formidable band?

[1] *The Times*, 2 August 1914, (special eight-page Sunday edition). The best survey of British press comment on foreign affairs, from 29 June 1914 to 5 August 1914, is A. J. Dorey, 'Radical Liberal Criticism of British Foreign Policy, 1906–14' (unpublished Oxford D. Phil. thesis, 1964), pp. 411–36.

[2] Holt's Diary, 2 August 1914, Holt MSS.

[3] A. J. P. Taylor, '1914: Events in Britain', *The Listener*, 16 July 1964.

From December 1911 about eighty Liberals who were keenly interested in foreign affairs were organized in a private backbench group called the Liberal Foreign Affairs Committee. The driving forces behind the Committee were radical, and critical of both the direction and conduct of Grey's policy. After a surge of enthusiasm lasting through 1912, the Committee had lost a great deal of its impetus by 1914. Though remaining suspicious of British foreign and military policies, and especially hostile to the development of the entente with Russia, the radicals had warmed a little to Grey's handling of the Near East crisis in 1913. Anglo-German relations appeared thereafter to be on a better footing. The government had given assurances that there were no secret agreements which would restrict the nation's freedom of action in time of war. And with politics dominated by domestic controversy, relative quiescence on foreign policy issues was hardly surprising. Nevertheless, under the sustaining leadership of Noel Buxton, Philip Morrell, and Arthur Ponsonby, the Foreign Affairs Committee continued to provide the principal forum for dissenting opinion on foreign policy. It was natural that, when European affairs again demanded attention, it was to that forum which Liberals turned.

A dozen radicals met on July 29 and instructed Arthur Ponsonby to write to Grey urging British neutrality. Ponsonby's letter, after being passed to the Prime Minister for information, eventually found its way back through Maurice Bonham Carter, Asquith's secretary, to Arthur Murray, Grey's parliamentary private secretary, in whose papers it now rests. The Foreign Affairs Group's message was meticulously penned in Ponsonby's own hand:

Dear Grey,

The Liberal Foreign Affairs group called together a small representative meeting of members this afternoon to discuss the present critical situation in Europe. I was instructed to forward to you the enclosed resolution which was passed unanimously and to inform you of what took place.

The most complete confidence was expressed by the meeting in yourself and there was a keen desire to support you in your efforts to restrict the area of warfare to the two powers immediately concerned. We are most anxious to take no action which would embarrass you in the delicate negotiations which you are now conducting and it was decided that our proceedings should not be reported to the press.

The tone of some of the newspapers and the somewhat alarmist reports of the mobilization of our forces have very much upset Liberal members and grave fear was expressed lest public opinion might become inflamed. It was decided that everything possible should be done to counteract the influences which already seem to be working for our participation in what may prove to be a general European conflict. On this point very strong views were expressed and it was the feeling of the meeting that we could not support the Government in any military or naval operations which would carry this country beyond its existing treaty obligations. It was felt that if both France and Russia were informed that on no account would we be drawn into war even though they and other European powers were involved it would have a moderating effect on their policy.

We decided for the present not to publish our resolution but to forward it to you first. We are meeting again tomorrow to consider if further steps such as a general meeting of Liberal members or the publication of a resolution would not be advisable. We are most anxious to assist and not to hinder you and if you should feel inclined to suggest any course which you think we might usefully take we would at once consider it.

Knowing how fully occupied you must be I have not ventured to propose seeing you but I would come at any time should you desire to talk with me.

Yours sincerely,
ARTHUR PONSONBY

Resolved:
That this meeting having had its attention drawn to statements in *The Times* and other organs of the press that this country may be involved in the war which has broken out in the East, desires to express its view that Great Britain in no conceivable circumstances should depart from a position of strict neutrality and appeals to His Majesty's Government to

give effect to this view while continuing to offer its good offices in every promising way to secure the restoration of peace.

ARTHUR PONSONBY	ARNOLD ROWNTREE
W. H. DICKINSON	H. NUTTALL
THOMAS LOUGH	D. M. MASON
C. N. NICHOLSON	G. J. BENTHAM
P. MOLTENO	
P. MORRELL	
N. BUXTON	

According to a covering note which Arthur Murray sent with Ponsonby's letter to Bonham Carter, Grey, having promptly summoned Ponsonby, told him that he could not make any definite statement to him until he had consulted the Prime Minister. But Ponsonby himself left a record of what Grey had said to him which reveals that the Foreign Secretary gave, if not a 'definite statement', at least an apparently candid expression of his thinking:

He could make no open statement of our determination not to be drawn in.

The doubt on this point was useful to him in negotiating.

To assure Russia-France that they would not get our support might have the opposite to a pacific effect.

We were absolutely free and working for peace.

On the whole would prefer our keeping quiet for this week.

The movements of the fleet were only necessary moves and in no way preparatory.

He would show the P.M. our communication.[1]

True to their word, neither on July 29 nor on the following day did Ponsonby and his associates attempt to bring public pressure to bear on the government. However, after question time on Thursday July 30, twenty-two members of the Foreign Affairs Group met to hear Ponsonby's report of his meeting with Grey and to decide on their next move. Again Ponsonby was instructed to write, this time to the Prime Minister. The message of the radicals was that 'Great Britain on no account should be drawn

[1] Ponsonby's 'Notes of Grey's Statement to me on July 29th [19]14', Ponsonby MSS.

into a war in which neither treaty obligations, British interests, British honour or even sentiments of friendship are at present in the remotest degree involved.' So determined was the conviction of 'Liberal members', Ponsonby wrote, that 'any decision in favour of participation in a European conflict would meet not only with the strongest disapproval but with the actual withdrawal of support from the Government'.[1]

Ponsonby's blunt warning was backed by a threat to ask the Foreign Secretary an awkward private-notice question in the House the following day. But, as Asquith was quick to perceive, Ponsonby was in no position to make threats. Although he claimed that the views he expressed were those of representative men, shared by 'nine-tenths of the party', Ponsonby had to admit that he was not 'as yet able to speak actually for more than 30 members'. Even this was an exaggeration, if only those who attended the meetings of the Foreign Affairs Group are counted as being in Ponsonby's camp. Moreover, a careful reading of the letter to Grey on the previous day as well as that to Asquith on the 30th showed significant qualifications in the neutralist declarations. So long as Belgium was not menaced, it was true to say that British treaty obligations were not involved; and it was at least arguable that interests, honour, and friendship were not decisively relevant either. But, as the Prime Minister could scarcely have failed to notice, Ponsonby wrote of Britain that it was in no way 'at present' involved—an obvious hint that the Foreign Affairs Group was undecided about whether Belgium would make any difference.

Perhaps encouraged by this chink in his critics' opposition, Asquith saw no necessity to try to alter the opinions of the uncounted number of Liberals whom he supposed did share Ponsonby's view. Winston Churchill, however, moved swiftly to try to quell the incipient revolt. Churchill received a letter from Ponsonby on July 31 urging him to 'use all your influence towards moderation'. Replying immediately, Churchill agreed in principle that 'Balkan quarrels are no vital concern of ours'. But he reminded Ponsonby of the menacing circumstances which would have to be considered if France and Belgium were drawn into the

[1] Ponsonby to Asquith, 30 July 1914 (draft), Ponsonby MSS.

conflict. 'It wd be wrong at this moment to pronounce finally one way or the other as to our duty or our interests.'[1]

Thus, enjoined to be silent, assured that peace was the ministry's objective, the radicals were disarmed. They clutched at rumours of cabinet splits. But there was little that they could do to affect the course of events. A party meeting might be called but would it do any more than advertise differences? What else could be done? Move the adjournment of the House of Commons? Ask for information? Give notice of a motion that the House would not grant supply for any British intervention? Declare that Great Britain had no interests at stake?[2] Almost any action would have involved implied or direct criticism of the government. Grey asked for a period of grace. And there was no reason to suppose that the government wanted war. The veteran radical Lord Bryce wrote to J. A. Spender: 'I have so far dissuaded any public action which might seem to imply distrust of the Govt, wh we ought so far, to credit with desiring to keep the country out of the mêlée.'[3] Could Liberals have confidence in the government?

> I believe that the great majority of the Cabinet are absolutely sound on keeping England out of the war, but there is a minority of a different view and one dreads the influence of Churchill ... Grey is working his hardest and doing his utmost to prevent a general war.[4]

So wrote the Quaker M.P. for West Leeds, Edmund Harvey, to his father. Most Liberals, whatever their previous criticisms of Grey's foreign policy, trusted him in this crisis. Whether they trusted him or not, they were obliged by lack of information to refrain from premature protest. 'We felt', wrote Christopher Addison a few weeks later, 'as helpless as rats in a trap, as indeed we were.'[5] At 5.15 p.m. on Friday, July 31, the Foreign Affairs

---

[1] Ponsonby to Churchill, 31 July 1914. Randolph S. Churchill, *Winston S. Churchill,* Companion Volume II, part 3, 1911–1914 (London, 1969), pp. 1990–1. Churchill to Ponsonby, 31 July 1914. Randolph S. Churchill, *Winston S. Churchill:* vol II, Young Statesman, 1901–1914 (London, 1967), pp. 715–16.

[2] The radical M.P., Alexander MacCallum Scott, pondered over the alternatives for two hours, without being able to decide on a desirable line of action. (MacCallum Scott's Diary, 31 July 1914, MacCallum Scott MSS.)

[3] Bryce to Spender, 31 July 1914, Spender MSS (Add. MS. 46392, f. 161).

[4] T. E. Harvey to W. Harvey, 30 July 1914, Harvey MSS.

[5] Addison's Diary, 30 August 1914. Christopher Addison, *Four and a Half Years,* 2 vols (London, 1934), vol. I, p. 32.

Group met for the second time in one day. In the morning they had agreed not to press a planned question in the House. Now they decided to take no 'definite step' until after the week-end. By then, although they could not know it, it would be too late.[1]

The Liberals were not without companions in their trap. Their parliamentary allies rendered themselves equally powerless to sway the course of events. The majority of the Labour Party and the Irish Nationalists came swiftly to heel when war was declared. Alone among the constituent organizations of the Labour Party, the Independent Labour Party maintained its opposition to war after British intervention was certain. There were many Labour voices for peace as late as August 3. But the principles of international socialism were largely abandoned during the next few days. Like the eighty-strong Liberal hard core conjured up by Mr Taylor, Labour's war resisters soon melted into the precincts of Westminster, preferring patriotic anonymity to the notoriety of untimely pacifism. Sadly reporting the story of the Parliamentary Labour Party's change of front on the war, *The Socialist Review* recorded in September 1914 that 'the defection began early and soon became a stampede'.

On behalf of the Irish Nationalists, John Redmond said in the House of Commons on August 3:

> ... while Irishmen generally are in favour of peace, and would desire to save the democracy of this country from all the horrors of war, while we would make every possible sacrifice for that purpose, still, if the dire necessity is forced upon this country, we offer to the Government of the day that they may take their troops away, and that, if it is allowed to us, in comradeship with our brethren in the North, we will ourselves defend the coasts of our country.

Redmond's speech was taken by many to be an offer of unconditional military assistance. This was a misconception understandable in the heat of the moment; however, there was no mistaking the direction of his sympathies, and there were soon to

[1] Additional details on the radicals in July 1914 may be found in two unpublished doctoral theses: K. G. Robbins, 'The Abolition of War: A Study in the Organization and Ideology of the Peace Movement, 1914–1919' (Oxford, 1964); and J. E. Lindsay, 'The Failure of Liberal Opposition to British Entry Into World War I' (Columbia, 1969).

be more concrete pledges of Irish co-operation. In recognition of Redmond's speech, and in the hope of stimulating a patriotic spirit in Ireland, Churchill named a new battleship *Erin*; the First Lord also promised to 'use every influence I possess' to work for a modus vivendi on Home Rule on lines acceptable to Redmond.[1]

From the leaders of the Conservative opposition, solidarity with the government came unsolicited. Bonar Law had doubts about the attitude of his party if Belgian neutrality remained inviolate. He expected unanimity if the Germans did invade Belgium.[2] For themselves, the leading Conservatives—Bonar Law, Lord Lansdowne, Arthur Balfour and Austen Chamberlain—were all agreed, as they told Asquith in a letter on August 2, that 'any hesitation in now supporting France and Russia would be fatal to the honour and to the future security of the United Kingdom'.

Bonar Law was careful, until Sunday, August 2, not to take any action which might look as though he was seeking to sway the cabinet's decision. As Austen Chamberlain recorded in a contemporary memorandum: 'Winston had invited Bonar Law and F. E. Smith to dine with him and Grey on Sunday night, but Bonar Law had thought it was undesirable for him to accept this invitation lest he should appear to be intriguing with a section of the Cabinet behind the Prime Minister's back.'[3]

Lansdowne, the last Conservative foreign secretary, also did not attempt at first to put pressure on the government; but he believed, as he wrote in 1919, 'that the war might have been avoided if Grey had been in a position to make a perfectly explicit statement as to our conduct in certain eventualities'.[4]

The Conservatives were convinced in August 1914 that it was their own letter to the Prime Minister on August 2 and its declaration of support for intervention on behalf of France and Russia which tipped the balance in the cabinet in favour of war. This belief, as the subsequent narrative will show, was unfounded. Nor was it true that the Conservative Party itself was absolutely of one mind about Britain's proper course. Lord Hugh Cecil, for example, wrote to Churchill urging complete neutrality. True, his brother,

[1] Churchill to Redmond, 5 August 1914. Denis Gwynn, op. cit., p. 362.

[2] Robert Blake, *The Unknown Prime Minister:* The Life and Times of Andrew Bonar Law, 1858–1923 (London, 1955), pp. 220–4.

[3] Sir Austen Chamberlain, *Down the Years* (London, 1935), p. 97.

[4] Lansdowne to Lord Loreburn, 28 April 1919 (copy), Lansdowne MSS.

Lord Robert Cecil, wrote immediately afterwards to warn Churchill that, as Austen Chamberlain put it, 'Hugh spoke for no one but himself.' This, like so many other statements made in these tense days, was an understandable exaggeration; and many silent Tories doubtless felt as impotent and bewildered as the radicals. But there was no possibility that any substantial number of Conservatives would publicly oppose British intervention. As early as July 30 the Liberal Edmund Harvey accurately sensed that there was no hope of effective united action with the tiny group of Conservative neutralists:

> The overwhelming mass of the Tory party seem to regard war as inevitable & some seem to be eager to take the best chance of smashing Germany. Bentinck & a few others are for peace, but I am afraid they would be swept away by the rest of their party if they tried to protest.[1]

[1] Harvey to W. Harvey, 30 July 1914, Harvey MSS. After Sir Edward Grey's speech in the House of Commons on August 3, Hugh Cecil encountered Churchill in the 'aye lobby'. According to the only eye-witness, Cecil 'flew toward him, took Churchill by the collar, shook him violently, and cried "You did it! You did it" ... He cast Churchill off and turned back the way he had come—a broken man, his face wet with tears.' (Francis Neilson, *My Life in Two Worlds*, 2 vols [Appleton, Wisconsin, 1952], vol. 1, p. 325.)

3 Grey Speaks

For all but a handful of civil servants, journalists, and ministers' wives, the decisive moment in the crisis for those outside the cabinet was the Foreign Secretary's statement to the House of Commons in the afternoon of Monday, August 3. Until Sir Edward Grey had spoken, combining an analysis of the considerations which had to weigh in British policy with incidental references to the salient incidents of the previous week, it was impossible for the ordinary Member of Parliament to attempt a balanced appraisal of the situation. No student of these events can fail to be struck by the importance which contemporaries attached to Grey's speech. 'The greatest speech delivered in our time or for a very long period,' wrote Lord Hugh Cecil.[1] The Speaker described it as 'one of the most remarkable speeches to which it was ever my fate to listen'.[2] Asquith, though admitting that there were 'some of his usual ragged ends', found it 'extraordinarily well reasoned and tactful and really cogent'.[3]

Did Grey's performance warrant praise of this order? It cannot be denied that the occasion was momentous. What is puzzling is the reception Grey was given. 'The speech had hardly been prepared at all,'[4] his parliamentary private secretary testified. Indeed, as the newly elected Conservative Member for Oxford University remembered, 'it bore no trace of preparation'.[5] The speech was undistinguished in style or logic. Its presentation of

[1] Cecil to Wilfrid Ward, n.d. G. M. Trevelyan, *Grey of Fallodon* (London, 1946), p. 265.

[2] James William Lowther, Viscount Ullswater, *A Speaker's Commentaries*, 2 vols (London, 1925), vol. II, p. 167.

[3] Asquith to Venetia Stanley, 3 August 1914, Montagu MSS.

[4] Lt.-Col. Arthur C. Murray, *Master and Brother:* Murrays of Elibank (London, 1945), p. 123.

[5] Rowland Prothero, Lord Ernle, *Whippingham to Westminster* (London, 1938), p. 265.

the government's case was fumbling and evasive. It is only possible to account for the paradoxical sense of relief which Grey brought to the majority of his listeners, by appreciating the anxious and perplexed state of mind which the obscurity of the government's intentions had produced.

Even on the periphery of the inner circle uncertainty had reigned. The case of the Parliamentary Under Secretary at the Board of Education is instructive. In spite of friendly relations with several senior ministers—Walter Runciman being particularly communicative—Charles Trevelyan tried in vain to keep abreast of events. A chance encounter with Grey, soon after the Austrian ultimatum to Serbia, had aroused Trevelyan's suspicions. 'So obvious was it that he [Grey] disliked the idea of neutrality that I got extraordinarily uncomfortable, without knowing what it all meant.' But, until August 2, Trevelyan 'trusted the government'. When Grey spoke to Parliament, the information upon which a neutralist case might earlier have been founded was at last divulged. For Trevelyan and the other radicals it was too late:

> I was prepared for bad news, but in no way for the barefaced, deliberate appeal to passion. He gave not a single argument why we should support France. But he showed he had all along been leading her to expect our support and appealed to us as bound in honour. However, I only want to record here that the Liberals, very few of them, cheered at all, whatever they did later, while the Tories shouted with delight.[1]

What was it about Grey's words which could produce reactions so different as those of Lord Hugh Cecil and Charles Trevelyan? The explanation is implicit in a comment of Cecil's about 'the extraordinary dexterity with which he dealt with the weak spot of his argument'. The weak spot was the nature of Great Britain's obligation to France. Grey explained the historical development of the military conversations which had taken place between the British and French general staffs since 1906. But he stopped short of urging that they entailed any obligation to act. 'With wonderful

[1] This quotation, and the two preceding ones, are from Trevelyan's 'Personal account of beginning of the War, 1914,' undated, but written at the end of August 1914, Trevelyan MSS.

skill', Cecil wrote, 'he did not argue the point, but he changed to a note of appeal to the individual conscience, thereby disarming criticism ... without any departure real or apparent from perfect sincerity.'[1] The same 'wonderful skill' was applied to justifying the assurance given to the French government that Great Britain would not stand aside if the German fleet entered the Channel or launched hostile operations through the North Sea against French coasts and shipping. Not honour but interest, Grey maintained, dictated this guarantee.

In the early stages of his speech Grey was feeling his way, trying to find the tone to which the House would respond. The evening papers, rushing out extra editions to record the announcement from the Foreign Secretary, at first caught only his indecisive opening remarks. Arthur Lee, the Conservative spokesman on military and naval affairs, later remembered that, as he lay recuperating from an appendix operation, 'the first stop-press reports of his speech which reached my bedside plunged me into depths of gloom, as he seemed to be vacillating on the brink and irresolute on the point of honour'.[2]

Only when Belgian neutrality had been brought before the House, did Grey venture to raise the question of 'our respect and good name and reputation before the world'. But the dominant note throughout was the need to protect British shores, British commerce, and British interests. 'The magnitude of the impending dangers in the West of Europe' left few choices for British policy. 'We must be prepared for the consequences of having to use all the strength we have at any moment—we know not how soon—to defend ourselves and to take our part.'[3]

In the end, Grey left the House in no doubt that decisive British action could not be long delayed. What would that action be? There was a moment when he seemed to hint at conditional neutrality.[4] But his tone of anti-Germanism—'the only adverse

[1] G. M. Trevelyan, op. cit., p. 265; see also Arthur Balfour's remark: 'It was wonderful how in his war speech he drew you on to the irresistible conclusion that war was inevitable for us.' (Sir George Riddell's Diary, 11 September 1914. *Lord Riddell's War Diary* [London, n.d., ? 1933], p. 31.)

[2] Viscount Lee of Fareham, *A Good Innings and a Great Partnership;* being the Life Story of Arthur and Ruth Lee, 3 vols (privately printed, 1939), vol. 1, pp. 530–1.

[3] Grey's speech is in 65 *H.C. Deb.*, 5s, cols 1809–1827.

[4] '... some of the press the following day supposed that conditional neutrality was what Grey had been talking about, and it says even less for the clarity of the speech ...

criticism possible', Asquith told Pease[1] — pointed in a different direction.

After Grey spoke, a despondent group of twenty-eight Liberals resolved that there was no sufficient reason for British intervention and that negotiations should continue. Two of the number opposed the resolution; three abstained. The majority of the Foreign Affairs Group did not attend this meeting, or any of the meetings, in the crisis period.[2] At first they were baffled. And, to many of them, Grey's exposition of the government view was little help in clarifying the position. Their continued confusion is understandable. Grey gave no clear lead because he had no mandate to do so. His speech reflected the failure of the cabinet, even in the decisive hours, to face up to the implications of the strategic arrangements and foreign policy of the previous eight years.

The one massive virtue of Grey's speech was its stumbling manner, mistaken this time, as so often before, for honesty. Here was a man, it seemed, who had struggled for peace. Fifteen Liberals rose to their feet to beg that the struggle be continued; but the mood of the House was turning against them. Grey had allayed most doubts about the government's pacific intentions; and he had provided plausible excuses for those who could not support a war without them. His statement, Christopher Addison concluded, 'crushed out all hope of peace and of our being able to keep clear'.[3] Liberals who had floundered over the Bank Holiday

---

that at first sight the German Ambassador was encouraged by it.' (A. J. Dorey, op. cit., p. 439.)

[1] Pease's Diary, 3 August 1914, Gainford MSS. Considering the way in which Asquith deployed far more damning anti-German arguments on August 5, it must be supposed that on the 3rd, he was either still clinging to hopes that Germany would recoil from the brink or, more likely, exaggerating for Pease's benefit his reluctance to provoke the Germans.

[2] Robbins, op. cit., chapters 1 and 2. The opponents of the August 3 resolution were Christopher Addison and Sir George Scott Robertson; the abstainers, Thomas Lough, Sir M. Levy, and Joseph King. Addison, Robertson, Lough, and King signed the neutralist resolution on July 30. Addison, in his diary entry on August 30 (*Four and a Half Years*, vol. 1, pp. 31–2), seems to have confused the two meetings. The records of the Foreign Affairs Group in the Ponsonby MSS do not include any reference to a resolution on July 31; but Addison later thought that at a meeting on that day he had been in a minority of four, against nineteen, voting against an unqualified call for neutrality. There were, as Addison rightly recalled, two meetings on the 31st; but no resolutions were proposed at either of them. (See *The Times* and *The Manchester Guardian*, 1 August 1914.)

[3] Addison's Diary, 30 August 1914. Christopher Addison, op. cit., vol. 1, p. 32.

week-end were thus thrown a lifebelt on Monday afternoon. Some, like Alexander MacCallum Scott, even discovered restoratives in their own back pockets. War, they observed, might be the best way of destroying the old order and inaugurating a new era of international relations:

Grey's masterly speech today and the increasingly aggressive tone of Germany's words and deeds make me review my position.

I do not think any of his arguments alone convince me.

1. He wants to make Britain part of the European system of politics. I do not.

2. He feels an obligation of honour to assist our friend — France. I do not.

3. His acknowledgement that there was no binding agreement and his appeal to each man to look into his own heart to find whether there was an obligation struck me as rather sharp practice.

But

1. I am impressed by Pringle's contention that the issue is which policy is to prevail in Europe, the policy of blood and iron alone or the policy of enforcing international obligations.

2. Peace armaments are becoming intolerable. May we not use this calamity to set up an international court of arbitration in Europe. Will they try?[1]

It is not possible to say how typical this position was. However, it is clear that there was no foundation for a large parliamentary opposition to war. On August 6, not a single voice was heard in opposition to the Vote of Credit. Like Richard Holt, the great majority of Liberals, overwhelmed by the tragedy, soon adopted the official explanation of British participation. A week after he had expressed his incredulity that a Liberal government could drag the country into war, Holt admitted a change of mind:

I had thought we might & should have kept out of the War but when Germany decided on an unprovoked attack

[1] MacCallum Scott's Diary, 3 August 1914, MacCallum Scott MSS. W. M. R. Pringle had spoken in support of Grey in the House of Commons.

upon Belgium whose neutrality Germany equally with ourselves had guaranteed it seemed impossible for us to stand by. Germany has acted with great brutality & haste & is, in my judgment, the party mainly responsible for this war.[1]

[1] Holt's Diary, 9 August 1914, Holt MSS.

4 A Cabinet Divided

How did the cabinet divide in the anxious July and August days? We may take as a starting point Lord Crewe's comment on the account written by Lord Morley:

> He seems to have thought that the Cabinet was divided between those who, like himself, were determined to keep out of war at any price, and those who were only anxious to find an excuse for taking part in it. Whereas the great majority belonged to neither class.[1]

From the contemporary records of Asquith and his colleagues, it is possible to be a little more precise than Crewe. It is true that there were few out-and-out neutralists, and probably no determined warmongers. Up to August 1, Asquith saw Grey, Churchill and himself on the one hand, Morley and Simon on the other, as marking the extreme positions. Morley and Simon gave the impression that they believed that there were no circumstances which could justify British intervention. Such an uncompromising policy, if it had been generally agreed, would have forced Grey to resign, and Asquith would have taken the same course. Morley and possibly Simon, it appeared, would not stay in a war cabinet whatever its reasons for intervening. After the mid-day meeting of the cabinet on August 2, the Prime Minister was convinced that a split was imminent. 'There is a strong party ... against any kind of intervention in any event,' he wrote.[2] Churchill recalled the same danger, 'an invincible refusal on the part of the majority to contemplate British intervention'.[3]

[1] Crewe's statement, 2 May 1936. G. M. Trevelyan, op. cit., pp. 256–7.
[2] Asquith to Venetia Stanley, 2 August 1914, Montagu MSS.
[3] Winston S. Churchill, *The World Crisis, 1911–1914* (London, 1923), p. 214.

D

To Churchill, the division in the cabinet presented awkward problems. He felt compelled, with Asquith's indulgence, to take precautionary measures in anticipation of his colleagues' collective approval. Simultaneously, fearing a Liberal split, he made overtures to the Conservatives, through F. E. Smith and Arthur Balfour, about the possibility of coalition.[1] It is a mistake to suppose that Churchill relished the approach of war, or that his mind was wholly occupied with the deployment of his naval forces. Admittedly, he confessed to the 'hideous fascination' which the preparations held for him. Yet his imagination was harnessed till the end to the cause of peace. Could not, he wondered 'those stupid Kings & Emperors ... assemble together and revivify Kingship by saving the nations from hell'.[2] Thus, in midnight speculation, he rehearsed for his wife a proposal presented more decorously to the cabinet on July 29.[3] Knowing better than any other member of the cabinet the tragedies of war, he participated to the last in the strivings for peace. He did not hesitate, however, to make every preparation that could be made to protect the nation should the fight for peace be lost.

The greatest burden of 1914 was on the shoulders of Sir Edward Grey. People habitually spoke not of Asquith's foreign policy, or even of the government's policy, but of Grey's policy. Grey's actions have been minutely dissected by several generations of historians; and the main outlines of his conduct are not in dispute. Until the latest possible moment, he refused either to give guarantees to France or to threaten Germany. He believed that both steps, if taken too soon, entailed more danger than hope. For nearly a month after the assassination of the Austrian Archduke, he sought to influence Germany to restrain Austria; and he tried

[1] Lord Beaverbrook, *Politicians and the War, 1914–1916* (London, n.d., ? 1960), pp. 16–19; Robert Blake, op. cit., pp. 220–1; the Earl of Birkenhead, *F.E.: The Life of F. E. Smith, First Earl of Birkenhead* (London, 1965), p. 241; Winston S. Churchill, op. cit., pp. 215 and 218.

[2] Churchill to Clementine Churchill, 28 July 1914 (midnight), quoted in Randolph S. Churchill, op. cit., p. 710. The familiar picture of Churchill embracing war as though he could not wait for bloodshed derives mainly from Margot Asquith's recollection of him on the evening of August 4 'with a happy face striding towards the double doors of the Cabinet room'. (*The Autobiography of Margot Asquith*, 2 vols [London, 1920 and 1922], vol. II, p. 196.) Churchill, in his review of this volume, demonstrated a number of factual errors in Margot Asquith's account. There is good reason to doubt whether her story has any basis in reality.

[3] Pease's Diary, 29 July 1914, Gainford MSS.

to persuade the Russians to adopt a conciliatory course. But he did not realize until late in July that he had been deceived by the Germans. Having concluded that the German refusal of a conference of ambassadors in London marked an almost irreversible step towards general war, Grey seemed after July 27 at a loss for constructive initiatives. After the Russians had begun to mobilize on July 29 his last hopes were dashed. Instead of thrashing in futile opposition to the inevitable, he directed his efforts to bracing his colleagues for the worst.

Grey's critics later attributed his almost fatalistic attitude to the crippling effect of his policy from 1906 to 1914. Why did he refuse to state plainly, even on August 3, terms on which Great Britain would either join in or stand apart from a continental war? His own explanation, a few months after war began, rested partly on common sense, partly on constitutional propriety: 'The idea that one individual sitting in a room in the Foreign Office, could pledge a great democracy definitely by his word, in advance, either to take part in a great war or to abstain from taking part in it, is absurd.'[1]

The absurdity was not apparent to all. When the facts relating to the Anglo-French and Anglo-Russian naval and military conversations were made public, it was possible to interpret Grey's unenterprising diplomacy in another way. Parliament had been told in response to repeated inquiries, that there were no engagements restricting Britain's freedom of action in Europe. Clearly, if there were no engagements, no pledge of assistance could be given to France or Russia. But, as Grey revealed on August 3, the government's obligations obviously went further than had ever been admitted. Grey had emptied his quiver of diplomatic options. His own, and Asquith's lack of candour about pre-war policy, not any constitutional nicety, was the stumbling block. As a disenchanted journalist wrote after reading the diplomatic documents, 'the Mediterranean naval arrangement with France, years ago, was a deadly piece of self-committal'.[2]

Grey's conscience would not permit him to reject the strongly-

[1] Grey's Memorandum, April 1915. G. M. Trevelyan, op. cit., p. 250.
[2] C. E. Montague to C. P. Scott, 11 August 1914, *Manchester Guardian* MSS.

worded advice of his Assistant Under-Secretary, Sir Eyre Crowe:

> The argument that there is no written bond binding us to France is strictly correct. There is no contractual obligation. But the Entente has been made, strengthened, put to the test and celebrated in a manner justifying the belief that a moral bond was being forged. The whole force of the Entente can have no meaning if it does not signify that in a just quarrel England would stand by her friends.[1]

Grey was not at first inhibited by the indecision of his colleagues. Reminiscing, early in May 1915, about the outbreak of war, he said that 'one of his strongest feelings ... was that he himself had no power to decide policy, & was only the mouthpiece of England'.[2] As long as the country had nothing to say, Grey was a muted instrument. A few old Balkan tunes were given an airing. That was all. The protracted disputes in cabinet may have worried the French and encouraged the Germans; and Grey did feel unable to press the cabinet to authorize formal assurances to the French, assurances which might have helped to steady the Russians. But, so far from being distracted by dissension, Grey found that the gravity of the situation conduced to restraint in discussion. 'We kept', he remembered, 'to that on which we were all agreed—the endeavour to prevent war altogether.'[3]

Grey was aware that there was an 'anti-war group' of his colleagues meeting privately. The group was, in Grey's view, sufficient in number and influence to have broken up the cabinet. Yet he made no attempt to counteract the group's activities, or to convert any of its members. It was better, he believed, that the country should not go to war at all, than that it should have to be manœuvred into it against strong opposition. In fact, Grey had more sympathy with the 'anti-war group' than he dared to express.

[1] Memorandum by Sir Eyre Crowe, 31 July 1914, BDXI, No. 369, pp. 228–9.

[2] Eleanor Acland's War Diary, c. 7 May 1915, Acland MSS. Mrs Acland was the wife of Francis Acland, Under-Secretary of State for Foreign Affairs.

[3] Viscount Grey of Fallodon, *Twenty-Five Years, 1892–1916*, 3 vols (London, 1928), vol. ii, pp. 186–7. Dr Zara Steiner and Dr Michael Ekstein, in an unpublished paper on the July crisis, have restated the traditional argument that Grey's 'hands were tied' by the cabinet. Although I am not completely convinced by their case, I am grateful to Dr Steiner and Dr Ekstein for permitting me to read their work in draft form.

He felt as strongly as any of them the horror that war would bring. He was impressed too with the argument that war would produce economic dislocation on a huge scale. According to Sir Eyre Crowe (whose anti-German attitude makes him something less than an impartial witness), the Foreign Secretary thought 'that if we went to war the commercial interests of this country would be ruined & we must *not* go to war'![1] Crowe and his chief, Sir Arthur Nicolson, chafed at the way in which Grey seemed to drag his feet, stumbling, inexplicably and indefensibly. But it is hard to believe that the Foreign Secretary seriously argued an economic case against war. It was not an argument he ever deployed in cabinet, though he might well have been tempted to respond to impatient counsel from Crowe by echoing predictions just transmitted by alarmist colleagues at the Treasury and the Board of Trade. On the other hand, in addressing the House of Commons Grey contended that Britain was unlikely to suffer more by participation in the war than by abstention. This massive miscalculation, based on the assumption of naval war alone, at least revealed genuine fears about the distressing consequences which European war would have for even a neutral Great Britain.

[1] Henry Wilson's Diary, 31 July 1914, Wilson MSS. Wilson, the Director of Military Operations, was aghast at hearing Crowe's story. Wilson called daily at the Foreign Office in the war crisis to hear the latest news from Crowe and Sir Arthur Nicolson, the Permanent Under-Secretary of State. However, by the autumn of 1914, Nicolson no longer enjoyed Grey's confidence and was not always a reliable guide to the Foreign Secretary's thinking. (See Zara S. Steiner, *The Foreign Office and Foreign Policy, 1898-1914* [Cambridge, 1969], ch. III.)

5 The Waverers and Lloyd George

Most accounts of the pre-war crisis mention the activities of an 'anti-war' or 'peace' group in the cabinet. In estimating the size and composition of this group ten names are usually listed: Lord Morley, John Burns, David Lloyd George, Lewis Harcourt, Lord Beauchamp, Sir John Simon, J. A. Pease, Walter Runciman, Herbert Samuel and T. McKinnon Wood.[1] This list includes seven ministers who lunched at Lord Beauchamp's house in Belgrave Square on August 2, with the addition of Pease, who arrived at Belgrave Square after lunching with Asquith, and Burns and Runciman.[2] Of the remaining nine members of the cabinet, only one, Hobhouse, should be added. Hobhouse was, according to Morley, present at a conclave in Harcourt's room at the House of Commons. His support for Lloyd George in the 1913–14 naval estimates crisis left no doubt about his radical inclinations, and Lord Beaverbrook identifies him as one of those who campaigned for neutrality.[3]

Runciman is the most doubtful candidate for inclusion in a 'peace' group. When Beauchamp was entertaining six of his colleagues for lunch on August 2, Runciman was with Charles Masterman at Reginald McKenna's house in Smith Square. Masterman was to recall seven months later how, on that 'Fateful Sunday', Runciman was 'not amongst the Peace Palaverers and not amongst the War Desirers'. The self-appointed task of McKenna, Masterman and Runciman was, according to Masterman, 'to keep the old

[1] See, for example, Roy Jenkins, op. cit., p. 325, fn. 1.
[2] Pease's Diary, 2 August 1914, Gainford MSS. Samuel arrived late and 'but for an act of self-denial on the part of Lord Morley, there would have been nothing left but a ham!' (Sir Almeric Fitzroy's Diary, 2 August 1914. Sir Almeric Fitzroy, *Memoirs*, 2 vols [London, n.d., ? 1923], vol. 11, p. 559).
[3] Lord Beaverbrook, op. cit., p. 20.

machine united and so keep the possibility of a Liberal Party alive'. However, Runciman spent much time in the company of the 'peace palaverers' who appear to have counted him as one of themselves; and he identified himself with them when he came to explaining his decision to remain in the ministry.[1]

There is enough evidence about Lord Haldane, Augustine Birrell, Lord Crewe, Reginald McKenna, Winston Churchill, Charles Masterman, Grey, and Asquith himself for them all to be excluded from any supposed peace group. Haldane, who had been Secretary of State for War when Britain's continental strategy was devised, was closely identified in outlook with Grey and Asquith, and convinced that German ambition had to be foiled.[2] Grey was, from July 27 onwards, living at Haldane's house in Queen Anne's Gate. The Foreign Secretary, Asquith, and Haldane had a long discussion together late on July 29 and thereafter acted in concert until the country was at war. Crewe usually was a faithful collaborator in Asquith's tactical procrastinations, and there is no evidence that he played a different role in this crisis. In a letter to Venetia Stanley, Asquith located Crewe among the 'moderating intermediate body' neither pressing for mobilization nor obdurately resisting intervention.[3] Masterman worked for unity but was dubbed a jingo, rather playfully, by Lloyd George.[4] Birrell was sure that Great Britain would sooner or later be forced into the war and was not prepared to trust any German promise to refrain,

[1] Masterman to Runciman, 14 February 1915, Runciman MSS. Lord Morley was uncertain about whether Runciman had been at the Beauchamp lunch. Jack Pease, hurriedly trying to write his recollections of the day's events, included Runciman in the list of people at Beauchamp's. Samuel does not mention him in his contemporary account. It is possible but unlikely that Runciman went to Beauchamp's after lunching with McKenna, and arrived before Pease. (John, Viscount Morley, *Memorandum on Resignation, August 1914* [London, 1928], p. 15; Pease's Diary, 2 August 1914, Gainford MSS; Samuel to Beatrice Samuel, 2 August 1914, Samuel MSS, A/157/697, f. 52; see also Sir Valentine Chirol to Lord Hardinge, 4 August 1914, Hardinge MSS, vol. 93, p. 296.)

[2] Richard Burdon Haldane, *An Autobiography* (London, 1929), pp. 273–5; Major-General Sir Frederick Maurice, *Haldane, 1856–1928*, 2 vols (London, 1937 and 1938), vol. 1, pp. 353–4.

[3] Asquith to Venetia Stanley, 2 August 1914, Montagu MSS. See also James Pope-Hennessy, *Lord Crewe, 1858–1945: The Likeness of a Liberal* (London, 1955), pp. 144–5.

[4] *Lord Riddell's War Diary*, pp. 3, 5–6; Masterman to Lloyd George, cabinet note, (?2) August 1914, Lloyd George MSS, C/14; Lucy Masterman, *C. F. G. Masterman: A Biography* (London, 1939), pp. 270–1.

for example, from attacking the French coast.[1] He held aloof from the advances of Loulou Harcourt who was trying to rally the forces of neutralism.

Only with McKenna is there any obscurity. In 1911 he had, as First Lord of the Admiralty, resisted the adoption of the General Staff's continental strategy. His opposition to the Anglo-French military conversations took him to the brink of resignation. Although no proof exists, it seems likely that he opposed the sending of an expeditionary force to France when the issue arose on August 1; certainly, for four days, this view prevailed. This does not mean that McKenna was against war. Asquith's description of him as 'sensible and loyal', and of forming a 'moderating intermediate body' with Samuel and Crewe, is the best indicator of his behaviour. Masterman spoke of him as sharing Runciman's efforts to fight for time.[2]

At close range, though from different perspectives, both Churchill and Harcourt assumed that the group of seven which lunched at Lord Beauchamp's house on August 2 had views as well as appetites in common. However, on closer scrutiny, the members of this group appear to have shared little more than a reluctance to renounce the pacific and isolationist positions with which they were publicly identified. The purpose of their meeting was not to co-ordinate tactics which would thwart the Prime Minister and Foreign Secretary. Had they chosen to do so, they could undoubtedly have smashed the ministry. But they were not bent on destruction. They came together to clear their own minds, to continue the discussion of issues that could not be resolved even in three-hour cabinets. The one thing which the majority of them did, eventually, have in common was that they actually remained in the ministry. To label them as a 'peace' or 'anti-war' group blurs

---

[1] Augustine Birrell, *Things Past Redress* (London, 1937), pp. 232–5. See also Leon Ó. Broin, *The Chief Secretary:* Augustine Birrell in Ireland (London, 1969), p. 108.

[2] Masterman to Lloyd George, cabinet note, (?2) August 1914, Lloyd George MSS, C/14. Lord Beaverbrook wrote that McKenna supported landing the B.E.F. in Belgium so that it would attack 'against the right rear of the German turning movement'. (*Politicians and the War*, p. 39.) No contemporary source corroborates this story, which, in any case, refers to the days after Britain entered the war. Correspondence in the Beaverbrook MSS reveals that both McKenna and his wife Pamela supplied information to Beaverbrook when he was preparing his book for the press. I am grateful to Mr A. J. P. Taylor for confirmation of this point.

the distinctions between their views. It is also an injustice to those of their colleagues who were no less peacefully inclined but were readier to accept the logic of events over which they had little control.

In origin, the idea of a 'peace group' owes something to journalistic convenience, something to wishful thinking, and something to hostile polemic. After fifty years, a misleading simplification is no longer necessary. It is easier and more accurate to describe the group's behaviour than its motives. What they all did, whatever their reasons, was waver. And it is more instructive for the historian to look for the ways in which the majority of the waverers differed from the resigners, than to try to construct a neutralist case common to them all.

Between Morley and Beauchamp, for example, there were significant differences of temperament and conviction. Morley's attitude, Pease reminisced, was that of 'a broken man in old age who has no confidence in his own ability as an administrator in a time of war'. Nor did he 'possess the courage at his time of life to accept responsibility for a policy which he disliked much but which he could not condemn'.[1] The last two days of peace were, for Morley, 'really *lacerating*'. He consoled himself with 'the hope that I have run my course and kept the faith'.[2] Provoked by the posthumous publication of Morley's *Memorandum* on the outbreak of war, Beauchamp tartly explained in a letter to *The Times*, on 25 October 1928, how Morley's position had differed from that of some of those who were originally associated with him:

> There was the question of the Anglo-French Entente and there was the question of Belgian neutrality. No one who remembers the anguish and anxiety of those days, or who reads again the daily papers of that time, will hesitate to confirm Lord Morley's opinion that the first dominated the last. But then, all of a sudden, almost incredible, appeared the fact that Germany was determined to violate her solemn pledge. What wonder, then, if those who might agree with Lord Morley on the one issue, separated themselves from him on the second? His memorandum shows that the feminine

[1] Lord Gainford's Typescript Memoirs, p. 22, Gainford MSS.
[2] Morley to J. A. Spender, 6 August 1914, Spender MSS (Add. MS. 46392, f. 163).

sensibility of his intellect condemned equally those who disagreed with him on either point.

The position of Serbia may, or may not, have been of vital importance to the British Empire. There was no doubt about the neutrality of Belgium. To Lord Morley the first issue was of paramount importance. There were, on the other hand, those who agreed with him on Serbia until the Belgium question overwhelmed it. They thought that the dangers to the British Empire here involved far outweighed in magnitude the Serbian problem.[1]

Beauchamp's summary did not do justice to Morley's opinions; and there is more fantasy than history in his portrayal of the way in which the issue of Belgian neutrality came before the cabinet. It became part of the waverers' mythology that the German invasion of Belgium was a shock to British, French, and Belgians alike. The German action, it was said, was unbelievable until it had happened. 'No one anywhere', as Mr A. J. P. Taylor has put it in a characteristically succinct contribution to the mythology, 'foresaw the massive German invasion of Belgium. No one knew that this was the only German war plan.'[2] These assertions, as will shortly be demonstrated, are far from the reality. For Beauchamp, and for almost all of his temporary allies except Morley, the Belgian factor was a central, and not at all unexpected, element in their calculations.

John Burns was at once the most resolute and the least coherent of all the waverers. None of his colleagues ever quite understood why he decided to resign.[3] It was obvious that he realized quicker than most of them that they were, under the subtle management of Grey and Asquith, drifting into an irreversible anti-German position. He was determined to bear no portion of the responsibility for war; and the cabinet's decision on August 2 to close the Channel to the German fleet seemed to him to point inevitably to naval war followed by land war. The decision to protect the coasts

---

[1] *The Times*, 29 October 1928. Beauchamp was, no doubt, stung by an unkind story that Morley told at his expense. (See Morley, op. cit., p. 27.)

[2] A. J. P. Taylor, *Politics in Wartime*, and other Essays (London, 1964), p. 88.

[3] Grey did not understand why either Burns or Morley resigned, though he felt sure that the resignations 'were based on deep and sincere conviction, not on any pusillanimity or opportunism'. (Viscount Grey of Fallodon, op. cit., vol. II, p. 218.)

and shipping of France symbolized 'an alliance with France with whom no such understanding had hitherto existed'.[1] His watchwords were: 'Splendid Isolation. No Balance of Power. No Incorporation in the Continental System.'[2] And these resounding phrases could not be reconciled with Grey's inferences from the entente with France.

In querying the wisdom of being drawn into quarrels in which Great Britain had no real concern, Burns was not alone. Samuel, too, jibbed at being dragged at French and Russian coat-tails. But Samuel—whose stand on these matters seems to have been very similar to Lloyd George's—did not let distaste for the Entente policy cloud his judgment of where British interests lay. The Foreign Editor of *The Times*, Henry Wickham Steed, thought that Samuel stood firm with the Prime Minister, the First Lord of the Admiralty, the Foreign Secretary, and the Lord Chancellor in defence of the British obligation to uphold Belgian neutrality.[3] By his own account, Samuel believed from the beginning of the crisis that British obligations under the Belgian treaty were 'definite and unavoidable'; and, although he expressed some doubts at the time, he later said that he had believed that the contingency contemplated by that treaty was certain to arise. Because he was not convinced that British support for France was obligatory he was out of sympathy with Grey and Churchill. He strove, therefore, to restrict argument on the French issue, being certain that Belgium would settle the matter without destroying cabinet unity.[4] Asquith placed Samuel in the same category as McKenna and Crewe: the 'moderating intermediate body'. Although not grouped with the moderating intermediaries, the Secretary of State for Scotland, McKinnon Wood, was another who was far from being a rigid non-interventionist. Some of the Conservative leaders who tried to assess the situation on August 3 thought that

---

[1] Words inserted by Burns in Morley, op. cit., p. 8; see also Burns's Diary, July 27 to 3 August 1914, Burns MSS (Add. MS. 46336).

[2] Burns's Diary, 23 September 1915. William Kent, *John Burns: Labour's Lost Leader:* A Biography (London, 1950), p. 238. Burns was referring to a conversation he had had with Lord Fisher who had asked him why he had resigned.

[3] Henry Wickham Steed, *Through Thirty Years, 1892–1922: A Personal Narrative,* 2 vols (London, 1924), vol. II, p. 16.

[4] Typescript of an article by Samuel published in *The Manchester Guardian Weekly,* 25 October 1928, Samuel MSS, A/45.

he was among those 'likely to go'.[1] But the usually well-informed Sir George Riddell listed him as an ally of Masterman, working for compromise. Unfortunately, for McKinnon Wood, as for Masterman and several other ministers, no documents survive to enable a fuller account of his views to be compiled.[2]

Several varieties of opinion were represented in the waverers' camp. What remains to be discovered is how, from this diversity of views, a common intention emerged. What combination of ideas, personal influence, and events led nine of the eleven waverers to adhere to the ministry? The answer is not to be found in leadership. For one of the most striking features of the group is that it was leaderless. Of the two who resigned, neither Morley nor Burns had the stature or the energy to lead an anti-war faction. If Asquith had been free to choose which of his ministers should be dropped in August 1914, he would have had difficulty in finding any other pair whose efficiency or public credit made them more dispensable. Neither Morley nor Burns constituted a greater threat to the government from outside than from within.

It is correct to speak of the waverers, in G. P. Gooch's words, being 'shepherded by Harcourt'.[3] Harcourt's appetite for intrigue was undiminished by years of indulgence. And, through long experience, he had acquired a certain facility in the lesser arts of political management. Morley noticed that he was soon 'organizing opinion ... in favour of neutrality';[4] and Beauchamp, McKinnon Wood, Hobhouse, and Pease, as well as Morley had responded to his overtures. But he provided no intellectual or moral impetus. Beauchamp's prominence was attributable entirely to the fact that his London mansion, Halkyn House, was close to Westminster and large enough to be a convenient meeting place. It is doubtful whether any of the other waverers could have catered for so large a group. Simon, probably the most articulate of the waverers, already carried more weight than many older men, but he was still too junior to be an effective standard-bearer. For inspiration and fighting leadership, Lloyd George was the most obvious candidate. And, because of the outstanding position which he occupied in the Liberal Party and the nation, Lloyd George's

[1] Austen Chamberlain's Memorandum, 3 August 1914. Sir Austen Chamberlain, *Down the Years* (London, 1935), p. 103.   [2] *Lord Riddell's War Diary*, p. 3.
[3] G. P. Gooch, *Recent Revelations in European Diplomacy* (London, 1940), p. 376.
[4] Morley, op. cit., p. 4.

actions were crucial. He alone was a big enough figure to lead a significant number of men out of the government. For this reason, the key to Asquith's handling of the war crisis—and his supreme achievement in that crisis—was the unerring touch with which he played his principal lieutenant.

Lloyd George was amply qualified for the role of leader of an anti-war party. For years he had championed economy and re-ductions in naval and military expenditure. In 1914 he had three times publicly declared that Anglo-German relations were im-proving, twice after the murder of Franz Ferdinand at Sarajevo. 'In the matter of external affairs', he had said at the Guildhall on July 9, 'the sky has never been more perfectly blue.' Fourteen days later, he spoke in the Commons of improved feeling between the two great empires: 'There is none of that snarling which we used to see.'[1] As the news from the Continent grew worse, colleagues and friends sought to win him to the neutralist cause. C. P. Scott of *The Manchester Guardian* added private counsel to his columns of daily exhortation. Robertson Nicoll, editor of the influential *British Weekly*, wrote to report that the Free Churches would oppose any war.[2] Scott, in particular, kept up the pressure until the struggle was hopeless. He cabled from Manchester on August 3 to convey the 'feeling of intense exasperation here at prospect of Government embarking on war'. He concluded with an ominous warning: 'No man who is responsible can lead us again.'[3]

Had Lloyd George dared to consult his revered old uncle, Richard Lloyd, the advice would have been the same. 'Curiously enough,' his brother William noted many years later, 'this is the one question of importance on which he never asked for an opinion or guidance from Uncle Lloyd or myself. I wonder if he feared what the answer would have been?'[4] Predictability rather than fear probably accounted for this lapse in communication. Lloyd George could have had no more doubt about his uncle's views than about the wishes of most of the government's followers in the House of Commons. Perhaps if he had declared himself at an early moment he might have been able to create a powerful anti-war

[1] Thomas Jones, *Lloyd George* (London, 1951), p. 47.
[2] *Lord Riddell's War Diary*, p. 11.
[3] J. J. Hammond, *C. P. Scott: of The Manchester Guardian* (London, 1934), p. 181.
[4] William George, *My Brother and I* (London, 1958), p. 239.

contingent. Dissident elements in the cabinet, radical backbenchers, and neutralists in the country might have joined forces for a great crusade. But it is doubtful. The prospect of numerous defections from the cabinet and the foundation of a great peace movement understandably affected Asquith's calculations. The danger was too great to be ignored. As we have seen, however, rank-and-file Liberals vacillated; uncertain and divided, they were an unimposing force. Their behaviour, together with the history of Lloyd George's relations with them, made an alliance improbable from the beginning.

Even if the radicals had stood firm there is no reason to suppose that they would have looked to Lloyd George for leadership. His occasional speeches in favour of economy and friendship with Germany could not disguise the wide difference in outlook which separated Lloyd George from the Ponsonby/Buxton group. To have remained in Asquith's government as a committed and practising dissenter would have required a fixity of principle and purpose far beyond Lloyd George's capacity or inclination. And, especially after 1911, his view of continental affairs had diverged from conventional radical attitudes. In the Agadir crisis he quickly grasped, as Sir Arthur Nicolson of the Foreign Office noticed with approval, 'the point that it is not merely Morocco which is at stake'.[1] By taking the initiative and issuing a firm rebuke to Germany in his Mansion House speech, Lloyd George had displayed a new interest and a new direction in his own thinking about foreign affairs. He never relinquished his role as principal advocate of limited naval expenditure. But he was impressed by the strategic arguments of Churchill and Henry Wilson. His main concern was always social policy; and in the field of social reform he continued to enjoy the confidence and support of most radicals. On foreign policy, however, his pronouncements after 1911 were more frequently delivered as blows in a cabinet struggle for economy than as balanced statements of personal conviction. The pro-Boer Liberal group, of which Lloyd George had been so prominent a member, had passed into history; and those who dissented from Grey's policies in the pre-war years had grown

---

[1] Nicolson to Lord Hardinge of Penshurst, 14 September 1911. Harold Nicolson, *Sir Arthur Nicolson, Bt, First Lord Carnock: A Study in the Old Diplomacy* (London, 1937), p. 347.

accustomed to looking for leadership outside the cabinet. So, in July and August 1914, the neutralist radicals did not seek guidance from Lloyd George; nor he refuge with them.

While he did nothing which could be construed as a move to take command of the neutralist forces, Lloyd George unashamedly took whatever credit accrued to one who was supposed to be inspiring a peace group. Yet the recollections and contemporary records of those who were present show conclusively that he neither organized nor directed the thinking of the waverers. He readily joined the discussions of those who were least prepared to support British intervention. But the evidence is clear that he did not dominate the group.

If his voice was not the loudest, it was not because he opposed the war any the less, or was less surprised than his fellow ministers at the sudden development of the crisis. (As late as Friday, July 31, both Asquith and Lloyd George were confirming plans to spend the week-end away from London, Asquith in Anglesea, Lloyd George in Dieppe.) The Chancellor did not expect war; and he did not want it. But, no matter what his personal feelings, if war could not be avoided then both duty and self-interest dictated that he should remain at his post. During the worrying days of 1911 he had recognized that a time would come when German ambition might have to be checked by a combination which included a British expeditionary force. Some observers had then been startled by his apparent bellicosity. He had actually contemplated British troops 'pivoting on Antwerp'.[1] If he had forgotten the lessons impressed upon him three years earlier by Henry Wilson, he was reminded on August 1 in a plainly worded memorandum by one of Wilson's disciples, Major A. H. Ollivant, a General Staff officer seconded to Churchill. Ollivant had been instructed by Churchill 'to lecture Lloyd George on the European military situation'.[2] His survey of strategic principles and mobilization schedules concluded that:

Germany's chief object, as far as this country is concerned, lies in preventing the arrival of the British expeditionary

[1] Churchill to Lloyd George, 31 August 1911. Randolph S. Churchill, op. cit., pp. 530–1; Lloyd George to Churchill, 27 August 1911, Frank Owen, *Tempestuous Journey*, Lloyd George His Life and Times (London, 1954), p. 212.
[2] Henry Wilson's Diary, 1 August 1914, Wilson MSS.

army. Its absence from the battlefield will exercise an influence out of all proportion to its numerical strength…There is reason to suppose that the presence or absence of the British army will determine the action of the Belgian army. It will very probably decide the fate of France.[1]

It is conceivable that, for a short time, as he wrote in his *War Memoirs*, Lloyd George thought that, by delaying her entry into the war, Britain might be able to build up her army and then dictate terms to the belligerents.[2] But there is no evidence, apart from his own later testimony, that he ever pressed this view upon his colleagues or friends.[3] Indeed, when he discussed German strategy with C. P. Scott on July 27, his assumption was quite incompatible with this suggestion. Germany, he said, would attempt to strike and cripple France and then would deal separately with Russia. If the British fleet were not interposed in the North Sea the Germans could 'land a force behind the French forces advancing *to meet the German invasion across Belgium*'.[4] He clearly saw both that Germany would attack across Belgium and that without British help the French would quickly be beaten.

Even if the French held out for some time against a German onslaught, it was not easy to dismiss Churchill's argument that the German occupation of the ports at the mouth of the Rhine, Scheldt, and Ems would be a serious menace to Great Britain.[5] Neither Lloyd George nor any of the other waverers was so naive

[1] 'A Short Survey of the Present Military Situation in Europe', Typescript Memorandum by Major A. H. Ollivant, 1 August 1914, Lloyd George MSS, C/16/1/14. A longer extract from Ollivant's memo is printed in the appendix on Military Planning before the Outbreak of War.

[2] David Lloyd George, *War Memoirs*, 6 vols (London, 1933–6), vol. 1, pp. 71–3.

[3] There is a note in the Lloyd George MSS (C/13) written by Lloyd George on 11 Downing Street notepaper, dated by Frances Stevenson, 3 August 1914, which reads: 'Whilst others fighting our business confined to starving [sic] women & children including our own. What will be the effect on Italy, Belgium & Holland.' This suggests a policy of naval blockade rather than neutrality. But the tone of irony and distaste suggests that Lloyd George was meditating on someone else's argument rather than his own. Randolph S. Churchill, op. cit., p. 719, cites this document, but prefaces it by the sentence, 'Ready to defend ourselves,' which comes from another document, dated 1 August 1914. Neither of these documents was a note to Churchill as Mr Churchill supposed. Both were private jottings.

[4] C. P. Scott's Memorandum, 27 July 1914, Scott MSS (Add. MS. 50901, ff. 144, 146). This document, in which Scott summarized Lloyd George's remarks on the European situation, is extensively quoted in J. L. Hammond, op. cit., pp. 177–8.

[5] Pease's Diary, 29 July 1914, Gainford MSS.

as to think that Great Britain had no interest in the security of the
Low Countries. The strange thing was their reluctance to admit
their concern even to each other. There was much posturing and
mouthing of phrases; but the overriding strategic facts were
wilfully neglected. Referring to the cabinet as a whole, the late
Lawrence Hammond wrote:

> It is perhaps not surprising that this little group of men,
> worn with eight years of arduous contention, faced at home
> with such confusion as no Government had faced since 1832,
> abroad with such confusion as no Government had faced since
> 1803, divided among themselves about their duty to Europe
> and their duty to Great Britain, seeing the chief danger of
> the hour and the future, some in Germany, others in Russia,
> groped and hesitated when they found themselves in the path
> of the storm.[1]

Due allowance must be made for the honest confusion which
Hammond explained. But there was something more than groping
and hesitation; there was deliberate evasion of issues. Neither
Asquith nor Grey asked for an unequivocal decision on the extent
of the British commitment under the French entente; and the
waverers gratefully refrained from forcing their colleagues to
accept a cripplingly restrictive interpretation. Meanwhile, the
waverers met and talked in private.

[1] J. L. Hammond, op. cit., p. 181.

6 'A *casus belli* wh everyone here wd understand'[1]

Lloyd George, Harcourt, Beauchamp, Simon, Pease, and Runciman gathered at 11 Downing Street at 10.15 a.m. on August 2.[2]
There, they 'all agreed we were not prepared to go into war now,
but that in certain events we might reconsider position, such as the
invasion wholesale of Belgium.'[3] Rarely has so eminent a company
of British politicians indulged in such an elaborate exercise in
mutual and self-deception. It should be noted that the conspicuous absentees from this meeting were Morley and Burns.
Neither would have tolerated the sham.

When Morley joined an enlarged group at lunch with Beauchamp, he was unimpressed by their resolution. John Burns had
announced his resignation after the morning cabinet had decided
to assure the French that Britain would protect French coasts and
shipping against attacks by the German fleet. What would the
waverers do? Morley remembered their meeting:

> It wore all the look of an important gathering, but was in
> truth a very shallow affair. On the surface they were pretty
> stalwart against allowing a mistaken interpretation of entente
> to force us into a Russian or Central European quarrel. The
> general voice was loud that 'Burns was right', and that we
> should not have passed Grey's proposed language to Cambon.
> They all pressed the point that the Cabinet was being rather
> artfully drawn on step by step to war for the benefit of France
> and Russia. If I, or anybody else, could only have brought
> home to them that the compound and mixed argument of
> French liability and Belgian liability must end in expedition-

[1] Churchill to Lloyd George, 31 August 1911, commenting on a possible infringement of Belgian neutrality by Germany. (Randolph S. Churchill, op. cit., p. 531.)

[2] The cabinet was to meet next door at 11.00 a.m.

[3] Pease's Diary, 2 August 1914, Gainford MSS.

ary force, and active part in vast and long-continued European war, the Cabinet would undoubtedly have perished that very evening.[1]

Morley was right to perceive that none of his colleagues sensed what sort of conflict they were about to enter. Whether, with complete foreknowledge, they would have acted differently is another matter. For all their expostulations about being 'artfully drawn', their resistance was notably muted. Talk was all; nobody suggested action.

On many points of detail Morley's memory betrayed him; but it is difficult to dispute the accuracy of his instinct about the waverers' state of mind. He remembered thinking that:

> the precipitate and peremptory blaze about Belgium was due less to indignation at the violation of a Treaty than to natural perception of the plea that it would furnish for intervention on behalf of France, for expeditionary force, and all the rest of it. Belgium was to take the place that had been taken before, as pleas for war, by Morocco and Agadir.[2]

The odd thing was that Morley himself did very little to influence his colleagues. He came among the waverers by invitation but, like Lloyd George, he did not take a leading part in their discussions. Nor did he try to sway the opinions of those who explicitly dissented from him. Augustine Birrell, an old friend of Morley's who was 'by no means enamoured' of Grey's policy, could not remember any occasion when 'on this vital question of our pre-war policy he ever addressed a word to me for my soul's benefit, and this was all the more surprising because he was never indisposed to sermonise after a most seductive fashion'.[3]

In fact, Morley expressed himself at the time rather less decisively than his memoir of these events discloses. At cabinet on July 29, for example, Pease noted that he said: 'I shall not be a party to any intervention between Austria and Serbia. France may be a different thing.'[4]

For the majority of the waverers, it was to be Belgium not

[1] Morley, op. cit., p. 15.
[2] Ibid., p. 14.
[3] Augustine Birrell., op. cit., pp. 233–4.
[4] Pease's Diary, 29 July 1914, Gainford MSS.

France which was the ostensibly 'different thing'. And, in truth, when they talked as though a German invasion of Belgium *might* have changed the situation they were simply saving face. The invasion of Belgium did not convert Lloyd George, or any of the others; it provided a pretext for an otherwise humiliating *volte face*. As far as Lloyd George's behaviour is concerned, his widow's testimony provides important, if not conclusive, corroboration of this interpretation. Frances Stevenson was at No. 11 Downing Street throughout the first week-end in August. As private secretary and intimate companion she was well placed to observe the Chancellor's moods: 'My own opinion is that L.G.'s mind was really made up from the first, that he knew we would have to go in, and that the invasion of Belgium was, to be cynical, a heaven-sent excuse for supporting a declaration of war.'[1]

Had it not been for the need to prevent the slightest suspicion that he was anything other than a most reluctant interventionist, Lloyd George might well have written to Grey in August 1914 as he had in September 1911:

> War is by no means inevitable but it is becoming an increasing probability. It is so much in the reckoning as to render it urgently necessary for us to take every step which would render the issue of war more favourable always provided that such a step does not increase the chances of precipitating a war.[2]

The behaviour of the majority of the waverers was consistent with their holding views like this. Their instinct was for patience. 'Do fight for unity,' Masterman implored Lloyd George.[3] And this was precisely what Lloyd George did. 'If patience prevails and you do not press us too hard,' he scribbled to Churchill across the cabinet table, 'we might come together.'[4] Belgium could bring unity; but only if the will existed to make it the basis of unity. There is evidence that Lloyd George argued that the German invasion plan might have involved the merest infraction of Belgian neutrality, and that he tried to persuade a number of his

[1] Frances Lloyd George, *The Years that are Past* (London, 1967), pp. 73-4.
[2] Lloyd George to Grey, 1 September 1911, Grey MSS, FO 800/101.
[3] Masterman's cabinet note, (?2) August 1914, Lloyd George MSS, C/14.
[4] Lloyd George to Churchill, undated cabinet note, (?1) August 1914, Lloyd George MSS, C/14.

friends that the 'little bit' of Belgian territory in question would not warrant British intervention. He told C. P. Scott on August 3 that he had urged the cabinet not to go to war if the German occupation of Belgium was limited to the 'sort of nose of land running out by Luxembourg'.[1] Was this a serious proposal? Lord Beaverbrook, who also records this story, seems to have believed it.[2] It seems indisputable that Lloyd George did, at some stage, speak in this sense. But he was shamming. He was reaping the benefit of neutralist noisemaking while certain that the hypothesis he was propounding would be falsified by events. A similar judgment may legitimately be passed on the version of the story recorded by Scott on 4 September 1914. Scott asked Lloyd George:

> to what point he had pushed his opposition to our taking part in the war. He said he would have resigned rather than consent to our going to war if Germany would have agreed not to violate Belgian territory or even if she would have agreed only to pass over the small projecting piece between Luxembourg and France, and he said Grey had, under pressure, agreed that if Germany would respect Belgian neutrality he would not insist on supporting France (perhaps, G. said, he knew she wouldn't), but he admitted that these terms had never been presented to Germany and said he 'regretted it'.[3]

After the event it was understandable that Lloyd George should wish to emphasize how reluctant he had been to support intervention. But there is no convincing evidence that he actually fought hard for the adoption of the neutralist policy which he outlined to Scott a month after the war had begun. What is certain is that Lloyd George had faced the possibility of war with Germany in 1911, and he had not flinched. He had agreed then with Churchill that, as Churchill put it, the 'violation' of Belgium 'wd be an undoubted *casus belli*, independently of other "griefs"'.[4] In the

[1] Scott's Memorandum, 4 August 1914, Scott MSS (Add. MS. 50901, ff. 148–50).
[2] Lord Beaverbrook, op. cit., p. 23.
[3] Scott's Memorandum, 4 September 1914, Scott MSS (Add. MS. 50901, f. 160).
[4] Churchill to Lloyd George, 31 August 1911. Randolph S. Churchill, *Winston S. Churchill*, vol. II, p. 531; for Lloyd George's qualified approval of Churchill's proposals for action if the Morocco negotiations failed, see Lloyd George to Churchill, 5 September 1911. *Winston S. Churchill*, Companion Volume II, part 2, pp. 1121–2.

following year when the Committee of Imperial Defence discussed plans for economic warfare against Germany, Lloyd George had been the strongest advocate of partially blockading Belgium and the Netherlands if, in the event of war, they tried to remain neutral. 'The first six weeks of war would be all-important,' he told his colleagues. 'We could not afford to lose a moment when war broke out.'[1] No matter how indecisive he may have sought to appear in July 1914, there is no reason to suppose that Lloyd George had receded in any degree from his firm, committed position in the discussions of 1911 and 1912.

What of the attitude of the other waverers towards Belgium? Was their devotion to Belgian independence and inviolability so deeply rooted that the very mention of a possible infringement aroused their indignation? So they later wished it to be believed. But the truth was different. When it suited them to dispute the binding nature of the British obligation to Belgium they did so unashamedly. Plausible arguments came readily to their tongues. The outlines of a neutralist case were presented in a letter which Charles Trevelyan, not himself a member of the cabinet, wrote to Walter Runciman:

I draw a great distinction between
a. Germany marching through Belgium for military purposes to get at France; and
b. Germany seizing Antwerp and the whole of Belgium.

I am quite clear that our civilization ought not to go into the melting-pot for the first contingency. Even our ancestors never intended to prevent merely the passage of troops. What they were thinking of was Belgian Independence. The letter of an obligation (if it really exists) is not enough to justify us in fighting because of such a considerable but still limited outrage against Belgian neutrality.

For that reason I strongly deprecate any statement by us in general terms that we require the observance of Belgian neutrality.

Belgian independence is another matter. But I am bound to

[1] Minutes of the 120th Meeting of the Committee of Imperial Defence, 6 December 1912, p. 7, Mottistone MSS.

say that I shall require to see the occupation of Antwerp etc. before I believe that it is more than bluff on Germany's part.

Now that war is declared, England must say that she is not joining in to help France. If that is done, as it ought to be tomorrow, I am bound to say that I should expect the result to be that Germany would limit her operations rather than risk incurring our definite hostility.

I ask you therefore to make up your mind not to allow us to be dragged into war:

(1) for the sake of preventing the Germans making a limited strategical use of Belgium however irritating it may be;

(2) by not distinguishing in our dealing and communications with Germany between such a passage of troops and the complete conquest of Belgium;

(3) by taking for granted that Germany will necessarily do all the things she threatens.[1]

At least some of Trevelyan's points were heard at 10 Downing Street. For example, Jack Pease noted on August 2 that 'Harcourt [was apparently] not prepared to rely on the Treaty of 1839 as necessarily binding. Simon was arguing also that 80 years had created wholly different circumstances'.[2]

Moreover, in assessing the candour of the waverers, it cannot be argued that the probable route of a German attack on France was a secret. To say, as Asquith's official biographers did, that until Luxembourg was invaded, it was only a 'hypothesis' that Germany would invade Belgium, is to give a misleading impression.[3] A similarly false emphasis is given by Crewe's statement, in 1936, that the invasion of Belgium was 'likely...[but] by no means certain'.[4]

Haldane's recollection was different. He wrote in his memoirs: 'I had always thought that this would be their mode of attack on France.'[5] Fortified by the knowledge acquired in the years when

[1] Trevelyan to Runciman, (?2) August 1914, Runciman MSS.
[2] Pease's Diary, 2 August 1914, Gainford MSS. Words in brackets added later by Pease.
[3] Spender and Asquith, op. cit., vol. II, p. 89.
[4] G. M. Trevelyan, op. cit., p. 257.
[5] Richard Burdon Haldane, op. cit., p. 275.

he reorganized the army, Haldane was probably the best-informed student of military affairs in the ministry. As Haldane knew, it was not merely a hypothesis, but the considered and unanimous prediction of the responsible British military authorities that the German route to France was through Belgium. Of course, the waverers could argue that German transit through a corner of Belgium would not justify British intervention. And there were high military authorities who held the view that the major thrust of the German attack would not be north and west of the Meuse. Indeed, *The Times* military correspondent, Colonel Repington, wrote in 1921 that:

> ... in the years immediately preceding the war some of our soldiers and the French came to false conclusions on the subject of a German attack, gravely underestimated the enemy's strength, misunderstood his strategy, and never took sufficiently into account the danger that the Germans would make their main effort through Belgium.[1]

Repington was convinced that German strategy, after 1911, involved a wide enveloping movement through Belgium.[2] However, General Wilson predicted that only Belgian cowardice or neglect would enable the German armies to penetrate north of the Meuse.[3] Wilson, as Director of Military Operations, laid great stress on the need for an understanding with Belgium. But the suspicions of the Belgians, and their fear that conversations with any power or group of powers would imply that rival powers could not be trusted, had made it impossible for any plans for military co-operation to be devised.[4] Early in 1915, writing to General Sir Neville Lyttelton from G.H.Q., British Army in the Field, Major-General Sir William Robertson recalled what he could of the arrangements that had been made:

[1] Lieut.-Col. C. à Court Repington, *The First World War, 1914–1918:* Personal Experiences, 2 vols (London, 1920), vol. 1, pp. 14–15.

[2] Lieut.-Col. Charles à Court Repington, *Vestigia* (London, 1919), pp. 304–9, refers to Repington's pre-war articles in *The Times*.

[3] Basil Collier, *Brasshat:* A Biography of Field-Marshal Sir Henry Wilson (London, 1961), p. 127. See the appendix on Military Planning.

[4] See the useful article by Jonathan E. Helmreich, 'Belgian Concern over Neutrality and British Intentions, 1906–1914', *Journal of Modern History*, vol. xxxvi, No. 4 (December 1964), pp. 416–17.

... some kind of unofficial permission was given to Barnardiston to discuss matters generally with the Belgian Chief of the Staff, as to what the Belgian Army could do and would be prepared to do in co-operation with ourselves in the event of Belgium being invaded. I feel certain that there was never any intention of our intervening unless Belgium were invaded, nor was it ever supposed that we could prevent the country from being invaded, for the simple reason that we did not propose to act until invasion practically took place.[1]

Robertson had left the War Office in 1907 and knew nothing of any results of Colonel Barnardiston's discussions, though he believed that 'nothing definite ever was settled'. What had been settled could have been quickly explained to the cabinet. But, as Henry Wilson noted in disgust: 'No C.I.D. has been held, no military opinion has been asked for by this cursed Cabinet who are deciding on a question of war.'[2]

The cabinet received no official briefing. The ineffectual Chief of the Imperial General Staff, Sir Charles Douglas, was brushed aside by Asquith and Grey.[3] Nevertheless, Asquith himself made sure that the crucial strategic point about Belgium was put before his ministers at least as early as July 29. Pease wrote in his diary that 'the Prime Minister said that if the Germans attacked France they would certainly go through Belgium, and would hesitate to attack in any other way.'[4]

Asquith evidently did not dwell on this prediction. Some of his audience did not grasp at once the significance of what he had said. Only Jack Pease thought the point important enough to record it. Yet, after fourteen years, Herbert Samuel had not forgotten that:

the information which was before us was categorical that the German strategic plan did involve the invasion of Belgium

---

[1] Robertson to Lyttelton, 24 January 1915 (copy), Grey MSS, FO 800/102. Lieut.-Col. N. W. Barnardiston was the British Military Attaché in Brussels. For a comment on the 'curious legend' that the British Army planned to invade Belgium, see Viscount Haldane, *Before the War* (London, 1920), pp. 180-2, and Jonathan E. Helmreich, loc. cit.

[2] Henry Wilson's Diary, 31 July 1914, Wilson MSS.

[3] Lieut.-Col. C. à Court Repington, *The First World War, 1914-1918*, vol. 1, p. 20.

[4] Pease's Diary, 29 July 1914, Gainford MSS.

and that there was no likelihood that it would be changed in any circumstances or on any conditions. There was every reason to believe that the Belgians would resist.[1]

Crewe testified to the same effect. Although he had changed his mind eight years later (probably after corrupting his memory by reading Spender and Asquith's *Life* of Asquith), Crewe wrote to Samuel in 1928 that 'there was general agreement that Belgium would be invaded'.[2] 'General agreement' put it, perhaps, too conclusively. There were doubters. And there were those who did not want to believe. To those who were uncertain Churchill addressed a barrage of contradiction. He repeatedly re-stated what Asquith had said on the 29th: that Germany would only attack France through Belgium, 'all her preparations had been made to this end...she neither could nor would adopt any different strategy'.[3] On August 1, Churchill wrote categorically to F. E. Smith: 'Germany must march through Belgium.'[4] Further, he put before all his colleagues the strategic danger to Britain 'if Belgium was occupied by Germany'.[5] Nobody wanted to utter self-fulfilling prophecies. And brains as yet unattuned to the imminence of war, sought, as if by instinct, to discount the likelihood of events that might draw Britain into conflict. Eyes closed. Heads bent towards sand. With characteristic simplicity, Pease proposed to his colleagues 'that we should not in conversation allude to a possible German invasion of Belgium'.[6] The subject was, by tacit consent, dropped. Having weighed the precedents, a working compromise was reached. Asquith summarized the conclusions of the cabinet of July 29 in his report to the King:

It is a doubtful point how far a single guaranteeing State is bound under the Treaty of 1839 to maintain Belgian neutrality if the remainder abstain or refuse.

The Cabinet consider that the matter if it arises will be one of policy rather than of legal obligation.[7]

[1] Samuel's typescript article, 25 October 1928, Samuel MSS, A/45/1.
[2] Lord Crewe to Samuel, 26 November 1928, Samuel MSS A/45/2; see also Crewe's statement of 2 May 1936, G. M. Trevelyan, op. cit., pp 256–7.
[3] Winston S. Churchill, op. cit., p. 200.
[4] Lord Birkenhead, op. cit., p. 241.
[5] Pease's Diary, 29 July 1914, Gainford MSS.
[6] Ibid.
[7] Spender and Asquith, op. cit., vol. II, p. 82.

Historians have overlooked the real pusillanimity of this formula. What was decided was not, as many have supposed, that a German invasion of Belgium would not automatically entail British intervention to maintain Belgian neutrality. The words plainly refer to a much more qualified contingency than a mere German invasion. All that was ever contemplated was whether Great Britain *alone* would be obliged to come to Belgium's aid, if the other guaranteeing states abstained or refused to do so.[1] It was, therefore, implicitly assumed either that France would herself violate Belgium or refuse to defend her. That either possibility should for a moment have clouded the issue of the only genuine threat—the threat of unprovoked German attack—is scarcely conceivable. It is so fantastic that it has hitherto escaped notice. Nevertheless, it is true. Pease's request that his colleagues should not allude to the possibility of German invasion found its answer in this Belgian formula: a pathetic dodge from an imaginary dilemma.

Why the cabinet did not at this stage, as Grey wished, consider what it would do if France were also prepared to respect and defend Belgian neutrality is a mystery. If the waverers, as some of them later maintained, would have been united in support of Belgium, it is curious that they failed to convey this fact to Asquith and Grey. Lloyd George wrote in 1933:

> Had the question of defending the neutrality and integrity of Belgium been raised there would not have been a dissentient voice on that issue. Lord Morley and John Burns might conceivably have stood out...But such a proposal was never submitted to our judgment.[2]

But it is no reply to say that the question was never posed in this way; for it was open to any member of the cabinet to propose a formula for discussion. The truth is that, until the necessity for a plausible *casus belli* was perceived, Belgium was not the focus of attention. John Burns, for example, seems to have been satisfied that the situation had been reviewed on July 29 'from all points of

[1] The cabinet was reminded on July 29 that Gladstone's Law Officers in 1870 held that 'the Powers were really jointly & severally responsible for the fulfilment of the [Belgian] Treaty' of 1839. (Pease's Diary, 29 July 1914, Gainford MSS).

[2] Lloyd George, op. cit., vol. i, p. 71.

view'.[1] In coming, one by one, to realize the significance of Belgium, the cabinet could not be hurried. When deciding for peace or war, 'each must be led by his own conscience',[2] Herbert Samuel wrote to his wife on July 30. By then a powerful minority of minds was already decided. But five days earlier, Asquith himself, talking with Edwin Montagu, was heard to say that Great Britain was under no obligation to Belgium.[3] It was hardly surprising that some of Asquith's colleagues continued a little longer to ignore the 'acts and tacit promises' by which they were encircled.[4]

[1] Burns's Diary, 29 July 1914, Burns MSS (Add. MS. 46336, f. 126).

[2] Samuel to Beatrice Samuel, 30 July 1914. John Bowle, *Viscount Samuel: A Biography* (London, 1957), p. 119.

[3] Lady Ottoline Morrell's Journal, 25 July 1914. Robert Gathorne-Hardy, loc. cit.

[4] Lord Esher's Journal, 3 August 1914. Oliver, Viscount Esher (ed.), *Journals and Letters of Reginald, Viscount Esher*, vols III–IV (London, 1938), vol. III, 1910–15, p. 174.

7 'The march of events will be dominating'[1]

The drift to intervention began with defensive precautions. 'So amazingly rapid' was the development of events, according to Lord Crewe, 'that we all feel as though we were living in a novel by Wells, and in no real world'.[2] On Monday, July 27, warning telegrams were dispatched to all naval, military, and colonial stations initiating a 'precautionary period'. Churchill and the First Sea Lord, with the concurrence of the Foreign Secretary, had already postponed the dispersal of the First and Second Fleets after their test mobilization. This action was approved by the cabinet.[3] 'I am still inclined to be pessimistic about the outlook,' Herbert Samuel wrote to his wife after the Monday evening cabinet, 'but we are doing our best to localize the conflict...Fortunately the P.M. & Grey are very fit and in good physical trim—very necessary when we are in a double crisis like this.'[4] Haldane, writing the same evening to his mother, thought 'there is just a chance of peace in the Near East'.[5] The situation was, at any rate, hopeful enough to permit the postponement until the following day of a discussion of the 'precise obligations in regard to the neutrality of Belgium'.[6]

On the 28th Samuel continued to be pessimistic. Having given up their London house for the Whitsun recess, the Samuel family

---

[1] Churchill to Lloyd George, undated cabinet note (1 August 1914). Randolph S. Churchill, op. cit., p. 719.

[2] Crewe to Lord Hardinge of Penshurst, 6 August 1914, Hardinge MSS, 76, f. 108. Part of this letter is quoted, from the copy in the Crewe MSS, in James Pope-Hennessy, op. cit., pp. 144–5.

[3] Asquith to King George V (cabinet letter), 28 July 1914. Spender and Asquith, op. cit., vol. II, p. 81. This letter summarized the discussion at the previous evening's cabinet.

[4] Samuel to Beatrice Samuel, 27 July 1914, Samuel MSS, A/157/687, ff. 19–20.

[5] Haldane to Mary Haldane, 27 July 1914, Haldane MSS, 5991, f. 276.

[6] Asquith to King George V (cabinet letter), 28 July 1914. Spender and Asquith, op. cit., vol. II, p. 81.

was separated and Samuel, finding temporary refuge in the Royal Palace Hotel, wrote daily letters to his wife. To this fortuitous separation, and to the extraordinary freedom with which Asquith and his ministers conveyed confidential information to their family circle and friends, we owe some of the most interesting accounts of the development of events. Samuel's letter on the 28th passed on the news that Austria had declared war on Serbia:

> That was clearly inevitable. There is a strange silence from Russia, which may mean that she intends to keep quiet, or which may mean that she is carrying out the preliminaries to her mobilisation without alarming the Germans prematurely. The great difficulty for Russia arises from the vast distances over which her armies have to be brought. The Germans can mobilise much more quickly and may be able to throw all their weight upon France before Russia is ready to move effectively. The Russians of course are fully alive to this and may possibly be refraining from showing their hands as long as possible.[1]

Writing presumably a few hours earlier than Samuel, Haldane had told his mother that 'things look a little less threatening in the East. I believe that there is no Power that really wants war. The next twenty-four hours will decide.'[2] The news that Austria had declared war on Serbia reached the Foreign Office at 6.45 p.m. At 5.00 p.m. the Admiralty had ordered the First Fleet to proceed to its preliminary war stations in the North Sea.[3]

The following day between 11.30 a.m. and 2.00 p.m. there was, as Samuel wrote, 'a long and grave Cabinet'. Asquith, Grey, and Haldane had sat up until 1.00 a.m. in the morning considering the implications of the declaration of war by Austria. What would Russia do? It seemed to Samuel that:

> Matters are taking the course which I foresaw on Friday [July 24] they would take. Russia will mobilise her southern

[1] Samuel to Beatrice Samuel, 28 July 1914, Samuel MSS, A/157/689, ff. 24-5.
[2] Haldane to Mary Haldane, 28 July 1914, Haldane MSS, 5911, f. 277.
[3] Brigadier-General J. E. Edmonds, *Military Operations France and Belgium, 1914* (London, 1922), vol. 1, p. 24. This volume was the first in the *History of the Great War*, based on official documents, compiled by direction of the Historical Section of the Committee of Imperial Defence.

armies tomorrow. It remains to be seen whether or not
Germany regarding war as inevitable will then at once strike
at France. There is a slight hope that, under the influence of
the Emperor and Bethmann-Hollweg, the Chancellor, she may
not do so. But her alliance with Austria binds her to intervene
if Russia does, and if she were to hold back now she may well
say that the only effect would be to give Russia time to complete her mobilisation which is so much slower than her own.
I still think that the probabilities are that the fuse which has
been fired will quickly bring a catastrophic explosion. You will
have seen that the P.M. said in the House to-day that the position is one of extreme gravity.

We nineteen men round the table at Downing St. may soon
have to face the most momentous problem which men can
face. Meantime our action is held in suspense, for if both
sides do not know what we shall do, both will be the less
willing to run risks.[1]

By the afternoon of July 29, the situation was unmistakably
'very critical' as Haldane reported to his mother. Grey's optimism
was drained, though he remained 'marvellously cool & concentrated'. But Haldane believed 'there is still hope.'[2] John Burns
recorded in his diary that the cabinet had 'decided not to decide'.[3]

Although he was given no clear lead by the morning cabinet
meeting, Grey told the German Ambassador, Lichnowsky, on the
afternoon of the 29th that his own friendly tone should not be
misconstrued as evidence that Britain would stand aside if
Germany and France were at war. This was a thinly veiled warning. The Foreign Secretary did not, however, give the French
Ambassador any encouragement. Even if France and Germany
were in conflict, Cambon was told, 'we were free from engagements, and we should have to decide what British interests required us to do'. Grey had been authorized only to indicate to the
German and French Ambassadors that Great Britain could not,
at that stage, pledge itself in advance 'either under all conditions
to stand aside, or in any conditions to join in'. Notwithstanding
this refusal to move to commitment, after Churchill had described

---

[1] Samuel to Beatrice Samuel, 29 July 1914, Samuel MSS, A/157/691, ff. 29-31.
[2] Haldane to Mary Haldane, 29 July 1914, Haldane MSS, 5911, f. 279.
[3] Burns's Diary, 29 July 1914, Burns MSS (Add. MS. 46336, f. 126).

the steps that he had taken, the cabinet decided that the time had come to open the War Book, and put the Precautionary Measures, on land and sea, into operation.[1] After a short delay—'no one', recalled Lord Hankey, 'had the slightest idea how to start the ball rolling'—officers and men on leave and furlough were recalled to duty, coastal defences were manned, and warning telegrams dispatched to the fleets.[2] Asquith, sending his regular bulletin to Miss Stanley at 6.00 p.m. on the 29th, reported: 'I have just finished an Army Council—concerned entirely with arrangements during the "precautionary period". Rather interesting because it enables one to realise what are the first steps in an actual war.'[3]

Asquith's bland comment and Hankey's jocular reminiscence concealed a disturbing state of affairs. The War Book prepared by the Committee of Imperial Defence under Hankey's direction had not taken for granted that British involvement in war would mean the speedy transference of an expeditionary force across the Channel. It was bad enough that several ministers forgot or did not understand their responsibilities to alert their departments after the cabinet decision to be in 'a state of readiness'. What was potentially much more dangerous was the failure of the C.I.D. to have done what most ministers thought it had done: effectively co-ordinate military and naval planning. In fact, while Churchill and the War Office had worked out plans on the assumption of a British 'continental strategy' Hankey continued, at least until July 31, to believe that the dispatch of an expeditionary force at the beginning of war was undesirable. Moreover, Hankey seems to have been kept in ignorance of the departmental plans which had been made.[4]

In thinking that it was an open question whether or not Britain would send an expeditionary force if she entered the war, Hankey shared a view which was common in the cabinet. On Thursday, July 30, General Sir John French was called to the War Office and

<hr/>

[1] Asquith to King George V (cabinet letter), 30 July 1914. Spender and Asquith, op. cit., vol. II, p. 81, referring to the cabinet on July 29.

[2] Edmonds, loc. cit.; Lord Hankey, *The Supreme Command, 1914–1918*, 2 vols (London, 1961), vol. I, p. 155–6.

[3] Asquith to Venetia Stanley, 29 July 1914 Montagu MSS.

[4] I am grateful to Mr Nicholas d'Ombrain for drawing my attention to letters and papers in the Esher and Corbett MSS which reveal Hankey's role. See also Hankey to Balfour, 12 October 1913, Balfour MSS (Whittingehame), 39.

informed privately by the Chief of the General Staff that he had been selected to command the expeditionary force, if one should be sent. But a decision on this vital matter remained to be taken.

July 30 also saw an important shift towards a stiffening of the British position. Grey had come to the conclusion that a militarist faction had gained the upper hand in Berlin. His attempts to restrain the Austrian government by appeals to the Germans were, he realized, futile. With Asquith's concurrence, the Foreign Secretary took it upon himself to reject a German proposal, transmitted by Sir Edward Goschen, the British Ambassador in Berlin, that Great Britain should pledge neutrality in return for a German guarantee of the territorial integrity of Belgium and metropolitan France after hostilities had ceased. The suggestion that Great Britain should stand aside while Belgium was invaded and Germany helped herself to French colonies provoked Grey to 'a white heat of passion'. The Prime Minister himself wrote to Miss Stanley of the 'rather shameless' German offer.[1] In the inflamed indignation of the moment, the Foreign Secretary persuaded Asquith to sanction an immediate reply. 'There was to be a Cabinet that afternoon,' Grey later wrote, 'but we agreed that the answer might be sent without waiting for the Cabinet.'[2]

In *Twenty-Five Years*, Grey wrote of his certainty that 'the Cabinet would agree that this bid for neutrality could not be accepted'.[3] Grey further recalled that 'in the afternoon...the Cabinet...approved what had been done'.[4] In fact, however, the cabinet did not meet in the afternoon of July 30. It did not meet again until the morning of the 31st. There is no official record of the meeting on the 31st, Asquith having communicated with the King in person rather than writing his customary letter. For

[1] Asquith to Venetia Stanley, 30 July 1914, Montagu MSS.

[2] Viscount Grey of Fallodon, op. cit., vol. II, pp. 175–81; Goschen to Grey and Grey to Goschen, 30 July 1914, *BDXI*, Nos. 293 and 303, pp. 185–6, 193–4; Grey's 'white heat of passion' was reported by his secretary (Sir William Tyrrell) to Francis Acland and recorded in Eleanor Acland's War Diary, 8 August 1914, Acland MSS.

[3] Viscount Grey of Fallodon, op. cit., vol. II, p. 180.

[4] Ibid., p. 181. See also Spender and Asquith, op. cit., vol. II, p. 87. Spender, following Grey's account, assumed that there had been a cabinet on July 30. Hence his comment on 'the limit of the intervention which the cabinet contemplated on 30th July'. He further confused himself into dating Grey's refusal to make any pledges to the French and German Ambassadors to the 30th instead of the 29th, forgetting, perhaps, that Asquith's cabinet letter of the 30th referred to the previous day's meeting.

evidence of what actually did happen in the cabinet when the German feeler was reported to it we must rely on Pease's diary:

> The P.M. alluded to ingenuous part Bethman-Hollweg had played—how he had written a letter through German Ambassador suggesting that we should abstain from the war if Germans at end of war left Belgium intact & their independence. Grey told him that without cabinet sanction he could not bargain treaty obligations away & if Germany wanted peace we were working for same end & believed if we could jointly bring it about it would do more to cement good feeling than any abstention now from war, & that he Grey would use his best offices to bring about a more permanent understanding & thought it would be then possible that the better relations which had been established cd take definite form.[1]

What was the cabinet's reaction to this news? Sir Eyre Crowe had minuted on Goschen's telegram that 'Germany practically admits the intention to violate Belgian neutrality'.[2] If the waverers were unwilling on the 29th to take the word of Asquith or Churchill, here surely was hard evidence that pointed in the same direction. The German proposals were such as 'we might have thrown aside without consideration and almost without answer', Asquith told the House of Commons on August 6.[3] Sir Stanley Buckmaster, the Solicitor-General, told Christopher Addison on August 4 that after the receipt of the German Chancellor's message, Simon, Harcourt, and Pease changed their minds about resignation and 'decided to stick to the ship'.[4]

In fact, however, we have seen that the cabinet was still very

[1] Pease's Diary, 31 July 1914, Gainford MSS. Grey's letter to Goschen on 30 July 1914 was not, in fact, couched in this form. The Foreign Secretary said nothing about not having a free hand or needing cabinet authority. He simply rejected the German proposal as unacceptable. When Lichnowsky probed further on August 1 about possible conditions for British neutrality, Grey apparently did not bring the German inquiry to the attention of his colleagues. John Burns complained of seeing the relevant telegram for the first time in the government's white paper. (Lord Courtney of Penwith to C. P. Scott, 14 August 1914, *Manchester Guardian* MSS; Grey to Goschen, 1 August 1914, *BDXI*, No. 448, pp. 260–1).

[2] Crowe's Minute, 30 July 1914, *BDXI*, No. 293, p. 186.

[3] Asquith's speech on the Vote of Credit, 6 August 1914, quoted in full in Spender and Asquith, op. cit., vol. II, 111–16.

[4] Addison's Diary, 30 August 1914. Christopher Addison, op. cit., vol. I, p. 35.

far from overt unity on July 31. If Pease, Harcourt, or Simon told Buckmaster that they had made up their minds on the 31st it is strange, to say the least, that Asquith still had doubts about the latter two until August 3. It cannot be denied that the waverers might easily, on the 31st, have professed their support for Belgium and dispelled the Prime Minister's doubts about their attitude. The opportunity was there; the will was not.

It could not be argued that the gravity of the situation was any longer in doubt. Asquith wrote that it was 'at least one degree worse than it was yesterday', and thought the prospect 'very bleak'.[1] Few would have disputed Haldane's phrase that 'things are trembling in the balance'.[2] Indeed, as Samuel's nightly letter to his wife reveals, the day had been full of incidents and consultation. Writing just before midnight on July 30, Samuel recounted:

Events are marching swiftly along the path that has been traced. Russia is mobilising her northern armies now. Germany will probably mobilise to-morrow. Both are most reluctant to go to war. But the headstrong recklessness of Austria is too much for them. Austria, which is really embarking on war in order to prevent the break-up of her own dominions is utterly selfish and cares nothing at all whom else she involves. The French, most unwilling of all, are dragged in by their Russian alliance, and cannot abstain without treachery. It will be the most horrible catastrophe since the abominations of the Napoleonic time, and in many respects worse even than they.

There was a violent scene yesterday between Sazonoff [Russian Foreign Minister] and the German Ambassador at St. Petersburg. At two this morning, the ambassador came back anxious to find a way of escape from the conflict. (Private). There is still a faint hope of an accommodation being reached, but it is an exceedingly faint one.

Samuel expected that the cabinet meeting on July 31 would be decisive; and it was a measure of how seriously the Prime Minister was treating the ever-worsening news from the Continent that Samuel had to warn his wife that he might have to remain in

[1] Asquith to Venetia Stanley, 30 July 1914, Montagu MSS.
[2] Haldane to Mary Haldane, 30 July 1914, Haldane MSS, 5911, f. 281.

London over the week-end for additional cabinets. 'Tomorrow,' Samuel confided in his letter on July 30:

> we have a fateful Cabinet and have to decide what this country shall do. It may be that the Cabinet will split, but I don't think it will. I had half an hour's talk at midnight last night with Grey. It is marvellous how serene, and indeed cheerful he keeps—cheerful, that is, in his demeanour, not in his outlook. I have had a word or two with L-G and some of the others, and to-night I dined at Hobhouse's with McKinnon Wood, and we had a long talk.[1]

In spite of Samuel's prediction, the cabinet in the morning of July 31 was not ready to come to an irrevocable decision. Perhaps, like Haldane, many clung to the belief that there was still hope until 'the armies have crossed the frontiers'.[2] At any rate, all that the cabinet could agree to, after listening to Asquith's summary of the German neutrality proposal, was that 'British opinion would not enable us to support France—a violation of Belgium might alter public opinion, but we could say nothing to commit ourselves.'[3]

The waverers, it seemed, were playing a complicated game of cabinet brinkmanship. Why did they prevaricate? Some, perhaps hoping to the last that neutrality might be possible, feared that the mere definition of a *casus belli* would enable Grey to manoeuvre the country into further entanglement with France and Russia. Others, like Pease, felt that the issuing of any sort of statement of terms might provoke Germany into acting more aggressively than she intended. Some, Morley in particular, still believed that 'the character of the joint guarantee which Belgium enjoyed was such as to limit its efficacy to occasions when all the parties to it were in accord'.[4] Most members of the wavering group behaved as though they thought that a solution would turn up if only they

---

[1] Samuel to Beatrice Samuel, 30 July 1914, Samuel MSS, A/157/692, ff. 34-5; see also Samuel to his mother, Clara Samuel, 30 July 1914, Samuel MSS, A/157/467, f. 1087.

[2] Haldane to Elizabeth Haldane, 31 July 1914 (3.00 p.m.), Haldane MSS, 6012, f. 46.

[3] Pease's Diary, 31 July 1914, Gainford MSS.

[4] Sir Almeric Fitzroy's Diary, 1 August 1914. Sir Almeric Fitzroy, op. cit., vol. II, pp. 558-9, summarizing a conversation with Morley.

could go on evading any decision that would limit their freedom of action. Lloyd George, and probably Samuel, had a definite idea of what that solution would be: Belgium would be invaded; and it would issue a moving appeal for help. For this providential deliverance, Frances Stevenson, Lloyd George's personal secretary, offered up fervent prayers.[1]

Despite the caution of his colleagues, Grey, in the late afternoon of July 31, 'took a diplomatic step that contemplated the contingency of war'.[2] The French and German governments were asked whether they were prepared to respect the neutrality of Belgium provided that all other Powers did the same.[3] An equivocal German answer was predictable.

During the cabinet on July 31 Lewis Harcourt pencilled a note to Jack Pease: 'It is now clear that *this* Cabinet will not join in the War.'[4] Asquith admitted in the evening that 'the general opinion at present—particularly strong in the City—is to keep out at all costs'.[5] And at the cabinet Asquith had referred to Arthur Ponsonby's letter which claimed that nine-tenths of the Liberal Party would probably withdraw support from the government if it entered the war.[6] As the week ended, and ministers prepared themselves for further long discussions on Saturday, and perhaps even Sunday, the leading non-interventionists in the ministry felt confident that if Britain were led into war, it would be by a coalition or Conservative government and not by the existing Asquith cabinet.

Nevertheless, in spite of the mounting tension and difficulty of the government's position, most of its members remained remarkably placid. 'Nothing untoward happened at the Cabinet to-day,' Samuel calmly reported to his wife.[7] Edward Grey, no longer believing in any avenue of escape, methodically read and

---

[1] Frances Lloyd George, op. cit., p. 74.

[2] Viscount Grey of Fallodon, op. cit., vol. II, p. 181.

[3] Grey to Sir Francis Bertie, 31 July 1914. *BDXI*, No. 383, p. 234. Samuel states in his *Memoirs* (p. 101) that the whole cabinet approved this step; but there is no contemporary evidence that the cabinet was even consulted in advance.

[4] Harcourt to Pease, undated cabinet note (31 July 1914), Gainford MSS, Harcourt's emphasis.

[5] Asquith to Venetia Stanley, 31 July 1914, Montagu MSS.

[6] Asquith to Ponsonby, 31 July 1914, Ponsonby MSS. Asquith said that he had brought the letter's 'contents to the notice of the Cabinet'.

[7] Samuel to Beatrice Samuel, 31 July 1914, Samuel MSS, A/157/694, f. 39.

answered the ominous dispatches from British representatives all over Europe. Grey's parliamentary private secretary tersely recorded the events and prospects of the day in his diary: 'The European crisis is at its height. War in my opinion cannot be averted. Dined with Edward Grey at Brooks's and played billiards with him.'[1]

At the Saturday cabinet meeting, Churchill was refused permission to go ahead with full naval mobilization. No account of this cabinet was sent to the King; but Churchill has explained in *The World Crisis* that his colleagues 'took the view after a sharp discussion that this step was not necessary to our safety'.[2] According to the Prime Minister, 'Winston [was] very bellicose'; and it seems clear that the First Lord accepted the cabinet's refusal to authorize the calling out of the Fleet reserves and the final naval preparations only after strenuous and prolonged argument. 'It is no exaggeration to say', Asquith informed Miss Stanley, 'that Winston occupied at least half of the time.'[3] In his letter to Miss Stanley, Asquith conveyed important information:

> We came, every now & again, near to the parting of the ways: Morley & I think the Impeccable [Simon] are on what might be called the Manchester Guardian tack — that we shd declare now & at once that in *no circumstances* will we take a hand. This no doubt is the view for the moment of the bulk of the party ... Grey, of course, declares that if an out & out & uncompromising policy of non-intervention at all costs is adopted, he will go ...
>
> I am still *not quite* hopeless about peace tho' far from hopeful. But if it comes to war I feel sure (this is entirely between you & me) that we shall have *some* split in the Cabinet. Of course, if Grey went I should go, & the whole thing would break up. On the other hand, we may have to contemplate with such equanimity as we can command the loss of Morley and possibly (tho' I don't think it) of the Impeccable.

Curiously, while he had come to the conclusion that the estimate of neutralist strength in the Liberal Party offered by Arthur

[1] Arthur Murray's Diary, 31 July 1914, Elibank MSS, 8814, f. 122.
[2] Winston S. Churchill, op. cit., p. 216.
[3] Asquith to Venetia Stanley, 1 August 1914, Montagu MSS.

Ponsonby and the Foreign Affairs Group was accurate, Asquith believed that he could scrape through the crisis into war with only a single resignation from the cabinet. Nothing in Asquith's account provides an explanation for this somewhat inconsistent optimism. The cabinet had 'parted in a fairly amicable mood' and agreed to meet again, unprecedently, on the next morning, a Sunday. But what had happened to bolster Asquith's confidence? In fact, a vital decision—perhaps the most significant decision of the war crisis—had been taken at the Saturday cabinet. No letter to the King records this decision; nor has any contemporary eye-witness version of the discussion which preceded it yet come to light.[1] However, a telegram from Grey to Sir Francis Bertie in Paris discloses the crucial point. The Foreign Secretary had seen the French Ambassador after the cabinet:

> I said that we had come to a decision: that we could not propose to Parliament at this moment to send an expeditionary military force to the Continent. Such a step has always been regarded here as very dangerous and doubtful. It was one that we could not propose, and Parliament would not authorize unless our interests and obligations were deeply and desperately involved.[2]

No expeditionary force! Could there have been any greater victory for those who sought to prevent British participation? On the surface, the decision was a triumph for the neutralists. It also met the wishes of Reginald McKenna, who had fought the expeditionary force plan when he was First Lord of the Admiralty and of Walter Runciman who, according to Charles Trevelyan, was 'very proud at some stage at having secured a decision against it'.[3] Winston Churchill explained in *The World Crisis*:

> The differences which had prevailed about entering the war were aggravated by a strong cross-current of opinion ... that if we participated it should be by naval action alone. Men of great power and influence, who throughout the struggle

[1] Pease was absent in the north of England on Saturday and his second-hand account is incomplete.

[2] Grey to Bertie, 1 August 1914. *BDXI*, No. 426, p. 253.

[3] Trevelyan's 'Personal account of beginning of the War, 1914', Trevelyan MSS. For McKenna, see above p. 56, fn. 2.

laboured tirelessly and rendered undoubted services, were found at this time resolutely opposed to the landing of a single soldier on the Continent. And, if everything had not been prepared, if the plan had not been perfected, if it had not been the only plan, and if all military opinion had not been industriously marshalled round it—who shall say what fatal hesitancy might not have intervened?[1]

To decide against using the expeditionary force made nonsense of the whole British continental strategy. The Anglo-French military conversations and the expectations which they had aroused were utterly repudiated. When Grey told his Permanent Secretary, Sir Arthur Nicolson, of the decision, Nicolson exclaimed: 'But this is impossible, you have over & over again promised M. Cambon that if Germany was the aggressor you would stand by France.' Grey replied, 'Yes, but he has nothing in writing!'[2] Did not Grey, or Churchill, or Asquith, or Haldane understand the implications of what they were doing? Or were they responding to the waverers' brinkmanship with a devious game of their own? Perhaps they had every intention of reviving the question as soon as the Germans moved into Belgium, confident that at such a propitious moment the decision could be reversed. It is tempting to adopt an explanation that assumes prescience as well as deviousness on the part of the ministers most responsible for national defence. And, as far as Churchill and Haldane are concerned, it is hardly conceivable that they could have believed that the expeditionary force could safely be delayed for days, let alone held in England for two or three months.[3]

[1] Winston S. Churchill, op. cit., p. 231.

[2] Henry Wilson's Diary, 2 August 1914, Wilson MSS. Nicolson had come to the conclusion, as early as April 1914, that the dispatch of an expeditionary force in the event of war was 'extremely remote'. (Nicolson to Sir George Buchanan, 7 April 1914, FO 800/373.)

[3] In conversation with Lord Lansdowne on August 4, Haldane clarified the reasons which had governed the decision not to send the expeditionary force 'at the very outset': it would have dangerously weakened Great Britain; the 100,000 men might have been surrounded and annihilated by the Germans; and, in any case, the neutrality of Italy meant that the French had a number of additional troops free to defend the frontier with Germany. (Lansdowne's Note of a Conversation with Haldane, 4 August 1914. Lord Newton, *Lord Lansdowne:* A Biography [London, 1929], pp. 440–1.) However, to loyally defend a cabinet decision to a leader of the opposition is a different thing from believing it to be right or endorsing the opinions

It is impossible to be so sure about Grey and Asquith: Grey admitted later to having thought, until persuaded otherwise by professional military opinion, that the British army should 'be kept in reserve till the first shock of the German onset was over'.[1] The Foreign Secretary defended the decision to withhold the expeditionary force, to Cambon and in Parliament, on the grounds that the need to protect Egypt and India and other parts of the empire 'when even the conditions of naval warfare and the possibility of protecting our coasts under these conditions were untried, [made it] impossible safely to send our military force out of the country'. And he convinced Nicolson, as we have noted, that he meant what he said. He had, however, made a significant qualification: the decision 'dealt only with the present moment'.[2] The unanswerable question is how long was the 'present moment' envisaged to be? Asquith also wrote on Sunday, August 2 that the government did not contemplate 'the immediate despatch of an expeditionary force'. This was the expression he used in a memorandum sent to Andrew Bonar Law. In a note for Miss

---

of those who do favour it, a point that seems to have escaped Lord Newton and Lord Beaverbrook (op. cit., pp. 38–9). Balfour's letter to Haldane, on 4 August 1914, put the case for dispatching the expeditionary force, but it did not necessarily imply that Haldane took a different view. It may have been intended for other eyes or to embolden Haldane to dispute the matter further with his colleagues. It is true that Haldane gave Balfour the impression later that day of being woolly and indecisive. But Haldane himself later wrote: 'I had desired to send off all the six divisions from the outset.' If his real views were not apparent to the Conservative leaders, the explanation should be sought first in his habitually nebulous verbal expression, and, second, in his acute embarrassment at the cabinet's decision. (Balfour to Haldane, 4 August 1914. Sir Frederick Maurice, op. cit., vol. I, pp. 358–9; Balfour's Memorandum of a Conversation with Haldane, 5 August 1914. Kenneth Young, *Arthur James Balfour*: The Happy Life of the Politician, Prime Minister, Statesman, and Philosopher, 1848–1930 [London, 1963], p. 349; Richard Burdon Haldane, op. cit., p. 277; Asquith remarked on Haldane being 'diffuse ... and nebulous' at the cabinet on Saturday, August 1 in a letter to Venetia Stanley [Montagu MSS].) A suggestion that the expeditionary force might be kept at home for three months and enlarged was sent to Haldane on August 4 by Sir Douglas Haig. Haig changed his mind the next day, as John Terraine explains in his important biography, *Douglas Haig:* The Educated Soldier (London, 1963), pp. 70–4. See also, Stephen E. Koss, *Lord Haldane:* Scapegoat for Liberalism (New York and London, 1969), pp. 117–18.

[1] Viscount Grey of Fallodon, op. cit., vol. II, p. 283. Grey states that Haldane was 'alone among civilians in supporting the immediate despatch of the whole expeditionary force'. (p. 282).

[2] Grey to Bertie, 2 August 1914. *BDXI*, no. 487, p. 275; 65 *H.C. Deb.*, 5s, col. 1824, 3 August 1914.

Stanley also written on Sunday, Asquith wrote with ambiguous finality: 'The despatch of the Expeditionary Force to help France at this moment is out of the question and would serve no object.'[1] If, by 'this moment' Asquith meant one or, at most, two days, that was certainly not the understanding of most of his wavering colleagues. But Asquith's real intentions are impenetrable. They are only more obscured by a strange episode recorded by General Wilson. 'At 11.30 a.m.,' Wilson related in his diary on August 1, 'Squiff wrote to C.I.G.S. saying training was not to be suspended, & "putting on record" the fact that the Govt had never promised the French the E.F.!!'[2] It is questionable whether such a formal move was necessary unless a lengthy delay was expected, though the Prime Minister, with an eye to posterity, may have wished to make the commitment of the expeditionary force appear to result from a consideration of British interests rather than obligations to France. What is most difficult to understand is why Asquith should have sent such a message to the Chief of the Imperial General Staff *before* a cabinet decision had been taken, especially as Asquith himself accepted Henry Wilson's judgment that the Germans would attack through Belgium. It must at least be admitted as a possibility that Asquith had himself come to believe that some delay might not have disastrous consequences. Or, more likely, that he doubted whether he, Grey, Haldane, and Churchill could persuade the rest of their colleagues to agree to anything more than a British naval commitment. We know that Grey and Haldane had arranged to see Asquith half an hour before the cabinet was due to meet. But the purpose of this private gathering—if it actually took place—can only be surmised.[3]

Whatever was in Asquith's mind, probably more than half of the cabinet acquiesced in the ensuing developments on the basis of a limited and erroneous conception of what British participation in a European war would mean. The cabinet discussions of August 2 and 3 rested on the premise that the British role in the war, if there were to be a British role, would be on the high seas. 'The naval war will be cheap,' Churchill assured Lloyd George, 'not

---

[1] Asquith's Memorandum for Bonar Law, 2 August 1914. Robert Blake, op. cit., p. 224; Asquith to Venetia Stanley, 2 August 1914, Montagu MSS.

[2] Wilson's Diary, 1 August 1914, Wilson MSS. The training to which Asquith referred involved the movement of troops away from their mobilization points.

[3] Haldane to Mary Haldane, 1 August 1914, Haldane MSS, 5992, f. 1.

more than 25 million a year.'[1] For reluctant interventionists, the consequences of taking a hard line over Belgian neutrality seemed, henceforth, more circumscribed. The worst contingency was a naval commitment which the Germans might prudently decline to challenge.

As ministers returned wearily to their homes on Saturday evening, a pervasive and fatalistic spirit of unity began to take a grip on the cabinet. Samuel, having had no more than half an hour for lunch, spent four hours from 2.00 p.m. until 6.00 p.m. in the company of Lloyd George, Haldane, Harcourt, McKenna, Simon, and Runciman, arranging measures with the bankers to avert financial panic. Before dining and re-joining the cabinet committee at 9.30 p.m., he scribbled a quick note to his wife. Samuel reported that while all hope of peace had not been abandoned, the cabinet had 'decided our course'. 'We may', he went on 'be brought in under certain eventualities. A suggestion of mine [not to send the expeditionary force?] was adopted by the Cabinet which may a good deal affect the issue.' Much, as Samuel concluded, depended on 'Germany's attitude to the neutrality of Belgium'.[2]

If Samuel believed that a decision about the expeditionary force settled 'our course', other members of the ministry realized that there was a great deal still to be resolved. 'It is fearfully difficult to steer,' Haldane confided to his mother.[3] John Burns admitted in his diary that the cabinet had been serious and united. But, he wrote, 'no decision as in all our minds there rested the belief and hope for agreement.'[4] Edward Grey, who had been dealing with dispatches since 3.30 a.m., took refuge again in the evening at his club with Arthur Murray, his parliamentary private secretary. In the next twenty-four hours, Grey sensed, the remaining straws of hope would be swept away. Murray's diary records: 'Edward Grey and self dined at Brooks's and played billiards. He told me that he would have his "tussle" with the Cabinet tomorrow.'[5]

[1] Churchill to Lloyd George, undated cabinet note, (?1 August) 1914. Randolph S. Churchill, op. cit., p. 718. This note provides a rare glimpse of Churchill acting disingenuously. No doubt the gravity of the impending disaster impelled him to shake aside customary restraints.
[2] Samuel to Beatrice Samuel, 1 August 1914, Samuel MSS, A/157/696, f. 45.
[3] Haldane to Mary Haldane, 1 August 1914, Haldane MSS, 5992, f. 4.
[4] Burns's Diary, 1 August 1914, Burns MSS (Add. MS. 46336, f. 128).
[5] Murray's Diary, 1 August 1914, Elibank MSS, 8814, f. 126.

8 To the Edge

On August 1, Grey was permitted by the cabinet to warn the German Ambassador that it would be 'extremely difficult to restrain public feeling' if one combatant violated Belgium. The French government, however, could be given no more than a promise that Grey would ask his colleagues to consider whether they would be prepared, in view of the fact that the French fleet was concentrated in the Mediterranean and that therefore the French northern and western coasts were exposed, to guarantee to defend those coasts against German attack.[1] Late that night London learned that Germany had declared war on Russia. In the early hours of the next morning Churchill, ignoring the standing decision of the cabinet, finalized the naval mobilization. Asquith had given a grunting assent.[2] Later on Sunday morning news reached London that the Germans had invaded Luxembourg; Belgium alone could be their next destination. Any other strategy would be madness. At 11.00 a.m. the cabinet assembled. For one hour, a second, and almost a third they argued. At last, in time for a late lunch they adjourned. What had they decided? Walter Runciman sensed the importance of the occasion. Unlike Pease, Harcourt, and Burns, he was not a diarist, but now he pencilled a minute of the discussion and conclusions. It served to clarify his own thoughts as well as to record precisely what had been said:

Grey proposes definitely
    (I) To announce to France & Germany that if the German ships enter the Channel we should regard that as a hostile act.

[1] Grey to Bertie, 1 August 1914; Grey to Goschen, 1 August 1914. *BDXI*, Nos. 447–8, pp. 260–1. The disposition of the French and British fleets had been fixed by a naval agreement of 1912.
[2] Winston S. Churchill, op. cit., pp. 217–19; Winston S. Churchill, *Great Contemporaries* (London, 1937), p. 148.

(II) On Belgian neutrality, we do not commit ourselves at present. We are consulting Parliament.

Crewe would not hesitate to go to war over the English Channel. Several others agreed.

McKenna suggested instead that the Channel should be neutralised to both.

Grey says that to niggle is not worth while. If the Channel is closed against Germany it *is* in favour of France, & we cannot take half measures—either we must declare ourselves neutral, or in it. If we are to be neutral he will go, but he cannot blame the Cabinet if they disagree with him. He therefore asks for a sharp decision.

P.M. read letter from Bonar Law in which he & Lansdowne promise that they will support us in going in with France. P.M. reads his summary of considerations to weigh with Cabinet & proposed to say in Parlt. that we cannot allow the Channel to be violated. We must come to a decision on neutrality of Belgium now.[1]

At the top of this memorandum, written on the Prime Minister's notepaper, Runciman later pencilled the words: 'The Cabinet which decided that war with Germany was inevitable.' In retrospect, Runciman perhaps put too definite an interpretation upon the conclusions of this long meeting. Another unpublished account, written to Beatrice Samuel by her husband from the Royal Palace Hotel on Sunday night, provides a fuller picture both of the course of the discussion and the decisions taken:

The morning Cabinet almost resulted in a political crisis to be super-imposed on the international and the financial crises. Grey expressed a view which was unacceptable to most of us. He is outraged by the way in which Germany and Austria have played with the most vital interests of civilisation, have put aside all attempts at accommodation made by himself and others, and, while continuing to negotiate, have marched steadily to war.

I expressed my own conviction that we should be justified in joining in the war either for the protection of the northern

[1] Runciman's Memorandum on the proceedings of the cabinet, 2 August 1914, Runciman MSS.

coasts of France, which we could not afford to see bombarded by the German fleet and occupied by the German army or for the maintenance of the independence of Belgium, which we were bound by treaty to protect and which again we could not afford to see subordinated to Germany. But I held that we were not entitled to carry England into the war for the sake of our goodwill for France, or for the sake of maintaining the strength of France and Russia against that of Germany and Austria. This opinion is shared by the majority of the Cabinet with various degrees of emphasis on the several parts of it.

We sanctioned a statement being made by Grey to the French Ambassador this afternoon, to be followed by a statement in Parliament to-morrow, that we should take action if the German fleet came down the Channel to attack France. (Almost the whole of the French fleet is in the Mediterranean.) But Burns dissented, feeling that Germany may regard this declaration as an act of hostility and may declare war on us because of it. He is for neutrality in all circumstances. It is probable that he will resign to-night ... [1]

It is clear from the accounts of both Samuel and Runciman that the cabinet had at last moved towards a precise clarification of the conditions on which it would be prepared to enter the war. In his memoirs, Grey attributed the proposal to forbid German use of the Channel as a base for hostile operations to the 'anti-war quarter' of the cabinet. But the very fact that this proposal was agreed to only after what Asquith described as 'much difficulty' and at the price of one briefly postponed resignation, should have cast doubt on Grey's statement. In reality, it was Grey himself, after being asked for an assurance by the French Ambassador, who raised the subject with his colleagues. And, as Runciman's note reveals, it was probably Crewe who gave the idea the strongest support.[2] It was, of course, possible to hope that neutralizing the Channel might prove a way of keeping Britain out of the conflict. As it turned out, the German government

---

[1] Samuel to Beatrice Samuel, 2 August 1914, Samuel MSS, A/157/697, ff. 50-2.
[2] Crewe, in answer to Professor Temperley's questionnaire, wrote on 8 May 1929: 'I had fancied that I had first raised the point.' Spender MSS (Add. MS. 46386, ff. 54-5).

was quite ready, subject to British neutrality, to pledge not to attack the French coasts.

But the probability or otherwise of a German attack on the French coasts does not seem to have been deeply considered on August 2. Jack Pease did, however, ask a highly pertinent question: 'If we tell the Germans they may not move their fleet & come out is not that tantamount to a declaration of war?' Grey replied that it was not; but, he added, 'I believe war will come & it is due to France they shall have our support.'[1] A number of the cabinet remained convinced that British support was not France's 'due'. Asquith believed that:

> there is a strong party including all the 'Beagles' and re-inforced by Ll. George, Morley & Harcourt who are against any kind of intervention in any event. Grey, of course, will never consent to this, & I shall not separate myself from him. Crewe, McKenna, & Samuel are a moderating inter-mediate body.[2]

The significant points about this analysis were two. First, that although Crewe, McKenna, and Samuel had initially taken different positions on the Channel question, they could be characterized as forming a 'moderating intermediate body'. Second, that, although the 'Beagles' (Simon, Beauchamp, and possibly McKinnon Wood and others) were seen to share Burns's determination to keep out, Lloyd George, Morley, and Harcourt only 'reinforced' them. Lloyd George appears to have said very little at this meeting. But Morley, disregarding strategic probabilities, acknowledged the force of the argument that 'we could not acquiesce in Franco-German naval conflict in the narrow seas on our doorstep, so to say'.[2] Morley was attracted particularly by the 'doorstep argument' because it made a warning to Germany 'defensible apart from French entente'. Harcourt, also realizing that the naval arrangements since 1912 left France defenceless on the North Sea and Channel, passed a note to Pease confessing 'I can't decline this.'[4] Samuel nursed a lingering hope that 'Germany will neither

[1] Pease's Diary, 2 August 1914, Gainford MSS.
[2] Asquith to Venetia Stanley, 2 August 1914, Montagu MSS.
[3] Morley, op. cit., p. 12.
[4] Harcourt to Pease, undated cabinet note (2 August 1914), Gainford MSS.

send her fleet down the Channel nor invade Belgium.' As he told his wife, if it should prove possible both to keep England at peace and protect the French coasts and the Franco-Belgian border from German attack, 'without firing a shot' this would be a brilliant stroke of policy'. Samuel concluded: 'For this object I have been working incessantly all the week. If we do not accomplish it, it will be an action of Germany's and not of ours which will cause the failure, and my conscience will be easy in embarking on the war.'[1]

Clearly, a major hurdle had now been taken. The cabinet had adopted a course that carried with it the possibility of having to go to war at the side of the French. This was an emotional break-through which dissolved the waverers' unity. If British security, as Samuel cogently argued, was incompatible with German con-quest of Belgium and the northern coasts of France, what prin-ciple remained around which the waverers could fight together against British participation?

Although Sunday morning's decision carried with it the theoretical possibility that Britain might be plunged into war, there was still uncertainty in the situation. After lunch Grey motored to the Zoo to spend an hour meditating among the birds.[2] Asquith reviewed the position for Miss Stanley:

Happily I am quite clear in my own mind as to what is right & wrong. I put it down for you in a few sentences.

1. We have no obligation of any kind either to France or Russia to give them military or naval help.

2. The despatch of the Expeditionary force to help France at this moment is out of the question & wd serve no object.

3. We mustn't forget the ties created by our long-standing & intimate friendship with France.

4. It is against British interests that France shd be wiped out as a Great Power.

5. We cannot allow Germany to use the Channel as a hostile base.

6. We have obligations to Belgium to prevent her being utilised & absorbed by Germany.[3]

[1] Samuel to Beatrice Samuel, 2 August 1914, Samuel MSS, A/157/697, ff. 54–5.
[2] Edmund Gosse to Earl Spencer, 3 August 1914. The Hon. Evan Charteris, *The Life and Letters of Sir Edmund Gosse* (London, 1931), p. 367.
[3] Asquith to Venetia Stanley, 2 August 1914, Montagu MSS.

The bland disingenuousness of the first and third points, and the breathtaking strategic ignorance of the second, reveal the extent to which the cabinet's deliberations had resulted in a convergence of views. Neutralists like Harcourt were finally prepared to specify a *casus belli*; but the Prime Minister in turn was forced to repudiate in principle an obligation to France for whose creation he bore a large responsibility. Everyone, in the end, could justify action in defence of British security.

Belgium was the last fence. 'We are consulting Parliament,' Runciman had written. But, already, on Sunday morning, Runciman had agreed in private conclave with Lloyd George, Harcourt, Beauchamp, Simon, and Pease, that 'the wholesale invasion of Belgium' might cause them to reconsider their position.[1] And, as has already been seen, at lunch at Beauchamp's after the morning cabinet, the same group (with the addition of Samuel and McKinnon Wood) had further discussed its position. By the early evening, just before the cabinet was about to re-assemble, a number of the waverers were ready to meet Crewe and Birrell at Lloyd George's official residence, 11 Downing Street. As Samuel's letter to his wife shows, the gathering at Halkyn House, and the meeting with the interventionists, Crewe and Birrell, marked the final and decisive steps towards cabinet unity:

I lunched at Beauchamp's and afterwards there was a talk between L.G., Harcourt, Beauchamp, Simon, McKinnon Wood, Pease, Morley and myself. They all agreed with my formula except Morley, who is now so old that the views he expresses are sadly inconsequent and inconsistent. I went from there to see McKenna, whom I found in bed, tired out. He concurred. After an hour at the L.G.B. taking various emergency measures I went to Downing St and saw the P.M. and told him the situation. At 6 several of us, including Crewe, met again at Lloyd George's. When the Cabinet resumed at 6.30 the situation was easier, the point of contention was not pressed, and with the exception of the two I have mentioned [Burns and Morley] we remain solid.[2]

[1] See above, p. 66.
[2] Samuel to Beatrice Samuel, 2 August 1914, Samuel MSS, A/157/697, ff. 52–3.

Samuel went on to relate how close the cabinet had been to breaking up:

> Had the matter come to an issue, Asquith would have stood by Grey in any event, and three others would have remained. I think all the rest of us would have resigned. The consequence would have been either a Coalition Government or a Unionist Government either of which would certainly have been a war ministry.

The fragility of the situation was revealed in the cabinet letter to the King, recording the evening's meeting: 'It was agreed,' Crewe reported on the Prime Minister's behalf, 'without any attempt to state a formula, that it would be made evident that a substantial violation of the neutrality of that country would place us in the situation contemplated as possible by Mr Gladstone in 1870, when interference was held to compel us to take action.'[1]

However guardedly Crewe expressed the collective view, the point of no return had been reached. On a pencilled note passed across the cabinet table, John Simon appealed to Burns to 'stay at any rate for *tomorrow's cabinet*. I am disposed to think 7 or 8 of us may be with you.' But Burns's reply was terse and unyielding: 'It is then too late.'[2] Burns was right. Within hours Morley and Simon wrote to the Prime Minister that they must join Burns in resignation. Beauchamp 'chipped in' the next morning to make a third balker at the Belgian obstacle. Lloyd George and Pease urged their resigning colleagues to stay, or at least to delay their departures.[3] Germany had demanded unimpeded passage through Belgium. This, Lloyd George told Morley, 'changed Runciman's line and his own'. Further news of German bellicosity shook the determination of Simon and Beauchamp and undermined the residual reservations of the other waverers. Late in the evening, it emerged that Asquith had won over Simon; and Beauchamp had also retracted.[4] Another waverer, Hobhouse, seems already to have made up his mind to stay after the Sunday evening cabinet.

---

[1] Crewe to King George V (cabinet letter), 2 August 1914. Spender and Asquith, op. cit., vol. II, p. 82.

[2] Simon to Burns (with note by Burns), 3 August 1914, Simon MSS.

[3] Pease's Diary, 3 August 1914, Gainford MSS; Morley, op. cit., p. 26; Asquith to Venetia Stanley, 3 August 1914, Montagu MSS.

[4] Morley, op. cit., pp. 24, 27–8.

He told John Burns on August 7: 'I did not want Germany to destroy us in detail, as I believe she hoped to do.'[1]

The last danger to the substantial unity of the cabinet had been the possibility that the Belgians would not resist a German attack. Without a Belgian plea for help, the waverers would have had inhibiting qualms about turning Belgian territory into the battleground of Armageddon. Grey later maintained that even if Belgium had acquiesced voluntarily in the passage of German troops, Britain would have been 'entitled to send troops to vindicate the neutrality and resist the violation of it'.[2] Grey's colleagues did not have to show whether they were prepared to take advantage of this alleged right. At first the evidence of Belgian intentions had been encouraging if not conclusive. On the morning of August 1 the Belgian government, replying to an inquiry sent by Grey the day before, stated that it would do the utmost in its power to maintain neutrality, and both desired and expected that its neutrality would be observed and upheld by other Powers.

This message, transmitted by the British Minister in Brussels, reached the Foreign Office at 12.25 p.m., too late to play any part in the cabinet discussion on the 1st.[3] G. M. Trevelyan, in his life of Grey, drew attention to a further communication from Brussels, received in London at 1.25 p.m. on August 2:

> Minister for Foreign Affairs states that Belgian Government have no reason whatever to suspect Germany of an intention to violate neutrality. He says that Belgian Government have no considered idea of appeal to other guarantee Powers, nor of intervention should a violation occur; they would rely upon their own armed force as sufficient to resist aggression, from whatever quarter it might come.[4]

It was, no doubt, in accordance with this futile resolve that two divisions of the Belgian army were mobilized on the French border, one on the coast (to hinder a British landing), and one

[1] Hobhouse to Burns, 7 August 1914, Burns MSS (Add. MS. 46303, f. 72).
[2] Viscount Grey of Fallodon, op. cit., vol. ii, p. 210, see also the evidence cited in Michael G. Ekstein-Frankl, 'The Development of British War Aims: August 1914–March 1915'. unpublished Ph.D. thesis, University of London, 1969, pp. 139–40.
[3] Sir Francis Villiers to Grey, 1 August 1914. *BDXI*, No. 395, p. 240.
[4] Villiers to Grey, 2 August 1914. *BDXI*, No. 476, p. 271; G. M. Trevelyan, op. cit., p. 255.

deployed to watch Germany. Trevelyan saw nothing odd about
the statement of Belgian intentions on August 2. He did not comment on the minute by G. R. Clerk, a senior clerk at the Foreign
Office, who pointed out that 'It is impossible for the German
troops to get out of Luxemburg without crossing Belgian territory except through a narrow bottle-neck into France.'[1] If the
German main force were to advance over Belgium, the Belgian
Army could not conceivably have been sufficient to resist aggression for long. No British cabinet minister could have been under
any illusion about that. For British policy, the only thing that
mattered was the Belgian determination to resist any infringement
of neutrality; and of that determination both these communications from Brussels were, in different ways, convincing indi-
cators. Samuel later testified:

> We did not know definitely what course Belgium would take.
> We had to contemplate the possibilities of (a) acquiescence,
> (b) formal resistance, (c) vigorous resistance. For my own
> part I thought (c) was probable. It is certainly not the case
> that the whole Cabinet expected (a) or (b).[2]

The plea of the King of the Belgians on August 3 was ample
proof that 'vigorous resistance' would be offered. In a telegram to
King George V, King Albert asked for 'diplomatic intervention...
to safeguard the neutrality of Belgium'. But, by the early afternoon
of August 3, when Grey saw the telegram, it was obvious that
diplomatic intervention would be brushed aside by the Germans.
Military action alone could effectively defend Belgian neutrality.[3]
From that moment there was no likelihood that the cabinet would
be required either to resort to legal technicalities or moral
obligations to France as justifications for intervention. Cabinet
opposition ended. When ministers left Downing Street after the
morning cabinet on August 3, British participation in the war had
ceased to be problematical. So relieved were they at this one certainty, that Asquith and his colleagues neglected to discuss certain
contingent decisions. Churchill has stated that:

> Formal sanction had been given to the already completed
> mobilization of the Fleet and to the immediate mobilization of

[1] Clerk's Minute, 2 August 1914. *BDXI*, No. 476, p. 271.
[2] Samuel to J. A. Spender, 24 June 1929 (copy), Samuel MSS, A/45/4.
[3] Spender and Asquith, op. cit., vol. II, p. 92.

the Army. No decision had been taken to send an ultimatum to Germany or to declare war upon Germany, still less to send an army to France. These decisions were never taken at any Cabinet. They were compelled by the force of events, and rest on the authority of the Prime Minister.[1]

At 6.00 p.m. on August 3, the cabinet met to prepare its reply to Germany's ultimatum to Belgium. It was a brief meeting, as the House of Commons was shortly to reassemble. Rather than send a reply that might be used by Germany as a pretext for a surprise attack on Britain, it was decided to postpone consideration of what should be said until the following day. By then, further progress could have been made to place the nation unobtrusively on a war footing.[2]

On August 4, as Asquith recorded laconically, there was 'an interesting Cabinet'. The Germans had entered Belgium and announced their intention to force a passage if opposition was encountered. That simplified matters. Grey had already taken it upon himself to ask for an assurance that the demand made upon Belgium would be withdrawn. He proceeded to issue an ultimatum to Germany to desist. Unless a satisfactory reply was received in London by 11.00 p.m. (a time apparently chosen for the convenience of the Royal Navy),[3] the British government would be bound to 'take all steps in their power to uphold the neutrality of Belgium'.[4] No satisfactory reply was expected; none

---

[1] Churchill, *The World Crisis, 1911-1914*, p. 220. Asquith himself wrote out an order of mobilization in the early hours of August 3. It was brought to the War Office by Haldane at 11.00 a.m. At 1.09 p.m. it reached the Director of Military Operations who was aghast to read that the Prime Minister's order was incomplete. It sanctioned mobilization in the name of the cabinet (though the cabinet had not yet given any authorization), but not, as all the expeditionary force plans required, embarkation. Not until 4.00 p.m. on August 4 was mobilization actually ordered. The telegram was dispatched from London at 4.45 p.m. and taken down at Salisbury six minutes later. A similar telegram was received by Sir Douglas Haig at Aldershot at 5.03 p.m. Only on August 6, was it settled that the Expeditionary Force would go to the Continent. (Sir Frederick Maurice, op. cit., vol. 1, p. 355; Repington, *The First World War*, vol. 1, p. 19; Wilson's Diary, 3 August 1914, Wilson MSS; Austen Chamberlain, op. cit., p. 104; Haig's Diary, 4 August 1914, Robert Blake [ed.], *The Private Papers of Douglas Haig, 1914-1919* [London, 1952], p. 67.)

[2] Pease's Diary, 3 August 1914, Gainford MSS.

[3] I am grateful to Mr Martin Gilbert for this information from the Admiralty papers.

[4] Asquith to Venetia Stanley, 4 August 1914, Montagu MSS; Grey to Goschen, 9.30 a.m., and 2.00 p.m., 4 August 1914, *BDXI*, Nos. 573 and 594, pp. 306, 314.

was received. In the words of Asquith's official biographers: 'The consequential steps were taken for granted.'[1] The nation awoke on August 5 to find itself at war.

[1] Spender and Asquith, op. cit., vol. II, p. 93.

9 Into Battle

Asquith's delay in bringing the cabinet to awkward decisions did not, in itself, stave off the collapse of the ministry. Few of his ministers were tired of power. Not one of them was a pacifist. All that most of them needed was an excuse to stay. Asquith made sure that they would have one. First he registered his belief that German war plans required the invasion of Belgium. Then he waited until the Belgian pretext emerged. His own apparent failure to understand the purpose of the British expeditionary force also contributed to unity. Opposition to intervention was markedly diminished by the understanding reached on August 1 that the British role could only be naval. Blockade and the protection of commerce would be a cheap and honourable discharge of the nation's obligations. But the vital element was Belgium. What Asquith realized was that men like Simon, Pease, Harcourt, and above all, Lloyd George, were prisoners of their own pacific images. Supporting a war demanded of them a reversal of lifetime commitments. Belgium, as Asquith sensed, would relieve them of unbearable embarrassment.

In all these momentous events, much hinged on the actions of Lloyd George. 'What', Asquith asked Samuel on August 2, 'is Lloyd George going to do?'[1] It was impossible to be certain. But there were reasonable grounds for optimism. Neither Lloyd George's behaviour in 1911 nor his interests in 1914 pointed to resignation. As Chancellor of the Exchequer, an established party leader, all his plans were inextricably linked with the Liberal Party and Liberal government. He had built, and proposed to continue building, his political career on domestic issues. He was no longer a comparatively unknown Welsh backbencher with a name to make; and the convictions and radical enthusiasm which

[1] Samuel, op. cit., p. 104.

had propelled him into the van of the anti-Boer war crusade burnt less fiercely after eight years of power. Since December 1905 he had been in the front rank of the Liberal ministry, bearing a full share of responsibility for the whole range of Liberal achievements. The People's Budget and national insurance had enhanced his own political stature, though they had at the same time multiplied his enemies. He had survived the damaging revelations of the Marconi inquiry. He was known to possess a predilection to compromise over Ulster and therefore had emerged comparatively unscathed from the worst of the Home Rule crossfire. Over female suffrage, his professed support for the cause secured him the sympathy of the constitutional suffragists although it did not procure immunity from militant harassment. And in Wales, as he ascended the heights, no attack or insinuation from any quarter could permanently harm a reputation which was growing to heroic, almost legendary proportions. Nor did even 'a staggering rebuff over his financial plans'[1] in 1914—a ruling by the Speaker made it necessary to postpone a new system of grants to local authorities envisaged in the Finance Bill—damage the engaging resilience which time and again carried him through the buffetings of party warfare.

Looking forward to the general election planned for 1915, Lloyd George's colleagues were committed—some of them grudgingly, it is true—to a platform and strategy largely of his devising. The Land Campaign, with vast implications for employment, housing, and welfare, as well as land tenure and the development of rural resources, had begun under Lloyd George's personal sponsorship. Temporarily retarded when the Marconi outcry was at its loudest, the campaign had regained its initial momentum and was, by midsummer 1914, poised for a massive assault on the lukewarm urban voter.[2] Westminster's preoccupation with Irish and constitutional issues had loosened the government's grip on many electoral strongholds; and the repeated rejection of Liberal reforms by the Tory-dominated House of Lords had made it impossible for the Liberals to carry out the programme to which they were pledged. Scouting the political horizon, an old associate of Lloyd George, the journalist, Harold Spender, had

[1] Runciman to Sir Robert Chalmers, 24 June 1914, Runciman MSS.
[2] Lloyd George to Runciman, 12 June 1914, Runciman MSS.

recognized the potential of a counter-attack against the forces of privilege. 'Your land artillery', wrote Spender, 'is moving over the wreckage of broken hopes.'[1] The way was open for some new rallying cry. It needed only Lloyd George's oratorical genius to translate a full programme of rural promises into a gospel for the towns as well. For, whatever their jealousies and disagreements, there was not one of his colleagues who could gainsay his mastery of the public meeting and the developing art of political publicity. If anyone could bring electoral victory, Lloyd George was undeniably the man.

Confidence in Lloyd George's continued hold upon a position of great authority and power in national affairs was perfectly justified in 1914. It is, however, important to notice that his stock in the centre of the political world—with colleagues and opponents, journalists, and hostesses—was subject to very much larger fluctuations than the image which he had established with the mass of the electorate. 'If', as a critical biographer remarked, 'candid friends and even compatriots admitted a strong element of egotism in his nature and a certain element of "gammon" in his speeches, the public at large did not resent, perhaps hardly perceived, these traits.'[2] To this large measure of public tolerance, could be added a further degree of mass indifference to the fine points of style and tactics which went into the making of a parliamentary reputation. It would be a fundamental error to identify transient sensations in the House of Commons with lasting movements in the political firmament. And it would be no less an error because gossiping or malicious contemporaries made the same mistake. Nevertheless, politicians lived in an atmosphere of exaggerated prophecies of doom and jarring ambition. Daily moving through this unwholesome environment, few men remained unaffected. They uttered extravagant words, and often they believed them. It is thus that we must explain the difference between the standing of Lloyd George in the counsels of the Liberal chiefs and his popularity in the country.

Some of Lloyd George's colleagues, it must be admitted, paid him generous tribute. 'Those who had only heard his powerful

---

[1] Harold Spender to Lloyd George, (?) March 1914, Lloyd George MSS, C/11/1/22.

[2] Charles Mallet, *Mr Lloyd George* (London, 1930), p. 41.

and eloquent speeches in the country', said Edward Grey to a private dinner of the Welsh Parliamentary Party on July 29, 'could not realize how patient and wise he could be in Council.'[1] Others, however, were more sparing in praise. Envying his successes, they gloated over his setbacks. Although he had amassed a large fund of popular approbation, his schemes of social amelioration and tax reform were not universally acceptable even in his own party. Some of the government's by-election defeats after 1912 were attributed to the unpopularity of the National Insurance Act. Earlier, there had been a pocket of resistance on the Liberal back benches against parts of the 1909 Budget; and a number of the same men joined again in June and July 1914 in 'a combined remonstrance by businessmen & some survivors of the Cobden–Bright school of thought against the ill-considered & socialistic tendencies of the Government finance'.[2] This 'Holt cave', as it was called, after its leading spokesman Richard Holt, enjoyed the sympathy of a number of Lloyd George's colleagues. 'Indeed,' Holt himself believed, 'a great many of the Cabinet secretly agreed with us: inter alia—McKenna & John Burns.'[3]

Among those ministers who were sympathetic to Holt and his allies, Walter Runciman may be included. Runciman outlined the origin of Lloyd George's troubles in 1914 in a frank letter to the Governor of Ceylon, Sir Robert Chalmers. Chalmers, an old friend of Runciman, had been Permanent Secretary to the Treasury under Lloyd George; he was no stranger to the Chancellor's ideas and method of work. Runciman wrote to Chalmers without inhibition, revealing the extent to which the Budget fiasco had been a personal jolt to Lloyd George's prestige as well as a major disruption of the government's plans. Lloyd George, Runciman explained:

> ... is taxing heavily in order to meet the claims of his friend at the Admiralty and he aimed at gilding the pill by a heavy set of subsidies to the local authorities. The subsidies are even yet undefined. Some of the financial purists on our side ... declared that they would not vote taxation for undefined objects: they said in private very freely that they refused to

[1] J. Herbert Lewis's Diary, 29 July 1914, Lewis MSS.
[2] Holt's Diary, 19 July 1914, Holt MSS.
[3] Ibid.

trust the Treasury with any money except what was clearly earmarked & voted by the House. Publicly they laid their case down in a manifesto which on constitutional grounds was unanswerable. The P.M. insisted on L-G respecting it and the Infant [Herbert Samuel, President of the Local Government Board] had to come down to the House ... to announce on L-G's behalf that...that part of the Budget is dropped & 1d less is now to be raised in Income tax ... You can imagine the blow this has been to L-G—and the dreadful muddle which we are now let in for. Banks and local authorities and electioneering Radicals are all enraged; our programme and legislation are horribly upset ... We are indeed in a precarious plight, and but for the follies of Bonar and his Orange and Tariff Reform colleagues we should be easily displaced.[1]

In a few months, this reverse would no doubt have been forgotten. Yet, while the controversy flared, and until it was edged from the centre of attention first by gun-running to Ireland and then by the European crisis, Lloyd George's standing at Westminster was at low ebb. In assessing his own position as war spread across Europe, neither he nor Asquith could ignore this most recent loss of favour. Thus the popular judgment that in 1914 the Chancellor of the Exchequer was the undisputed second man of his party, the acknowledged heir apparent to the Liberal leadership, needs careful qualification. Asquith's sudden death might have precipitated Lloyd George to the top. But, if Asquith had remained free to make his own arrangements, the probability is that he would have preferred another successor—Simon or McKenna perhaps—and would have timed his departure accordingly.

Moreover, although it is possible to do no more than speculate, it must be doubted whether in 1914 Lloyd George's dreams were occupied by the premiership. Certainly, in the aftermath of a disastrous budget, it seems more likely that sheer survival in high office would have been uppermost in his mind. Because his position was fundamentally insecure—depending not on patronage, family connection, or wealth, but on unique personal qualities—

[1] Runciman to Chalmers, 24 June 1914, Runciman MSS.

he could not afford to take the risk of resignation. The hazard was easy to predict: he might never recover from opposition to a short successful war. A long war would probably lead to a coalition in which the Chancellor of the Exchequer was more likely to be included than a man who had declined to accept responsibility for British intervention. In either case Churchill at the Admiralty might forge ahead in power and popular esteem. Other rivals would prosper. And less magnanimous men than Churchill could not be trusted to welcome Lloyd George's return if once he should leave the ministry. Fortunately for both Asquith and Lloyd George, Churchill could be relied upon to plead with his friend to stay in the cabinet:

> I am most profoundly anxious that our long co-operation may not be severed. Remember your part at Agadir. I implore you to come and bring your mighty aid to the discharge of our duty. Afterwards by participating in the peace we can regulate the settlement and prevent a renewal of 1870 conditions.[1]

Churchill's eloquence was hardly necessary. Sir George Riddell described precisely the position Lloyd George had reached by August 2: he was 'in favour of intervention in certain circumstances'.[2] Since there could be no war without those circumstances he was in effect, if not in appearance, a war man. He could afford to dissociate himself from Asquith's and Grey's insistence on the need to support France, believing that events would inevitably throw them together.

By concealing his intentions without actually lying, Lloyd George deceived his less alert associates. Yet his vacillation, like that of some of his colleagues, was partly genuine. As Chancellor of the Exchequer, he had become aware earlier than many other members of the cabinet of the threat which war posed to European financial stability. The fear of economic collapse spread from the City to the ministry with astonishing rapidity.

---

[1] Churchill to Lloyd George, undated cabinet note, (?1 August) 1914, Lloyd George MSS, C/14. Agadir was on other minds. J. L. Garvin of *The Observer* wrote: 'If we leave our friends to fall we are done as a people ... Oh Agadir, Agadir and your courage then!' (Garvin to Lloyd George, 2 August 1914, Lloyd George MSS, C/4/13/3.)

[2] *Lord Riddell's War Diary*, p. 8.

In cabinet, Lloyd George told his colleagues about the pessimism of the financial community. According to Lord Morley's account:

He informed us that he had been consulting the Governor and Deputy Governor of the Bank of England, other men of light and leading in the City [sic], also cotton men, and steel and coal men, etc., in the North of England, in Glasgow, etc., and they were all *aghast* at the bare idea of our plunging into the European conflict; how it would break down the whole system of credit with London as its centre, how it would cut up commerce and manufacture—they told him—how it would hit labour and wages and prices, and when the winter came, would inevitably produce violence and tumult.[1]

Some historians have supposed that these views were those of Lloyd George himself. But they were not. He transmitted news; he did not say that he endorsed commercial opinion. Like Sir Eyre Crowe, he was quite capable of recognizing 'pusillanimous counsels'.[2] One thought which did impress itself upon him was the fear, most ably expounded by Morley, that Russia might become predominant in Europe.[3] At dinner with Simon, Charles Masterman, and Ramsay MacDonald at Sir George Riddell's house on August 2 he dwelt on the Russian menace.[4] In 1916, he said, the Russian army would be larger than those of Germany, France and Austria combined. Nevertheless, earlier in the evening,

[1] Morley, op. cit., p. 5.

[2] Memorandum by Crowe, 31 July 1914, *BDXI*, No. 369, p. 228. Crowe attributed panic in the City to the machinations of German financial houses. His stress on the subject was probably prompted by the remarks of Grey which are quoted from Henry Wilson's Diary on p. 53 above. For the foreign editor of *The Times*'s story of the 'dirty German Jewish international financial attempt' to bully *The Times* into advocating neutrality see Henry Wickham Steed, op. cit., vol. II, pp. 9–12. On Asquith's opinion of businessmen at this time, see Spender and Asquith, op. cit., vol. II, p. 102.

[3] Morley, op. cit., pp. 6–7.

[4] MacDonald was spending the week-end with Robert Donald. 'L.G. was there on the Saturday but he was recalled to Town ... On Sunday came [a telephone call]. L. G. wished him to go to London at once. MacDonald replied that he had no means of transport, whereupon L. G. said he would send out a car for him, and MacDonald went.' (Memorandum of H. A. Taylor's interview with J. R. MacDonald, 2 October 1933, Taylor MSS.) Whatever path Lloyd George was to choose, it was sensible to keep in contact with MacDonald as long as possible.

he spoke 'very strongly' about the observance of Belgian neutrality. And to the urgings of Riddell and Masterman that the hypothetical Russian threat was secondary to the present danger of annihilation of France by Germany, he offered no reasoned reply.[1] MacDonald noted in his diary that Lloyd George was 'jingo', a conclusion which perhaps more accurately reflected MacDonald's unhappiness than the Chancellor's convictions.[2]

Preoccupied with their own private struggles of conscience, Morley, Simon, Runciman, and several others were temporarily convinced that Lloyd George was firmly aligned with them. Morley was sceptical. He admitted in his 'Memorandum on Resignation' that he could not make out 'what exactly brought Lloyd George among us, and what [were] the passing computations for the hour inside his lively brain.'[3] Simon, on the other hand, apparently was deluded, for a short time at least, into thinking that he could exert 'decisive influence' over Lloyd George.[4] Runciman had no illusions about his own influence, but he too seems to have missed the drift of Lloyd George's remarks:

> In course of conversation with about one half of our Ministerial colleagues in No. 11 on the afternoon of that day [August 2] he told us that he would not oppose the war, but he would take no part in it, and would retire for the time being to Criccieth. He would not repeat his experience of 1899–1902. I remember him saying that he had had enough of 'standing out against a war-inflamed populace'.[5]

Recalling these events many years later, Runciman's memory was shaky on details.[6] It is unlikely that at this meeting Lloyd George would have made an unqualified declaration against having any part in a war since he had already, with Runciman, specified cir-

---

[1] *Lord Riddell's War Diary*, pp. 4–5.

[2] I am indebted to Mr David Marquand for this reference to the MacDonald Diary.

[3] Morley, op. cit., p. 16.

[4] Ibid., p. 14.

[5] Statement by Runciman, undated, *c.* 1945). Lt.-Col. Arthur C. Murray, op. cit., p. 120.

[6] Runciman may have been confusing the meeting at Beauchamp's and the later gathering at 11 Downing Street. The Downing Street meeting was at 6.00 p.m., not 'in the afternoon'. Years later, however, a bright midsummer evening could easily have been mis-remembered as an afternoon.

cumstances which might change his position.[1] In any case, if
Runciman's impressions can be relied upon at all, the most signi-
ficant point to emerge from this Sunday meeting was Lloyd
George's determination *not* to lead a peace movement.

Asquith was not present at any of the waverers' informal
gatherings during the pre-war crisis. There was, however, no
secrecy about them; and it was not hard for him to keep abreast of
the movement of opinion. On Sunday, August 2, Samuel and
Pease both reported to the Prime Minister on their colleagues'
deliberations; and, as has been seen, a group of waverers met
Crewe and Birrell on that Sunday evening to further the search
for unity.[2]

Asquith took careful note of the fluctuations in Lloyd George's
position. He observed one day that the Chancellor was 'nervous'.[3]
On August 1, he noticed that 'Lloyd George—all for peace—is
more sensible and statesmanlike for keeping the position still
open.'[4] Every day of delay could only make it easier for the
Chancellor to stay at his post. On July 23 Lloyd George had said
of Anglo-German relations that they were 'very much better than
they were a few years ago' and that before long a reduction of
armaments expenditure might be justified.[5] The Prime Minister,
as Mr Roy Jenkins writes, 'had to allow a little time for Lloyd
George to recover from this extravagance and for other ministers
to move with the pressure of events'.[6] The crucial point was that
without a standard-bearer the waverers would fall down within
the government and not outside it. They were not a solid bloc,
acting together throughout the crisis, eager to follow Lloyd
George in revolt. Lloyd George's influence was symbolic. If he
went, it would be awkward for those who stayed. If he stayed, it
would deprive those who left of some of their moral force.

[1] See above, p. 66.
[2] Viscount Samuel, op. cit., p. 104; Pease's Diary, 2 August 1914, Gainford MSS.
[3] Undated and unattributed quotation. Spender and Asquith, op. cit., vol. II,
p. 101.
[4] Asquith to Venetia Stanley, 1 August 1914, Montagu MSS.
[5] 65 H.C. Deb., 5s, cols 727-8. According to the British Ambassador in Paris,
Grey himself thought in late June 'that the German government are in a peaceful
mood and that they are very anxious to be on good terms with England, a mood
which he wishes to encourage.' (Bertie's Memorandum, 27 June 1914, Bertie MSS,
FO 800/171.)
[6] Roy Jenkins, op. cit., p. 326.

Exactly the same considerations applied to Lord Morley and, to
a lesser extent, to John Burns, John Simon, Jack Pease, and the
other waverers. It was his realization of the symbolic function of
Morley's resignation which drew from Lloyd George on August 3
the frank exclamation: 'But if you go, it will put us who don't go,
in a great hole.'[1]

Those who did not go made the best of their hole. Asquith
used every persuasive device at his disposal to soothe troubled
consciences. His letter to Morley, interrupting a dry-toast break-
fast on August 3, could not have helped digestion:

> To lose you in the stress of a great crisis is a calamity which
> I shudder to contemplate...I therefore beg you, with all my
> heart, to think twice and thrice, and as many times more as
> arithmetic can number, before you take a step which im-
> poverishes the Government and leaves me stranded and al-
> most alone.[2]

Morley withstood the emotional assault. A different approach
worked with Simon. The Attorney-General was unhappy at the
thought that his own defection might precipitate coalition. No
binding promise was given, but Simon's path was softened by a
hint that, if he stayed, his ability would shortly be recognized by
promotion.[3] What weighed with the rest? Between them they
soon produced a convincing battery of arguments to justify
fighting against Prussian militarism, for the sanctity of treaties,
for the 'five-foot five' nations, and even for British interests.

In explaining 'the most terrible decision of my life', Loulou
Harcourt steered the most rigidly logical course. He had never
recognized a binding obligation to any other Power. It was less
than eight months since he had remonstrated with Grey about the
use of the 'mischievous and misleading' term 'Triple Entente' to
imply a much wider understanding with France and Russia than

---

[1] Morley, op. cit., p. 23.

[2] Asquith to Morley, 3 August 1914 (midnight). Ibid., pp. 29–30. 'I part company
with my colleagues in more sorrow than I expected. The pang is sharp,' Morley told
Haldane on August 5. (Haldane MSS, 5910, f. 253.)

[3] See the exchange of letters between Simon and Asquith on August 2, 3, and 4
in the Simon MSS; Charles Trevelyan's 'Personal account of beginning of the War,
1914', Trevelyan MSS; and Addison's Diary, 30 August 1914 (Christopher Addison,
op. cit., vol. 1, p. 35).

was warranted by the government's commitments. 'I object to "Triple Entente",' Harcourt had told Grey on 8 January 1914:

> because no such thing has ever been considered or approved by the Cabinet.
>
> In fact the thing does not exist. We had an 'Entente' with France over Morocco, with some obligations which are now happily resolved.
>
> This 'Entente' left behind it greatly improved relations between the two countries, but no mutual obligations of any kind whatever.
>
> At a later date we came to an 'understanding' with Russia over Persia—and *over* nothing else.
>
> It is true that there is an alliance between France and Russia (in which we are not concerned) and that when we are acting with one of these Powers we are likely to find ourselves in agreement with the other.
>
> But none of these facts entail any community of action between the three in European diplomacy...[1]

It is true that Harcourt had, in an anxious moment, implored Lloyd George to 'speak for us' because it seemed that 'Grey wishes to go to war without violation of Belgium.'[2] In cabinet, he actually followed Lloyd George in saying that the invasion of a neutral state made all the difference to him—a view which a few days earlier he was not even prepared to admit as a possibility and which he did not choose to adopt in public after August 4.[3] Slow as Harcourt and his allies were to admit it, Belgium was an

[1] Harcourt to Grey, 8 January 1914, Grey MSS, FO 800/91. Grey replied on January 10 that it was a mistake to assume that there was any misapprehension in Russia or France about British obligations. If Harcourt wanted the cabinet to discuss the matter, Grey was willing to do so. But, he concluded, 'the best course...is to let things go on as they are without any new declaration of policy. The alternatives are either a policy of complete isolation in Europe, or a policy of definite alliance with one or the other group of European powers. My own desire has been to avoid bringing the choice between these two alternatives to an issue; and I think we have been fortunate in being able to go on as long as we are.' Harcourt beat a polite retreat.

[2] Harcourt to Lloyd George, undated cabinet note, (?2) August 1914, Lloyd George MSS, C/14.

[3] Pease's Diary, 3 August 1914, Gainford MSS.

obvious cause with public appeal. But British interests, not sentiment or obligations, were what really mattered:

> I have acted not from any obligation of Treaty or of honour, for neither existed, and it has been part of my work for the last four years to make it perfectly plain that such was the fact, but there were three overwhelming British interests which I could not abandon:
> (1) That the German fleet should not occupy, under our neutrality, the North Sea and English Channel.
> (2) That they should not seize and occupy the northwestern part of France opposite our shores.
> (3) That they should not violate the ultimate independence of Belgium and hereafter occupy Antwerp as a standing menace to us.[1]

Like Harcourt, Runciman also maintained, when asked by the historian Harold Temperley in 1929, that the Belgian security treaty was never for him 'the big fact'. His thoughts, he told Temperley, were centred on the importance for Britain of free passage through the English Channel. In talking to Grey (as he did at lunch on August 1, for example) Runciman may perhaps have indicated that this was his line. But he did not declare himself in this sense either privately to the other waverers or in the cabinet.[2]

Perhaps the most effective political weapon in the Prime Minister's armoury was the threat of coalition. It was rumoured (according to Sir Valentine Chirol in a letter to Lord Hardinge on August 4) that the King had told Asquith that, if the ministry collapsed, he would summon Asquith and Lord Lansdowne and ask them to form a 'National Defence Government'. By writing to the Prime Minister on August 2 to offer 'unhesitating support' to the government in any measures which were thought necessary to aid France and Russia, the Conservative leaders had also given some credence to the possibility of coalition.

Addressing himself to the waverers, Asquith argued that, if they went, coalition might be necessary. To Churchill, and perhaps

---

[1] Harcourt to F. G. Thomas, 5 August 1914 (copy), Harcourt MSS.
[2] Runciman to Temperley, 4 November 1929, Spender MSS, (Add. MS. 46386, ff. 72–6).

Grey, coalition might have been acceptable. But the Prime Minister himself put forward the view that the Conservatives were neither led by, nor included amongst their number, men competent to direct the nation's affairs at a time of crisis. 'Coalitions', he added, 'have hardly ever turned out well in our history.'[1] As well as encountering the Prime Minister's studied pessimism, the idea of coalition suffered by being associated with Churchill. The very fact that this ex-Tory favoured union with the Conservatives might have been enough to persuade some of the waverers that their own continued presence in the ministry was essential.

Morley found Asquith's implicit denigration of Balfour, Bonar Law, and Austen Chamberlain 'grotesque'.[2] Nevertheless, in justifying his own resignation, Morley actually tried to dissuade his colleagues from following; their future responsibilities to the Premier, to the party, and to the constituencies were, he argued, different from his. They were younger; and 'long issues [were] committed to their charge'.[3] It was not until later that the special advantage to the nation of being led into war by a Liberal cabinet was fully appreciated. Morley did not stress this idea; nor is it recorded that anyone else did so. Yet it is a recurring theme in the memoirs of those who played a part in these events. A Liberal decision for war was the best assurance of Labour and Irish Nationalist support, of national unity. In Lloyd George's words:

> War had been declared by a party which by tradition and training regarded war with the deepest aversion, and has more especially since the days of Gladstone, Cobden and Bright, regarded itself as specially charged with the promotion of the cause of peace.[4]

[1] Charles Trevelyan's 'Personal account of beginning of the War, 1914', Trevelyan MSS; Morley, op. cit., p. 25. Asquith's comment on the Conservatives was offered as a reason why it would be inadvisable for the Liberal government to resign and be replaced by Conservatives. But his judgment on the Conservatives' capacity for leadership applied also to the consideration of their usefulness as members of a coalition.

[2] Geoffrey Robinson's Notes of a Luncheon with Lord Fisher, 18 January 1915. John Evelyn Wrench, *Geoffrey Dawson and Our Times* (London, 1955), p. 118. Geoffrey Robinson (later Dawson), the editor of *The Times*, was on his way to lunch with Lord Fisher, and met Lord Morley in the street.

[3] Morley, op. cit., p. 16.

[4] Lloyd George, op. cit., vol. 1, p. 220.

What was the frame of mind of the waverers as they braced themselves for war? Perhaps the sincerest and most illuminating expressions of their feelings came from Pease and Runciman. Pease's adherence to the government partially counterbalanced the loss of Morley and Burns. As a Quaker and President of the Peace Society, Pease's anti-war credentials were unimpeachable. His decision, and the way in which he justified it, ensured that Lloyd George would not be immediately isolated from the un-reconciled pacifists and nonconformists. Pease's easiest course, as he pointed out to a correspondent, would have been to say that he hated war so much that he could not make himself responsible for its conduct:

> But having carefully thought the whole question over for some days I have come to the conclusion that Friend as I am by conviction it would be a cowardly and selfish act on my part to seek my own rest of mind and leave to my colleagues the distasteful and hateful work.[1]

Runciman, in a letter to Charles Trevelyan, stated the position which he professed to share with Lloyd George, Harcourt, and Pease. They all considered it to be their duty to remain at their posts 'and with our full strength devote ourselves to the terrible work of the organization of industry and food supply, and of defence'. Runciman was almost certainly thinking primarily of a duty to alleviate the distress which he believed would be caused by unemployment and the disruption of trade. Like most politicians he was committing himself not to mobilization for total war but to mitigating domestic suffering while the Continental tangle was sorted out. Of course, he was miserable; but that was no reason why the Liberal government should destroy itself. No personal feelings would be 'sufficient to justify us in handing over policy and control to the Tories'.[2] Before it was known that Simon and Beauchamp had decided to withdraw their resigna-

---

[1] Pease to J. B. Hodgkin, 4 August 1914 (copy), Gainford MSS. The Society of Friends promptly recognized 'that our Government has made most strenuous efforts to preserve peace, and has entered into the war under a grave sense of duty to a smaller State towards which we had moral and treaty obligations'. ('To Men and Women of Goodwill in the British Empire: A Message from the Religious Society of Friends', 7 August 1914, Acland MSS.)

[2] Runciman to Trevelyan, 4 August 1914, Trevelyan MSS.

tions, Samuel had written: 'Our participation in the war is now inevitable.' As for those who declined to remain in the cabinet: 'Those four men have no right to abandon us at this crisis—it is a failure of courage...The Prime Minister goes on out of sheer sense of duty.'[1]

So the waverers stayed. On Monday, August 3, Lloyd George drove with Samuel and some others through cheering crowds to the House of Commons. The Chancellor of the Exchequer was warmly welcomed by the excited throng in Whitehall. But, for the moment, such demonstrations of enthusiasm and affection gave him no pleasure. 'This is not my crowd,' he said. 'I never want to be cheered by a war crowd.'[2]

By the following day, however, his spirits had lifted. 'In a week or two', he wrote to his friend Alick Murray, 'it might be good fun to be the advance guard of an expeditionary force to the coast of France, and run the risk of capture by a German ship!'[3]

[1] Samuel to Beatrice Samuel, 3 August 1914, Samuel MSS, A/157/698, ff. 60-1.
[2] Samuel to Beatrice Samuel, 3 August 1914, 10.00 p.m., Samuel MSS, A/157/699, ff. 63-4.
[3] Lloyd George to Murray of Elibank, 4 August 1914, Murray of Elibank MSS, 8803, f. 132.

Part II From Truce to Coalition

1 Radical Murmurs

Getting his cabinet—and especially Lloyd George—into war with the minimum of embarrassment for everyone was a triumph for Asquith. It gave him and his party a new lease of life. But the delicacy with which the Prime Minister found it necessary to handle his Chancellor was a hint that the leader's grip, on both the party and the nation, was far from secure. In the first days of August, many of Asquith's colleagues had seemed to be on the verge of resignation. Only Lloyd George, however, by leaving the government, could have shaken Asquith's hold on power or seriously impaired the unity of the nation.

Having committed himself to war, Lloyd George's fortunes were for the time being indissolubly linked with those of his chief. And, preoccupied with the massive problems of financial adjustment, Lloyd George as Chancellor of the Exchequer was not usually summoned, nor did he seek entry, to the informal meetings at which war policy was decided in the opening weeks of the conflict. From August 4, the Prime Minister, Secretary of State for War, First Lord of the Admiralty, and Foreign Secretary necessarily and properly concentrated their attention on the urgent problems of mobilization for Continental warfare. Within forty-eight hours the cabinet had reversed its prohibition on the use of the expeditionary force.

Later on August 6, Asquith recorded that the cabinet that morning 'decided with much less demur than I expected to sanction the despatch of the Expeditionary Force of four divisions'.[1] There was only one plan for co-operation with the French and that plan had already been disrupted by the delay in committing the army. At two meetings of an *ad hoc* council of war, attended by Asquith, Grey, Haldane, and Churchill, and a miscellaneous assembly of military and naval leaders, the professionals showed

[1] Asquith to Venetia Stanley, 6 August 1914, Montagu MSS.

121

themselves as ignorant and confused about British plans and capabilities as the cabinet had been in the previous week. But Henry Wilson's timetables prevailed. Preliminary points of embarkation and concentration were settled; and attention turned to the manifold contingent arrangements for mobilizing the men and resources of the Empire.[1]

While the nation thus began to gear itself for war, the world of politics itself underwent a transformation. The anti-war clamour died away. The rhetoric of civil violence in Ulster and England was silenced. The surface hostilities of party, class, and sex gave way to united protestations of patriotism. Momentarily, the old antagonisms were swept aside. Hastily created neutrality agitations collapsed as quickly as they had been started. The two resignations from the cabinet passed with scarcely a murmur of protest. Burns and Morley were not going to be missed. Charles Trevelyan's departure from the Under-Secretaryship of the Board of Education caused hardly more comment.[2] He too could be replaced. 'Happily,' Asquith told Miss Stanley, 'il n'y a pas d'homme nécessaire.'[3] Yet the flight of these three to the back benches was a harbinger of the strain on both ministry and party that would assuredly accompany their conduct of war.

How long could the nation's unity be preserved? For those with eyes to see, the precarious position of the Liberal government was easily discernible.

Trevelyan's resignation, for example, was far wider in its implications than might have been guessed from his comparative lowliness in the Liberal hierarchy. Unlike his contemporaries, Walter Runciman and Herbert Samuel, he had not received the advancement to which he could feel reasonably entitled. He had entered Parliament before he was thirty. An active proponent of social reform and land taxation, he was soon established as one of the most promising younger members of the party. He combined

[1] Haig's Diary, 5–6 August 1914. Robert Blake (ed.), *The Private Papers of Douglas Haig, 1914–1919*, pp. 68–70; Wilson's Diary, 5–6 August 1914, Wilson MSS. Pease's Diary, 5–6 August 1914, passes over the decision to employ the Expeditionary Force without comment.

[2] Burns decided not to make a resignation speech in the House of Commons. Trevelyan believed that custom forced him to take the same course. (Charles Trevelyan's 'Personal account of beginning of the War, 1914', Trevelyan MSS.)

[3] Asquith to Venetia Stanley, 4 August 1914, Montagu MSS.

enthusiasm for ameliorative progressive Liberalism with inheritance of a strong family tradition of constitutional and administrative reform. Nevertheless, despite his connections and abundant attributes, he languished for six years in junior office, frustrated by the preferment of less talented men, and constrained by loyalty to defend the actions of the government even when, as in the field of foreign affairs, he had deep misgivings about the direction of policy.

It would not be correct to think of Trevelyan's resignation as the petulant gesture of a disappointed aspirant for power. What his action does reveal, however, is a sense of betrayal shared with, and strongly felt by, a number of kindred spirits on and beyond the fringes of Liberalism. The fact that Grey and Asquith had led the nation into war came to Trevelyan as a profound shock. He had wrestled incredulously with the possibility of British intervention. 'What are we bound to do?' he asked in a note of self-examination:

Are we bound to sacrifice all other interests, all our civilization—if these are engaged in our keeping out of war [?]
Never thought before that obligation to sacrifice everything.[1]

When Grey revealed the cabinet's position on August 3, Trevelyan realized at once that 'there is no use blinking the big differences.' As he wrote sadly to Walter Runciman, 'The Entente was an alliance after all, no less real in Grey's mind because it was not written.'[2] Even before his resignation, Trevelyan had been in touch with Norman Angell and other leading neutralists. He spent a large part of August 1 in helping to organize a Neutrality Committee—an action which was hardly consistent with the loyalty that he owed to the government to which he still belonged. 'I ... could do nothing overt,' Trevelyan admitted, 'as being in the Government, but helped to warn and stir up.'[3] Within hours of becoming a private member, the ex-parliamentary secretary was plunged into co-ordinating those radicals inside and outside Parliament who could not reconcile themselves to war. He met with twenty or thirty Liberals who wanted to work with the Labour

[1] Note by Trevelyan, undated (?2 August), 1914, Trevelyan MSS.
[2] Trevelyan to Runciman, 4 August 1914, Runciman MSS; see also Trevelyan to Asquith, 3 August 1914 (copy), Trevelyan MSS.
[3] Trevelyan's 'Personal account...1914', Trevelyan MSS.

Party; and on August 6 he became chairman of a parliamentary group of thirty M.P.s 'to watch the war & secure peace as soon as possible'.[1] With Ramsay MacDonald, Norman Angell, E.D. Morel, Philip Morrell, Arnold Rowntree, and Bertrand Russell he formed the Union of Democratic Control. For a month this group operated without publicity. But a blaze of allegations in *The Morning Post, The Globe,* and other Tory papers about a 'secret pro-German conspiracy' forced the U.D.C. to come into the open with a declaration of policy. 'The Union has been created', they declared, 'to formulate and organize support for such a policy as shall lead to the establishment and maintenance of an enduring peace.'[2] Specifically, U.D.C. documents supported 'democratic control' of foreign policy, reduction of armaments, and international organization to secure agreements to guarantee peace—objects that had long appealed to members of the Liberal Foreign Affairs Committee.

Within the ranks of the dissident radicals there were conflicting views about the most effective course which might be followed. Some M.P.s, like Wilson Raffan and Sir William Byles, argued that there was no chance of an unprejudiced hearing for the U.D.C. platform.[3] George Macaulay Trevelyan, counselling his brother with the wisdom of history, warned:

I shouldn't try to make 'Bright Crimean' speeches against the war in the House—still less elsewhere, while its issue is in doubt, because even then only Bright could have done it, and that war was a game, just as the Boer War was; this is life and death. You will all be more effective for peace when the time comes if you show patriotism now and don't make yourselves wildly unpopular. Until the issue of the war is essentially decided there is and must be the old anti-Napoleonic feeling of 'In Britain is one breath.' I feel that in my bones.[4]

Arrayed against British involvement in war were some of the nation's most perceptive students of politics as well as men per-

[1] Trevelyan to Mary Trevelyan, 7 August 1914, Trevelyan MSS.
[2] F. Seymour Cocks, *E. D. Morel:* The Man and His Work (London, 1920), p. 224.
[3] P. Wilson Raffan to Trevelyan, and Sir William Byles to Trevelyan, 21 October 1914, Trevelyan MSS.
[4] G. M. Trevelyan to Trevelyan, 8 August 1914, Trevelyan MSS.

sonally experienced in the manœuvrings of the political arena.
Sage advice was available in many quarters. Francis Hirst, editor
of *The Economist*, sketched what was probably the ideal strategy
for dissenters: 'associate for particular purposes with all the people
who are in agreement on a particular purpose'. Thousands of
people, Hirst argued, would co-operate to prevent martial law,
others to prevent the suppression of public criticism, others in
defence of free trade, others in opposition to 'the indefinite and
unlimited export of British troops to the Continent', others, perhaps, 'to mitigate the barbarous war against commerce and contracts'.[1]

Had Hirst's advice been followed, formidable pressures might
have been focused on the government. There were however, siren
voices calling for more dramatic and open activity. Discreet
manipulation and the quiet conversion of opinion were not totally
satisfying to militant internationalists. MacDonald's stand, for
example, appeared to Graham Wallas to require a concentrated
effort to discredit the government. MacDonald asked, in a letter
to *The Nation*, whether the people who had led the country into
war could be trusted to make the peace.[2] But, attacking the integrity of Grey, however justifiably, was a futile, self-destructive
policy. Moderate Liberals found MacDonald's accusations offensive. 'I do not believe he is a straight man or a brave man,' wrote
the West Riding M.P., Gerald France, '& he has to my mind put
himself beyond the pale by his untrue & wicked libel against Grey
re France & the neutrality of Belgium.'[3] Such was Grey's stature
that there was only one safe way to attack him—by denouncing
'secret diplomacy'. This impersonal evil could, as Bertrand Russell
pointed out, be taken as Grey's alias.[4]

When inquisitive journalists flushed the U.D.C. into the public
gaze, most of its leaders put their case with the minimum of
personal invective. But the speeches, lectures, pamphlets, and
articles condemning the pre-war diplomacy swelled into a surging,
though narrow and partly subterranean, stream of dissatisfaction
with the political leadership which brought Britain into war. As

[1] Hirst to Trevelyan, 12 August 1914, Trevelyan MSS.
[2] Wallas to Trevelyan, 29 August 1914, Trevelyan MSS; *The Nation*, 29 August
1914.
[3] France to Trevelyan, 27 September 1914, Trevelyan MSS.
[4] Russell to Trevelyan, 2 October 1914, Trevelyan MSS.

month followed unpromising month, new trickles of impatient criticism began to surface. To the sin of entering the war was added that of failing to end it quickly. And, most ominously for the safety of the government and the stability of the Liberal Party, the critical voices included not only the unashamed pacifists on the one hand and the notorious jingoes on the other, but men who, having begun the war with the utmost reluctance, were transformed by their involvement in the struggle into ardent patriots.

Dissent of all sorts was inevitable. What could not be predicted with certainty was the likely extent and intensity of opposition. It did not take long to establish the fact that the attacks of the U.D.C. and its associates, notwithstanding their cogency, attracted little support at Westminster or in the country. For the first two years of war Trevelyan, Morrell, Ponsonby, and their allies were little more than a nuisance to the government. By impugning the honesty of the Prime Minister and the Foreign Secretary, they actually provoked a reaction in the government's favour. The unpopularity of the U.D.C. was a temporary comfort but an ultimate disaster for Asquith. In the haven of the U.D.C., radicals seeking an early peace and a reformed international system found like-minded men from different parties. When the time came for Liberals to be counted in 1916, and again in 1918, a small but influential number no longer felt allegiance either to the Prime Minister or his party.

2 Parliament

From the beginning of hostilities, seeds of doubt about the British case were widely sown. But for every one that flowered, many more were stifled by patriotism. 'It is painful to break silence, painful to keep silence,' wrote Lord Courtney of Penwith to C. P. Scott on August 8. Courtney was troubled by the publication in the Foreign Office White Paper of a dispatch (No. 123) showing that 'Lichnowsky made advances, almost offers to Grey to give up the neutrality of Belgium and the integrity of France and her colonies, in fact all that lay in dispute, and even asked what were our own conditions if we would only formulate them.'[1] Courtney kept silence.

If the war could not be justified by a 'scrap of paper' it could not be terminated to relieve guilty consciences. War itself provided its own continuing justification. When, in December 1914, the Germans shelled Scarborough, Hartlepool, and Whitby—'our first sample of Hunnishness on our own shores'—Eleanor Acland reflected:

> It comes just when we are getting rather bored with the other reasons for fighting, just to remind us that the reason for going on is that we have begun; just to show us once again what the inward gist of Potsdam is... The repetition of a good cry soon gets monotonous, & we want to have our blood stirred by something that really pricks.[2]

Mrs Acland, speaking for herself and her husband, spoke also perhaps for those hundreds of M.P.s whose contribution to the war effort was limited to speaking on recruiting platforms and silently consenting to emergency legislation. 'An M.P. is as useless

[1] Courtney of Penwith to Scott, 8 August 1914, *Manchester Guardian* MSS.
[2] Eleanor Acland's War Diary, 19 December 1914, Acland MSS.

as an empty soda bottle just now,' Josiah Wedgwood complained[1] Winston Churchill 'showered commissions on Members of the House of Commons to lead his amphibian Forces, till the War Office, in sheer self-defence, had to do the same'.[2] On September 17, Wedgwood and Baron de Forest were made lieutenant-commanders and Geoffrey Howard became a lieutenant in the Royal Naval Volunteer Reserve. By January 1915, 184 M.P.s were in the armed services, of whom 41 were Liberals and 139 Conservatives. But for the majority of middle-aged and elderly parliamentarians the exhilaration of active service was no more than a dream. Cut off from the smell and noise of battle they were pledged to duty at Westminster. In the historic but stuffy Parliament buildings, the endemic frustrations of backbench life were now to be aggravated by the attraction of imagined glamour across the Channel.

Could epidemics of irritation and controversy be contained? A healthy party, with smoothly functioning channels of communication between leaders and followers, might have expected to survive the strain; but a heavy load would fall unavoidably on the Chief Whip and his subordinates. How well was the Liberal Party served by its managers? In Percy Illingworth the Liberals had an amiable but uninspiring Chief Whip. Asquith described him as 'shrewd, resourceful, inclined by nature to be pugnacious, and capable of giving a good account of himself in any company either with his tongue or his fists'.[3] Illingworth had achieved the difficult feat of remaining on good terms with the opposition Chief Whip throughout the years of exasperation before the outbreak of war. He lacked the suavity of his predecessor, the Master of Elibank; and he did not possess vast resources of Parliamentary guile. Nevertheless, with vigilance and strict discipline, he had steered the government through the dangerous stages of the Home Rule Bill. His 'unusual blend of unbending Nonconformist and hearty sportsman made a nature which could sympathize with the varying elements of his flock'.[4] Yet sympathy, essential as it was in maintaining trust and harmony, was not enough. Despite the introduction of a number of procedural and mechanical improve-

---

[1] Wedgwood to Runciman, 25 August 1914, Runciman MSS.
[2] Lord Wedgwood, *Testament to Democracy* (London, 1942), p. 40.
[3] Asquith, *Memories and Reflections*, vol. 1, p. 192.
[4] Obituary by J. W. G.[ulland], *The Westminster Gazette*, 5 January 1915.

ments in the gathering and recording of parliamentary intelligence, Liberal organization had been recognizably in need of reform in the closing months of peace. Edwin Montagu complained to Asquith of the 'pathetic weakness of our Whips' Office'.[1]

At the root of the trouble in the party machine was the over-working of the Chief Whip. The increasing pressure of parliamentary business was making it impossible for the same man, in addition to his daily duties at Westminster, to supervise the choice of candidates, the control of party funds, and the direction of party affairs in the country. The Tories had recognized this two years earlier and placed Arthur Steel-Maitland at the head of a reorganized party machine. Montagu was convinced, as he told the Prime Minister in May 1914, that: 'We have seen nothing in our time like the Conservative by-election organization, and I believe, as I have so often said to you before, that the time has come to split the office of Liberal Whip as the Tories have done, and as I suggested to you in November 1908.' As another well-informed critic pointed out about Liberal organizational weakness: 'It is no fault of the Chief Whips, who work themselves to death, but it is because there shld be under the Chief Whip, someone who combines political instinct with a love of electoral machinery.'[2]

The need for change was recognized in high places. 'Grubby little complications which a competent, authoritative, man could deal with daily, but which, because there is no one whose particular business is just this, cumulatively clog the wheels'[3]—these obvious defects impelled Lloyd George to take counsel with Lord Murray of Elibank who, although nominally retired from politics, kept a close watch on matters of organization. In June 1914, Asquith agreed with Lloyd George and Murray that party management in the country should be divided from parliamentary business. A party organizer, with functions and responsibilities clearly separate from those of the Chief Whip in the House of Commons, was to be appointed. For this important new post several men were considered. Lloyd George had told Sir George Riddell on May 24 that Wedgwood Benn 'was the best man

[1] Montagu to Asquith, 27 May 1914 (copy), Montagu MSS.
[2] Cecil Beck to Charles Masterman, 26 May 1914, Lloyd George MSS, C/5/15/5.
[3] Ibid.

I

available' to assume some of Illingworth's burden.[1] Murray was 'divided in his mind between [Arthur] Ponsonby and [Christopher] Addison'. The former Chief Whip's opinion, as reported by Lloyd George to the Prime Minister, was that Percy Illingworth 'would be more likely to accept tranquilly the appointment of an outsider than one of his own subordinates like Wedgwood Benn'.[2] It was important for the success of the scheme that it should not begin by offending Illingworth's susceptibilities. For this reason, Wedgwood Benn, whose inventions and formidable system of record-keeping had recently brought discernible increments of efficiency to the operations of the Whips' Room in the House of Commons, could not be advanced. Wedgwood Benn's promotion would have implied some reflection on the capacity of his chief.

The proposed changes and the new appointment had not been settled before the outbreak of war. 'Illingworth', Riddell recorded, 'would not agree.'[3] From the point of view of the cohesion of the Liberal Party, particularly in the House of Commons, the consequences of this delay are important, though difficult to measure. Had one of the two top party jobs fallen to Christopher Addison, he, as one of Lloyd George's most loyal adherents, would have been strongly placed either to take the initiative in preparing the ground for a possible seizure of power within the party—if Lloyd George ever contemplated such a move—or to work from the inside at preserving party unity. What might have happened if Arthur Ponsonby had held the reins of the party machinery in his hands is almost impossible to imagine. It is surprising that he, as the leader of a body of opinion overtly critical of the government's conduct of foreign policy, could have been considered at all for such a post. If he had accepted the task it must be doubted whether he would have stuck to it when the cabinet opted for war. But if he had accepted, he too, in a different way, could have done much to allay the suspicions of the government's radical critics. He might have done something to prevent the drift of radicals out of the party instead of taking a prominent place in the war-time and post-war exodus.

---

[1] Riddell's Diary, 24 May 1914. Lord Riddell, *More Pages From My Diary, 1908–1914* (London, 1934), p. 214.

[2] Lloyd George to Asquith, 5 June 1914, Lloyd George MSS, C/6/11/15.

[3] Riddell's Diary, 9 January 1915. *Lord Riddell's War Diary*, p. 50.

The failure to make the arrangements which were obviously necessary to revitalize the party machinery had one indirect but far-reaching consequence. In December 1914, Percy Illingworth fell ill; he died a few weeks later. To replace him, Asquith's first thought was J. H. Whitley, who had served since 1911 as Deputy Speaker. Whitley refused, ostensibly on grounds of health, but also because, as he told Herbert Samuel, 'I feel that the highest permanent interests of Liberalism lie in the maintenance of the Commons in efficiency as the instrument of democratic government, & for me, or anyone, to step out of the Chair to the Chief-Whipship would be to some extent to lower the position temporarily placed in my trust.'[1] Whitley, of course, knew that he had the reversion to the Speakership; and it was this office which he was determined to have when Lowther, the Conservative incumbent, stepped down from the Chair.

Lloyd George's favourite for Chief Whip was Neil Primrose, the popular younger son of Lord Rosebery, who had been serving with his regiment since the beginning of the war. But Asquith did not share Lloyd George's enthusiasm. Nor, evidently did Asquith's friend, Venetia Stanley: 'Your veto on Neil for Chief Whip', the Prime Minister wrote to Miss Stanley on January 16, 'is heartily endorsed by both Violet [Asquith] and Bongie [Maurice Bonham Carter, Asquith's secretary]. I wonder why Ll.G. is so enamoured of the idea? I am beginning to think that *faute de mieux*, it will be the line of least resistance to promote Gulland.'[2]

The trouble with Primrose was not that he lacked ability—he became Under Secretary at the Foreign Office a few weeks later—but that he would have had to be brought in over the heads of the existing Whips and those who had temporarily left the Whips' Office to join the forces. Whitley, when asked for his suggestions, had first proposed the wealthy young Buckinghamshire landowner, Sir Harry Verney, who had entered the government in August 1914 as the junior minister at the Board of Agriculture. Asquith believed that Verney's ability and interests were suitably recognized by his existing appointment.[3] Of Whitley's other

[1] Whitley to Samuel, 15 January 1915, Samuel MSS, A/155, ff. 128–9; Pease's Diary, 12 January 1915 (entry referring to January 7), Gainford MSS; Asquith to Venetia Stanley, 14 January 1915, Montagu MSS.
[2] Asquith to Venetia Stanley, 16 January 1915, Montagu MSS.
[3] After the name of Illingworth's successor had been announced, John Gulland

suggestions, the only one which impressed Asquith was Francis Acland, Grey's Under Secretary at the Foreign Office. Acland was undeniably capable; but he had a 'suffragette' wife, and Asquith found him 'a rather angular man'.[1]

Whitley's refusal created difficulties. 'The more I consider the problem', Asquith had told Miss Stanley on January 10, 'the less hope have I of finding any other suitable man.' Acland, Verney, Primrose, even Churchill's cousin, Freddie Guest, who was dropping stage whispers about his own qualifications, all had points in their favour and equally weighty disqualifying attributes—a wife with the wrong opinions about woman suffrage, an obtrusive deficiency in intelligence or experience, or a character too robustly assertive for the tactful role of chief pacifier and gentle disciplinarian.

However, after several days of indecision, Asquith's mind fastened on an alternative solution. With no outstanding man available, the opportunity had arisen to revert to the plan of reorganization which had been discussed the previous June. The development of Asquith's thinking may be followed in extracts from two letters to Miss Stanley, both written on January 17:

> To go back to the Whipship, about wh. I talked to the Assyrian [Edwin Montagu]—he suggested [Donald] Maclean, quite an impossible person—I am not sure that I shall not have to fall back upon Gulland (for the House) and Benn (for organization & the country).

> I talked again over the question of Chief Whip with the Assyrian & Bongie before dinner. On the whole, they were disposed to acquiesce in my tame and (as you say) 'uninspiring' conclusion to put it in commission between Gulland & Benn.

As Illingworth was beyond embarrassment, there was no longer any obstacle to promoting Wedgwood Benn to the post of principal organizer in the country. Asquith had agreed with Lloyd

---

wrote to Verney: 'From what I read in the papers I was lighting my torch to escort you in triumph to the Chief Whip's room, but alas! you could not be spared from the growing of wheat.' (Gulland to Verney, 31 January 1915, Verney MSS.)

[1] Asquith to Venetia Stanley, 14 January 1915, Montagu MSS.

George seven months earlier that Benn was 'the best man for the job'.[1] In June 1914, Benn would have been delighted with the appointment. But, after five months of war, the pert, energetic, ex-Junior Whip had other plans. He had put on the uniform of a cavalry officer. 'The task of organizing conflicting Parties in Parliament seemed ridiculous and distasteful,' he wrote many years afterwards.[2] It seemed all the more ridiculous when lengthy prorogations and the suspension of party warfare left 'practically nothing to do on the floor of the House'.[3]

Asquith had proposed that Wedgwood Benn should be a sort of Joint Chief Whip, sharing the burden with John Gulland, who had worked as Scottish Whip under Illingworth. Gulland was to enjoy the title of Chief Whip, and have mainly parliamentary duties. Wedgwood Benn was to be in charge of what Gulland described to his sister as 'the very harassing work of English candidates and constituencies'.[4] On learning that Benn was unavailable, the Prime Minister appointed Gulland to succeed Illingworth with the full power and responsibility of his predecessor. It was a fateful appointment. Of all the conceivable Chief Whips canvassed by the party leaders and in the press in January 1915, Gulland was one of the least fancied. Apart from Wedgwood Benn, half a dozen names—Jack Seely and Geoffrey Howard, as well as Primrose, Verney, Whitley, and Freddie Guest (whose claims were strengthened, according to one report, by his possession of 'a good social position and a house in Park Lane'[5])—all had strong claims. And, in the event, any one of them might have served the Prime Minister and the Liberal Party more successfully than Gulland.

Gulland proved unequal to the demands of the war-time House of Commons. He was bequeathed a Whips' Office that was undermanned and short of experience. The loss of Henry Webb, Geoffrey Howard, and Freddie Guest, as well as Wedgwood Benn, had multiplied Illingworth's difficulties in the last months of 1914.

[1] Asquith to Lloyd George, 7 June 1914, Lloyd George MSS, C/6/11/16.
[2] Autobiographical Note by Lord Stansgate, undated, Stansgate MSS.
[3] MacCallum Scott's Diary, 3 December 1914, MacCallum Scott MSS.
[4] Runciman to Sir Robert Chalmers, 7 February 1915; Runciman to Hilda Runciman, 12 January 1915, Runciman MSS; Gulland to Elsie Osborne, 21 January 1915, Gulland MSS.
[5] *The Manchester Despatch*, 4 January 1915 (press-cutting in the Illingworth MSS).

With Illingworth gone, the team that remained—Gulland, Walter
Rea, Cecil Beck, and William Jones—was seriously ill-equipped.
The death of Jones a little later further depleted Gulland's force.
Gulland himself was disappointingly ineffectual. Asquith had
admitted to Venetia Stanley that his new Chief Whip was 'lacking
in personality and authority'. And though Gulland was credited
with a strong strain of native shrewdness, the Prime Minister
did not expect to receive the same unflinching, if occasionally
disagreeable, argument which Illingworth had always been prepared to offer.[1] Asquith was right. Gulland's personality left so
little impression on his contemporaries that it is difficult for the
historian to reconstruct a satisfactory picture of his activities.
What does survive, however, is clear evidence of his lack of
acumen, and even of that unsubtle but reliable 'nous' which had
attracted Asquith to Illingworth. The limitations of Gulland's
predecessor had been obvious enough. Nevertheless, he had com-
manded a personal allegiance in the Liberal ranks, and a respect in
the Tory and Labour organizations, that Gulland never matched.
In retrospect it was the good qualities of 'honest Illingworth'[2]—
as Walter Runciman had rather patronizingly described him in
June 1914—which his colleagues wistfully recalled. Gulland aimed
at maintaining the morale of the Liberals, believing that 'they only
ask for an opportunity of work'.[3] Undeniable as was the general
desire to make a contribution to the war effort, discontents were
soon to go much deeper and to demand more effective palliatives
than Gulland seemed capable of producing.

[1] Asquith to Venetia Stanley, 17 and 21 January 1915, Montagu MSS.
[2] Runciman to Chalmers, 24 June 1914, Runciman MSS.
[3] Gulland to Runciman, 25 February 1915, Runciman MSS. See also Gulland's
circular letter to ministers, 22 February 1915, urging all departments to take
advantage 'of the willing services of as many members as possible'. (Grey MSS,
FO 800/90.)

3 Truce

Since January 1910, the Liberal government had depended for its parliamentary majority on the votes of the four-score Irish Nationalists and forty Labour members. The loose alliance continued into the war. Labour and Irish leaders—apart from the notable exceptions who have already been mentioned—pledged patriotic support to the ministry. The Labour Party joined in the work of the Joint Parliamentary Recruiting Committee. But Redmond and Carson refused to appear together on recruiting platforms; and the Nationalists did not begin a recruiting campaign of their own until Home Rule reached the statute book in the middle of September. Redmond and Arthur Henderson gave tokens of their own good faith. They could not, however, guarantee the indefinite loyalty of their parties. Nor, indeed, could Bonar Law and Lansdowne.

The one way in which Asquith could have bound up the fortunes of the opposition with his own was the way of coalition. Churchill had been eager for coalition when war broke out. So too, on the other side, had F. E. Smith. Their leaders, however, gave the idea no encouragement. Asquith used the threat of coalition to dissuade Simon and Beauchamp from resigning. Bonar Law refused to countenance Churchill's unofficial overtures and made no move on his own initiative.

Many years later, Ramsay MacDonald said that he had been asked to join the government when war began.[1] It is conceivable that Asquith may have toyed with the idea of taking in Mac-Donald as a hostage to ensure Labour co-operation. It is more likely that some other ministers, Lloyd George among them, talked tantalizingly in MacDonald's presence about the attractions

[1] Hankey's Note of a Conversation with MacDonald, 30 September 1930. Hankey, *The Supreme Command, 1914–1918*, vol. I, p. 167.

of coalition. Lloyd George might even have deliberately explored the Labour leader's reactions with a view to proposing that the Prime Minister should make a formal approach. The opportunity for such probing certainly occurred when MacDonald dined with Sir George Riddell on August 2, for Lloyd George, Simon, and Masterman, as well as Riddell, were present that evening.[1]

MacDonald could, of course, have been brought into the ministry whether or not the Conservative opposition had been invited to join a national government. And whatever Asquith thought about the desirability of securing MacDonald's services—on which subject no evidence has come to light—the Prime Minister certainly had no enthusiasm for coalition with the Tories. The sentiments of Bonar Law and his associates were equally cool. The Conservatives had little to lose by patriotically, supporting the government from outside. Asquith, on the other hand, had much to gain by winning the war unaided.

In any case, for the time being, coalition was scarcely possible. Tempers inflamed by Ireland and Welsh Disestablishment needed time to cool. A political truce was the best immediate solution. It was quickly agreed, and normal party warfare in the constituencies was suspended.

'I am', wrote Asquith to Bonar Law on 8 August 1914, 'anxious above all things that, in the circumstances which surround us, no impression should be given to the world that we are, any of us, intent on the pursuit of domestic controversy.'[2] This was the appropriate sentiment for the hour. But Asquith destroyed any likelihood of cordiality by going ahead with the enactment of Home Rule and Welsh Church legislation. The government's action on Home Rule infuriated a large section of the opposition despite the efforts of Crewe, Harcourt, Grey, and Haldane to mollify the Conservative leaders.[3]

A number of Conservative leaders protested after only a few days of war. 'How is it possible,' one asked, 'to let political warfare run riot within the H. C. and proclaim a truce of God every-

---

[1] *Lord Riddell's War Diary*, pp. 3–5; Lucy Masterman, 'Reminiscences of Lib-Lab days', *New Outlook*, No. 50 (January 1966), p. 21.

[2] Asquith to Bonar Law, 8 August 1914, Bonar Law MSS, 34/3/20.

[3] Balfour to Bonar Law, 12 August 1914, Bonar Law MSS, 34/3/36; Harcourt to Bonar Law, 14 August 1914, Bonar Law MSS, 34/3/41; Note of Conversation between Lansdowne and Crewe, 21 August 1914, Lansdowne MSS.

where else. Such a policy is unthinkable.'[1] It was not only the wild
men who choked on Home Rule. After one injudicious intervention by Arthur Balfour, Lloyd George wrote with undisguised
dismay to Austen Chamberlain:

> Last Monday's debate was one of the most depressing inci-
> dents I have ever witnessed in the House of Commons ... Mr
> Balfour's interposition ... was angry, petulant and shrewish
> ... Mr Balfour is an ex-premier who has even now great
> Imperial responsibilities, and no speech from Redmond
> could have justified the rather truculent zeal with which
> Mr Balfour advertised our differences to the Enemy at a
> moment of supreme crisis in our fate.
>
> These differences ought to be settled. It is our patriotic
> duty to find a settlement and I wish I were convinced Mr Bal-
> four was doing his best to achieve that end.

That Ireland could not be treated merely as an irritating distrac-
tion was a lesson which Lloyd George made clear in his conclud-
ing sentences:

> I should be sorry if differences as to Home Rule should pre-
> vent co-operation between parties in resisting the common
> enemy. If we go out of office then I promise you that as I
> think this war a righteous war I shall give all the support in
> my power to a Unionist Government in bringing it to a
> triumphant conclusion.

Chamberlain felt the sting. He hastened to reassure Lloyd
George that as long as the war lasted he would not withhold support nor 'do anything to embarrass the government of my
country'. Nevertheless, there ought, he argued, to be reciprocal
sacrifices. If the opposition were debarred from taking 'any of
those measures of agitation, or more', which they had planned,
there was a corresponding obligation upon the government to
refrain from carrying 'in a controversial form the measures which
were in dispute between us'.[2]

[1] Memorandum (by Arthur Balfour), undated (7 August 1914), Bonar Law MSS,
34/3/16. See also Blanche E. C. Dugdale, *Arthur James Balfour: First Earl of Balfour,
K.G., O.M., F.R.S.*, etc., 1848–1930, 2 vols (London, 1939), vol. II, p. 90.
[2] Lloyd George to Chamberlain, 2 September 1914; Chamberlain to Lloyd George,
3 September 1914, Lloyd George MSS, C/13/14/3,4. Most of Lloyd George's

Unhappily, as several painful years had shown, there was no uncontroversial way of passing Home Rule. A cabinet committee decided on September 7 that the Bill should be placed on the Statute Book under the operation of the Parliament Act as soon as possible. At the same time, a short measure postponing the operation of the Home Rule Act for a definite period was also to be passed. The government's intentions were announced on September 15. Both the Home Rule and Welsh Church Bills were to be immediately enacted. A suspensory Bill would defer their operation for twelve months or until the end of the war, whichever was the longer; and during the suspensory period the government undertook to introduce an Amending Bill dealing with the area to be excluded from the Home Rule Act. Asquith told the Commons that, in view of the tremendous exhibition of patriotic spirit in Ulster, the employment of force to coerce the recalcitrant counties was 'an absolutely unthinkable thing.'

Asquith's temporary solution was the price of Nationalist loyalty. John Redmond accepted it gracefully. Had anything else been offered, he feared that he would have lost control of the Irish situation.[1] The Tories, after a violent speech from Bonar Law, left the House of Commons in a body. The Prime Minister described the scene in a private letter:

> This afternoon has been quite dramatic. I made a quiet, rather humdrum speech, pitched purposely in a low key, which was well listened to by the Tories as a whole. Then Bonar Law followed with his usual indictment of us, and me in particular, for lying and breaking faith, treachery, etc. He was so offensive that both Illingworth and McKenna, who were sitting by me, left the House, lest they should be unable to overcome their impulse to throw books, paperknives and other handy missiles at his head. He did not really make out much of a case, and watching his people carefully I do not think they were at all united or enthusiastic. At the end of his speech the whole Tory party walked out the House by way of washing their hands of responsibility for our

letter, and all of Chamberlain's, may be seen in Sir Charles Petrie, Bt, *The Life and Letters of The Rt. Hon. Sir Austen Chamberlain*, K.G., P.C., M.P., 2 vols (London, 1940), vol. II, pp. 3–5.
[1] Redmond to Illingworth, 27 August 1914, Illingworth MSS.

wicked ways. It was not really a very impressive spectacle, a lot of prosaic and for the most part middle-aged gentlemen trying to look like early French revolutionists in the Tennis Court. Still, it was unique in my, or anybody's, experience ...[1]

The government's actions earned not only ill-tempered outbursts on the floor of the House of Commons, but measured private protests. Lord Robert Cecil wrote at length to Edward Grey explaining one current of Unionist opinion:

As soon as war became inevitable we all hastened to assure the Govt. of our support in any measures that they might think necessary & contributed not a little to the extinction of all opposition on the Ministerial side of the House. We were told that our interests & position should not suffer & rather vague—studiously vague as I must now suppose— assurances were given to us that controversial politics would be avoided. We absolutely relied on those pledges. We not only supported the Govt.—we treated them with the utmost friendliness. Several of their Bills—such as the Housing Bill— not urgently necessary were passed without opposition though many of our party strongly objected to their provisions. Our Press was equally scrupulous. With scarcely one exception ordinary political topics were avoided by them though Radical contemporaries continually published arrogant & offensive articles on the Irish question. Our papers left it to them to fire under the protection of a flag of truce.

As time went on & no definite statement of Government policy was forthcoming, Unionists began to be uneasy. Several of us spoke to Mr Bonar Law who always replied that we were unnecessarily anxious, that he was in communication with Mr Asquith & he was certain that the Prime Minister meant to deal fairly with us. By this he was understood to mean that either the Bill would be hung up till next Session or that at the very least we should be given terms no less satisfactory than those of which we believed

[1] Asquith to Venetia Stanley, [15] September 1914, Montagu MSS. This note is dated September 14 by Asquith but clearly refers to the events of the following day.

ourselves to be certain last July. This elaborate play-acting—
for I can call it nothing else—went on until the Govt. had not
only secured every possible concession from the opposition
but had also used their assistance to beat down all resistance or even criticism from their own side. Having got all
they want they now turn round & reject everything in the
nature of a compromise.[1]

The accuracy of Cecil's version of the government's actions
could, of course, have been challenged. But that was not the
point. Verisimilitude was irrelevant. The important fact was that
a grievance was deeply felt, and powerfully expressed; and,
making due allowance for hyperbole, Cecil's dismay was sincere
and shared by a large number of Conservatives. As Cecil angrily
put it to a widely reported meeting of Unionist M.P.s at the
Carlton Club on September 14: 'They would have to treat the
Government as one would treat cardsharpers ... they no longer
regarded them as gentlemen and as no longer fit for the society
of gentlemen.'

What were to be the ground rules of war politics? In its strictest
sense the political truce was an agreement—originally signed
on 28 August 1914 by Percy Illingworth, Lord Edmund Talbot,
and Arthur Henderson—to do no more than avoid contested
elections for vacant seats. The agreement was understood to run
until 1 January 1915 or the end of the war, whichever was the
sooner. It was to be renewed 'by general consent'. At the second
renewal on 5 February 1915, a small but important alteration was
made: 'In the case of the resignation of a Member the three
signatories shall consult in confidence before the truce shall be
held to cover the same.'[2] Thus the parties registered their mutual
suspicions, forestalled tactical evasions of the spirit of the truce,
and tightened their grip on wayward followers. Wholesale resignations became impossible.

While the truce could be narrowly defined, its spirit implied

[1] Cecil to Grey, 11 September 1914 (copy), Cecil of Chelwood MSS, (Add. MS.
51073, ff. 70–4). For evidence of Cecil's own attempts to find a compromise over
Home Rule and Welsh disestablishment, see Lord Edmund Talbot to Bonar Law,
11 August 1914, and 14 August 1914 (enclosing Cecil to Talbot, 13 August 1914),
Bonar Law MSS, 34/3/31,42.

[2] The signed agreements are in the Asquith MSS, vol. 26, ff. 12–38.

the burial of old differences. As the officers of the National Liberal Federation wrote to their members in the first week of war: 'The immediate duty of all good citizens is to render such service as each can best perform in movements which know no Party distinction.' The relief of distress and the regulation of food supplies were among the original non-partisan tasks. But recruiting quickly became the dominant joint endeavour. On August 27, the chief whips of the 'great political parties', together with the Conservative Party Chairman, Arthur Steel-Maitland, and General Sir Henry Rawlinson of the War Office met to discuss how 'the grave issues of the War should be fully comprehended by the people, and thereby to give a powerful impetus to recruiting'.[1] Four days later at a larger meeting of whips and military and party officials, it was resolved to form a Parliamentary Recruiting Committee. Asquith, Bonar Law, and Arthur Henderson became joint presidents, and plans were made for the co-ordination of canvassing and propaganda throughout the country.

Asquith secured from his opponents practical co-operation and a tolerable interment of disputed issues; but he seemed to make little effort to seek a warmer understanding with his former adversaries. Many Conservatives were convinced that their gestures of good will were not being reciprocated by the Liberals. And soon it was apparent to the government that the opposition's self-restraint could not be treated as a permanent condition. Speaking immediately after Bonar Law's melodramatic departure from the House on September 15, John Redmond noted ironically that 'having told the world that the Government of this Empire is made up of men devoid of honour, devoid of truth, devoid of decency, [Bonar Law] wound up his speech by saying that his one desire in life was to support the Government in this crisis'. There could hardly have been a nobler resolve for an opposition spokesman to utter, nor one so onerous to execute, when the personality no less than the policies of the Prime Minister were so unpalatable to his opponents.

Inside the Conservative Party, Walter Long was one of the first front-bench personalities to articulate dissatisfaction. Long

[1] Minutes of the Parliamentary Recruiting Committee, 27 and 31 August 1914. Add. MS. 54192.

summarized the balance of advantage from the truce in January 1915:

> The Opposition has given up contesting by-elections and propaganda work in the country. The Government pursues its course of domestic legislation, retarded and truncated it is true, but nevertheless by no means entirely suspended. It expects from the Opposition entire acquiescence in its war policy, resents criticism of its actions in connection with the war, hints indeed at a joint responsibility when mistakes are pointed out, but takes great care that all praise for successes shall be showered exclusively upon itself.[1]

Long, of course, exaggerated the extent to which the truce actually operated in the Liberals' favour. But the Liberals themselves had no illusions about how fragile the Tory self-denying ordinance was. 'The political truce is very thin,' wrote Walter Runciman, 'and has never included McKenna who is attacked by every Tory newspaper and many Tory members of both Houses... If things go wrong we shall be flayed.'[2]

[1] Memorandum by Long, 27 January 1915, Balfour MSS (Add. MS. 49693, ff. 192–3).
[2] Runciman to Chalmers, 7 February 1915, Runciman MSS.

4 Anxieties

The outcry against McKenna was a striking indication of the public mood. As Home Secretary it was his responsibility, acting in accordance with the recommendations of the naval and military authorities, to supervise internal security operations — rounding up spies, and taking precautionary measures against hostile acts by resident enemy aliens. These duties McKenna executed with his usual competence. But, because of insufficient attention to publicity, he failed to dispel the widespread fear that spies and enemy agents were roaming round town and country in dangerous numbers. No official statement on enemy espionage was issued until 8 October 1914. Six days earlier, Lord Charles Beresford, in a speech at Aberdeen, had blamed the loss of three cruisers on the activities of a German spy ring. This charge and other loose talk was rebutted by McKenna in the House of Commons of November 12. But, in a short debate that day, several speakers referred to what Sir Henry Dalziel called 'solid ground for anxiety'. And Lord Haldane provoked choleric splutterings from the Tory benches in the House of Lords by appearing to display more concern for the welfare of innocent aliens than for the maintenance of British security.

Anxieties persisted. 'The public is being worked up to a state of frenzy,' McKenna told Kitchener on October 16.[1] Even Maurice Hankey, the normally level-headed secretary to the Committee of Imperial Defence, succumbed briefly to the prevalent alarmism. At the beginning of December 1914, Hankey addressed a memorandum to the Prime Minister surveying the problem. Aliens had been dealt with in a report of 17 October 1914 which was circulated to the cabinet as a matter of urgency, it being considered at that time too pressing to await the next

[1] McKenna to Kitchener, 16 October 1914, Kitchener MSS, PRO 30/57/75.

meeting of the C.I.D. 'I have never been able to discover', Hankey wrote, 'whether the Cabinet actually discussed the Report.' In fact, on October 22, the Home Office ordered the arrest of all unnaturalized male Germans, Austrians, and Hungarians aged between seventeen and forty-five. However, Hankey noted that the policy of interning enemy aliens of military age was dropped 'apparently because the accommodation was not available'.[1]

By the end of November it was officially estimated that there were 25,000 Germans and Austrians of military age at large in London. Only 3,000 police were on duty by day and 6,000 at night. There were also some special constables who, with the police, guarded most of the vulnerable points in the metropolis. The military had been partially withdrawn from these duties. The aliens were unarmed and their houses had been searched; but they could still inflict great damage if determined to do so and organized.[2]

Hankey sent a copy of his memorandum to Arthur Balfour, who, at Asquith's invitation, was participating in the discussion of high policy. Balfour professed to being in complete agreement that action was necessary. 'I suppose', he wrote, 'the real difficulty is finding accommodation for 25,000 persons. But this ought not to stand in our way.'[3] In his customary unruffled manner, Balfour gave no indication that anything more than the minimal amount of intellectual effort would be needed to sort out the difficulty. Hankey, however, whose flexible brain was engaged in that exercise, could not find an easy solution. The thousands of men enrolled in Kitchener's new armies had absorbed all the available accommodation. And, more fundamentally, the Prime Minister could not be persuaded that anything needed to be done. 'I saw the Prime Minister about my Memorandum,' Hankey unhappily reported to Balfour, 'and he heard me at full length and read the Memorandum. At the end of our interview his only re-

---

[1] Hankey, Secret Memorandum to Asquith, 4 December 1914 (typescript copy), Balfour MSS (Add. MS. 49703, ff. 110–12). Hankey makes no mention of his anxieties when discussing aliens in *The Supreme Command*, vol. 1, p. 220. Kitchener told Asquith and Pease that the War Office had originally stopped interning aliens without his knowledge and against McKenna's wishes. (Pease's Diary, 20 October 1914, Gainford MSS.)

[2] Hankey's Secret Memorandum, 4 December 1914, loc. cit.

[3] Balfour to Hankey, 5 December 1914 (copy), Balfour MSS (Add. MS. 49703, f. 113).

mark was that he was entirely unconvinced! I feel that I have made my protest, and can do no more.'[1]

Asquith's scepticism and McKenna's apparent complacency did not satisfy the scaremongers. Lord Northcliffe, who considered himself anything but an unduly suspicious or 'scarey' person, was convinced, for example, that spies were active in government offices. 'It is beyond question that, for some reason, the Government are protecting spies—and spies in high places.' Who were these sheltered infiltrators? On the vital details, Northcliffe was vague. 'There are persons who speak of recent contributions to the Liberal exchequer, but I do not like to think of anything of the sort,' he wrote mysteriously.[2]

Liberal ministers could not deal with the problem of enemy aliens as a straightforward matter of security. For there was pressure of a different kind from that generated by Northcliffe being brought to bear upon the government. An exchange of letters between L. T. Hobhouse, Professor of Sociology at London University and one of the most influential Liberal writers of the preceding twenty years, and the Attorney-General, John Simon, illustrates the tenderness of Liberal consciences. Hobhouse wrote on October 22:

> I wish to put it to you whether nothing can be done by the Government to stop the outbreak against Germans in this country. It is not for me to criticise any action of the Government in interning men of military age. But the Press agitation is going far beyond this & is producing a very dangerous state of mind. Apart from the humanitarian aspect of the question, it is clear that any outbreak, any unjust or unreasonable action whether by the police or by the mob, will do us untold harm in neutral countries wh. hitherto have respected our calmness, & will also lead to retaliation on English people in Germany. My belief is that it is entirely a newspaper agitation wh. is however gradually catching on with the ordinary man. There is nothing that can now stop it but a strong warning from a trusted member of the government of the evil consequences wh. may ensue.

[1] Hankey to Balfour, 8 December 1914, Balfour MSS (Add. MS. 49703, f. 116).
[2] Northcliffe to Bonar Law, 6 November 1914 (copy), Northcliffe MSS.

K

As a former leader writer for *The Manchester Guardian* and *Tribune*, Hobhouse knew something of the mechanics of press agitation. And Simon accepted his argument that anti-German feeling was not entirely spontaneous. But there were 'other considerations to be borne in mind', as Simon explained:

(1) The position now, with German troops at Ostend, and only a narrow piece of sea between them and this country, is strategically quite different from the position at the beginning of the War, when there was the whole of Holland and Belgium between the two forces. *If* any attempt was made at raid or invasion, the distance to be traversed is trifling, and the thing would come very quickly.

(2) Experience has shown that the German Navy is extraordinarily well informed of our movements, and though I have the greatest detestation of spy mania, I do not think it is open to doubt that there are a number of unidentified persons in this country, who have been making treacherous communications, and who were not known to us at the beginning of the war.

(3) The stricter measures now taken do not portend the keeping of all German and Austrian subjects under lock and key, but are a necessary preliminary to weeding out and restoring to ordinary activities those who are altogether above suspicion...

(4) Your remark about retaliation is not unfair, but it is to be remembered that Germany has taken this step at the beginning of the War, and is maintaining it with the greatest rigour. I may add that nothing is being done here save interning men of military age.

...just as there is the greatest danger in one section of the population being led to extravagance by a press agitation, so, I venture to think that there is a danger of another section thinking what is being done is a mere piece of gross tyranny and stupid surrender to panic.[1]

Whether or not there was much substance to Northcliffe's fears, or to the many similar views expressed in public by worried

[1] L. T. Hobhouse to Simon, 22 October 1914; Simon to Hobhouse, 26 October 1914 (copy), Simon MSS.

M.P.s, is doubtful. Simon believed that 'all available influence ought to be thrown on the side of reasonableness'. The reasonable side did not go unheard. There is no doubt, however, that the challenges to McKenna's policy contributed to the undermining of confidence in the ministry. As Lloyd George was to recall:

> His policy towards residents of enemy extraction in this country was thought to be too protective, too indifferent to the dangers which might arise from espionage ... Mr McKenna's rigid and fretful answers, though always technically complete, were provocative.[1]

McKenna was not alone in restricting the scope and number of his parliamentary statements and press announcements. A government which had, in years past, been so 'leaky' as to provoke censure from the Prime Minister, became overnight a citadel of reticence. Few ministers realized how delicate a growth was public confidence in war-time, or what constant nurture was needed to ensure the support of the great organs of opinion. Asquith was shrewd enough to notice, after a month of war, that the newspapers were complaining of a 'starvation diet'. 'For all that the public know', he told the ex-war correspondent, who now presided over the Board of Admiralty, 'they might as well be living in the days of the prophet Isaiah, whose idea of a battle was "confused noise & garments rolled in blood".'[2] But, apart from consenting to eat a hearty meal with American journalists, and to answer a few of their questions 'off-the-record', the Prime Minister gave little encouragement to those of his colleagues and advisers who tried not only to muffle the indiscretions of the press but to enlist its power in the national interest.[3] Only at the beginning of April 1915 did Asquith make any attempt to put the relationship between the press and the government on a practical working foundation. After a Downing Street conference between the Newspaper Proprietors' Association and senior ministers, Sir George Riddell undertook to act as the representative

[1] Lloyd George, *War Memoirs*, vol. I, pp. 220–1.
[2] Asquith to Churchill, 5 September 1914, Churchill MSS. Asquith's text was Isaiah 9:5.
[3] Asquith's meeting with the American journalists was suggested and arranged by J. St Loe Strachey, the editor of *The Spectator*. (Strachey to Asquith, 8 September 1914 [copy], and subsequent correspondence in the Strachey MSS).

of the press in dealings with the First Lord of the Admiralty and the Secretary of State for War. During the first week of May 1915, six accredited press correspondents took up residence at G.H.Q. in France. They were never officially recognized by Kitchener but they remained in France until the end of the war.[1]

Although improvement came eventually, the official attitude towards the release of details about British military operations in the opening phase of the war was so restrictive and obsessively secretive that irreparable harm was done to the relations between government, newspapers, and the high command. As late as November 10, John Simon was querying the value of 'the War Office view that military science requires a permanent state of mystification'.[2] It had been the intention of the General Staff to allow a contingent of accredited correspondents to accompany the Expeditionary Force to France. Press representatives were present at army manœuvres for several years before 1914. But when war broke out the standing policy was reversed. The policy of the French military authorities was adopted. Permission for journalists to go to the front was refused. Not until September 14 was an official 'Eye-Witness' detailed to supply reports to the newspapers. Meanwhile, there began a period of tension between journalists and the military and political authorities. Enterprising newspapermen filed copy from forbidden zones. A hastily improvised Press Bureau in London had to cope with the examination of material which might better have been handled at G.H.Q. in France. Under the Defence of the Realm Act, the publication of many categories of information potentially helpful to the enemy was prohibited. Severe penalties and trial by court-martial were authorized.

Apart from the compulsory censorship of all messages transmitted by cable, no other form of compulsory vetting was prescribed. The Press Bureau was charged with the duties of issuing official statements, censoring telegrams, and giving advice to all journalists who voluntarily sought clearance of proposed articles.[3]

[1] *Lord Riddell's War Diary*, ch. III.

[2] Simon to the Archbishop of York, 10 November 1914 (copy), Simon MSS.

[3] Major-General Sir C. E. Callwell, *Experiences of a Dug-Out, 1914–1918* (London, 1920). Chapter XVII deals with the press and the War Office in 1914–15. On the powers and working of the Press Bureau, see Sir Edward Cook, *The Press in War-Time: With Some Account of the Official Press Bureau* (London, 1920).

The officials of the Press Bureau were 'left to work out its scope and methods as experience might suggest'.[1] Soon they became responsible not only for the issue of statements from naval and military authorities but for all information emanating from government departments which was relevant to the war.

In the meantime, for month after month, the press was denied the privilege of gathering war news at its source. Starved of that steady stream of information without which it was impossible to place particular items in perspective, editors generally opted for a hopeful tone. For the first few weeks there was no hint of impending disaster. When the first-hand accounts of the retreat from Mons appeared in *The Times*, melodramatically sub-edited in an after-dinner haze by F. E. Smith, the first director of the Press Bureau, politicians and public alike reacted with anger and incredulity to the account of defeat.[2] When genuine successes followed the rarely reported setbacks, it was equally impossible for even professional observers to form a coherent picture of the trend of events.

There was no lack of newspapermen to tell political friends of the folly of excessive secrecy. Among them, conspicuous for his dedication to the national cause in general as much as for his victimization of certain particular individuals, was Lord Northcliffe, proprietor of both *The Times* and the *Daily Mail*. Unable to obtain a satisfactory hearing from anyone in authority, Northcliffe explained to Bonar Law that the question of war correspondents was something of far greater significance than the satisfaction of journalistic curiosity. Not only was it important to convey to the British at home some impression of the scale of the conflict in which they were involved; it was also regrettably necessary to dispel any appearance of discrimination against newspapermen on the basis of their peace-time political allegiance. F. E. Smith defended himself in September 1914 against the

---

[1] Sir Edward Cook, op. cit., p. 42.

[2] The dispatches giving details of the defeat and retirement of British troops were written by Arthur Moore and Hamilton Fyfe. Fyfe's autobiographical version of the episode may be found in *My Seven Selves* (London, 1935), pp. 180–2. See also Sir Edward Cook's Diary, 2 September 1914, Cook MSS; *The History of The Times;* vol. IV, The 150th Anniversary and Beyond, 1912–1948: part I, 1912–1920 (London, 1952), pp. 222–7; Tom Clarke, *My Northcliffe Diary* (London, 1931), p. 68; Reginald Pound and Geoffrey Harmsworth, *Northcliffe* (London, 1959), p. 469.

allegation that the Press Bureau's staff was 'unduly Tory'. He told Lloyd George: 'You know me well enough to know whether I care in work like this whether men are (or were) Tories or Radicals.'[1] But as Northcliffe made clear to Bonar Law, the embers of Home Rule were ready to flare at the slightest puff of controversy:

I am not at all interested in the question of 'war correspondents', but I do think it important for the nation, for the soldiers at the front and the recruits at home, as well as to ensure a proper realization of our efforts by the French and Russians (both of whom are dissatisfied) that some account should be published of the things that happened weeks ago. The Battle of Ypres was the greatest battle in which the British Army has been engaged throughout the whole of its history. The campaign in its entirety is of a magnitude and bearing not understood by the nation at large, and the result is that the people have not put forth the effort of which they are capable.

Could you possibly put the question to Sir John French — 'Is it by your wish, or is it not, that the deeds of the British Army have been obscured?' Is it not possible for Sir John French to invite skilled writers, as is done by the French Army? ... the French are in the habit of inviting correspondents; and if the French, why not the British? The grumbling that one hears in London as to the command in France is beyond question considerably due to the mysterious silence regarding past events — events well known to the Germans and therefore not dangerous to publish.

As to the treatment of newspapers by the British Army during this war; I do not think that the many distinguished writers who have been treated like criminals by Sir John French's orders will readily forget the matter, more especially as in certain instances the treatment has been meted out with particular severity to newspapers that took prominent part in the anti-Home Rule agitation. Sir John French's right-hand man in this connexion is the well-known General Macready. I do not think I need say more.[2]

[1] Smith to Lloyd George, 9 September 1914, Lloyd George MSS, C/3/7/5.
[2] Northcliffe to Bonar Law, 4 February 1915 (copy), Northcliffe MSS. General

Northcliffe's strictures on the policy of secrecy were typical of journalistic opinion. The editor of *The Spectator* was almost alone among newspapermen in expressing the opposite view:

I cannot flog myself up into any great excitement over the matter—whether I know about gallant deeds a couple of months after they have happened instead of knowing them red hot. I want to win, not to talk about winnings or losings, and hot news is as dust in the balance compared with the slightest conceivable grain of actual gain.[1]

St Loe Strachey's belief was that 'in times like this it is the duty of journalists to obey, not to argue'.[2] What neither Strachey nor Asquith grasped was that obedience was less likely to come from an angry press than from men treated as responsible professionals and patriots.

Macready was appointed G.O.C. Belfast District early in 1914 and was thus implicated in the alleged plot to coerce Ulster.

[1] Strachey to Masterman, 8 October 1914 (copy), Strachey MSS.

[2] Strachey to Sir Stanley Buckmaster, 3 November 1914 (copy), Strachey MSS.

5 Symbols of Unity

To lay the blame for mismanaging press relations at the feet of Sir John French and General Macready was to miss the root cause of the trouble. Responsibility lay as much with politicians as with generals. And one member of the cabinet, above all, could by a word have put matters right. But it was this one man, the Secretary of State for War, Lord Kitchener, who was personally responsible for the restrictions on the press. Kitchener, whose very name had been made legend by the newspapers he now frustrated, was at once the almost unfettered dictator of military affairs and the heroic leader at whose bidding men enrolled daily by the thousand to serve their sovereign and nation.

Kitchener's appointment to the War Office, although widely acclaimed at the time, was perhaps the most ominous event of the early weeks of the war. The Prime Minister had been acting as Secretary of State for War since March 1914 when Jack Seely had to surrender his seals for mishandling the Curragh incident. In war conditions, it seemed obvious that the War Office demanded the undivided energies of a strong man. And the instincts of Asquith and Haldane (who returned for a few days to his old department during the July/August crisis) coincided with the clamour which was speedily launched in the Northcliffe press and supported by J. A. Spender of *The Westminster Gazette*.[1] Kitchener, it was said, should be installed in the vacant place. He would symbolize, as a soldier not a party man, the nation's unity in time of danger; he would promise, by his very presence, the prospect of resounding victories.

There was a flaw in this reasoning. It was logical to find some employment for the kingdom's best-known serving officer. But why the War Office? Of course, Kitchener was not merely 'an

[1] Wilson Harris, *J. A. Spender* (London, 1946), p. 160.

ageing ignorant man armed only with a giant's reputation', as one exuberant American scholar has described him.[1] He was, after all, a Field-Marshal, the effective ruler of Egypt, the former Commander-in-Chief in India, and at sixty-four, no older than several of Asquith's senior colleagues. He could bring to the government something which no Liberal politician possessed—a mystique that transcended reservations about ability or age and, after enveloping his own reputation, left something to spare for less glamorous colleagues. Nevertheless, it is true that in the excitement of welcoming the new recruit, no one paused to question whether he could actually do the job. Walter Runciman, for example, hailed Kitchener's appointment as a master-stroke: ' ... amongst other advantages which he [Asquith] no doubt foresaw — the old wizard—was the political convenience of having the unattackable K. at the War Office and at his board.'[2]

After seven weeks of war, the Secretary of State's authority was so firmly established that Arthur Balfour observed: 'I doubt whether he [Asquith] possesses any influence with either K. or Churchill in military matters, or whether, if he does possess such influence, he would care to exert it ... '[3] Kitchener had stepped at once to the Prime Minister's right hand. He was given immense power over military affairs. Asquith did indeed have confidence in his ability. For a few months his colleagues, awed by the legend incarnate in their midst, habitually deferred to Kitchener's judgment. Stories of the new minister's impact on his subordinates reverberated around Whitehall and Westminster. The first army council over which he presided was 'Hell with the lid off', reported Sir Charles Harris, Financial Director at the War Office.[4] General Callwell, who stepped into Henry Wilson's shoes as Director of Military Operations two days before Kitchener arrived at the War Office, saw his new chief as a 'giant amongst the pigmies'.[5] Absent for years from Britain, Kitchener had no sympathy or patience with the domestic dissensions which distracted other members of the government from the business of

[1] Paul Guinn, *British Strategy and Politics, 1914 to 1918* (Oxford, 1965), p. 32.
[2] Runciman to Chalmers, 7 February 1915, Runciman MSS.
[3] Balfour to Bonar Law, 26 September 1914 (copy), Balfour MSS (Add. MS. 49693, f. 185).
[4] Eleanor Acland's War Diary, 6 August 1914, Acland MSS.
[5] Callwell, op. cit., p. 54.

war. 'I am rather worried about this Irish question,' he told Churchill on August 22. As though the Nationalists and Unionists were rival tribes of squabbling dervishes, he went on: '*We ought to force a settlement or proclaim a truce*. In these times it seems to me wicked to carry on with people so divided as they are on the subject.'[1]

A sway so imperious could not last unchallenged. In his office first, and then in cabinet, the imposing façade began to crack. 'Cramped by defective knowledge of the army system',[2] Kitchener failed to make good use of the Special Reserve and Territorial Forces at his disposal. He allowed the War Office general staff to disperse to the front, leaving ill-qualified deputies to learn vital tasks, untutored and in haste. He consulted few of his own staff, and was as Lord Hankey has written, 'extremely reticent in matters of moment', in dealing with his political colleagues. The art of delegation to subordinates was as alien to his manner of working as the practice of free discussion among equals to which his fellow ministers were accustomed. Gradually, the suspicion spread, reinforced by his incorrigible myopia over the supply of munitions, that Kitchener's taciturnity concealed not unassuming mastery but frighteningly limited competence.

To one man in Britain, the discovery that Kitchener's defects outweighed his virtues was hardly a revelation. Lord Curzon, who had as Viceroy fought and lost to Kitchener in India ten years earlier, knew from experience how awkward, irascible, and inscrutable 'K' could be. After one particularly distressing House of Lords' debate early in 1915, Curzon wrote to Lord Lansdowne:

K. told us *absolutely nothing*. He simply plays with us & the public, delivers a few generalities about the war which any schoolboy who has read the morning papers could compile in 10 minutes. As to what the Govt. are after about recruiting who can tell? K. literally discourages it by his frosty remarks. Other members of the Govt go about pleading for men! Where does the truth lie? I suppose it is all a matter of equipment, arms & ammunition.

My belief is that these 6 armies are largely a piece of stage

---

[1] Kitchener to Churchill, 22 August 1914, Churchill MSS, Kitchener's emphasis.
[2] Callwell, op. cit., p. 48.

bluff. French as you may have heard—(very confidential) will have none of them, does not want the armies or the Generals, wants to make new armies out of his old ones, and objects to all these schemes being launched over his head. Things are so acute between him and K. that I believe Asquith is to go over to France to see French & try to put matters straight.

I sit & smile as all these tales are poured into my ear. I know my K., and it tickles me to hear St John [Brodrick, Lord Midleton, Secretary of State for India under Balfour, at the time of the Kitchener/Curzon dispute] telling me the very things in the very words about that great warrior which I was flouted & overruled by a certain Govt for persisting in telling them some years ago.

'Will have everything in his own hands,' 'Listens to no one,' 'Knows no scruples,' 'Will tell any lie,' 'Threatens to resign unless he may have his own way,'—these are the things I now hear 20 times a day from the very lips to whom he was the Law & the Prophets.[1]

Yet even among Kitchener's detractors there were those who had to admit to his striking qualities. Margot Asquith who had long distrusted him was moved to record in November 1914:

K's whole soul and mind is in the war. *Everything is subordinate to it*. His loathing of war is a factor in human life; his perfect appreciation of the horrors of it, his ungrudging gift of all his time and his powers to finishing this war all raise him in one's estimation.[2]

It was Margot's seventeen-year-old daughter Elizabeth who summed up the simple fact which, for all his failings, made Kitchener secure at the War Office. He was, if not a great man, at least a great poster. In the public mind he remained unassailable. His transfixing gaze was an indispensable recruiting asset, his abundant prestige the best protection available to the government against an irritable Parliament and press.

Even Kitchener's influence could not save the government

[1] Curzon to Lansdowne, 6 January 1915, Lansdowne MSS.
[2] Margot Asquith's Diary, (?19 November) 1914, Oxford and Asquith MSS.

from every blunder and controversy. Nor could the Whips, by any appeal or inducement in their gift, have stifled the genuine impulses of inquiry and protest which stirred among their flock.

The House of Commons could be muzzled but not silenced by the party truce. The Treasury Bench, especially when some eager M.P. ferreted with awkward questions for unpalatable revelations, began to be a trial to busy ministers. 'Parliament is assembled once more,' wrote a jaded President of the Board of Trade in February 1915, 'a nuisance in time of war.'[1] But, if all probing and criticism could be not quashed, those who might have been expected to give a lead in opposition could sometimes be diverted into other occupations. Participation without power was freely dispensed to those susceptible to official invitation. Ramsay Mac-Donald, John Burns, and Walter Long, for example, found themselves employed as members of the Government Committee on the Prevention and Relief of Distress. After seven weeks and 'a frightful amount of drudgery work' all three were eager to be free. As MacDonald told Charles Trevelyan: 'Long feels that we are being made fools of by the Cabinet and I believe will go at the first opportunity.'[2]

MacDonald did not let his duties prevent collaboration with the U.D.C. He appreciated how dangerous it would be to neglect propaganda: ' ... if public opinion is left to be controlled by the influences that now alone play upon it, it will be impossible for us to do anything with it before long.'[3] Seeing his own position clearly, he was soon disgusted with his fellow Labour M.P.s who ignored obvious chances to exploit the truce. 'If the Labour Members had not been mostly fools they would have conducted their recruiting campaigns as an anti-conscription propaganda.' Pained by abuse and falsification of his views, MacDonald felt especially sourly about Lloyd George. There had been a moment when it seemed as though they might be colleagues in office or

[1] Runciman to Chalmers, 7 February 1915, Runciman MSS.

[2] MacDonald to Trevelyan, 24 September 1914, Trevelyan MSS. Burns may not have been as anxious for freedom as Long and MacDonald. 'He hangs about the L.G.B. on his committee work, a political shadow.' (Lord Gladstone to Lord Buxton, n.d. *c.* November 1914, Buxton MSS.) Buxton, who had been President of the Board of Trade, 1910–14, succeeded Gladstone as Governor-General of South Africa in February 1914.

[3] MacDonald to Trevelyan, 10 September 1914, Trevelyan MSS.

opposition. Now, as their paths diverged, perspectives altered too. 'The little Welshman is slim,' MacDonald warned Charles Trevelyan. 'The government may find that before the war is over.'[1]

Several prominent Conservatives were invited to participate in government deliberations or to hold semi-official executive posts. Austen Chamberlain and Earl St Aldwyn came to Lloyd George's aid at the Treasury. 'Austen was at all our meetings and played an honourable part. St Aldwyn was useful mainly with the joint stock bankers,' Walter Runciman told Sir Robert Chalmers on 7 February 1915.[2] Balfour reactivated his membership of the Committee of Imperial Defence, and was also invited to meetings of the war council that was established in November 1914 as 'a supplement to the Cabinet for exploring some of the larger questions of policy'.[3]

However valuable all these Conservative brains were to the government, there was no gainsaying the advantage of disarming potential critics and dividing them from their friends. The tasks of opposition were not lightened by the presence of leading Conservatives deep in the counsels of the Prime Minister and his colleagues. Moreover, for the majority of Conservatives, there were no more avenues for criticism than there were opportunities for useful service. After being out of office for eight years, their frustrations were daily nourished by the futility of patriotic politics. It seems hardly likely that Asquith could have been oblivious of Conservative feelings. His failure to address himself seriously to stabilizing the framework of political life, suggests that he was hoping, in defiance of the gloomy but authoritative predictions he had heard, for a quick victory.

The boys were not home by Christmas. And, as the chill realities of winter and the trenches filtered home, Conservative forbearance was severely strained. Bonar Law was urged by Curzon and Walter Long either to demand more private consultation or to renew parliamentary opposition. The idea of

---

[1] Ibid.; the preceding quotation is also from this letter.

[2] For St Aldwyn's role in framing the Budget of November 1914 and as an intermediary between Lloyd George and Chamberlain, see St Aldwyn to Chamberlain, 28 October 1914, Austen Chamberlain MSS, 13/4/43. For Chamberlain's understanding with Lloyd George, see Chamberlain to Lloyd George, 18 November 1914 (copy), Austen Chamberlain MSS, 13/4/31.

[3] Hankey, op. cit., vol. 1, p. 239.

coalition was a third alternative, never far from the surface. Churchill had written guardedly to Lord Robert Cecil in September that:

> No one can tell from week to week what the course of the war will be, or what political combinations may be necessary to secure its effective conclusion. No one can foresee the shape in which the political parties will emerge from the struggle.[1]

By January, Lord Hugh Cecil was convinced that his old intimate, Churchill, was not alone among ministers in being prepared, 'if circumstances made such a course feasible', to participate in 'some kind of coalition'.[2] Lord Hugh believed that Grey, Asquith, and Haldane had been glad to have opportunities of working with the opposition leaders. It could not be expected that Churchill would make an easy colleague; and 'Asquith has behaved so mendaciously that it is very repugnant to my feelings to contemplate any co-operation with him.' Nevertheless, as Cecil argued in a confidential memorandum to his brother, Lord Robert, there was much to be said for co-operation between moderate men on both sides. Such an alliance might not be created until the war was over. But, if it did come, it would have two desirable results. Unionist leaders like Bonar Law and Austen Chamberlain would be severed from the reactionary Tories of *The Morning Post* and *National Review* stamp; and an effectual party would exist to counter the industrial unrest which could be predicted for the post-war period.

In Lord Hugh's analysis, the significant omission from the list of 'dissentient moderate Liberals' with whom co-operation would be welcome was Lloyd George. The omission was deliberate; for in Cecil's eyes Lloyd George was the enemy of the future:

> ... he will be a leader very well qualified for the task of stirring up a dangerous spirit of class bitterness ... we ought to remem-

---

[1] Churchill to Cecil, 8 September 1914, Cecil of Chelwood MSS (Add. MS. 51073, f. 101).

[2] Lord Hugh Cecil to Lord Robert Cecil (private memorandum), 10 January 1915, Cecil of Chelwood MSS (Add. MS. 51157, ff. 34-43).

ber that to create an effective split in the Liberal Party is the
only real hope of saving ourselves from Lloyd George.

It would be easy with hindsight to scoff at this misreading of the
course of Lloyd George's career. But there were good grounds
until mid-1915 for suspecting that if he were to come adrift from
Liberalism Lloyd George would find a new home in the ranks of
Labour. There were few grounds for imagining that if he were
to be thrust from the Liberal Party he would be accepted as the
head of a predominantly Conservative peace-time government.

Cecil's strategy to prepare for a post-war coalition was simple.
Conservatives should take advantage of 'the rather sloppy sentiment (which I hate) about "no party feeling"', and begin to
build a golden bridge over which willing Liberals could cross. For
entirely different reasons Bonar Law resolved on a course whose
practical effect was the same. The Conservative leaders in both
Houses drew a sharp distinction between co-operation with the
government and the acceptance of partial responsibility for
government policy. In the House of Lords, Lord Lansdowne took
pains to repudiate the suggestion that there was a 'partnership'
between government and opposition and to disclaim having had
preliminary knowledge of major war measures.[1] Lansdowne trod
deliberately to the boundaries of the truth. For, while it would
have been false to suggest that the opposition had been consulted formally or induced to participate in the making of war
policy, individual members of the government had made considerable efforts to acquaint the leading Unionists with the progress of events. Lansdowne and Bonar Law received constantly,
from the War Office and Foreign Office, copies (paraphrased so
as to conceal the cypher) of incoming and outgoing telegrams,
almost as if they were members of the government. These telegrams were read out regularly at meetings of the shadow cabinet.
Lord Crewe conveyed confidential information to Lord Curzon
about British reverses in East Africa when Curzon was acting,
in Lansdowne's absence, as Conservative leader in the House of
Lords. And Arthur Balfour, from his vantage point on the war
council, was able to communicate to Lansdowne or Bonar Law
much of the fact and opinion upon which government policy was

[1] 18 H.L. Deb., 5s, col. 415, 2 February 1915.

based. Balfour's position was, in some respects, an awkward one, as he explained to Lansdowne in a long letter from Whittinge-hame, his Scottish home:

Jan 9th, 1915

Dictated
Private
My dear Clan,

I have just come back from a meeting of a Defence Sub-Committee of the kind I spoke to you about when I was at Bowood. It is, I suppose, the fourth; and there will probably be one next week, at which (though this is, of course, *strictly confidential*) Sir John French has been asked to be present.

I won't put down on paper anything about our pro-ceedings—partly because I could not do justice to them, partly because some of them at least are of a kind about which the less written, or even said, the better. The reason I write to you is that I have occasional qualms of uneasiness about my own position. I slid into this by insensible degrees: indeed, this particular sub-committee is itself almost an accidental growth. But, accidental or not, it *has* grown during these meetings in importance, and the process might conceivably continue. Already, some of its members occasionally de-scribe it among themselves as a 'Council of War'. The members besides myself are the Prime Minister, Kitchener, Grey, Churchill, Lloyd George, Crewe, & Haldane among Cabinet Ministers—Lord Fisher, General Wolfe Murray of the War Office, and Hankey. I am rather a curious addition to this collection, and the question arises, 'ought I, or ought I not, to say to Asquith that my presence on it puts me in a position so delicate and difficult that I am reluctant to con-tinue my services.'

Hankey, of the Defence Committee, with whom I have worked a good deal on very intimate terms, is almost passionately anxious that I should remain; and, so far, I do not think anything has occurred which could possibly put me in a difficulty. If one can imagine a debate arising upon questions of naval or military policy, I might—and almost certainly should—have to keep silence. But this seems a small matter. On the other hand, it is very easily conceivable that I might in Council give an opinion in favour of some course of action which, in the event, would lead to a disaster more or less serious. Such chances are inevitable. Would that seriously embarrass my friends? It is hard to say beforehand.

It must, of course, be remembered that the Defence Committee, (still less Committees of the Defence Committee) has no Executive power whatever. Its opinions do not relieve either the Government as a whole, or individual members of the Government like the Secretaries [sic] of State for War or the First Lord of the Admiralty, of an atom of their responsibility. Still, you have only got to look at the names I have mentioned to see that if the sub-committee is agreed, it is very unlikely that the Cabinet would think of disagreeing.

My personal ease and comfort would, of course, be much consulted by declining any further share in the work. I hate long journeys, and I am always having to take them. At the same time, if I can be of any use, I do not see how I can refuse my services. I am too old to fight, and this is all I can do for the general cause. I do not like to shelter myself behind objections which seem rather parliamentary than national. If any thoughts occur to you, do let me know.

Yours ever,

ARTHUR JAMES BALFOUR[1]

Balfour remained on the war council. But his unique situation was no consolation to Curzon and Long who were all the more conscious of being outside the privileged circle. 'As you know,' Curzon had told Lansdowne with obvious pique, 'I see no telegrams & only pick up things by chance.'[2] Curzon could have been worse off. There was much to be learned by chance as well as through the proper channels. Sir John French spoke freely to visiting Unionist politicians at the front. Henry Wilson purveyed a steady flow of details and interpretation to anyone willing to listen; and made a special effort to keep Bonar Law

[1] Balfour to Lansdowne, 9 January 1915, Lansdowne MSS.
[2] Curzon to Lansdowne, 20 December 1914, Lansdowne MSS.

abreast of military affairs. There was also a frequent traffic of soldier–politicians crossing the Channel on official and private missions of liaison, not to mention the professional intermediaries, like Lord Esher, and the talkative civil servants like Sir Francis Hopwood of the Admiralty, who displayed a remarkable disposition to retail unauthenticated gossip when their stocks of hard fact were exhausted. To the restless Curzon, Bonar Law made it clear that:

> ... much as I dislike the present position, there are only two alternatives open to us. One is to go on as we are doing without responsibility and with only a very limited amount of criticism ... or to face a coalition. The latter proposal I should certainly be against.[1]

Not all observers realized how much the Tories resented their impotence. Edward Grey, for example, wrote years later:

> In the very early days of the war, before any disaster had occurred, someone remarked to me that it was very patriotic of the Conservative Party to support the Liberal Government, when the war might be a triumph that would give the Liberal Government an assured lease of power for many years. It was amazing to me that anyone should be capable of such a reflection or of thinking at such a time in terms of party politics at all.[2]

Few leading Liberals could have been so insulated from political reality as Grey, whose vision of the domestic scene by 1914 seemed rarely to encompass anything beyond the banks of the Test and the Itchen. Nevertheless, Grey's attitude may not have been unique. The conversation had, after all, taken place before any disaster had occurred. And, at a time of national peril, any government could draw upon an extended fund of tolerance. Nowhere was the attitude of patriotic Unionists better expressed than in a letter written by Austen Chamberlain to Francis Acland early in December 1914. Acland had written from the Foreign Office inquiring whether Chamberlain thought that any good

---

[1] Bonar Law to Curzon, 29 January 1915. Robert Blake, *The Unknown Prime Minister*, p. 238.
[2] Viscount Grey of Fallodon, op. cit., vol. III, p. 220.

purpose would be served by the publication of an official pamphlet putting the British case on the outbreak of war. Chamberlain's reply was carefully drafted, in the expectation that it would be shown to the Foreign Secretary, and perhaps to other leading ministers:

I am deeply impressed by our undeserved good fortune in carrying our people so unanimously with us. There had been nothing beforehand in official speeches or in official publications to make known to them the danger that we ran or to prepare them for the discharge of our responsibilities and the defence of our interests. Those who knew most were silent: those who undertook to instruct the mass of the public were ignorant, and our democracy, with its decisive voice on the conduct of public affairs, was left without guidance by those who could have directed it properly, and was misled by those who constituted themselves its guides.

You may say that all this is past; but I think it has a very serious bearing on the present and even more upon the future. Now is the time, when people will read and ponder over these things, to form an enlightened public opinion which will support the Government through whatever sacrifices are needed in the weary months of war and will uphold them in insisting upon stable terms of peace. Now is our opportunity to lay the foundations in the minds of the public of a wise, responsible, & consistent foreign policy after the war is finished.

I urge, therefore, as strongly as I can, the publication of everything which can enlighten the public mind & form public opinion. No doubt the past action of the Government —as for that matter of all Governments—is open to criticism. I myself believe that if after Agadir or the earlier Moroccan crisis the Entente had been developed into an alliance we might very likely have avoided war at the present time, and even if this were not so, the outbreak of war would have found us better prepared to face its inevitable responsibilities and we should [have] avoided the extraordinary exacerbation of German feeling against us.

... you have a better assurance in our past action than in any

words of mine that there is no disposition on the part of any
section of the Unionist Party to make capital out of the difficulties of the Government or to say or do anything which can
embarrass them in the successful conduct of the war.[1]

Punch reflected and reinforced this goodwill in an extraordinary
panegyric by Sir Henry Lucy printed on 10 March 1915:

> A special Providence ordains that at such a crisis we have at
> head of affairs a strong man endowed with gift of lucid
> speech, which from its very qualities of simplicity and hon-
> esty of purpose frequently, without visible effort, rises to
> height of eloquence. Rarely in its history, perhaps never, has
> House found its sympathies, convictions and aspirations, so
> faithfully, so fully, so forcefully expressed as on several
> occasions during last seven months when Asquith has stood
> at Table and talked about the War, its prospects, and its in-
> evitable accomplishment.
>
> True, few Prime Ministers have been sustained and in-
> spired in equal degree by assurance of the confidence and
> sympathy of a unanimous nation represented by a united
> Parliament. That is a position difficult to win, hard daily to
> live up to. With increasing success the Premier has achieved
> both successes. His personality is worth to the Empire an
> army in the field, a squadron of *Queen Elizabeths* at sea.

Of course it was not true. But could it be believed? Perhaps
Asquith was not the man for long and disillusioning war. And
if he could not maintain unanimity, it was possible that a tired and
dispirited nation, yearning for fresh inspiration, might ordain a
new leader.

[1] Chamberlain to Acland, 7 December 1914 (copy), Austen Chamberlain MSS,
13/1/3.

6 Strains

For eight years before 1914, the trials of bitter party warfare had taken their toll on the health of Liberal ministers. Fatigue left its mark in greyed hair and lined faces. Parliamentary recesses often did not suffice to restore wearied bodies and frayed nerves. In quieter times, more than a half a century later, it is hard to imagine what agonies of adjustment must have been demanded of Asquith's cabinet in 1914. Plucked from the brink of civil upheaval only to be dropped into the unimagined horrors of continental war, they were, in a few weeks 'worn out with endless emergency work'.[1] After 'working at their highest efficiency, no dinners and week-ends',[2] Edward Grey, Walter Runciman, and Lewis Harcourt needed extended periods of rest. Time and again from August 1914 onwards Frances Stevenson thought that Lloyd George was on the verge of a physical breakdown. Only the occasional intervention of the Chancellor's trusted friend Lord Reading, who came into the Treasury as an unofficial relief, allowed Lloyd George to escape sometimes for a recuperative half-day. Private fears and anxieties had been added to the burdens of government which weighed upon the Prime Minister and his ministers. Almost every member of the cabinet had sons, brothers, nephews, close friends, and protégés, daily hazarding their lives. Some, as Margot Asquith noted, were 'shrivelled with grief'.[3] A letter from Grey to Percy Illingworth on September 14 told a familiar story:

> I hope my brother will come home alive but his left arm is amputated and that is irreparable. My nephew was in the

---

[1] Runciman to Chalmers, 7 February 1915, Runciman MSS.
[2] Beatrice Webb's Diary, 28 August 1914. Margaret I. Cole (ed.), *Beatrice Webb's Diaries, 1912–1924* (London, 1952), p. 28.
[3] Margot Asquith's Diary (?30 November) 1914, Oxford and Asquith MSS.

worst fighting on the 26th of August & has been missing since. It is a load of private grief to carry, but others have griefs as heavy or heavier.[1]

Grey, whose eyesight was irretrievably failing, would have resigned if Asquith had not prevailed upon him to stay. The others also persevered, giving fresh evidence of that determined clinging to office which had contributed so much to the cohesion of the pre-war ministry. Lewis Harcourt, for example, blandly glossed over the extent of his incapacitation after a heart attack. Writing to Lord Emmott he confessed:

... my heart has shown some signs 'rather serious' of failure in the last few days and all I have been able to extract from my doctor is permission to attend the Cabinets and to spend the rest of my time in bed, though doing paper work there and perhaps a few of the most essential interviews.[2]

Six months later Asquith told Lord Stamfordham that Harcourt managed his office well but he was no use in the House of Commons or on the special problems of the war.[3] What Asquith may not have known was the extent to which the work at the Colonial Office was, in fact, carried out by persons other than the minister. In particular, the Prime Minister might have been shocked to discover that between the hours of 8.00 p.m. and 10.00 a.m., at week-ends, and on any other occasions when the Colonial Secretary was absent from the office, full authority to act as Secretary of State had been unofficially vested in J. C. C. Davidson, a twenty-five-year-old unpaid private secretary. 'Every morning', Davidson has recorded, 'I took in a sheaf of telegrams in original and the replies I had sent, and never once did Harcourt repudiate me, although—as was only natural—he often added to instructions which I had sent, as I made it a rule to work on a minimum basis.'[4]

That anyone in Harcourt's physical condition should have contemplated, for a moment, continuing to undertake responsibility

---

[1] Grey to Illingworth, 14 September 1914, Illingworth MSS.
[2] Harcourt to Emmott, 3 November 1914, Emmott MSS.
[3] Stamfordham to the King, 19 May 1915, Royal Archives, GV K/770.
[4] Davidson's undated Memorandum. Robert Rhodes James, *Memoirs of a Conservative: J. C. C. Davidson's Memoirs and Papers, 1910–37* (London, 1969), p. 22.

for the administration of the Colonial Office is, to say the least, surprising. That he should have done it in time of war is so little short of incredible that it cannot be recorded without comment. How could Harcourt have failed to see the danger of neglecting the daily performance of his duties; or Asquith allowed a patently unfit man to impair the war effort? In Harcourt's case, the answer must be that the magnitude, the sombre reality, of the world conflict had not begun to penetrate his mind. The war, for the Colonial Secretary, was not mud and barbed wire in France, but a series of far-flung skirmishes in which the bravest of the Empire's manhood exhibited fine moral qualities and attested the virtues of imperial co-operation. Emerging from his sick-bed, Harcourt shared his experience of war with a gathering of the Victoria League on 26 January 1915:

> I wish you could see my daily and nightly sheaves of tele-grams, the despatches, the letters from the tropical firing line. You would live, as I have done for six months, in the thrills and the romance of thinly-defended frontiers, of gallantly captured posts, of conquest and reverse; of strategy and organisation. Sometimes a cruiser—more often a launch or a lighter—capturing a defended port or taking an enemy ship; bridges blown up or repaired; railways attacked or defended; wireless stations destroyed or erected—the ten-tacles of an impregnable and united Empire stretching out its embrace, unhasting, unyielding, the personification of the power of the seas.[1]

The thrills and the romance gave no comfort to the Prime Minister. He retreated from the war into undemanding female society and the secluded recesses of the Athenaeum. In the be-ginning, Walter Runciman testified, 'he never lost the regularity of his stride'.[2] As early as August 6 *The Daily Citizen* had carried a report that the Prime Minister's 'face is white and sunken, his hair looks white'. But, after the initial days of strain, Asquith ceased to display a 'racked expression' in public. And, to all appearances, he was justified in telling Lloyd George early in

[1] Lewis Harcourt, *A Free Empire in War Time*, a speech delivered to the Victoria League, 26 January 1915 (Westminster, 1915), Harcourt MSS.
[2] Runciman to Chalmers, 7 February 1915, Runciman MSS.

October 1914, 'You and I are the only ones who have stood this crisis really well. All the others are showing signs of wear and tear.' Lloyd George agreed, and spoke with admiration of his chief's tough-fibred, strong, body.[1] Underneath that sturdy exterior, however, the tangled strains of personal and public responsibility were unsettling the rhythm of Asquith's life. He continued to present a mask of equanimity to his colleagues. But behind that mask, the memory of vivid dreams lingered often after sleep had ended. He wrote about death in a playlet whose action presupposed his own suicide. He wrote ever more profusely to a young woman nearly forty years his junior, and frequently sought her companionship.[2] On at least one occasion his composure collapsed in public, to the unbridled fascination of reporters. It was the memorial service for Percy Illingworth at the Marylebone Presbyterian Church. A writer in *The Baptist Times* produced this picture of that sad January assembly:

> ... by far the most pathetic figure was the Prime Minister. His nature is not emotional; but he was visibly overwhelmed with grief at what is to him a heavy personal loss. Mr Lloyd George, who was next him, sang with much earnestness the last hymn 'Sun of my soul', and also joined in the hymn after the Benediction, 'Now the labourer's task is done', but Mr Asquith seemed unable to do so. At the 'Dead March' in *Saul*, the Prime Minister remained standing for a moment, and then, as if he could bear it no more, sank on his knees and buried his face in his hands. We have always felt a profound admiration for Mr Asquith, for his strength and courage, but we never realized how true it is that the tenderest heart is often found together with the most powerful intellect.[3]

From a closer vantage point than the reporter, Lloyd George noticed that Asquith 'sang vigorously all the words of all the hymns but ... there was not a note in tune the whole time. He sang in a dull, continuous, deep monotone. He was, however, doing his best and enjoyed his own singing!'[4]

[1] Riddell's Diary, 10 October 1914. *Lord Riddell's War Diary*, p. 34.
[2] Roy Jenkins, *Aqsuith*, pp. 333–7, 346–7.
[3] *The Baptist Times*, 15 January 1915, from a press cutting album in the Illingworth MSS.
[4] Addison's Diary, 19 January 1915. Addison, op. cit., vol. 1, p. 56.

It should not be thought that any exhibition of emotion signified a major weakening in Asquith's constitution. His intermittent displays of sentiment, unfailingly contrasted by observers with his supposed insensitivity and aloofness, had served him well before and were to do so again. Perhaps Illingworth's loss was a genuine grief to him. If so, he managed to contain his feelings in those private contexts where they might reasonably have been expected to have come to the surface. Walter Runciman, after dining with the McKennas on 12 January 1915, wrote to his wife:

> Pamela [McKenna] has just gone in to a 'Jolly' (new name for cards, frolic & frivolity) at the Francis McLarens where the P.M. and his ladies are dining & other people joining them afterwards. Reggie [McKenna] who disapproves of frivolities during the war refused to go.[1]

Evenings of bridge and chatter, afternoons with a novel in a club armchair, long week-ends away from London, all contributed to the lightening of the Prime Minister's cares. 'In these bleak times,' he admitted to the Lord Chancellor in April 1915, 'one needs all one can get of creature comforts.'[2] But nothing comforted as much as the company of the young woman who received his letters almost daily, and joined him as often as discretion allowed in the blurred anonymity of a closed car speeding through the countryside around London. Venetia Stanley, the beautiful, twenty-eight-year-old daughter of Lord Sheffield, was the Prime Minister's most intimate correspondent and frequent companion. Important not as a political influence upon Asquith but as an object of his attention and the recipient of his confidences, Miss Stanley cannot be ignored by students of Asquith's premiership. 'There is nothing (as you know)', Asquith wrote to her in February 1914, 'that I would not shew you: so great and deep is my trust.'[3]

In his letters to Venetia Stanley, appear some of Asquith's least inhibited comments on men and affairs. It was in one of these letters that he confided his opinion of Lloyd George in March

---

[1] Runciman to Hilda Runciman, 12 January 1915, Runciman MSS.
[2] Asquith to Haldane, 15 April 1915, Haldane MSS, 5911, f. 26.
[3] Asquith to Venetia Stanley, 5 February 1914, Montagu MSS.

1915. Though a wonderful person in some ways, the Prime Minister conceded, Lloyd George 'is totally devoid of either perspective or judgment'. Asquith had no antipathy to his colleague; it was rather that he found 'this volatile and versatile personage'[1] too incalculable for comfort. Perhaps, too, the mild disparagement of Lloyd George's qualities concealed a suppressed envy of the remarkable appreciation in the Chancellor's stocks since the previous August.

Asquith himself stood high in his colleague's estimation at the end of 1914, and in the ensuing few months was treated relatively kindly by the press. But Lloyd George's inspirational oratory had caught the nation's imagination to a far greater extent than the Prime Minister's balanced periods were ever likely to do. Because it was believed that Lloyd George had, as Lord Beaverbrook later wrote, 'approached the prospect of intervention with the greatest reluctance',[2] and had played no direct part in entangling Britain's destiny with that of France and Russia, he escaped the brunt of the radical criticisms of pre-war diplomacy. And, being Chancellor of the Exchequer, he avoided, as Churchill, Asquith, and Kitchener could not, becoming a focus of public impatience and disillusion fostered by the onset of stalemate in France. So notable was the improvement in Lloyd George's fortunes by January 1915 that Lord Reading, unstinting as ever in flattery, could speak of the 'highest pinnacle where you now are & must remain until a taller one is made for you'.[3]

[1] Asquith to Venetia Stanley, 4 March 1915, Montagu MSS. The letter was dated 3 March 1915, but written 'after midnight'.
[2] Lord Beaverbrook, op. cit. p. 23.
[3] Reading to Lloyd George, 2 January 1915, Lloyd George MSS, C/7/2/11.

7 The Highest Pinnacle?

Lloyd George's ascent to the pinnacle began with his widely praised handling of the financial crisis at the outbreak of war. Professor Victor Morgan has explained how 'imminent and terrible disaster' faced London accepting houses because of the threat of mass default by foreign customers. 'If the accepting houses had been ruined, they would have dragged down the bill-brokers, and possibly even the great joint-stock banks as well.'[1] The Bank of England, too, was alarmed by heavy demands on its reserves. Rapid intervention was essential. Bank Rate was raised to ten per cent, and the Bank was authorized to exceed the legal maximum fiduciary issue. A proclamation was issued to postpone payment on bills of exchange. Pressure on banks and discount houses was relieved by the extension of the Bank Holiday until August 6. The Treasury was authorized to issue one-pound and ten-shilling notes. By August 7, anxiety had abated and it was possible to reduce Bank rate to five per cent. Further action was required to revive the discount market, but the worst was over.

Many hands had contributed to the drafting and execution of the emergency measures. Sir John Bradbury, Lloyd George's senior official adviser, headed the Treasury team. The editor of *The Statist*, Lloyd George's old economic counsellor, Sir George Paish, gave helpful advice. Austen Chamberlain, the last Conservative Chancellor, responded to Lloyd George's inspired invitation to join the small group of Liberal ministers who were occupied with the intricate problems. But it was Lloyd George himself who bore the responsibility and reaped the plaudits for

[1] E. Victor Morgan, *Studies in British Financial Policy, 1914-25* (London, 1952), p. 8. See also Walter Runciman's Notes of a conference between London bankers and a cabinet committee, (?2) August 1914, Runciman MSS; and Lloyd George, op. cit., vol. I, pp. 100-16.

the success of the operation.[1] Mr Malcolm Thomson's verdict exaggerates the facts but accurately portrays the contemporary mythology: 'It was freely acknowledged, even by his bitterest political opponents, that the genius, resource and swift action of Lloyd George in face of this entirely unprecedented situation saved the country from very grave financial disaster.'[2] J. M. Keynes, in *The Economic Journal* for September 1914, judged the achievement of the Treasury more moderately: 'They have acted on the whole with rapidity and with courage, and have combined a regard for principle with practical good sense in action.' Of Lloyd George's personal contribution, Austen Chamberlain said in the House of Commons, 'the Chancellor of the Exchequer has handled a very difficult situation with great tact, great skill and great judgment'.[3]

Among his colleagues, as well, the Chancellor's efforts found favour. Walter Runciman was, for once, the author of a generous tribute to a man whose fitness as the supreme trustee of the nation's finances he had never been wont to exaggerate:

> L-G conducted numberless and endless conferences with the Banks & financial houses, with McKenna, Crewe, Harcourt and me to assist, & Rufus [Isaacs, Lord Reading] to act as hourly counsellor and guide to our courageous Chancellor of the Exchequer. L-G was at his best, & got such a command of the immediate problems by the end of the discussions that on currency, exchange, the principles of credit and banking, and general business necessities, the City and the great commercial centres have belauded him, & he well deserves the praise he has won.[4]

Within the Treasury, Lloyd George's rapid assimilation of the complex details and his responsiveness to official advice won him the almost disbelieving approval of his staff. In the eyes of civil servants, as Basil Blackett recorded in his diary, the Chancellor

---

[1] Among the other men involved in the crisis were Maurice Hankey and Sir John Simon who submitted memoranda to the Prime Minister on the practical and legal aspects of prohibiting the export of bullion and coin. These documents, and several briefs by Sir John Bradbury, are in the Asquith MSS, vol. 25, ff. 201–24.
[2] Malcolm Thomson, *David Lloyd George* (London, n.d., ?1948), p. 232.
[3] 66 *H.C. Deb.*, 5s, col. 73, 26 August 1914.
[4] Runciman to Chalmers, 7 February 1915, Runciman MSS.

moved in five days from being an economic ignoramus to 'quite a currency expert'. On August 1, Blackett wrote that 'the last few days suggest that Lloyd George could be dispensed with at the Treasury'. By August 8, it was a different story: 'It took some time to teach him, but he promises now to reach the front rank of financial experts, if his present knowledge makes him retain a taste for the pure finance side of the Treasury work which he has hitherto entirely neglected.'[1]

Much of the arduous financial negotiation in August was conducted in secrecy. But Lloyd George was questioned in detail, day-by-day, in the House of Commons. On August 4, he made a statement to the House on a proposed scheme of state insurance against war risks to shipping. Following the recommendations of a sub-committee of the Committee of Imperial Defence, the government undertook to reinsure eighty per cent of all war risks on vessels leaving port after the outbreak of war. The state was to receive eighty per cent of the premiums, charging no premiums on vessels already at sea when war began. Embarking on a 'novel and unprecedented' course, 'the first experiment of the kind undertaken by the state', Lloyd George expounded the scheme with studied restraint.[2] The technicality of the details and the moderation of the Chancellor could not, however, conceal the fact that a major shift in government policy had occurred. Christopher Addison noted happily that it was 'probably the most Socialistic measure, after Insurance, to which this Government has ever been committed'.[3]

The adoption of the shipping insurance plan resulted from Lloyd George's personal decision to recommend it to the government. Hours of discussion between ministers, officials, and independent experts on August 1 and 2 had produced no conclusion. 'It was obviously impossible', Lloyd George wrote in his memoirs,

---

[1] Basil Blackett's Diary, 1–8 August 1914. R. F. Harrod, *The Life of John Maynard Keynes* (London, 1963: first published 1951), pp. 196-7. The Chancellor's decisions were not, of course, above criticism. Sir John Bradbury wrote to Austen Chamberlain on August 13: 'I wish we could have got a more substantial *quid pro quo* from the bankers than the mere assurance of co-operation.' But Bradbury had to admit that 'it is difficult to see what form it could have taken.' (Austen Chamberlain MSS, 13/4/4.)

[2] 65 *H.C. Deb.*, 5s, cols, 1941-8, 4 August 1914.

[3] Addison's Diary, 30 August 1914. Addison, op. cit., vol. 1, p. 33.

'to leave our shipping hanging on a dead centre whilst politicans wrangled about the ideal nature and extent of state action to set it moving again.'[1] In this vital intervention, Lloyd George gave a glimpse of the powers of resource and determination that were to impress a new image upon both the world of politics and the nation at large. Beatrice Webb wrote of the Chancellor at the end of August that he 'showed at his best in his lack of self-consciousness, his freedom from pedantry, his alert open-mindedness, and his calm cheeriness'.[2]

Having dined with Haldane, Grey, Lord Reading, Edwin Montagu, and Lloyd George on 28 August 1914, Mrs Webb came away with the impression that Lloyd George was 'prepared for the boldest measures to re-establish credit and keep the population employed'. In the House of Commons three days later, the Chancellor announced an extension of the moratorium, and concluded that: 'There has been a provisional breakdown of credit but that will be re-established, and the moment the machine is set going there is no reason why, in spite of this terrible war, we should not be able to conduct our business very much as we have ever done.'[3]

By restricting his utterances to Treasury subjects and endorsing the philosophy of business as usual, Lloyd George exposed himself to the charge that he was merely handling the financial problems without, as Mr Taylor has put it, 'committing himself further'.[4] It is true that he made no publicized appearance in the country and issued no significant declaration to the press until September 8. What was the reason for this unobtrusiveness? Preoccupation with urgent affairs naturally accounted for part of the Chancellor's quietness. Was there also a cautious instinct operating to remind him of the time it would take for his pre-war speeches to be forgotten? When asked in mid-August by Sir George Riddell to make a speech explaining why the nation was

[1] Lloyd George, op. cit., vol. III, p. 1211.

[2] Beatrice Webb's Diary, 28 August 1914. Margaret I. Cole (ed.), op. cit., p. 28.

[3] 66 *H.C. Deb.* 5s. col. 524, 31 August 1914. Austen Chamberlain had advised against an unqualified extension of the moratorium for a month. But Lloyd George, having consulted some members of the government, decided that 'the balance of the argument' was in favour of continuing the moratorium without limitations through September. (Chamberlain to Lloyd George, 30 August 1914 [copy], and Lloyd George to Chamberlain, 1 September 1914, Austen Chamberlain MSS, 13/4/29, 30).

[4] A. J. P. Taylor, *English History, 1914–1945* (Oxford, 1965), p. 5.

at war, he replied cryptically that he did not feel like speaking. But, he reacted to indications of half-heartedness about the war from the Attorney-General with a homily on Britain's duty to small nations. 'I would rather see the British Empire bite the dust than allow poor little Belgium to be crushed by this hectoring bully.'[1]

Nevertheless, Mr Taylor has gone so far as to suggest that Lloyd George was keeping silent and deliberately refraining from endorsing the war, because in his heart he was still uncertain about whether British participation was justified. It is Mr Taylor's view that Lloyd George, doubtful of the outcome as well as the advisability of British involvement, was holding his peace until some definite sign pointed either to British success or failure. That sign, Mr Taylor contends, was the achievement of British and French troops in holding the German onslaught at the Marne.[2]

Two things make Mr Taylor's theory untenable. The first is that Lloyd George actually committed himself without reserve to the British cause while the Marne struggle was still in progress. The second is that, even on September 19 when a stirring speech at the Queen's Hall dispelled any possibility of doubt about his position, Lloyd George could by no means have been able to predict when, or in whose favour, the war would end.

Lloyd George's initial statement on the war has received little attention from historians. It came in answer to a deputation from the Association of Municipal Corporations, which he received in company with Herbert Samuel, President of the Local Government Board. The deputation presented itself, after thirty-five days of war, to ask the government to earmark a portion of the War loan so that it could be borrowed for municipal undertakings. The municipalities also desired to have the Trustee Act amended so that corporation mortgages—and those of all boroughs with more than 20,000 inhabitants—could be classified as trustee securities. This second request was rejected. To the first proposal, however, the government acceded, with the Chancellor urging that the money should be carefully spent, no unnecessary relief works being instituted in areas where distress was not severe. In

---

[1] Lord Riddell's War Diary, p. 14.
[2] These views were expressed in an unpublished lecture on Lloyd George and the First World War delivered at Nuffield College in January 1967.

the course of his brief speech to the members of the deputation, Lloyd George made some general reflections which were released in the press the next day:

> The first thing is that we should come out triumphant in this struggle, and as finance is going to play a very great part we must husband our resources ... in my judgment, the last four hundred millions may win this war ... The first hundred millions our enemies can stand just as well as we can, but the last they cannot, thank God; and, therefore, I think cash is going to count much more than we possibly imagine at the present moment. Of course, if we have great victories, and smashing victories, that is all right, but then they may not come yet. We may have fluctuations, and things may last long. We are fighting a very tough enemy, who is very well prepared for the fight, and he will probably fight to the very end before he will accept the conditions upon which we can possibly make peace, if we are wise.
> ... that is where our resources will come in, not merely of men, but of cash. We have won with the silver bullets before.[1]

For a minister unconnected with any of the traditional war-making departments, the provision of 'silver bullets' was a memorable way to be associated in the public mind with the real business of defeating the enemy. The address left no room for suspicion that Lloyd George was hedging on the war. His commitment was unambiguously to victory, decisive victory. Two days after the publication of these remarks, Winston Churchill, in a much more publicized speech at the London Opera House, gave grounds for hope that victory could be won. 'Everything that we have heard during four long days of anxiety', he said, 'seems to point to a marked and substantial turning of the tide.'[2]

Stemming the German attack was only the beginning. Respite on the Marne was dearly bought by sacrifice. The veteran Lord Roberts wrote to Lord Kitchener on 17 September 1914 about 'the serious want of officers available for duty after the heavy casualties that have taken place in some battalions'. Only the example and encouragement of the officers, Roberts reported, was

[1] *The Times*, 9 September 1914.
[2] *The Times*, 12 September 1914.

keeping the men going. The troops were 'dead beat'.[1] Whatever else the omens showed, they did not alter the Secretary of State for War's conviction that preparations had to be made for a long struggle. Hundreds of thousands of men were demanded. And, in addition to supplying 'silver bullets', Lloyd George, like his colleagues, was pressed into service on the recruiting platform. His first appeal to the men of military age was scheduled for Saturday, September 19, at a meeting of London Welshmen in the Queen's Hall.

Just over a week before he was due to appear at the Queen's Hall, Lloyd George received a parcel of pamphlets setting out the British case on the outbreak of war. Two of the pamphlets had been prepared, with the help of the Foreign Office, by Sir Edward Cook. The other, sent in typescript draft, was written for the use of schoolmasters by Jack Pease, President of the Board of Education.[2] From the plain catalogue of facts and arguments which were at his disposal, Lloyd George laboured for days to produce a speech of surpassing power. 'How we worked at that Queen's Hall speech!' Lady Lloyd-George has recalled. 'And how apprehensive he was before it was delivered! With his Boer War record he realised how important it was—a landmark in his career. People would have to be convinced of his sincerity.'[3]

Lloyd George's Queen's Hall message was simple. The British, small nation though they were, were not going to stand aside while 'the road-hog of Europe' careered unchecked across the continent:

> There is no man in this room who has always regarded the prospects of engaging in a great war with greater reluctance, with greater repugnance, than I have done throughout the whole of my political life. There is no man either inside or outside of this room more convinced that we could not have avoided it without national dishonour ... If we had stood by when two little nations were being crushed and broken by the brutal hands of barbarism our shame would have rung down by the everlasting ages.[4]

[1] Roberts to Kitchener, 17 September 1914, Kitchener MSS, PRO 30/57/73.
[2] Pease to Lloyd George, 11 September 1914, Lloyd George MSS, C/4/12/7.
[3] Frances Lloyd George, *The Years that are Past*, p. 75.
[4] David Lloyd George, 'Honour and Dishonour' (London, 1914), pp. 2, 7. Not

M

Moving from justification to patriotic exhortation, Lloyd George painted a grim and challenging future:

It will not be easy. It will be a long job. It will be a terrible war. But in the end we shall march through terror to triumph. We shall need all our qualities, every quality that Britain and its people possess. Prudence in council, daring in action, tenacity in purpose, courage in defeat, moderation in victory, in all things faith, and we shall win.[1]

Taut, simple phrases and flashes of imagery merged into a compelling appeal. At the end, in a thoroughly rehearsed peroration, Lloyd George turned to the theme of sacrifice — 'the great pinnacle of Sacrifice, pointing like a rugged finger to heaven'.[2] He had been apprehensive about the speech; and he was unhappy about its reception. In a letter to me on 7 April 1968, Lady Lloyd-George recounts that:

He was very uncertain about the last part — the peroration. He knew that he ought to have one, and I remember suggesting to him that the theme of sacrifice would appeal not only to his audience but to the country ... I remember that during the week-end I retired to bed with a temperature, and he came to my room to declaim. My brother, who had got his commission in the army, was also at Walton Heath that week-end, but he did not respond to the draft speech as L.G. would have liked ...

But the impact of the speech beyond the Queen's Hall was immediate and profound. There came a chorus of congratulation from men and women of all parties and of no party. A box of Lloyd George's favourite mild cigars arrived from Neil Primrose, Lord Rosebery's younger son. Probably the most welcome and most important letters were those from the proprietors and editors of the leading national newspapers. H. W. Massingham and J. A. Spender were no less laudatory than Emsley Carr of the

---

a single member of Asquith's cabinet had been prepared to go to war to save one of the little nations, Serbia, from 'the brutal hands of barbarism'.

[1] Lloyd George, 'Honour and Dishonour', p. 10.
[2] Ibid., pp. 11–12.

News of the World. 'I can't tell you', wrote Carr, 'how delighted I was to boom it amongst our *three* million readers.'[1]

The newspapers were loudest in their congratulations on Monday morning, September 21. Lloyd George 'laughed at the exuberance of *The Times*'. 'These people become almost sickly', he remarked, 'when one happens to fall in with their ideas.'[2] Nevertheless, Tory praises were welcome. Setting the seal on all these favourable responses, there came also a heartening letter from a little village in North Wales:

Tremendous! Tremendous!! Success!!!
Bravo! *Bravo*!! BRAVO!!! BRAVO!!!!
All efforts heretofore on war platforms buried in obscurity for good.[3]

Uncle Lloyd approved.

[1] For the letters of James Hawthorn, Hedley Le Bas, Earl Grey, Emsley Carr, G. W. E. Russell, Neil Primrose, Edgar Jones, J. A. Spender, H. W. Massingham, Harold Begbie, William Brace, and Colonel A. Lockwood, see Lloyd George MSS, C/11/2. The speech was nearly, but not quite, perfect. Robertson Nicoll and Pamela McKenna were offended by the word 'snug' in the peroration. (Riddell's Diary, 28 October 1914. *Lord Riddell's War Diary*, p. 37); and Lord Crewe wrote to say that 'Moslem dovecotes' were ruffled by an injudicious phrase. Referring to the Kaiser's blasphemous claims, Lloyd George had said 'there has been nothing like it since Mahomet'. The phrase was omitted from the authorized reprints of the speech (Crewe to Lloyd George, 2 letters, 2 October 1914, Lloyd George MSS, C/4/1/13, 14).

[2] Frances Stevenson's Diary, 21 September 1914, Lloyd George MSS.

[3] Richard Lloyd to Lloyd George, 21 September 1914, Lloyd George MSS, I/1/1/17.

8 The Chancellor's War

All over the British Isles, in the dominions and colonies and in allied countries, millions of copies of the Queen's Hall speech were distributed. Reprinted at first under the title 'Honour and Dishonour', it was later more dramatically entitled 'Through Terror to Triumph'. The Parliamentary Recruiting Committee published an authorized edition under the title 'Through Terror to Triumph'. The Caxton Publishing Company also produced a version—'Mr Lloyd George's Speech on the Road-Hogs of Europe'—from the text printed in *The Daily News*, which was subsequently revised by Lloyd George himself.[1] Richard Lloyd's enthusiasm was more than vindicated by events. Late in October, Harry Cust, Chairman of the Central Committee for Patriotic Organisations, but better known as one of London's most notorious libertines, was appalled to discover that, while the Queen's Hall speech was about to be officially translated into fourteen languages, no speech by the Prime Minister had been authorized for similar treatment by the Foreign Office or the propaganda group working under the direction of Charles Masterman.[2]

While the Queen's Hall phrases reverberated around the world, at home the war made unceasing demands. In the first week of October, a deputation from the War Emergency: Workers' National Committee called on the Chancellor of the Exchequer and the President of the Local Government Board. The Labour representatives were alarmed by a passage in Lloyd George's statement to the deputation from the municipalities in the pre-

[1] Frances Stevenson to J. M. Malcolm, 14 June 1915, Lloyd George MSS, D/20/1/24.
[2] Cust to Asquith, 23 October 1914, and enclosed memorandum by Claud Schuster (or Ernest Gowers?), Asquith MSS, vol. 26, ff. 50-2.

vious month. Some authorities had interpreted the Chancellor's words as an encouragement to neglect the relief of unemployment and distress. Lloyd George ridiculed the idea that he had intended municipalities to do nothing until 'they had a mob at the Town Hall threatening to batter down the doors and clamouring for bread'.[1] It was easy enough to show that his remarks had been misunderstood and Messrs Bowerman, Seddon, Webb, Gosling, and Middleton, as well as Miss Susan Lawrence, might legitimately have wondered whether so formal a meeting was necessary to disabuse themselves of a rather obvious misconception.

On a rather different matter, Labour's spokesmen, had they known of the Chancellor of the Exchequer's efforts, might well have been grateful. The cabinet gave much thought to the question of the scale of separation allowances to wives of recruits. A subsidiary question was whether or not *de facto* wives should also be entitled to an allowance. The Archbishop of Canterbury, as Frances Stevenson noted, 'does not wish them or their children to starve, but he does not wish them to be openly treated as deserving of relief—which is a piece of blatant hypocrisy.'[2]

Lloyd George fought hard to secure equal rights for any woman who could show that she had lived with a man as his wife. He argued that, in Scotland, many of the women would have been legally married, and that the 'holy institution of marriage' was therefore purely a matter of local convention. Moreover:

> it is not right to take the lives of the men for their country and after you have accepted the sacrifice to say that you do not approve of their morals and are afraid you cannot make decent provision for the women they have treated as their wives. If you are going to take this line, you ought to inquire into the morals of the man *before* you accept his life. Once you have accepted it, he has a right to *demand* an allowance for the woman he has lived with & their children—provided it is a bona fide union.

[1] Lloyd George's reply to the Workers' National Committee deputation, reported in *The Morning Post*, 8 October 1914. See also the fiery exchange of letters between Edwin Montagu and Herbert Samuel, 1 and 2 October 1914, and Montagu to Lloyd George, 2 October 1914 (copy), Montagu MSS.

[2] Frances Stevenson's Diary, 23 October 1914, Lloyd George MSS.

It should perhaps be added as a footnote that on the question of the scale of allowances, Lloyd George aligned himself with the financially prudent minority in favour of five shillings a week, rather than with the romantic minority of one—Churchill—in favour of seven shillings and sixpence.

When the time came for the introduction of a special war Budget on November 17, the indulgent tolerance of the emergency period in August could no longer be relied upon. The mood of politicians and public was beginning to change. The war was beginning to make a deep impression at home. 'The wastage from the original expeditionary force', Lord Crewe wrote euphemistically to Lord Lansdowne, 'has been terrific ... though there has been no epidemic, and no Crimean conditions of hardship.'[1] In England, as stalemate settled in France, there arose a fear of invasion which, despite the scepticism of Asquith, Lloyd George, and Churchill, for a time took a grip of many responsible men in Whitehall.

Some students of public finance later found fault with the failure of the Chancellor of the Exchequer to exploit the mood of the people and raise more of the cost of the war by taxation. 'The spirit of the House was willing,' Francis Hirst and J. E. Allen wrote in after-years, 'but the Minister hardly rose to the occasion, at least when he came to practical proposals.'[2] But this retrospective comment bore the imprint of another twelve years of partisan controversy. Hirst's contemporary remarks in *The Economist* were less harsh:

> The Government deserves all credit for having boldly faced an unprecedented emergency by calling upon the nation to make an unprecedented sacrifice. And we must commend Mr Lloyd George not only for promptitude and courage, but also for the directness and simplicity of the scheme which he laid before the House of Commons ... [3]

Until patriotic restraint gave way to anxious criticism, and hindsight replaced prediction, Hirst's original judgment remained typical. The success of the first War Loan, for example,

[1] Crewe to Lansdowne, 27 October 1914, Lansdowne MSS.
[2] F. W. Hirst and J. E. Allen, *British War Budgets* (London, 1926), p. 22.
[3] *The Economist*, 21 November 1914.

was greeted by the Chairman of Lloyd's Bank as 'one of the greatest—if not the greatest—achievements that have ever been recorded in the financial history of the nations'.[1] Three months later, however, Edwin Cannan, Professor of Political Economy at London University, struck a rather different note:

> I am sure the attempt to prevent anyone suffering anything, (except, of course, violent death, wounds and bereavement, which seem to be taken as a matter of course) from the war must fail, and the only question is in what kind of crisis the inflation of spending power caused by it will end.[2]

Cannan's fears were well founded. But, as an academic economist, he could afford to ignore the inhibiting political considerations that necessarily impinged on Treasury policy. Lloyd George's measures were, perhaps, too timid at the outset. Nevertheless, in his November 1914 Budget speech, he actually emphasized the desirability of raising as much money as possible by taxation. 'This', commented the First Commissioner of Works, Lord Emmott, two days after the introduction of the Budget, 'is quite right & if L. G. can ease the situation of the income-tax payers who have to find their increased contributions on profits made before the War out of losses (so to speak) made during the War, I think it will go through smoothly.'[3]

Lloyd George's difficulty was that he was in an unprecedented and unpredictable situation. As Chancellor he dared not assume a short war, and his original proposals were calculated as sufficient to run the war until July 1915.[4] Had he fully examined the financial implications of the war aims to which the government was already committed, he might have been more stringent from the beginning. Yet, to have done so, to have proclaimed that the government's objectives could not be achieved in less than the three years which Lord Kitchener predicted, might have started a panic. Did Lloyd George privately share Kitchener's opinion?

[1] Richard Vassar Vassar-Smith to Lloyd George, 26 November 1914, Lloyd George MSS, C/11/2/74.
[2] Edwin Cannan to Sir Thomas Whittaker, 24 February 1915. Edwin Cannan, *An Economist's Protest* (London, 1927), p. 16.
[3] Emmott's Diary, 19 November 1914, Emmott MSS.
[4] 68 *H.C. Deb.* 5s. col. 371, 17 November 1914.

Probably he did. And for those who could read between the lines he said as much in public:

> I am not going to presume to express an opinion about the duration of the War. There is no man, however equipped and however competent, who can express an absolutely reliable opinion upon that subject. There may be accidents which will shorten the War. There may be accidents that will lengthen the War. It depends upon questions military. It depends upon questions political. It depends upon subtle human considerations that are outside the purview of both. I am therefore not going to express an opinion. We are fighting a tough enemy. *We are fighting an enemy that cannot submit to any terms we can accept — to any terms we can prudently accept — without a smashing defeat* ... [1]

These sentences have attracted little comment. But they demonstrate that Lloyd George had already realized the need to prepare the country for a long struggle.[2] This realization can even be seen in the words that he spoke to the deputation at the Treasury on September 8. In those early days he seems to have hoped that Britain might fight more with cash than with men. 'We financed Europe in the greatest war we ever fought, and that is what won ... When the others were quite exhausted we were getting our second breath, and our third, and our fourth.'[3] The most obvious point about this appeal for economy was the hope (it could not be called an assumption) that British lives could be saved by paying France and Russia to bear the brunt of the killing. But it was also obvious that in a short war no third and fourth wind are required. It took only a few weeks for Lloyd

[1] 68 *H.C. Deb.* 5s. col. 353, 17 November 1914; my emphasis.

[2] On November 23 Lloyd George spoke privately of the war lasting until Christmas 1915. (Addison's Diary 23 November 1914. *Four and a Half Years*, vol. 1, p. 46.) Simon, Montagu, Emmott, and others were more hopeful. On October 20, Emmott wrote: 'I cannot even now believe that this war will be a matter of years. The waste is too heavy.' (Emmott's Diary, 20 October 1914, Emmott MSS.) Asquith is reported to have told George Macaulay Booth at about this time: 'This war is going to be over in a few months.' (Duncan Crow, *A Man of Push and Go:* The Life of George Macaulay Booth [London, 1965], p. 69.) On October 1, Sir John French predicted an end to the war in the spring. (Sir Henry Rawlinson's Diary, 1 October 1914, Rawlinson MSS.)

[3] *The Times*, 9 September 1914; see also 'E. T. Raymond' (E. R. Thompson), *Mr Lloyd George:* A Biography (London, 1922), p. 174.

George to appreciate that the British commitment could not be limited. With this view there also grew a determination not to squander lives on the western front.

While new-found friends like the *Daily Mail* spoke warmly to their readers of the Chancellor of the Exchequer's 'open-minded-ness, flexibility, and courage',[1] those valuable qualities were applied to finding ways of intensifying Britain's war effort. The problem had two aspects: how to mobilize men and resources most effectively, and how best to deploy them once they were available. Underlying the practical decisions that mobilization and strategy dictated, there were two conditioning factors. The precise mixture of men, arms, cash, and other supplies which Britain was to contribute to the allied cause logically depended on an antecedent decision about the kind of role for which Britain was fitted. And, in choosing between the several strategies open to British forces, either acting alone or with their allies, it was necessary to consider the objectives that were being sought, Britain's war aims. What was victory to mean?

Although the war had begun in Europe the scattered empires of friend and enemy were drawn ineluctably into the struggle. 'Neutralization-plans', said Sir Eyre Crowe, 'are a futile absurdity. What is wanted is to strike hard with all our might in all the four corners of the world.'[2] Peace could not be considered until all invading forces were evacuated from neutral and allied territory and guarantees were given that the belligerent Central Powers would sustain a permanent peace. Unless these cardinal points were agreed to, the Foreign Secretary told Colonel House, President Woodrow Wilson's personal emissary, in February 1915, England would continue the war indefinitely. Publicly, the government was committed to the Prime Minister's pledge given at the Guildhall on November 9:

> We shall never sheathe the sword which we have not lightly drawn until Belgium recovers in full measure all, and more than all, that she has sacrificed, until France is adequately secured against the menace of aggression, until the rights

---

[1] See, for example, the *Daily Mail*, 28 November 1914 and 30 January 1915.
[2] Minute by Crowe, 10 August 1914, FO371/2016. Wm. Roger Louis, *Great Britain and Germany's Lost Colonies, 1914–1919* (Oxford, 1967), p. 9.

of the smaller nationalities of Europe are placed upon an unassailable foundation, and until the military domination of Prussia is wholly and finally destroyed.

In pursuit of victory, the cabinet examined many schemes. The expeditionary force alone would not bring down Germany. A naval blockade would hasten the process by cutting off vital shipments of war material and food. Sensitive consciences—not yet anaesthetized by casualty lists from Flanders—were disturbed by the stringency of the blockade policy. Walter Runciman was warned by his erstwhile colleague Charles Trevelyan:

I feel great uneasiness about the trend of action of the Government towards trying to exclude German food-supplies passing through neutral countries ... I do implore you to take care what you are doing. It would be bad enough to alienate Dutch opinion. But it will be infinitely worse if you alienate the U.S.A. Remember that under very analogous circumstances the U.S.A. went to war with us against its will.[1]

Trevelyan feared that the government would act precipitately, especially if Winston Churchill's influence were not checked. 'But I hope you won't act rashly, however anxious the Navy is to justify its existence.'[2]

But the Foreign Office was alive to the danger of antagonizing the Americans. As Professor Link has written in the third volume of his biography of Woodrow Wilson: 'Conciliation of America was perhaps the Foreign Office's chief concern at this early juncture.'[3]

By the middle of October 1914 the war's phase of movement was coming to an end. Hankey wrote to Balfour: 'I think we are far off the stalemate that Lord K. spoke of. Sir John French's movement seems to be encountering a good deal of opposition, and the Russian news is not as yet very stimulating.'[4] Within a few weeks the time for understatement was over. The navy was in the ascendant. But on land the Russian 'steamroller' had been

[1] Trevelyan to Runciman, 28 August 1914, Runciman MSS.

[2] Ibid.; see also Trevelyan to Runciman, 5 October 1914, Runciman MSS.

[3] Arthur S. Link, *Wilson: The Struggle for Neutrality, 1914-1915* (Princeton, 1960), p. 116.

[4] Hankey to Balfour, 15 October 1914, Balfour MSS, (Add. MS. 49703, f. 56).

halted; and trenches from Switzerland to the North Sea marked the boundaries of a new variety of siege warfare. 'This war is going to be one of exhaustion,' said the official 'Eye-Witness' on November 2:

> ...and after the regular armies of the belligerents have done their work it will be upon the measures taken to prepare and utilize the raw material of the manhood of the countries concerned that final success will depend. This implies trained men—hundreds of thousands of trained and disciplined men.[1]

Recruits came forward initially in ample numbers. Kitchener's magnetism and the nation's patriotic ardour induced the flow of volunteers. Persuasive newspapers advertising from the pen of the young copywriter, Eric Field, and canvassing, as well as an imaginative poster campaign by the Parliamentary Recruiting Committee, had an immense impact on a society unused to government-sponsored professional assaults on the emotions.[2] But a future for Kitchener's magnificent new armies had to be settled. And the generals in the field had to be guaranteed an adequate supply of munitions and other equipment. To these problems, Lloyd George, like the other senior ministers, increasingly directed his thoughts.

[1] (Ernest D. Swinton), *Eye-Witness's Narrative of the War:* From the Marne to Neuve Chapelle, September 1914–March 1915 (London, 1915), p. 155.

[2] Eric Field, *Advertising: The Forgotten Years* (London, 1958), tells the story of the first recruiting publicity produced by Hedley Le Bas's Caxton Publishing Company. The Caxton Company's records for this period have been lost. The manuscript minute books of the Parliamentary Recruiting Committee have been deposited in the British Museum by the Committee's secretary, R. II. Davies. (See Add. MS. 54192.)

9 Strategy

'The War Lords', wrote Walter Runciman on 6 January 1915, 'are sad at their stalemate, & Winston in particular sees no success for the Navy (& himself) anywhere.' Runciman was optimistic; his colleagues, he said, were 'sure that by doing their best we shall succeed if not in a dramatic coup then in a sturdy endurance that will outlast German, or rather Prussian plunges'.[1] Even if a dramatic coup were in store, sturdy endurance as a method of waging war had a limited appeal. The war council and the cabinet weighed great strategic alternatives and investigated the promise of mechanical contrivance in tipping the balance against Germany and Austria. On 25 February 1915, the minutes of the war council record:

> Hankey proposed (a) igniting German crops and (b) distributing a 'blight' over the crops.
> Mr Lloyd George approved the idea: Mr Churchill saw no objection to burning the crops, but drew the line at sowing a blight, which was analogous to poisoning food. Mr Lloyd George did not agree. A blight did not poison but merely deteriorated the crop.[2]

Churchill's finely calibrated conscience gave him no trouble when he dealt with the desirability of entangling the United States in the war on the allied side. Walter Runciman, while trying to decide on new rates of insurance for neutral shipping, was assailed by the First Lord who wrote three letters in five days urging that the rates should not go up. 'My dear Walter,' began the first entreaty:

> It is most important to attract neutral shipping to our shores, in the hope especially of embroiling the U.S. with Germany. The

[1] Runciman to Hilda Runciman, 6 January 1915, Runciman MSS.
[2] Minutes of the war council, 25 February 1915, Asquith MSS, vol. 132.

German formal announcement of indiscriminate submarining has been made to the United States to produce a deterrent effect on traffic. For our part, we want the traffic—the more the better; & if some of it gets into trouble, better still. Therefore, do please furbish up at once your insurance offer to neutrals trading with us after February 18. The more that come, the greater our safety & the German embarrassment.[1]

The war could be lost on the oceans; but it could not be won there, except indirectly, as Churchill perceived, by embroiling the Americans. Not more ships, but more men were needed. 'Fresh forces are necessary to change the deadlock,' Kitchener told Sir John French at the beginning of January 1915.[2] And some outflanking operation was imperative. For, as Kitchener put it, 'the German lines in France may be looked upon as a fortress that cannot be carried by assault'. 'To force the line,' Lloyd George surmised, 'you would require at least three to one; our reinforcements would not guarantee two to one, or anything approaching such predominance.'[3]

By the end of December 1914, strategy demanded urgent attention. The urgency was not only military but political. Lloyd George alone in Whitehall and Westminster stressed the significance of the domestic aspect of stalemate. He underlined the point in a memorandum to the war council on 1 January 1915. This document is usually discussed as an example of his proclivity to an eastern strategy. While its recommendations differed in detail, the strategic assumptions of the Lloyd George document were not incompatible with the independent contemporary views of Churchill and Maurice Hankey. What was peculiar to Lloyd George was his stress on the political necessity of 'winning a definite victory somewhere'. His analysis of the state of public opinion was ominous:

There is a real danger that the people of Great Britain and of France will sooner or later get tired of long casualty lists

[1] Churchill to Runciman, 12 February 1915, and also February 13 and 16, Runciman MSS.

[2] Kitchener to French, 2 January 1915. Sir George Arthur, *Life of Lord Kitchener*, 3 vols, (London, 1920), vol. III, p. 85.

[3] 'Suggestions as to the Military Position', war council memorandum by Lloyd George, 1 January 1915. Lloyd George, *War Memoirs*, vol. I, p. 370.

explained by monotonous and rather banal telegrams from headquarters about 'heavy cannonades', 'making a little progress' at certain points, 'recovering trenches', the loss of which has never been reported, etc., with the net result that we have not advanced a yard after weeks of heavy fighting. Britishers have ceased to be taken in by reports which exaggerate slight successes and suppress reverses; neutral states have never been deceived by these reports...A clear definite victory which has visibly materialized in guns and prisoners captured, in unmistakable retreats of the enemy's armies, and in large sections of enemy territory occupied, will alone satisfy the public that tangible results are being achieved by the great sacrifices they are making, and decide neutrals that it is at last safe for them to throw in their lot with us.[1]

Where was the 'clear definite victory' to be won? The Baltic? Salonika? Syria? Gallipoli? On 29 December 1914, Churchill recommended 'the invasion of Schleswig-Holstein from the seas' to threaten the Kiel Canal and induce the accession of Denmark to the allied cause.[2] But the Dardanelles was soon the favourite, supported by both Kitchener and Churchill. However, Sir John French insisted that only rain, fog, and a shortage of men and high explosives prevented him from breaking through the German lines by direct attack. So, on 13 January 1915, the war council compromised. Preparations were to be made to send two extra divisions to French for an advance to the Dutch frontier. A naval expedition against Gallipoli was sanctioned. And Lloyd George, who wanted a thrust from the Aegean through Greece to help the Serbs, was thrown a sop. If the position in the western theatre were to become one of stalemate in the spring then, it was agreed, troops should be dispatched to 'another theatre and objective'. A sub-committee of the Committee of Imperial Defence could investigate and prepare for such an operation.[3] No one bothered to define what criteria of stalemate were to be applied in the spring. Somehow everyone forgot that it was the alleged stalemate in France which made alternative operations, such as the attack on

[1] Ibid., vol. 1, pp. 372-3.
[2] Churchill to Asquith, 29 December 1914 (copy), Churchill MSS.
[3] Hankey, op. cit. vol. 1, pp. 261, 267.

the Dardanelles, desirable. Deference to military advisers for the time being precluded the elimination of these tiresome logical contradictions.

Lloyd George was not satisfied with the January compromise. As the proposed sub-committee investigation was not confined to any particular theatre, it could be used as the basis for a movement of troops to Gallipoli as well as his chosen areas of Salonika and Syria. The Balkan tangle was Lloyd George's special concern. And he made no secret of his views. Lord Esher told Kitchener on January 29 that:

> Lloyd George talked a good deal about Serbia; he replied that he was aware of it, and had no objection, because, he said, should the Germans hear of it, they would probably strengthen any force that they intended to send against the Serbians; that to do this would mean loss of time, and that the longer the time before any attack on Serbia was made, the better, and the more troops that were withdrawn from other areas of operation for that purpose, the weaker would any direct attack upon the Eastern or Western frontier become.[1]

To Lloyd George, Kitchener wrote on the same day: 'I think we all see the danger.' Kitchener continued: 'The difficulty is that our forces are tied up in France and that the situation requires a fighting force in Servia.'[2] Convinced that the Balkan states would not commit themselves 'until they see khaki', Lloyd George called on his colleagues 'not to dilly-dally any longer'.[3] To Churchill he addressed a clever appeal:

> Are we really bound to hand over the ordering of our troops to France as if we were her vassal? We have already sent her thrice our promise. Strategy in France must necessarily be hers to declare. Outside we are free after taking counsel with

[1] Esher's Diary, 29 January 1915, Esher MSS.
[2] Kitchener to Lloyd George, 29 January 1915, Lloyd George MSS, C/5/7/12 Lloyd George, *War Memoirs*, vol. I, p. 402.
[3] Lloyd George to Kitchener, 29 January 1915 (copy), Lloyd George MSS, C/5/7/13; Lloyd George to Grey, 7 February 1915, (copy), Lloyd George MSS, C/4/14/25, quoted ibid., p. 404 and p. 413. Copies of this letter were circulated to several other ministers.

her to take our own course. French dilatoriness, timidity and selfishness helped to lose Antwerp. It would be criminal folly if we allowed it to compel us to look on impotently while a catastrophe was being prepared for the Allies in the Balkans.[1]

Antwerp, that 'eccentric expedition',[2] as *The Morning Post* described it, was a tender subject for Churchill. In October, he had tried, by personal intervention, to stave off Antwerp's collapse. With the aid of some two thousand marines and four thousand naval volunteers, the First Lord covered the retirement of the Belgian Field Army and encouraged the Antwerp garrison to fight on for several days. Two French divisions promised as a relief force did not arrive. Many of the British naval division were interned, or captured. Some died. And Churchill's reputation was severely battered. He was attacked in *The Times* by Walter Long — the first breach of the party truce. Several of his colleagues found fault with the way in which he conducted the operation. Lloyd George complained to Frances Stevenson that Churchill 'behaved in rather a swaggering way when over there, standing for photographers and cinematographers with shells bursting near him, and actually promoting his pals on the field of action'.[3] Churchill was accused in several newspapers and in London gossip of futile and flamboyant irresponsibility.[4]

Churchill did not rise to Lloyd George's anti-French bait. Nor, apparently, was he any longer animated by the notion of an anti-Austrian Balkan federation with which he himself had fired his friend's imagination in the first week of the war.[5] On February 7, the First Lord did warn Asquith of the imminent danger in the Balkans. 'Surely,' asked Churchill, 'in your position you cannot be content to sit as a judge pronouncing on events *after* they have

[1] Lloyd George to Churchill, 29 January 1915, Churchill MSS.

[2] *The Morning Post*, 15 October 1914.

[3] Frances Stevenson's Diary, 23 October 1914, Lloyd George MSS.

[4] A. MacCallum Scott, M.P., *Winston Churchill in Peace and War* (London, 1916), Chapter IX, is an informed contemporary account which contended, against Churchill's critics, that the First Lord was 'open to attack only by those who take the narrowest and most limited views of military operations, who would never sacrifice a pawn to save a piece' (p. 117).

[5] Emmott's Diary, 11 August 1914 (referring to August 7), Emmott MSS, records Lloyd George's early enthusiasm for a Balkan project.

taken place.'[1] But, in the ensuing weeks, the entrancing prospect of a master-stroke at the Dardanelles diverted Churchill's thoughts from the general problem of the Balkans. Lloyd George, less single-minded, found himself in a tactical dilemma. Late in February he leaned towards supporting Churchill's request for a sizable military force to be moved within hailing distance of Gallipoli. But he wavered on the use to which such a force should be put. On February 22 he wrote that a failure of the Dardanelles effort '...will be disastrous in the Balkans, and might very well be disastrous throughout the East...There must be a strong British force there available to support our friends.'[2]

Two days later, at the war council, his emphasis had altered:

Mr Lloyd George agreed that a force ought to be sent to the Levant, which could, if necessary, be used after the Navy had cleared the Dardanelles to occupy the Gallipoli Peninsula or Constantinople ... [He] hoped that the Army would not be required or expected to pull the chestnuts out of the fire for the Navy. If we failed at the Dardanelles we ought to be ready immediately to try something else. In his opinion we were committed by this operation to some action in the Near East, but not necessarily to a siege of the Dardanelles.[3]

With fading hope of success, Lloyd George fought on into March in an attempt to swing the cabinet round to a policy of territorial concession attractive enough to bring Bulgaria into the war on the side of the Entente.[4] Asquith recorded on February 26 that 'Lloyd George is anxious to go out as a kind of extra ambassador and emissary to visit all the Balkan States and try and bring them in'. The Foreign Secretary, not surprisingly, was 'dead opposed to anything of the kind'.[5] And Lloyd George's scheme of attacking Austria in alliance with the Serbians, the Roumanians, and the Greeks, met other obstacles before it was finally stymied by the Greek refusal to allow British troops to land at Salonika. It required men, and trained men were in heavy demand. Kitchener

---

[1] Churchill to Asquith, 7 February 1915 (copy), Churchill MSS.
[2] 'Some further considerations on the conduct of the war', cabinet memorandum by Lloyd George, 22 February 1915. Lloyd George *War Memoirs*, vol. 1, pp. 430–1.
[3] Minutes of the war council, 24 February 1915. Ibid., pp. 418–19.
[4] Mosa Anderson, *Noel Buxton* (London, 1952), pp. 73–7.
[5] Asquith to Venetia Stanley, 26 February 1915, Montagu MSS.

admitted privately at the end of January that he would prefer not to send out more troops until the end of April.[1] Moreover, as Sir William Robertson was later to point out, there were elementary strategic flaws in the Chancellor of the Exchequer's conception:

> ...we could not alter the geography of Europe which conferred upon the enemy the advantage of a central position... Mr Lloyd George's plan would gratuitously provide an additional means of utilizing this advantage, since the enemy could transfer troops by rail to the new front in, say, two or three days, whereas we, condemned to move on the outside of the circle by sea, would for the same operation take as many weeks.[2]

The Lloyd George plan, to which Asquith was at first sympathetic, entailed that the expeditionary force in France should be depleted, and that the troops thus assembled, together with new formations from England, should be sent to assist Serbia and strike at Austria.[3] Without knowing who the author of this idea had been, Henry Wilson wrote: 'Anything more insane I cannot imagine.'[4] Perhaps the only operation which, in Wilson's opinion, came close to this one in lunacy was the one which found favour in its stead: the Dardanelles adventure, 'Heaven help us,' Wilson implored on learning of the war council's decision to mount a naval expedition.[5] Churchill won assent for this plan—despite the misgivings of the First Sea Lord—by tenacious argument, and because he originally offered success without the commitment of troops away from France. 'It is not until all the Northern possibilities are exhausted that I wd look to the S of Europe as a field for the profitable employment of our expanding milty forces,' Churchill assured Sir John French on January 11.[6] Yet, notwithstanding this initial reservation and the hesitations of many ministers and official advisers, the Dardanelles operation, once begun, developed an irresistible momentum.

[1] Esher's Journal, 29 January 1915, Esher MSS.

[2] Field-Marshal Sir William Robertson, Bt., *Soldiers and Statesmen, 1914-1918*, 2 vols, (London, 1926), vol. II, p. 87.

[3] Asquith to Venetia Stanley, 21-22, 26 and 31 January, 8, 9, 13 and 17 February 1915, Montagu MSS.

[4] Wilson's Diary, 11 January 1915, Wilson MSS.

[5] Wilson's Diary, 17 January 1915, Wilson MSS.

[6] Churchill to French, 11 January 1915 (copy), Churchill MSS.

The prospect of carving up the Turkish Empire, though it was never part of Churchill's motivation, engaged the imaginations of several of his colleagues. Even the Conservative leaders were brought to a meeting of the war council to discuss 'the future of Constantinople & the Straits, and other cognate matters'.[1] Arthur Balfour had believed from the beginning of 1915 that if Turkey were completely paralysed the Russians would be able to bring troops from the Caucasus to Galicia and British troops could be taken from Egypt to German East Africa or 'some European theatre of operations'.

But there were longer-term considerations to be examined. At the war council on March 19, Lloyd George suggested that Germany ought perhaps to receive 'a bone of some sort' from the Turkish joint. To crush Germany altogether would prevent her from acting as a barrier to Russian ambition in Europe. While this and other proposals for dismemberment were under discussion, Kitchener, after much delay, agreed to provide troops to follow up the naval assault. The stakes grew higher. By April 8, the only hope that Henry Wilson had for the expedition was that it would fail, 'and to fail might, ought to, mean the *dégommé* of Winston & this would be cheap at the money'.[2]

Being a critic of the Dardanelles policy, frustrating though it was, had real advantages. Failure at the Dardanelles could not possibly be blamed on Lloyd George. Although, as John P. Mackintosh has said, 'the missing factor in the whole story is leadership from the Prime Minister',[3] it was not Asquith who suffered most by the ill-fortune of the expedition. Nor was it Kitchener, in spite of the great responsibility which he had for delaying the commitment of an adequate military force. The scapegoat was Churchill. Tragic though the Dardanelles fiasco was for the First Lord, its most significant political consequence was its effect on the reputation of Lloyd George. After April 1915, he was the only figure in the first rank of the Liberal Party who was untarnished either by responsibility for precipitating war or for setbacks in the field.

[1] Asquith to Lansdowne, 8 March 1915, Lansdowne MSS.
[2] Wilson's Diary, 8 April 1915, Wilson MSS.
[3] John P. Mackintosh, *The British Cabinet*, 2nd edn., (London, 1968), p. 353.

10 Munitions and Kitchener

In the middle of March 1915, the Prime Minister considered relieving Lloyd George of his Treasury duties, and creating for the ex-Chancellor of the Exchequer a post of 'Director of War Contracts or something of the kind'.[1] Two weeks earlier, Arthur Balfour had written to Lloyd George that he could see no possibility of improvement in the supply of shells and rifles 'unless you will take in hand the organization of the engineering resources of the country'.[2] For a few days in March Lloyd George seems to have thought over the idea of assuming personal responsibility for munitions production. In an undated note preserved in the Lloyd George papers there is a bald outline of a new Ministry of Contracts to be headed by Lloyd George. In the hand of Edwin Montagu, who cast himself as Deputy Minister and 'devil for George', was a short list of businessmen, politicians, and civil servants who would presumably have been associated with the ministry.[3]

Having come to the conclusion that 'we could double our effective energies if we organized our factories thoroughly',[4] Lloyd George tried from September 1914 to slash a way through what Montagu called the War Office's 'continued, bigoted, prejudiced reluctance to buy rifles or to increase the munitions of war'.[5] Short of removing munitions supply altogether from the control of Lord Kitchener, the only expedient that offered any prospect of improving a position that was widely recognized as

[1] Asquith to Venetia Stanley, 18 March 1915, Montagu MSS.
[2] Balfour to Lloyd George, 5 March 1915, Lloyd George MSS, C/3/3/1. Lloyd George, *War Memoirs*, vol. 1, p. 172. Balfour's letter and Lloyd George's reply were both composed with the aid of Maurice Hankey. (Hankey's Diary, 6 March 1915. Hankey, op. cit., vol. 1, p. 311.)
[3] Note by Edwin Montagu, (?March) 1915, Lloyd George MSS, C/14/3/19.
[4] David Lloyd George, 'Some further considerations on the conduct of the War', cabinet memorandum, 22 February 1915. Lloyd George, *War Memoirs*, vol. 1, p. 169.
[5] Montagu to Asquith (?March/April), 1915, ibid., p. 183.

unsatisfactory was the creation of committees with special authority co-ordinate with the War Office. But Kitchener obdurately obstructed the attempts of each body which tried to get to grips with the problem. In April, the Secretary of State for War created a committee of his own nominees, the Armaments Output Committee, chaired by George Macaulay Booth, the Liverpool shipowner. This body was outflanked by the Munitions of War Committee appointed a few days later by Asquith. Lloyd George was chairman of this 'Treasury Committee' as it was generally known. According to the official history: 'The Munitions of War Committee was in fact an embryo Ministry of Munitions.'[1]

The breakdown of munitions supply in the first half of 1915 was not the fault of Kitchener. The War Office contract system which he inherited was partly to blame, as was the reckless overcommitment of the armaments firms to production targets which they were incapable of reaching. Unselective recruiting for the armed forces complicated the problem by taking irreplaceable skilled men away from the factories. Kitchener himself seems to have realized from the beginning of his tenure at the War Office that the standing arrangements for munitions supply were unsuitable for war conditions. In conversation with Walter Runciman, Kitchener said that in a continental war the President of the Board of Trade should be made Joint Secretary of State for War, Supply Department. According to Hubert Llewellyn Smith, the Permanent Secretary at the Board of Trade, Kitchener went on to say:

> The old-fashioned little British Army was such an infinitely small proportion of the world's demand that looking after its equipment was not much more difficult than buying a straw hat at Harrods. But now I am going to need greater quantities of many things than have ever been made before, and I fancy this will be equally true of the Navy and perhaps the Flying Corps. Surely we cannot allow competition to arise, as will be inevitable between the Services unless there is some central control of the distribution of supplies.[2]

[1] *History of the Ministry of Munitions:* vol. 1, Industrial Mobilisation, 1914–1915: part I, Munitions Supply (London, 1922), p. 135.

[2] G. M. Booth's Diary, (?) August 1914, recording Llewellyn Smith's version of Runciman's account of a talk with Kitchener. Duncan Crow, op. cit. ,p. 71.

Whatever glimmer of understanding Kitchener revealed to Runciman, in practice, the only centralization which he encouraged was in his own office. The Secretary of State's attitude to the problem of supplying munitions can be explained partly by the fact that he was served by an incompetent Master-General of the Ordnance, Sir Stanley von Donop, partly by his own ignorance of both War Office and business procedures, and by his obsessional insistence on secrecy.[1] Since he objected to giving any figures about the number of men whom it was proposed would be under arms at a given date, the Treasury Committee had no firm basis for planning. Balfour was reduced to suggesting that Kitchener should be invited to state that *no* additions to the supply of arms would be in excess of the army's requirements.[2]

The critical attitude of Lloyd George to War Office procedures probably provoked as much resistance as it overcame. Kitchener's obstructionism sometimes only makes sense if it is interpreted as instinctive self-preservation. Accustomed all his life to taking and giving orders, the Secretary of State found the cut and thrust of cabinet discussion and comradeship a strange milieu. He took too seriously the casual charges thrown out in verbal combat. And his colleagues made insufficient allowance for his unfamiliarity with their mode of decision-making. Once, in quarrelling with Kitchener over his secrecy, Lloyd George 'let slip', Asquith noted, 'some injurious and wounding innuendoes which K. will be more than human to forget'.[3] Only extreme provocation would have wrung deliberately hurtful phrases out of Lloyd George. But a style of debate and personal criticism at which Liberal ministers were practised exponents made Kitchener resentful and defensive.

An early clash between Lloyd George and Kitchener had occurred over the creation of a Welsh division. 'George let fly at K. of K', Pease recorded on 28 October 1914, 'because he had taken Welsh regiments into his new army & prevented a Welsh division or corps being formed. He let him have it straight. K. said he would resign.'[4] Angered also by an order that Welsh

---

[1] Among many critical comments, the assessment of von Donop by a senior official at the Board of Trade, G. S. Barnes, was probably the most summary: 'Von Donop ought to be hung'. (Barnes to Lord Buxton, 21 May 1915, Buxton MSS.)

[2] Balfour to Lloyd George, 17 April 1915, Lloyd George MSS, C/3/3/6.

[3] Asquith to Venetia Stanley, 16 April 1915, Montagu MSS.

[4] Pease's Diary, 28 October 1914, Gainford MSS.

troops could not speak Welsh on the parade ground or in their billets, Lloyd George, on his own admission, 'spoke to Kitchener in a way that gentleman had never been spoken to before'.[1] According to Frances Stevenson's account of Lloyd George's version of the story:

> Kitchener got angry, and suggested that perhaps C. [Chancellor, i.e. Lloyd George] would like to take over the management of the W.O. Whereupon C. remarked that he was only one among 19, and must stand criticism in the same way as any other member of the Cabinet. He (K.) was not a dictator, and if things were not mended at the W.O. the Chancellor would criticize him in the House of Commons and in the Cabinet.[2]

This 'royal row', as Asquith called it, was quickly patched up.[3] But the surface civilities which ensued did not repair the breach of confidence, however well they screened barriers of mutual incomprehension. Lloyd George told Churchill at the time:

> I am in despair over the stupidity of the War Office. You might imagine we were alien enemies who ought to be interned at Frimley until we had mastered the intricacies of the English language sufficiently to be able to converse on equal terms with an East End recruit.[4]

Walter Runciman reported to Sir Robert Chalmers in February 1915 that 'K. gives most proper deference to our Welshman now'.[5] Yet Kitchener remained uncommunicative: 'were it not for Winston & L.G. asking Kitchener questions we shd have precious little enlightenment on military questions,' wrote a newcomer to the cabinet.[6]

By the middle of April 1915 Kitchener had accepted that Lloyd George had a special position in relation to munitions questions.

[1] T. P. O'Connor to Redmond, 27 February 1915. Denis Gwynn, *The Life of John Redmond*, p. 327.

[2] Frances Stevenson's Diary, 30 October 1914, Lloyd George MSS.

[3] Asquith to Venetia Stanley, 28 October 1914, Montagu MSS; Pease's Diary, 30 October 1914, Gainford MSS; Frances Stevenson's Diary, 2 November 1914, Lloyd George MSS.

[4] Lloyd George to Churchill, 28 October 1914, Churchill MSS.

[5] Runciman to Chalmers, 7 February 1915, Runciman MSS.

[6] Emmott's Diary, 4 January 1915, Emmott MSS.

And, in the next month, G. M. Booth effected a practical reconciliation between the overlapping committees concerned with armaments. Meanwhile, Lloyd George was once again engaged in preparations for a Budget; and he had taken up with characteristic energy the problem of excessive drinking by the working population. On this latter subject, the Chancellor of the Exchequer for once found common ground with the Secretary of State for War.[1]

[1] In a speech in the House of Lords on 15 March 1915, Kitchener referred to absenteeism, slack work, and irregular timekeeping caused 'in some cases [by] the temptations of drink'. (Sir George Arthur, op. cit., vol. III, p. 86.)

11 Men and Masterman

As he increasingly engaged his mind with the problems of war organization Lloyd George brought to the task three major qualifications: unflagging energy, receptiveness to new ideas, and a rare ability as a negotiator with management and labour.

The dynamism of the Chancellor of the Exchequer had never been questioned. And to the intense driving determination of his peace-time administration he added an element of ruthlessness in dealing with subordinates. 'In ordinary times one can spare time and tissue to soothe the vanities and jealousies of civil servants who magnify their offices—but these are not ordinary times,' he told Edwin Montagu.[1] Languishing as Governor of Ceylon, Sir Robert Chalmers, sometime Permanent Secretary to the Treasury, could have testified that even the Lloyd George of ordinary times was not a man to be dominated by his official advisers. Sir John Bradbury and Sir Malcolm Ramsay had to be taught the same lesson. After one particularly irritating example of departmental petty-mindedness, Lloyd George gave vent to his feelings in a letter to Montagu:

The fact of the matter is Bradbury is suffering from swelled head. His rapid promotion and the great advertisement given to his name by the new notes [Bank of England notes bearing Bradbury's signature] have been too much for his nerves. He talked to me yesterday—at least he started to talk to me—as if I were the boots and he were scolding me for deflowering his 'tweeny' maid without his consent. I soon reminded him of our relations ... Bradbury and Ramsay can

[1] Lloyd George to Montagu, 24 January 1915 (copy), Lloyd George MSS, C/1/2/5.

go to hell—the only fit abode for men who nurse grievances in a great crisis.[1]

If hell was the only place fit for civil servants who nursed grievances, limbo was the appropriate destination for politicians whose slackness and timidity impaired their contributions to the war effort. Relegated to the unglamorous activity of co-ordinating foreign propaganda, Charles Masterman was one of those who had time to reflect in 1915 on the inadvisability of falling afoul of the nation's most powerful men. Masterman's fall from the cabinet and disappearance from Parliament was an irreparable interruption to a career of rich promise. One of the Liberal Party's leading spokesmen on social reform, he had been elevated to the cabinet as Chancellor of the Duchy of Lancaster in February 1914. From being an acolyte, spreading the gospel of Lloyd George and Churchill, he was on the verge of standing on a level of equality with the prophets of reform. One obstacle frustrated him. He was obliged by the law of the day to resign his seat and submit himself for the electors' approval before taking the new office. Resign he did; win the support of the majority of his constituents he could not. He lost South-West Bethnal Green by twenty-four votes. He lost a vacant seat at Ipswich in May 1914 by a large margin. Then, for eleven months, from peace into war, he continued to attend the cabinet without having a place in the House of Commons.

Masterman had been reluctant to stand at Ipswich. He blamed Percy Illingworth and Lloyd George for encouraging him to try a dangerous contest; and he attributed the loss of many votes to Lloyd George's Insurance Act, which he had helped to pilot through the House of Commons. Lloyd George himself thought that Masterman had fought a bad campaign, unwisely failing to answer some of the attacks aimed at him by the Northcliffe press and the East Anglian Tories. According to Lord Riddell, Masterman and Lloyd George had, at this time, 'the only serious quarrel they had ever had'.[2]

---

[1] Lloyd George to Montagu, 24 January 1915 (copy), Lloyd George MSS, C/1/2/5; Bradbury was Joint Permanent Secretary and Ramsay was Assistant Secretary at the Treasury. I am indebted to Sir Horace Hamilton for illuminating comments on the Treasury officials under whom he served in this period.

[2] Riddell's Diary, 24 May 1914. Riddell, *More Pages From My Diary, 1908–1914*, p. 213.

Seven months later a fresh vacancy occurred at Swansea; and in the discussions over whether Masterman should be a candidate for this seat, there developed a tragic misunderstanding between the two men. Although he was not originally consulted about Masterman's candidature, Lloyd George came to believe that the Swansea opportunity was too good to be missed. The local party leaders were ready to welcome Masterman. But there was a difficulty. A Welsh candidate with nationalist support threatened to stand as an unofficial Liberal if Masterman, an outsider, was given the nomination. Masterman asked Lloyd George to see his opponent and persuade him to withdraw. This was a request which Lloyd George could not possibly oblige. Whatever his private sympathies, he could not, for his own or the Welsh Liberal Party's sake, be seen to be deeply involved in a manœuvre to prevent the nationalist from winning the seat, particularly as the Welshman in question, Jeremiah Williams, was a local man, popular, wealthy, and the son of a former M.P. for the same constituency. However, Lloyd George took pains to discover that the majority of the Swansea Liberal Party were in favour of Masterman's candidature; he left the Swansea party leaders in no doubt about his own preference for Masterman, and he advised Masterman to go down to Swansea and fight it out.

Fortified by the inquiries of Jack Pease, who was acting temporarily as Chief Whip, Lloyd George had come to the conclusion that, if Masterman declared himself in the contest, Jeremiah Williams would stand down. 'Personally,' Jack Pease wrote, 'I think Masterman's political career is in great danger, if any white feather is shewn now ... He has no personal ties by residence or interest in any constituency which is calculated to help him.'[1] This was also Lloyd George's opinion. Masterman, however, had misgivings about his chances in a Welsh constituency. He was concerned, too, that a local dispute might upset the electoral truce. For this reason, rather than immediately follow Lloyd George's suggestion to throw himself into the fight, he sought the advice of the Prime Minister. Asquith, as was to be expected, stated that he did not want a contest. This, Masterman all too readily interpreted as an instruction to stay away from Swansea

[1] Pease to Lloyd George, 1 January 1915, Lloyd George MSS, C/4/12/8.

altogether. On January 7 he declined the formal invitation of the Swansea District party to accept nomination.

It seemed to Lloyd George that Masterman was using the Prime Minister's formal wish to maintain the party truce as an excuse to evade a contest which, 'fearing personal issues and a doubtful result', as Pease put it, he had no desire to undertake.[1] It was hardly surprising that Lloyd George should be angered by his associate's timidity. He realized that Asquith could not officially sanction Masterman's candidature if it involved a contest. But bold action—to which the Prime Minister could have turned a blind eye—might have made a contest unnecessary. Although neither Masterman nor many of his contemporaries realized it, Lloyd George had gone out of his way to smoothe Masterman's path behind the scenes. Mrs Lucy Masterman, in her biography of her husband, writes as though Lloyd George's advice about Swansea amounted to irresponsible flouting of the Prime Minister's instructions.[2] What Mrs Masterman understandably does not point out is that her husband's cynicism and rudeness—for all that it was partly a protective shell and affected mannerism—and his insobriety, had lost him the active sympathy of a number of his colleagues. As the new Chief Whip, John Gulland, told Christopher Addison, the Prime Minister himself had 'grown tired and will make no special effort to keep him'.[3] Lloyd George did not desert or betray his friend. But he did, as Lady Lloyd-George has recently testified, 'regard this incident as a slight both to himself and to Wales, ... he did take great offence, and the two friends drifted apart'.[4]

To many politicians and observers of the Westminster scene, the estrangement between Lloyd George and Masterman had a different aspect—in spite of the fact that it was quickly ended when Masterman apologized in April for having treated Lloyd George badly.[5] A colleague suffering misfortune was apparently abandoned by a friend firmly entrenched in office and possessed of sufficient influence to have effected a rescue if he had chosen to do so. The truth was more complex. But the illusion, regret-

[1] Pease to Lloyd George, 1 January 1915, Lloyd George MSS, C/4/12/8.
[2] Lucy Masterman, C. F. G. Masterman, p. 270.
[3] Addison's Diary, 28 January 1915. Addison, op. cit., vol. 1, p. 60.
[4] Frances Lloyd George, op. cit., p. 45.
[5] Frances Stevenson's Diary, 18 April 1915, Lloyd George MSS.

tably shared by Masterman himself, fed the suspicions of those who, in subsequent months, began to have misgivings about what appeared to them to be a ruthless bid for power by Lloyd George.[1]

'There is no friendship at the top,' Lloyd George often said, repeating a friendly warning that had been given to him early in his career. And as one who had risen from obscure origins to backbench and then to ministerial fame, he had inevitably moved through and beyond the social circles of his youth and young manhood. Losing close touch with many of his old friends, he did not seek the embrace of established London society. Rather, he drifted into the company of men who, like himself, had carved out their own fortunes: among them, Sir George Riddell, proprietor of the *News of the World*, Harold Spender, political journalist, Rufus Isaacs, Jewish lawyer. Even Winston Churchill, Lloyd George's closest political ally, despite his aristocratic lineage and political birthright, was a maverick who owed the high place he had secured in national life to individual exertion and courageous espousal of a doctrine in which he believed.

In politics, Lloyd George never allowed himself the luxury of sentimental attachments divorced from respect and trust in a person's capacity for public business. Thus, although he admired Masterman's abilities, he could not condone his slackness and intemperance. In trying to get Masterman back into Parliament the Chancellor's motive was probably, in part, the hope of rehabilitating a useful colleague who had allowed misfortune to pierce his inhibitions. There was nothing in Lloyd George's actions in the Masterman affair to suggest that he was prompted by an impulse of pure friendship, if such a quality can be isolated.

Because so much of Lloyd George's existence was a political existence, most of those who developed more than a passing acquaintance with him did so as a result of mutual involvement in political affairs. In long hours of working together at complicated pieces of legislation, or in controversial negotiations, a sense of friendship could often be generated. For Lloyd George,

[1] For a fuller exposition of the background to the 'Masterman–Lloyd George split', see my article in *New Outlook*, No. 72 (July/August 1968), pp. 33–9; see also Mrs Masterman's admission: 'We did not know that the Swansea invitation was due to his [Lloyd George's] exertions or we would have handled the situation differently.' (*New Outlook*, No. 74 [October 1968], p. 50.)

however, the private courtesies and entertainments which resulted from such contacts were usually no more than passing elements in his working routine. He himself had neither the wealth nor the taste for social intercourse on the scale of the Asquiths, the Harcourts, or the Beauchamps. It followed, therefore, that new projects and fresh political responsibilities, in creating new personal relationships, severed old ones. Lloyd George's preoccupation with the work of the moment allowed him to terminate without a pang friendships which others cherished, thus contributing to a legend that he made use of people only as long as they served an immediate purpose. In an objective sense, whatever he felt about it, he did behave at times in a way that appeared ungrateful, and even cruel.

Yet, despite his repeated failures to sustain close personal relationships, Lloyd George possessed a unique facility for mediation and negotiation. With groups of men who, as well as being riven by disputes of their own, were sometimes distrustful of Lloyd George himself, he exercised an uncanny skill. As Walter Runciman once put it, describing the settlement of the railway dispute in 1907, 'geniality, finesse, & a certain bold art were the qualities which made his success'.[1] In an age when the fear of bureaucratic control was in vogue, a minister who rarely looked inhibited by a departmental brief enjoyed peculiar advantages. It could not be said by any deputation met by Lloyd George that he was 'practically run and controlled by his permanent officials'. Unlike his colleagues, of whom this complaint was heard several times at T.U.C. meetings before and during the war, he had a refreshing eagerness to talk what sounded like common sense.[2] He was one of the few ministers whom it was not correct to describe as 'strangely outside and ignorant of the labour movements in the country'.[3]

Lloyd George's skill as an industrial negotiator, well proven before the war, was to have special value after August 1914. It was that skill which enabled him, in March 1915, to capitalize

[1] Runciman to Hilda Runciman (?1907), Runciman MSS.

[2] For the complaint about excessive power in the hands of permanent officials of government departments see the speech by J. C. Gordon (Sheet Metal Workers), 7 September 1915. *Proceedings at the Forty-Seventh Annual Trades Union Congress*, p. 307.

[3] Lord Askwith, *Industrial Problems and Disputes*, p. 351.

on the workers' spirit of concession and produce agreements, known as the Treasury Agreements, with the unions mainly concerned in munitions work. For the duration of the war, the union leaders recommended to their members the cessation of restrictive practices and the surrender of their rights to stop work —privileges which had been won at great cost. In return, the government undertook to restrict the profits of munitions firms. Much of the preliminary discussion and planning for the Treasury Conference at which Lloyd George's persuasive powers were employed had been handled by officials from the War Office and Admiralty and Sir George Askwith of the Board of Trade. The ground had been well prepared:

> It remained only to persuade the Trade Union leaders, already more than half persuaded, that the Government were in desperate earnest both in their appeal to them and in their promise that labour should not be prejudiced after the War if they listened to the appeal ... On all those present weighed a consciousness that they were dealing not only in words, not even in vast industrial negotiations, but in the life and death of a people.[1]

In that setting, Lloyd George's eloquence was irresistible. He communicated a conviction that the concessions for which the government was asking were essential to the survival of the nation. Perhaps, like some of his colleagues, he saw a negotiated voluntary arrangement as a precursor to legislation. Perhaps, too, he shared Sir Edward Grey's desire for a voluntary agreement which would 'secure the goodwill of workmen and enable the Government to avert or settle strikes, while leaving the management of the works as now in the hands of the employers'.[2] Winston Churchill had argued vigorously against the suggestion that 'the workmen of armament firms have any grievance against their employers on the ground of excessive profits'. In Churchill's view, industrial discontent was a product of 'class envy and an

---

[1] Humbert Wolfe, *Labour Supply and Regulation* (London, 1923), p. 152. Wolfe served in the Board of Trade from 1907–15; he was secretary to the Treasury Committee on Munitions of War and Controller of the Labour Regulation Department in the Ministry of Munitions.

[2] Grey to Kitchener, 2 March 1915 (copy), Grey MSS, FO 800/102.

anti-war spirit, seeking a permissible form of expression'.[1] This was not the general opinion. Charles Masterman told the President of the Board of Trade that there was 'a very strong undercurrent of feeling that some people (no one quite knows who) are exploiting the working classes and making big profits out of the war'.[2]

Whatever were the facts about profiteering, an undercurrent of suspicion and resentment undoubtedly did exist. Lloyd George's original plan had been to use an amendment to the Defence of the Realm Act to institute compulsory arbitration in labour disputes. Excess profits could be distributed to the labour force in the form of wage awards. But, according to the *History of the Ministry of Munitions*, the proposed clauses were cancelled because of the fear that they might embarrass negotiations that were then in progress on the Clyde and in other places.[3] A week before the Conference at the Treasury, Lloyd George had introduced the Defence of the Realm Act No. II into the House of Commons. It was 'a very drastic measure for the control of private industry'.[4] Power was taken to convert any factory in the country to the production of war material under government control.

Parliament was taken by surprise. Not knowing of the shortage of munitions, many people felt that such a vast increase of public control was disproportionate to the needs of the hour. 'Is this Government going to end, having begun so well, as a panic Govt?' asked H. W. Massingham. 'Many shakings of heads there must be over L.G.'s speech & the measure it expounded.'[5] So large an encroachment on the area of private enterprise alarmed traditional Liberals. At the same time it did not satisfy Labour men that the interests of the working population would be safeguarded. Asked by Sir George Riddell why he personally had introduced the Bill, Lloyd George replied: 'All the others were afraid. They thought there would be a terrible row in the House of Commons. It was not my job, but I agreed to do it.'[6] Having done it, the Chancellor did his best to convince union leaders that,

[1] 'Armament Firms', cabinet memorandum by Churchill, 3 March 1915, *Cab.* 37/125/9.

[2] Masterman to Runciman, 19 February 1915, Runciman MSS.

[3] *History of the Ministry of Munitions*, vol. I, part II, pp. 63–4.

[4] Ibid., p. 64.

[5] Massingham to Runciman, n.d. (? March 1915), Runciman MSS.

[6] Riddell's Diary, 13 March 1915. *Lord Riddell's War Diary*, p. 68.

if they made sacrifices, the government would ensure that the benefits which resulted would not go into the pockets of any particular individual or class.[1] In fact, the Treasury Agreement of 19 March 1915 was no more than an expression of opinion. 'The rank and file', Sir George Askwith wrote after the war, 'were scarcely touched by the bargain.'[2] For a few months, however, it seemed that an agreement of substance had been reached. And for that boon the thanks of the nation accrued most of all to Lloyd George.

[1] There is a full report of Lloyd George's address in *Proceedings of the Forty-Seventh Trades Union Congress, 1915*, pp. 220–2.

[2] Lord Askwith, op. cit., pp. 382–3. Neither the General Federation of Trade Unions nor the National Union of Railwaymen had even been invited to the Treasury meetings. J. H. Thomas of the N.U.R. protested that 'this renders our position open to very serious misunderstanding'. (Thomas to Lloyd George, 18 March 1915; see also W. A. Appleton to Lloyd George, 19 March 1915, Lloyd George MSS, C/11/3/28, 30.)

12 'Another Little Drink'[1]

'LG is now off thinking of anything but drink,' Asquith commented at the end of March 1915.[2] On March 29, a deputation from the Shipbuilding Employers' Federation called upon the Chancellor of the Exchequer and the Secretary of State for Scotland to argue the case for total prohibition for the rest of the war. In response, Lloyd George was reported as saying:

I have a growing conviction, based on accumulating evidence, that nothing but root and branch methods will be of the slightest avail in dealing with the evil. I believe that to be the general feeling. The feeling is that if we are to settle German militarism we must first of all settle with the drink. We are fighting Germany, Austria and Drink; and, as far as I can see, the greatest of these three deadly foes is Drink.[3]

The campaign against excessive drinking and the consequent diminution of the output of munitions had begun with a speech by Lloyd George at Bangor on February 28. 'Drink is doing us more damage in the War than all the German submarines put together,' the Chancellor declared.[4] These vaguely calculated ravages hit the pockets of the arms manufacturers, as well as the ammunition supply of the army and navy; and it is clear that much of the initial enthusiasm for some measure of control of alcohol consumption came from the munitions firms. The public

[1] A song performed by George Robey in the revue, 'The Bing Boys'.
[2] Asquith to Venetia Stanley, 31 March 1915, Montagu MSS.
[3] *The Times*, 30 March 1915. The opinions of various armament and shipbuilding firms were reported in a letter and memorandum from Sir George Askwith to Lloyd George, 24 March 1915, Lloyd George MSS, C/3/2/3.
[4] *The Times*, 1 March 1915.

deputation of March 31 was preceded by 'a secret and confidential conference' on March 19 with representatives of Vickers.[1]

There were other supporters. The King took a pledge of abstinence until the end of the war. Lord Kitchener accepted the same restraint. The Conservative leaders agreed not to oppose a proposal for state purchase of the entire liquor trade if the government thought it necessary as a war measure.[2] On April 11, the government Chief Whip wrote confidently to his sister: 'L.G. has got a *very* big scheme on hand & as usual he will probably get his own way.'[3] But the nature of the scheme was uncertain. In the Prime Minister's eyes, Lloyd George's unpredictability on this matter demonstrated a lack of 'perspective or judgment':

His mind apparently oscillates from hour to hour between the two poles of absurdity: cutting off all drink from the working man, which wd. lead to something like a universal strike; and buying out (at this moment of all others) the whole liquor trade of the country, and replacing it by a huge State monopoly, which wd. ruin our finances and create a vast engine of possible corruption.[4]

Oscillating between the two poles of absurdity, Lloyd George's proposals encountered immovable obstacles. It was possible to produce much evidence—even 'overwhelming evidence' as Lord Northcliffe was told in a private appeal for help[5]—of the grave mischief caused by excessive drinking in the major munitions and transport centres. Strong action was justified. But strong action, as Asquith noted, carried with it all sorts of dangers. There was the danger that sweeping charges of incompetence, idleness, and insobriety would provoke a hostile reaction from those men—

[1] Memorandum by Sir Vincent Caillard, 19 March 1915, Lloyd George MSS, C/5/7/26. Caillard was a director of Vickers.

[2] Blake, *The Unknown Prime Minister*, p. 239; Bonar Law to Lord Robert Cecil, 1 April 1915, Cecil of Chelwood MSS (Add. MS. 51161, f. 215); Bonar Law to Chamberlain, 2 April 1915, Austen Chamberlain MSS, 13/3/39.

[3] Gulland to Elsie Osborne, 11 April 1915, Gulland MSS.

[4] Asquith to Venetia Stanley, 31 March 1915, Montagu MSS. Mr Jenkins (p. 338) incorrectly dates this letter to March 3. Asquith (op. cit., vol. II, p. 71) suppressed a number of important phrases in his version of this 'aide-memoire'.

[5] Lloyd George to Northcliffe, 15 April 1915 (copy), Northcliffe MSS.

probably a majority of workers—who were sober and industrious.[1] And there were the ultimately more formidable difficulties of negotiating a scheme of state purchase at a price acceptable to all parties, and of convincing the fanatical temperance forces that state control was not a greater evil than the existing practice of financing government spending through taxes on liquor.

Lloyd George wanted nationalization. *The Spectator* gave its editorial blessing to state purchase. *The Nation* carried an article in its favour by E. Richard Cross, an old associate of Lloyd George from Land Campaign days.[2] Confidentially, Strachey of *The Spectator* wrote: 'I love to see a man speak out plainly as you did and throw his cap over the wall and follow it, as I am sure you mean to do.'[3] Joseph Rowntree and George Lansbury wrote privately to commend what Rowntree called 'the bold course'.[4] Asquith, however, vetoed the 'Great Purchase Folly'. The hostility of many local optionists and abstainers, together with the complex problem of negotiating with 'the whole motley crowd of interests', convinced Asquith that a less ambitious scheme was needed.[5] In spite of Joseph Rowntree's prophecy that the opposition of the temperance forces would have no electoral significance, the Prime Minister encouraged Lloyd George to produce a substitute plan. This entailed additional taxes on the strongest alcoholic drinks, and state power, under the Defence of the Realm Act, to control the liquor traffic in areas producing or transporting war material. Kitchener and Churchill were 'doughty supporters' of the compromise suggestions; and the bankers could not argue, as they had against state

[1] This point was pressed by Sir Frederick Donaldson of the Woolwich Works in a letter brought to Lloyd George's attention on 5 April 1915, Lloyd George MSS, C/5/7/20. There was much contemporary talk of a 'general demoralisation' of the population. But, as one commentator wrote: 'The general lessening of regard for strict honesty is probably more of a revelation which has come about owing to the war than an actual creation of it.' (Cecil M. Chapman, 'War and Criminality', *Sociological Review*, vol. IX [Spring 1917], p. 84.)

[2] *The Spectator*, *The Nation*, 17 April 1915.

[3] Strachey to Lloyd George, 30 March 1915, Lloyd George MSS, C/11/3/41.

[4] George Lansbury to Lloyd George, 2 May 1915; Joseph Rowntree to Lloyd George, 7 May 1915. Lloyd George MSS, C/11/3/57,65.

[5] Asquith to Venetia Stanley, 15 April 1915, Montagu MSS. Several leading temperance advocates supported state purchase, among them Sir Thomas Whittaker and Charles Roberts, as well as Joseph Rowntree. (See especially, Charles Roberts to Lloyd George, 30 March 1915, Lloyd George MSS, C/4/1/17).

purchase of the whole trade, that the available supply of capital would be absorbed.[1]

The diluted proposals were presented to the House of Commons on April 29. A fortnight later the government had secured powers of purchase under D.O.R.A.; but of the taxation proposals nothing was left. A restriction on the sale of spirits less than three years old was the only salvage from the wreck. In the meantime, the Irish Parliamentary party had unanimously rejected the proposed taxes as 'grossly unjust and oppressive to Ireland'.[2] Terms which were rejected by the Irish could not prudently be imposed upon the British. 'The British liquor interests had triumphed under the banner of Irish industry,' one unhappy chronicler of these events concluded.[3] This was an oversimplification. Conservative leaders also condemned 'penal and crushing' taxes, though their protests savour of a belated gesture with an eye to the trade rather than heartfelt opposition.[4]

Asquith appeared undistressed by the government's failure to win approval for the stringent controls that Lloyd George wished to impose. The Prime Minister's role in all the discussions and negotiations over drink was negative. Notwithstanding the strong cabinet support of Runciman, McKenna, and others, Asquith seems to have taken the idea of nationalization, for example, less than seriously. While Lloyd George was being 'driven from pillar to post'[5] in the House of Commons and elsewhere, his chief remained in the background until the matter began to assume what, in Asquithian language, could be described as 'rational dimensions'.[6]

Like many M.P.s and most of his colleagues, Asquith did not emulate the King and the Secretary of State for War in taking

[1] Lloyd George to Samuel, 19 April 1915 (copy), Lloyd George MSS, C/7/9/11; Addison's Diary, 29 April 1915. Addison, op. cit., vol. 1, p. 73.
[2] Richard Hazleton to Lloyd George, 4 May 1915, and enclosed resolution, Lloyd George MSS, C/11/3/62; see also Sir Matthew Nathan to H. P. Hamilton, 1 April 1915, and John Redmond to Augustine Birrell, 7 May 1915, Lloyd George MSS, C/3/8/4,9.
[3] Henry Carter, *The Control of the Drink Trade:* A Contribution to National Efficiency, 1915–1917, with a Preface by Lord D'Abernon (London, 1918), p. 66.
[4] For the speeches of Lloyd George, as well as those of critics and opponents of the taxes, see 71 *H.C. Deb.*, 5s, 29 April and 4 May 1915.
[5] Sir Arthur Markham's phrase, 71 *H.C. Deb.*, 5s, col. 2063, 17 May 1915.
[6] Asquith to Venetia Stanley, 19 April 1915, Montagu MSS.

a pledge of abstinence for the duration of the war. Nor is there any evidence that the consumption of alcohol at Number 10 Downing Street was significantly diminished in this period. John Gulland wrote to his sister on April 11: 'I have started to make the House of Commons follow the King's example & be teetotal. With the Irish Members away it will be fairly easy.' It was not as easy as Gulland expected.[1] 'This drink agitation is saturated with humbug and hypocrisy,' Sir George Riddell told Lloyd George on April 10. 'I have come to think so too,' was the reply. 'It is the old story.' Riddell had been pressing Asquith to make a speech. The nation, as Lloyd George agreed, needed enlightening and 'waking up'.[2] The Premier did make a speech; it was at Newcastle, on April 20. The essence of Asquith's message, according to *The Annual Register*, was 'Deliver the Goods.'[3] But, in content, the speech was little different from Lloyd George's speech at Bangor two months before. In tone it was predictably less animated. Mr Spender, in discussing the temperamental divergence between Asquith and Lloyd George which was becoming apparent at this time, has written:

> Asquith was wholly sceptical as to the value of either agitation or imprecation in winning the War, and he thought it of high importance that both the Government and the public should keep an equal mind in face of adversity. Mr Lloyd George, in common with Lord Northcliffe, who took the same line in his many newspapers, believed in constantly whipping up both the Government and the public to effort and more effort, and imparting to others the sense of peril which they felt so acutely themselves.[4]

Pushing and probing the Nonconformists on the drink question, the trade unionists on restrictive practices, or the arms manufacturers on delivery delays, Lloyd George was as valuable to Asquith in failure as in success. What Lloyd George could not achieve with the consciences of temperance advocates, union leaders, or industrialists, probably could not be achieved at all.

---

[1] Gulland to Elsie Osborne, 11 April 1915, Gulland MSS.

[2] Riddell's Diary, 10 April 1915. *Lord Riddell's War Diary*, p. 74.

[3] *The Annual Register:* A Review of Public Events at Home and Abroad for the Year 1915, New Series (London, 1916), p. 93.

[4] Spender and Asquith, op. cit., vol. II, p. 122.

And having so resourceful a colleague, as well as a ministry replete with executive and imaginative talent, the Prime Minister was relieved from otherwise distasteful responsibilities. He was rarely called upon to meet and argue with disagreeable deputations. Nor was he often obliged to demonstrate the fecundity of his brain. Expert advisers could produce their schemes. The war council, the cabinet, or some informal group would canvass their merits. The Prime Minister adjudicated.

13 Patience 'the highest form of courage'[1]

It need hardly be said that the picture of a Premier attending to his duties in a somewhat desultory manner while his senior colleagues shouldered the real burdens of war is not the picture to which Asquith himself subscribed. After the war Asquith defended his own record. Following a luncheon at the Connaught Rooms on 3 June 1919, the ex-Premier first attempted to parody and then to rebut the story which had just been published by Lord French, the former Commander-in-Chief of the expeditionary force, of how the Liberal ministry had fallen in May 1915:

> I am represented ... as spending my time lolling in an armchair, occasionally arbitrating over the disputes of the different departments, waiting on the chapter of accidents, in the hope that somehow or other, the storm-tossed ship might drift safely into port ...
> ... what is the fact? ... It is no exaggeration to say that I was called upon at almost every hour of every day to take, on my own responsibility and initiative, decisions which might be, and which often were, of the most momentous consequences.
> I had to deal, not only with military and naval operations, the recruiting of new armies, transport, food supply, and labour problems, but also with inter-Allied finance, and, what at that time was a task of supreme importance and delicacy—Allied diplomacy.[2]

[1] A judgment by Lloyd George, Riddell's Diary, 11 October 1914. *Lord Riddell's War Diary*, p. 35.
[2] *The Great Shell Story: Mr Asquith's Reply to Lord French* (London, 1919), pp. 38-9.

In claiming to perform these duties, the Prime Minister posed something of a mystery to his colleagues, friends, and relatives. There were some of Asquith's associates who vouched, during the war and later, for his speedy and meticulous execution of business. But they were few. Referring to Asquith's reputation as an efficient worker before the war, Herbert Asquith wrote that, although he had lived with his father at Downing Street for two and a half years, 'I never discovered exactly how and when he did it.'[1] Two points are at issue: whether the Prime Minister was conscientiously and successfully attending to his duties; and whether he was credited with doing so by his colleagues and the wider political community. To the public at large, the Asquithian façade was unblemished down to May 1915. Within the cabinet, and in the opposition ranks, his capacity was questioned to an extent unparalleled in the years of his peace premiership.

The Chancellor of the Exchequer was especially dissatisfied. Lloyd George told Sir George Riddell on March 7 that the Prime Minister lacked initiative and took no steps to control and co-ordinate government departments. This was an old criticism, but its force was all the greater in time of war. 'The Prime Minister should direct and overlook the whole machine. No one else has the authority.'[2] Six weeks later Lloyd George said that he would not go on without Asquith. He did not want to be Prime Minister himself. The ceremonial trappings of the premiership would be hateful. In any case, why should he wish to vacate his position as Chancellor? 'As it is, I always get my own way unless the circumstances are such that there is really good reason why I should not.'[3]

Whatever Asquith's faults, Lloyd George thought that he could rely on the Prime Minister's loyalty. In return, the Chancellor gave not merely loyalty but enthusiastic service. Nevertheless, each week that passed saw increasing murmurs about the leadership of the nation. In April, Northcliffe spoke contemptuously of Asquith as 'indolent, weak, and apathetic'. Sir William Robertson Nicoll, editor of *The British Weekly*, referred to the Premier's

[1] Herbert Asquith, *Moments of Memory: Recollections and Impressions* (London, n.d., [?1937]), p. 141.
[2] Riddell's Diary, 7 March 1915. *Lord Riddell's War Diary*, p. 65.
[3] Riddell's Diary, 4 April 1915. Ibid., p. 81.

'nerveless hand'. And, interspersed with these manifestations of dissatisfaction, there came hints about one obvious path to reform in the central direction of the war effort. 'L.G. may be the man. He is the best of the lot,' Northcliffe opined. 'A general supervisor and stimulator is badly needed,' said Lord Reading invitingly.[1] But conversational musing and enticement amounted neither to grounds for Asquith's removal nor the basis of a bid by Lloyd George to replace him.

What can be observed in the first four months of 1915 is a developing consciousness in Lloyd George of his own enhanced standing and enlarged responsibility. His platform speeches, ever more unequivocally committing him to a war to the finish, struck British chords where once they had played Welsh, nonconformist, and Liberal notes. By March 1915, no one could say, as was said a few months previously, that he had 'entirely disappeared from public view'. Referring to the popular belief that some figure of household fame had been incarcerated pending trial for treason, one old Liberal had jokingly wondered early in November 1914: 'Perhaps he is the illustrious Prisoner in the Tower?'[2] Yet even by January, the Chancellor's problem was keeping out of the news rather than making it.

As a man whose name had more than once been dragged through the divorce courts, and as the central figure in the Marconi inquiry, Lloyd George was more conscious than most of his colleagues of the damaging effect of bad publicity. He fell in love, but did it without flaunting. He did not, at this period in his life, hazard his reputation in frequent casual liaisons. And, like those of his colleagues whose tastes were different, he could usually rely on English journalists not to intrude into his private affairs. However, he had acquired a sensitivity about certain subjects which, at the beginning of February, led to a trivial but instructive incident.

When he was in France for an allied conference, one of the largest French news agencies sent a brief report to London on

---

[1] Riddell's Diary, 13 March, 20–21 April 1915. Ibid., pp. 68, 78.

[2] Lord Burghclere to Lord Buxton, 4 November 1914, Buxton MSS. As Herbert Gardner, Burghclere had been President of the Board of Agriculture, 1892–5. He was offered the Under-Secretaryship at the Foreign Office in December 1905 but hedged his letter of acceptance with so many qualifications that Campbell-Bannerman treated it as a refusal.

February 3. 'Mr Lloyd George,' the report read, 'after a busy day in conference with ministers here, drove this evening to the Latin Quarter, in order to see it under war conditions.' After a delay of three days, the telegram was released by the Press Bureau and and circulated by the Central News Agency. Within hours, Central News had been informed that Lloyd George found the report inaccurate and offensive—a complaint that led to its immediate withdrawal, and an apology. Any semblance of frivolity, still less of loose living, at so serious a moment in England's history would raise eyebrows if nothing worse. Lloyd George's career depended on public confidence. His nonconformist supporters, in particular, were being sorely tried by the war. He could not, therefore, share the conclusion—ingenuous or disingenuous—of the agency spokesman:

> It still appears to me to be the most natural thing in the world that a minister from London visiting Paris should take a drive through the quarter of Paris which, next perhaps to Montmartre, presents the most striking instance of the contrast between the conditions of today and those of yesterday.[1]

This was one piece of information better concealed than publicized. For the most part, however, Lloyd George had no objection to wide dissemination of news about his activities. Having conquered the London Welshmen in his Queen's Hall speech, he had set out to persuade the rest of his fellow countrymen, English nonconformists, and working men throughout the land, that the British cause was just. 'I must first of all stir up my own country,' he told a Conservative M.P.[2] To Welshmen at Cardiff on 29 September 1914 he said: 'If we fail through timidity, through ignorance, through indolence, it will take generations before Welshmen will be able to live down the evil repute of faintheartedness at such an hour.'[3] Wales answered the call.

In wooing nonconformists generally, he had the powerful aid of Robertson Nicoll and Dr Clifford. Although Nicoll had at first

[1] Hugh Redwood (Evening Editor, Central News Agency) to Lloyd George, 7 February 1915, Lloyd George MSS, C/11/3/6.
[2] Lloyd George to Colonel A. R. M. Lockwood, 8 October 1914, Lloyd George MSS, C/11/2/49.
[3] *The Liberal Magazine*, vol. XXII, No. 253 (October 1914), p. 649.

opposed British intervention, he published a pro-war leader in *The British Weekly* on August 6. 'From that hour,' in the words of his biographer, 'his one absorbing care was how to secure victory.'[1] Nicoll recognized that Asquith's ponderous speeches would never 'set the heather on fire'. Only Lloyd George could arouse the national conscience south or north of the border. At a Free Church demonstration in the City Temple on November 10, Nicoll and Lloyd George joined Dr Clifford and R. J. Campbell in an appeal for recruits. The packed meeting heard an emphatic declaration from Nicoll about the Christian's duty. 'The devil would have counselled neutrality, but Christ has put His sword into our hands.'[2] Lloyd George was more restrained in interpreting the divine will:

> I never read a saying of the Master's which would condemn a man for striking a blow for right, justice, or the protection of the weak. To carry those principles too far is just the way to retard their advent ... The surest method of establishing a reign of peace on earth is by making the way of the transgressor of the peace of nations too hard for the rulers of men to tread it.[3]

By November, most traces of apology for his position had disappeared from Lloyd George's public statements. In private, too, he assumed an increasingly confident tone.

Replying to a well-wisher who had told him how valuable the reprints of the Queen's Hall speech had been in 'putting the British case for the War from the democratic point of view', he put his defence of the Liberal government's decision for war in capsule form:

> Since the Germans invaded Belgium I have never had the slightest doubt as to the justice of our intervention.
>
> It is hard for Liberals to have to support war under any conditions, but I feel we could have done no other in this case without disgracing the best traditions of our own Party.[4]

[1] T. H. Darlow, *William Robertson Nicoll: Life and Letters* (London, 1925), p. 236.　　　　　　　　　　　　　　[2] Ibid., p. 242.
[3] *The Times*, 11 November 1914.
[4] Lloyd George to the Hon. Alexander Shaw, 25 November 1914, Craigmyle MSS.

There was no going back from this position. Still, it was another three and a half months before Lloyd George was confident enough to make an explicit crusading appeal. At the end of February 1915, in a speech at Bangor that was notable for its new emphasis on the need for equipment rather than men,[1] he used unequivocal language: 'I make no apology ... for coming here to preach a holy war.'[2] This was a message which not all chapel-goers could swallow. But in the offices of the *Daily Mail* and *The Morning Post*, and the ante-chambers at Buckingham Palace, new friends were found to replace those who fell by the wayside.[3] The Queen's Private Secretary, Edward Wallington, agreed 'with every word'. H. A. Gwynne, editor of *The Morning Post*, admitted to being 'very glad to see the great emphasis you laid upon our united effort'.

Lloyd George's excursions into fields which were not purely financial were the basis of his magnified fame. Unlike Churchill or Kitchener he could claim little of the credit for military and naval successes, if there were any. Moreover, as Chancellor of the Exchequer his duties offered limited scope for favourable publicity. This is not to suggest that his activities were primarily devised to advance his own position. He admitted that 'the function of the Chancellor of the Exchequer upon these occasions is the least picturesque and the most perilous of all the combatants. He is simply a coal-heaver; he is filling the bunkers of the battleships and cursed by everybody as a nuisance.'[4] But his dominant motive was, like that of most of his colleagues, a sense

---

[1] 'This is an engineers' war, and it will be won or lost owing to the shortcomings of engineers. Unless we are able to equip our armies, our predominance in men will avail us nothing.' (Speech at Bangor, 28 February 1915. *The Liberal Magazine*, vol. xxiii, No. 259, April 1915.)

[2] The Bangor arrangements were made with great care, although the time and place — Sunday, in a theatre — might have been better chosen. For a St David's Day celebration the next day, Lloyd George was 'exceedingly anxious not to pack the floor of the Pavilion with a stodgy, fashionable crowd who will chill every enthusiasm in my own and everybody else's breast'. He insisted, therefore, that all the speeches were in Welsh, a stipulation which had the incidental advantage of keeping prominent Conservative politicians off the platform. (Riddell's Diary, 7 March 1915, *Lord Riddell's War Diary*, p. 67; Lloyd George to Sir Henry Lewis, 7 October 1914 [copy], Lloyd George MSS, C/11/2/60.)

[3] E. W. Wallington to Lloyd George, 1 March 1915, Lloyd George MSS, C/5/6/10; Gwynne to Lloyd George, 1 March 1915, Lloyd George MSS, C/4/16/1.

[4] 68 *H.C. Deb.*, 5s, col. 357, 17 November 1914.

of duty. He was too old to fight, except with the one weapon with which he excelled, words. When convinced that recruits were needed, or that the liquor traffic had to be controlled, he used the same eloquence which had always been at the service of social reform. To dismiss all his public utterances as humbug or self-advertisement is totally to misunderstand the man and his times.

Lloyd George had given himself completely to the business of war just as he had formerly devoted all his passion to social reform. Churchill told his brother: 'L.G. has more true insight and courage than anyone else. He really sticks at nothing—no measure is too far-reaching, no expedient too novel.'[1] In this wholeheartedness he was not unique. Some Liberals were incapable of reversing the ideas and habits of a lifetime. But for Lloyd George, the favourite propositions of Liberalism had always been defensible programmes rather than eternal verities. And the supreme trial of war found his doctrinal flexibility matched only by that of Lord Haldane. On 8 January 1915 Haldane declared in the House of Lords that compulsory military service, although as yet unnecessary, was not foreign to Britain. Further, he argued, that in a great national emergency, a time of 'final necessity', it was the nation's duty to resort to it. 'At a time of national necessity every other consideration must yield to national interest, and we should bar nothing in the way of principle if it should become necessary.'[2] This was a doctrine to which Asquith also, privately, subscribed. For Asquith, however, there were two riders. One was that men were as dispensable as principles. Hence Haldane was shortly dropped from the cabinet in response to Tory clamour, not because he was unsound on the war but because he had acquired an undeserved reputation for sympathizing with the enemy. The second was that Asquith's own principles —certainly those principles to which he was publicly committed —could only be abandoned with maximum delay and the greatest show of reluctance. As it happened, when Liberal rule came to an end in May 1915, only men were sacrificed. For a brief and indeterminate period principles were spared.

In the spring of 1915, Asquith's chief lieutenant had carved

[1] Churchill to Jack Churchill, 26 February 1915, Churchill MSS.
[2] 18 H.L. Deb., 5s, col. 378.

out a new place for himself in the British political scene. As early as March, J. L. Garvin wrote to Lloyd George with the assurance that 'I never make the least concealment of my belief that the man we have always to look to at the last is you as the only leader of popular genius we have.'[1] Popular genius or not, Lloyd George made mistakes. 'Why didn't L.G. call in the work-men after the masters' deputation had been heard?' asked H. W. Massingham at the time of the engineering employers' declaration for prohibition.[2] This was an opportunity missed.

Over Welsh Disestablishment, which flared again in mid-March, Lloyd George's position was inescapably awkward. Welsh M.P.s protested vehemently against the government's Bill to postpone the operation of the Disestablishment Act. The Chan-cellor could not please his Welsh friends without condoning their disregard of the political truce. He appealed to them for restraint, but was regarded by some of his former associates as 'selling the pass'.[3] However, hostile propagandists encountered in Wales an 'editorial dread of saying anything which may be construed into an attack or reflection upon the new St David'.[4] By rebuking those who indulged in sectarian controversy, Lloyd George earned the applause of Tories while the majority of the Welsh press remained faithful.[5]

No amount of friendly journalism could conceal the lack of enthusiasm which the second war Budget met in May. Criticism came from all sides of the House, particularly on the liquor taxation proposals. Were they necessary? Were they not punitive? Few tears were shed on their abandonment. As to the rest of the Chancellor's proposals, the House evinced only sporadic interest. Income tax was unchanged; and the optimists were encouraged by

---

[1] Garvin to Lloyd George, n.d. (1 March 1915), Lloyd George MSS, C/4/13/4.

[2] Massingham to Runciman, 8 April 1915, Runciman MSS.

[3] John Massie to Ellis Griffith, 19 March 1915, Griffith MSS, 468. Massie was a member of the executive of the National Liberal Federation. A Congregationalist Professor of Theology, he was M.P. for Cricklade, 1906–10. Griffith had resigned from the Under-Secretaryship at the Home Office in January 1915.

[4] Beriah G. Evans to E. T. John, 12 March 1915, John MSS. According to Evans, a journalist, who ten years earlier had been closely involved in Lloyd George's activities in Wales, 'everything affecting Lloyd George personally is still, in the Welsh press, taboo and sacrosanct'. John had been M.P. for East Denbighshire since 1910.

[5] See the correspondence of E. T. John in the John MSS; and Kenneth O. Morgan. *Wales in British Politics, 1868–1922* (Cardiff, 1963), pp. 278–9.

the way in which the Budget calculations were based on two alternative assumptions: the war would last another six months or it would last another twelve months. 'I see no attempt', MacCallum Scott wrote in his diary, 'to organise the national economy for a struggle which may be expected to last for years.'[1] In reality, Lloyd George had by then come to the conclusion that the war might last another three years.[2] To the House of Commons, he put with clarity the courses open to Britain in the allied combination. Britain could keep command of the seas, maintain a great army, and bear the burden of financing and supplying allied forces:

> We have raised enormous numbers of men in this country, but I say, speaking now purely from the point of view of finance, that the time has come when there should be discrimination, so that recruiting should not interfere with the output of munitions of war, and that it should interfere as little as possible with the output of those commodities which we export abroad, and which enable us to purchase munitions for ourselves and our Allies.[3]

This was an appropriate argument from the lips of a Chancellor of the Exchequer, perhaps even for a Minister of Munitions. But, if there was to be discrimination in recruiting, how should that process be organized? How, and by whom, should manpower be allocated? The options could be easily defined. Making the choice was another matter. And the choice, as even radical backbenchers were beginning to realize, could not be avoided. 'We ought at once to begin', MacCallum Scott wrote on May 4, 'making preparations for the great squeeze.'[4]

---

[1] MacCallum Scott's Diary, 5 May 1915, MacCallum Scott MSS.
[2] Riddell's Diary, 2 May 1915. *Lord Riddell's War Diary*, p. 84.
[3] 71 *H.C. Deb.*, 5s, col. 1015, 4 May 1915.
[4] MacCallum Scott's Diary, 4 May 1915, MacCallum Scott MSS.

Part III A National Government

1 'Supremely ridiculous suspicions'

'Supremely ridiculous suspicions are often held by eminently sane people.' Thus did Edwin Montagu rebuke Walter Runciman in April 1915 for appearing to suspect that Montagu was 'party to, helping in, or watching accessorily, an intrigue against the P.M.'[1] Attacks had been made on Asquith in *The Morning Post*, *The Observer*, and *The Times*. An article in *The Daily Chronicle* alleged that there was an intrigue against the Prime Minister under way. As the *Chronicle* put it on March 29:

> ... because the very facts of his occupation withdraw Mr Asquith from the public gaze, and because in his public appearance he preserves always that bearing of serene cheerfulness and that total absence of fuss which is not the least factor in his efficiency, it has been thought worth while to put about by innuendo and suggestion the pretence that he is not fit for his task.

Who was putting about these innuendoes? On March 25 Margot Asquith was visited by the editor of *The Nation* who brought 'a horrible tale'. According to the best authority, said H. W. Massingham, Churchill was intriguing to oust Grey from the Foreign Office and have him replaced by Balfour. Mrs Asquith's informant does not seem to have mentioned any movement against the Prime Minister himself.[2] Five days later, the day after the *Chronicle* article was published, the Postmaster-General, Charles Hobhouse, recorded details of a larger conspiracy. Churchill, Hobhouse wrote to Lord Buxton, had 'been at his old game again of intriguing all round'.[3] Working with Churchill

---

[1] Montagu to Runciman, 29 April 1915, Runciman MSS.
[2] Asquith to Venetia Stanley, 25 March 1915, Montagu MSS.
[3] Hobhouse to Lord Buxton, 30 April 1915, Buxton MSS.

were Balfour, Garvin of *The Observer*, and Lloyd George. Their aim was to dislodge Asquith as well as Grey. They had tried originally to enlist Kitchener for this struggle. Kitchener declined. Then, so Hobhouse's story continued, the Secretary of State for War was added to the list of targets; and Sir John French joined the plotters.

What truth was there in these stories? It may have been the case that Churchill would have preferred Balfour to Grey at the Foreign Office. 'There is no doubt', Asquith wrote, 'that Winston is at the moment a complete victim to B's superficial charm.'[1] And Churchill had, according to Montagu, suggested that Balfour should take temporary charge of the Foreign Office while Grey had a fishing holiday. Lloyd George, when asked by the Prime Minister what he thought of the Massingham story, replied that he believed it to be substantially true.[2] By this, it must not be supposed that Lloyd George was pointing his finger at Churchill as a plotter. All that Churchill was guilty of, in Lloyd George's opinion, was a preference for Balfour as Foreign Secretary. With Grey's eyesight failing rapidly, it was a change which had much to recommend it.

However, as neither Lloyd George nor Asquith could have failed to realize, there were two implications of great importance in the proposal to substitute Balfour for Grey. In the first place, the Foreign Secretary could not be moved without the Prime Minister's consent, and Asquith was unlikely, on grounds either of personality or policy, to desire the expulsion of one of his oldest friends and trusted associates. A plot against Grey was, therefore, necessarily a plot against Asquith. The two men stood, and would fall, together. Secondly, if Balfour were to be the new Foreign Secretary, the question of coalition would automatically be raised.

What was Lloyd George's role in these rumoured machinations? On the day that the *Chronicle* story appeared, Asquith told the Chancellor of 'the sinister and ... absurd interpretations which were being given to the articles in *The Times*, *Observer*, and *Morning Post*'.[3] Lloyd George, it was being said, was conspiring against

[1] Asquith to Venetia Stanley, 25 March 1915, Montagu MSS.
[2] Ibid.; and Asquith to Venetia Stanley, 21 March 1915, Montagu MSS.
[3] Asquith to Venetia Stanley, 29 March 1915, Montagu MSS.

his leader. There followed an emotional scene. Lloyd George defended himself earnestly. The real culprit, he argued, was Kitchener. For Kitchener, although responsible for the dearth of munitions, was immune to press criticism. The Tory press attacked Asquith as an easier, Liberal, target. Asquith's version of the dialogue continues:

> As for himself (L.G.) he declared that he owed everything to me, that I had stuck to him and protected him and defended him when every man's hand was against him, and that he would rather (1) break stones, (2) dig potatoes, (3) be hung and quartered (these were metaphors used at different stages of his broken but impassioned harangue) than do an act or say a word or harbour a thought that was disloyal to me, and he said that every one of his colleagues felt the same. His eyes were wet with tears, and I am sure that, with all his Celtic capacity for impulse and momentary fervour, he was quite sincere. Of course I assured him that I had never for a moment doubted him, which is quite true, and he warmly wrung my hand and abruptly left the room.

Clearly, Asquith enjoyed telling the tale. Equally obviously, he was not taking the talk of a Lloyd George plot very seriously. Lloyd George's behaviour indicated much greater concern at the *Chronicle* story. 'In a state of great anger and excitement', he had telephoned Sir George Riddell.[1] And, on March 30, he gave Riddell his version of his meeting with the Prime Minister. 'The old boy was in tears,' he said. Furthermore:

> I shall not let this rest. I have never intrigued for place or office. I have intrigued to carry through my schemes but that is a different matter. The Prime Minister has been so good to me that I would never be disloyal to him in the smallest detail. I may criticize him amongst ourselves, as I have no doubt he criticizes me, but we are absolutely loyal to each other.[2]

What worried Lloyd George was that he might be thought

[1] Riddell's Diary, 29 March 1915. *Lord Riddell's War Diary*, p. 70.
[2] Riddell's Diary, 30 March 1915. Ibid.

to be the inspiration of the *Chronicle* article. Robert Donald had commented on the hints in the Tory papers that a coalition, excluding Asquith, might be formed. Would it not seem that Donald, known to be on friendly terms with Lloyd George, had been subtly magnifying Tory propaganda at Lloyd George's behest?

Riddell did his best to calm his friend. Impossible! In the presence of the Prime Minister, Lloyd George accused McKenna of inspiring the *Chronicle*. McKenna denied implicating Lloyd George but defended the thesis that there was an anti-Asquith plot. This, countered Lloyd George, was further evidence of McKenna's continual imagining of non-existent conspiracies. After an hour of heated exchanges, Asquith soothed the fractured cordiality.[1] In a day or two the whole affair was over. The drink question brought McKenna and Lloyd George together. Asquith accepted their assurances of loyalty.

There was no plot against Asquith in March 1915. As for Lloyd George, he was growing fidgety about the premier's deficiency in driving power.[2] Not that he wanted to be rid of Asquith. Or that he wanted coalition any more than Asquith wanted it. Churchill's desire to stop the Conservatives from 'brooding morosely outside',[3] aroused no more enthusiasm in Lloyd George than it did in the Prime Minister. As Lloyd George told Frances Stevenson, it was the last thing he would wish for.[4] For that matter, even Churchill quickly cooled in his desire for coalition after one taste of a war council at which Lansdowne and Bonar Law were present.

On March 10 the Conservative leaders were invited to attend the war council's discussion of policy in relation to Constantinople and the future territorial settlement in the Straits region. 'They did not contribute very much,' Asquith thought.[5] When Lord Fisher suggested that the Conservatives should attend another meeting, Churchill replied: 'I don't think we want a war council on this. It is after all only asking a lot of ignorant people

---

[1] Asquith to Venetia Stanley, 30 March 1915, Montagu MSS.

[2] Riddell's Diary, 7, 13, and 27 March 1915. *Lord Riddell's War Diary*, pp. 65, 68, 70.

[3] Winston S. Churchill, *The World Crisis, 1915*, p. 198.

[4] Frances Stevenson's Diary, 8 April 1915, Lloyd George MSS.

[5] Asquith to Venetia Stanley, 10 March 1915, Montagu MSS.

to meddle in our business.'[1] For their part, Bonar Law and Lansdowne notified Asquith that they could not come to any future war council meetings. If they did, they feared that they would lose their grip on the Conservative party. So ended the only gesture towards co-operation which the government and opposition leaders were willing to make. There was one positive result. Henceforth, on Asquith's instructions, Hankey sent to the two Conservative leaders all the papers prepared for the war council.[2]

At Question Time on May 12, Handel Booth, the Liberal M.P. for Pontefract, asked the Prime Minister:

> ... whether, in view of the present War and in view of the steps necessary to be taken in order to grapple with the rearrangement of industry and social life consequent upon a prolonged struggle, he will consider the desirability of admitting into the ranks of Ministers leading Members of the various political parties in this House?[3]

Asquith's answer was brief and pointed. The government, he said, was indebted for suggestions and help from the leaders of all parties. But coalition was 'not in contemplation'. Nor was Asquith aware that coalition would meet with 'general assent'. Nobody contradicted this last remark. Exactly one week later the Prime Minister informed the House that 'steps are in contemplation which involve the reconstruction of the government on a broader, personal and political basis'.[4] During the next seven days, that reconstruction took place. When Parliament returned from its Whitsun holiday, a coalition government had been created.

[1] Churchill to Fisher, 15 March 1915, Lennoxlove MSS; see also Fisher to Churchill, 15 March 1915, Churchill MSS.

[2] Hankey's Diary, 17 March 1915. Hankey, *The Supreme Command*, vol. II, p. 289. In fact, only four papers were circulated to the war council between March 17 and the creation of the coalition two months later.

[3] 71 *H.C. Deb.*, 5s, col. 1642.

[4] 71 *H.C. Deb.*, 5s, cols 2392–94, 19 May 1915.

2 'This beneficent revolution'[1]

Coalition, an arrangement which one week had been 'not in contemplation', was an accomplished fact a fortnight later. What had happened to change the minds of the Liberal, Conservative, and Labour leaders? Two things. The dearth of munitions had become a public scandal. And Lord Fisher, after 'anxious reflection', had come to the conclusion that he could no longer continue as the colleague of Churchill at the Admiralty.[2]

Fisher resigned; and he made sure that Bonar Law knew that he had done so. For some weeks the Tory leader had been under pressure from his party manager, Arthur Steel-Maitland, to reconsider the idea of coalition.[3] The shell shortage, dramatically publicized in an article by Colonel Repington in *The Times*, had stirred up the Conservative back benches. Faced with the possibility of a rebellion in the ranks over shells, Bonar Law was certain that he could not guarantee to hold his followers in check if Fisher—who had many Tory sympathizers—went and Churchill stayed.[4] Early on Monday, May 17, Bonar Law visited Lloyd George at the Treasury to seek confirmation of his deduction that Fisher had resigned. Lloyd George did not deny it. Then, Bonar Law explained, a parliamentary crisis was unavoidable. Lloyd George's reply was crucial. Later in the day, the Conserv-

[1] H. H. Asquith, *The Great Shell Story*, p. 44.
[2] Fisher to Churchill, n.d., (15 May 1915). Arthur J. Marder (ed.), *Fear God and Dread Nought*, The Correspondence of Admiral of the Fleet Lord Fisher of Kilverstone: vol. III, Restoration, Abdication, and Last Years, 1914–1920 (London, 1959), p. 228.
[3] Steel-Maitland to Lord Robert Cecil, 26 May 1915, Cecil of Chelwood MSS (Add. MS. 51071, f. 108).
[4] On Unionist discontent, see Beaverbrook, *Politicians and the War*, pp. 84–8; and W. A. S. Hewins, *The Apologia of an Imperialist*, 2 vols, (London, 1929), vol. II, pp. 11–18 and ch. xiv.

ative leader told Lord Lansdowne and Austen Chamberlain
that:

> Lloyd George burst out passionately, saying that he entirely
> agreed with Bonar Law—that it was impossible that things
> should go on as they were, and inveighing against much in
> the conduct of the war. In particular he said that Kitchener
> had 'put lies into his mouth' as to the supply of munitions
> and that the situation was altogether intolerable.[1]

According to Lord Beaverbrook's account, Lloyd George told
Bonar Law: 'Of course, we must have a coalition, for the alternative is impossible.'[2]

It is not certain from the evidence available whether Lloyd
George or Bonar Law was the first to propose coalition. In
Austen Chamberlain's contemporary memorandum, it appears
that, immediately after Lloyd George's passionate outburst, Bonar
Law drafted a letter to Asquith, saying that:

> having regard to Fisher's resignation things could not go on
> as they were, that in his opinion the time had come for a
> coalition, and that whilst he was ready, especially in view of
> the delicate situation in Italy ... to postpone public discussion
> if Asquith could give him the assurance that he was consider-
> ing the whole position and that Fisher's resignation would
> not be acted upon in the meantime, he must if such a de-
> claration were refused question Asquith on the subject in
> the House that afternoon.[3]

Lansdowne and Chamberlain persuaded Bonar Law to alter
his direct reference to coalition and to write instead in support
of 'some change in the constitution of the government'. But
before this revised letter could be sent, the Prime Minister

---

[1] Chamberlain's Memorandum, 17 May 1915, Austen Chamberlain MSS,
2/2/25.

[2] Beaverbrook, op. cit., p. 107; Beaverbrook's account of the events of May 1915
draws heavily on a memorandum by J. L. Garvin. As Eye-Witness with the Canadian
troops, Beaverbrook was in France until May 18. I am grateful to Mr A. J. P. Taylor
for information on this point from the Beaverbrook MSS. See also Riddell's Diary,
20–23 May 1915. *Lord Riddell's War Diary*, pp. 91–3.

[3] Chamberlain's Memorandum, 17 May 1915, Austen Chamberlain MSS, 2/2/25.

telephoned for Bonar Law to come at once to Downing Street.

Austen Chamberlain recorded that:

> Asquith now stated that he had arrived at the same conclusion and that he had been intending to inform his colleagues at the end of this week. He produced a scheme for the distribution of offices, not complete in itself, but showing that he had been seriously thinking of the matter and had advanced some way in its consideration. He and Lloyd George both stated that it was absolutely necessary to get rid of Kitchener.

After a fifteen-minute discussion, agreement was reached. For Asquith the Kitchener umbrella was now too threadbare a protection against a storm in the House of Commons. Much of the ministry's credit had gone. Haldane had been subject to a campaign of vilification for alleged pro-Germanism. McKenna's handling of the aliens question was still under fire. Grey was pining for release or relief from the work that was slowly blinding him. Churchill was becoming a growing liability. 'Everyone seems terribly depressed except me,' Hankey wrote on May 14.[1] Coalition, therefore, offered a timely rescue, especially if suggested, as it was, by the Conservative leader himself. 'An entirely new departure', as Asquith described it to his colleagues later on May 17, was both opportune and imperative.[2]

Coalition came quickly. It was a time of telephone calls and unpremeditated conversations rather than correspondence. None of the principals was a diarist. Lacking the sources with which to build alternative hypotheses, most historians have adopted a version of these events not much different from that which was first offered in the 1920s by Lord Beaverbrook. Mr A. J. P. Taylor threw out a footnote of doubt in his *English History*. 'I am not sure', Mr Taylor ruminates, 'that Lloyd George played so passive a part. Perhaps he pushed Law forward.'[3]

But only Dr Stephen Koss has attempted to overturn the

[1] Hankey's Diary, 14 May 1915, Hankey, op. cit., Vol. I, p. 315.
[2] Asquith to the cabinet, 17 May 1915. Asquith, *Memories and Reflections*, vol. II, p. 95.
[3] A. J. P. Taylor, *English History, 1914–1945*, p. 30, fn. 2.

traditional interpretation with a detailed, documented study.[1]

In his article, 'The Destruction of Britain's Last Liberal Government', Dr Koss has attempted 'to answer at least some of the riddles posed by the formation of the first war-time coalition' by dissecting 'several newly discovered pieces of "solid evidence" '.[2] The conclusions to which Dr Koss has come are startling. If they are accepted they require a new appraisal of the motives and behaviour of most of the leading participants in the events of May 1915. Dr Koss's thesis is so potentially disturbing to received opinions, especially concerning the role of Churchill, that it demands the most careful and cautious scrutiny.

The Koss thesis may be summarized as follows:

1. The fall of the Asquith government in May 1915 cannot be attributed to the crisis at the Admiralty created by Lord Fisher's refusal to serve any longer as First Sea Lord under Churchill.

2. The most important of the causes contributing to the fall of the government was the 'so-called shells scandal'.[3]

3. The shell scandal did not, as is usually supposed, originate with a leak of information from a member of the British expeditionary force to Colonel Repington, the military correspondent of *The Times*. Nor, according to Dr Koss, did Sir John French act entirely on his own initiative when he sent emissaries to leading politicians in London with information which confirmed Repington's story. Behind, and enveloping, French and Repington was a wider conspiracy. Arthur Balfour, David Lloyd George, and Winston Churchill intrigued to achieve 'the disruption of the *ancien regime*'.[4] Repington was probably briefed and 'unquestionably inspired'[5] by Churchill who conferred with him in France on the week-end of May 8–9.

4. The downfall of the Liberal ministry was precipitated by the publication of Repington's dispatch and the accompanying editorial, 'Shells and the Great Battle', in *The Times* on 14 May 1915.

[1] Stephen E. Koss, 'The Destruction of Britain's Last Liberal Government', *Journal of Modern History*, vol. XL, No. 2 (June 1968), pp. 257–77. This article is reprinted with a few small alterations in Dr Koss's book, *Lord Haldane:* Scapegoat for Liberalism (New York and London, 1969), Ch. VII.

[2] Koss, op. cit., pp. 257–8. The phrase 'solid evidence' is Mr Taylor's.

[3] Ibid., p. 261.

[4] Ibid., p. 273.

[5] Hobhouse to Buxton, 10 June 1915, Buxton MSS, quoted in ibid., p. 265.

Asquith did not choose to create a coalition because of the fear of criticism. He acted not to forestall parliamentary opposition over munitions or the Admiralty but 'to avert pressures from within the government that had taken him completely by surprise'.[1]

How convincing are the evidence and arguments of this case? Professor Trevor Wilson has emphasized recently that the shell scandal antedated the resignation of Lord Fisher, and that the problem of munitions supply was a threatening political issue before news of Fisher's departure had spread outside official circles.[2] Dr Koss goes further. To him, it appears, the disruption at the Admiralty was of little consequence. 'It remained possible for Asquith either to retain Fisher's services or to replace him without reconstructing the ministry.'[3] This, it must be admitted, was Asquith's first impression. Until the morning of May 17, the Prime Minister seems to have intended to do no more than consult the Conservative leaders about the steps to be taken concerning both the Admiralty and the shells disclosure.[4] Churchill, too, was sure that Fisher could be dismissed without danger.

But Bonar Law thought otherwise. Not only were his followers unlikely to be docile if Fisher were allowed to go, he himself had little confidence in Churchill and the Dardanelles venture. Bonar Law's attitude, quickly and directly conveyed, convinced both Lloyd George and Asquith that coalition was inevitable. No Liberal government could continue successfully in the teeth of well-founded Conservative attacks.

There can be no doubt that all three of the creators of the coalition acted to avert the parliamentary storm that would certainly have ensued if both the shell shortage and Fisher's resignation were raised simultaneously in the Commons. Dr Koss's contention that 'prominent Liberals ... found it impossible to reconcile the admiralty crisis with the ensuing cataclysm' is itself hard to reconcile with the evidence which exists.[5] It is unlikely that many 'prominent Liberals' could have been so obtuse as not to appreciate the danger, national as well as party,

[1] Koss, op. cit., p. 266.
[2] Trevor Wilson, *The Downfall of the Liberal Party*, pp. 53–5.
[3] Koss, op. cit., p. 259.
[4] Churchill, *The World Crisis, 1915*, p. 364; Violet Bonham Carter, *Winston Churchill as I Knew Him*, pp. 393–4.
[5] Koss, op. cit., p. 260.

if Westminster were torn with bitter political strife at a time of national emergency.

With many Tories only too eager to exploit the government's difficulties, coalition was a natural solution to the additional dilemma created by the Fisher–Churchill dispute. 'The thing seemingly which has immediately precipitated the crisis, apart from the growing misgiving as to the arrangements for war supplies', Christopher Addison wrote, 'is the impossibility of Fisher and Winston getting on together any longer.'[1] Charles Masterman wrote to Herbert Samuel: 'Why the fact that Winston quarrelled with Fisher should mean your giving up the L[ocal] G[overnment] B[oard] is a *non sequitur* which today and tomorrow will find difficult to understand.'[2]

But this sympathetic remark does not prove that Masterman was mystified by the 'cataclysm'. In a letter of condolence to a former colleague who had just been asked to accept 'a temporary suspension of Cabinet rank',[3] Masterman was making no more than a polite reference to one particular consequence of coalition.

In discounting the significance of the events at the Admiralty, Dr Koss seeks to persuade us that Fisher was not the sort of man who would have 'resigned unconditionally, particularly if he realized that he might topple a government in the process'.[4] Quoting from letters by Fisher and his champion, the Duchess of Hamilton, Dr Koss succeeds only in demonstrating the very fact which made it inconceivable for Asquith to invite Fisher to stay: the First Sea Lord had taken leave of his senses. He was, Asquith told Lord Stamfordham, 'somewhat unhinged otherwise his conduct is almost "traitrous" '.[5] Churchill put it more succinctly: 'Fisher went mad,' he wrote to Kitchener.[6] The series

---

[1] Addison's Diary, 17 May 1915. Addison, *Four and a Half Years*, vol. 1, p. 78; see also Haldane's Memorandum, 29 May 1915, Sir Frederick Maurice, *Haldane*, vol. 1, pp. 364–5.

[2] Masterman to Samuel, 26 May 1915, Samuel MSS, A/48/11; Koss, op. cit., p. 260.

[3] Asquith to Samuel, 26 May 1915, Samuel MSS, A/48/5, partly quoted in Viscount Samuel, *Memoirs*, pp. 108–9.

[4] Koss, op. cit., p. 259.

[5] Stamfordham's Memorandum, 19 May 1915, Royal Archives, GV K/770.

[6] Churchill to Kitchener, 21 May 1915 (copy), Churchill MSS, partly quoted in Philip Magnus, *Kitchener: Portrait of an Imperialist* (London, 1961), Grey Arrow edition, p. 324.

of megalomanic demands which Fisher sent to Asquith on May 19—when coalition was obviously in prospect—show that the admiral simply did not care about the political implications of his actions.[1] 'Yesterday', Fisher wrote to Bonar Law on May 17, 'a member of the Cabinet told me that the present Government is on the verge of being smashed by my going! I DOUBT IT, but I WILL GO!'[2]

If Fisher was actually surprised at the disruption which his resignation caused, then his grasp of contemporary realities had declined so far that he was no longer fit to continue in his office. In fact, he was not surprised. He was, in his own words to Pamela McKenna, 'out-manœuvred'.[3] He had deliberately staked his own career in a calculated attempt to frustrate the war council's Dardanelles policy. '*It was better*', he told Arthur Balfour on June 5 1915, '*to wreck the Government than the Navy*.'[4] In confusing, for a short time, the Prime Minister's courtesy with cordiality, Fisher gave an additional indication that his sensitivity to the political environment was failing as rapidly as his ambitions were expanding. There was further evidence of his declining perception. On May 17, Asquith wrote him a brief note, marked 'secret', stating that 'a considerable reconstruction of the Government is in contemplation' and asking him, in the public interest, to 'neither say nor do anything for a day or two'. From this letter Fisher deduced that Churchill was to be ejected from the cabinet.[5] Wishful thinking turned the bare announcement of reconstruction into a premiss which pointed to Churchill's elimination. But the Prime Minister's letter contained no warrant for the subsequent deduction.[6]

In any case, whatever Fisher thought he was doing, or thought Asquith's intentions were, is irrelevant. What matters is that

---

[1] Fisher to Asquith, 19 May 1915. Marder (ed.), op. cit., vol. III, pp. 241–2.

[2] Ibid., p. 238. The cabinet minister was probably Grey. (See Fisher to Balfour, 5 June 1915. Ibid., p. 254.)

[3] Fisher to Pamela McKenna, 29 May 1915. Ibid., p. 250.

[4] Ibid., p. 254, Fisher's emphasis.

[5] Ibid., pp. 239, 250.

[6] Fisher told his wife that the Prime Minister had said that Churchill had been 'definitely dismissed'. Perhaps Asquith was referring to the fact that Churchill was to leave the Admiralty. Perhaps the Prime Minister said nothing but Fisher inferred that Churchill was to go. (Fisher to Lady Fisher, 26 May 1915. Ibid., p. 249.) The 'secret letter' was almost certainly the letter printed by Marder on p. 239.

Fisher's action had consequences outside Asquith's control. The fact that Asquith accepted the suggestion of coalition with alacrity does not necessarily indicate that he found Fisher's resignation a convenient pretext. It is more likely—as indeed most previous scholars have agreed—that he realized that a double crisis was more than the ministry could withstand. Asquith's rapid accommodation to the coalition idea shows that he had long appreciated that coalition might some day be necessary: as soon as he saw that the time had come he made no difficulty. Had he wished to stall and delay he could perhaps have done so. But coalition was so obviously the answer to the government's predicament that he made no attempt to resist it.

3 The Conspirators

The most interesting and original part of Dr Koss's argument is his contention that the destruction of the government was planned and carried out by a network of conspirators. At the centre of the plot, it is asserted, were three men: Lloyd George, Churchill, and Balfour. Repington, French and J. L. Garvin were also involved. 'Steps were initiated by Winston Churchill and ... Balfour, French and Lloyd George were eager accomplices.'[1]

What are the sources for this story? Dr Koss speaks of 'several newly discovered pieces of "solid evidence" '.[2] Of the documents cited, one stands out. No fewer than eight separate references are made to a letter from Charles Hobhouse, the Postmaster-General, to Lord Buxton. This letter, snipped into tantalizing phrases, is the origin and principal support of the conspiracy theory. Dr Koss accepts without reservation every statement which Hobhouse made. In order to make an independent judgment of the value of Hobhouse's testimony, it ought to be seen as it was written, connected and complete. Here is the relevant portion of the letter, written on 10 June 1915:

> I will tell you the story as it is known to me.
>
> For some time past Churchill has been intriguing against K. sometimes in conjunction with Gen. French as of late, sometimes, as earlier, with Ll.G.
>
> They made a joint attack on K. and Grey in Cabinet about a month ago; and then W.S.C. went to France and while there unquestionably inspired an attack on 'K' by Repington of *The Times*, wh though I think justifiable was very treachery [*sic*], & certainly disloyal.

[1] Koss, op. cit., p. 264.　　　　[2] Ibid., pp. 257–8.

Meanwhile Ll.G. and A.J.B. had resumed their colloguing of 1909, never long interrupted. A.J.B. was given a room at the Admiralty, and against the wishes of the Cabinet & without their knowledge taken to the Bd. of T. Committee on supplies. He thus knew of the difficulties at the Dardanelles and the quarrel between W.S.C. and Ld Fisher.

The latter on Thursday 13th or 14th sent a note to the P.M. and another to W.S.C. to say he wd. not stay at Admiralty if the latter remained there and nothing would make him recede from that position. Then A.J.B. put a pistol at P.M.'s head threatening debates and disclosures at W.O. and Admiralty.

The P.M. resists [*sic*] at first, & then (advised by Ll.G. I think, who *alone* was consulted I know) capitulated. On Monday (17th) afternoon we received a circular note, written between lunch and questions asking us to resign. I was the first to see it: R. McK[enna] was in my room the second. McK. and Runciman went to consult Grey, & found he knew nothing of it, & while they were talking in comes Haldane. 'Have you heard the news[?]' 'No, from the Dardanelles?' 'No, from Downing St.' So he is told, turns his usual ghastly colour, & nearly collapses. Meanwhile the P.M. is in closest communion—to recall C.B.—with the two villains of the peice [*sic*] & they form the new Cabinet with the aid of their Tory friends. Fisher still refuses to stay, this time if W.S.C. is in the Cabinet, so the latter goes to A.J.B. who announces he will not join unless Fisher is dismissed. And all this in the name of the nation ...[1]

Before proceeding to build his interpretation on the allegations made by Hobhouse, Dr Koss concedes that Hobhouse's prejudices against 'certain colleagues'—specifically Lloyd George and Churchill—are obvious. Nevertheless, we are told, Hobhouse's account of the 'Cabinet crisis' remains 'more complete, more dramatic, and more far-reaching in its historical significance than any other first-hand account that has come to light'.[2] Does this letter warrant such a judgment on its importance? So far

[1] Hobhouse to Buxton, 10 June 1915, Buxton MSS.
[2] Koss, op. cit., p. 262.

as the conspiracy charge is concerned, it is not first-hand. Hobhouse had actually visited the front on the week-end of May 8–9; and on May 9 spent some time with the British Ambassador in Paris where, according to the Ambassador's diary, 'he talked a lot of rubbish about the justice of Russia's claim to hold Constantinople and the Straits'.[1] But no authentic eye-witness account of intrigue resulted from Hobhouse's excursion.

So far as the account of Asquith's decision for coalition is concerned, Hobhouse's letter is not only incomplete but demonstrably inaccurate. All of the statements which can be checked are either disproved by credible witnesses or so trivial as to be worthless. The whole account is so riddled with factual errors that the few allegations for which no corroborative or incompatible testimony exists must be treated with the utmost scepticism. The fact is that Hobhouse was uninformed and strongly biased. His version of what caused the destruction of the government is of use to historians only as an example of the kind of fabricated gossip which usually accompanies political crises.

Consider first some of the points of detail in Hobhouse's story which cast doubts upon his reliability as a witness and a collector of political intelligence. He speaks, for example, of colloguing between Lloyd George and Balfour in 1909. This is presumably a reference to the discussions about the possibility of coalition in *1910* which involved not only Lloyd George and Balfour but Asquith, Grey, and Crewe as well. Hobhouse was too junior at that time to be privy to the discussions, and his information — though confidently uttered — is patently fragmentary.[2]

Hobhouse goes on to suggest that Balfour had been improperly brought into the counsels of the government after the outbreak of war; and that Balfour's knowledge of the Dardanelles operation and the Fisher–Churchill dispute derived from the fact that he had a room at the Admiralty and had been clandestinely installed as a participant in the deliberations of the 'B[oar]d of T[rade] Committee on supplies'. So ludicrous a misconception does little credit to Hobhouse's grasp of what was happening around him.

[1] Sir Francis Bertie's Diary, 9 May 1915. Lady Algernon Gordon Lennox (ed.), *The Diary of Lord Bertie of Thame, 1914–1918*, 2 vols (London, 1924), vol. I, p. 163.

[2] The best published account of the coalition negotiations of 1910 is by Peter Rowland, *The Last Liberal Governments: The Promised Land*, 1905–1910 (London, 1968), ch. xvi; see also Roy Jenkins, *Asquith*, pp. 216–17.

There was no such body as the 'Board of Trade Committee on Supplies'; and, if there had been, its terms of reference were hardly likely to have led into discussion of the points at issue between Fisher and Churchill.[1] The committee which Hobhouse had in mind was probably the Cabinet Munitions of War Committee to which Balfour was appointed by the Prime Minister along with Lloyd George, Edwin Montagu, Arthur Henderson and a group of businessmen, military advisers, and civil servants. Moreover, to suppose that it was his occupation of a room at the Admiralty which gave Balfour access to strategic debates is to ignore the more obvious and legitimate channels of communication which were open to him.

It was public knowledge that Balfour had been invited by the Prime Minister to continue sitting on the Committee of Imperial Defence. And it was well known at Westminster that Balfour was also frequently in attendance at meetings of the war council. If he knew about the secrets of the government's strategy, and was familiar with its personal dissensions, it was not through unauthorized disclosures but because he was entitled to know. Asquith complained that Churchill told Balfour 'a lot of things which he ought to keep to himself, or at any rate to his colleagues'.[2] But the Prime Minister knew, and was indeed responsible for, the fact that Balfour was thoroughly conversant with the major lines of government policy.

Even on the elementary level of chronology, Hobhouse was imprecise and unreliable. He dated Fisher's letter of resignation to "Thursday, 13th or 14th'. Yet the letter was written and sent on Saturday, May 15. There is, of course, no reason why Hobhouse should have known when Fisher's letter was sent. But that is precisely the point. If he could not find out, or remember, the date of one of the most controversial and widely publicized events of the crisis, it cannot be supposed that his reconstruction of other events is any more accurate.

Consider the general accusation that Churchill had intrigued

---

[1] There is no mention of a Board of Trade Committee on Supplies in N. B. Dearle, *Dictionary of Official War-Time Organizations* (London, 1928), nor do the Board of Trade archives confirm its existence. There was a 'Co-ordinating Committee on Trade and Supplies' of the Committee of Imperial Defence to which Hobhouse may nave been referring.

[2] Asquith to Venetia Stanley, 25 March 1915, Montagu MSS.

for some time against Kitchener, in collaboration with French and Lloyd George. In an earlier letter to Buxton, Hobhouse had mentioned Balfour and J. L. Garvin as co-conspirators. But in none of his letters did he produce evidence which supported the charge.

It must be admitted that Hobhouse referred to an attack made in cabinet on Kitchener and Grey by Lloyd George and Churchill. Could this be evidence of an intrigue? We are told nothing of the subject of the 'attack' or the merits of the case; we are offered nothing which would indicate that the attack was premeditated and concerted; nor are we given any evidence that there might have been an ulterior motive behind the attack. In fact, in describing the same incident to Buxton six weeks earlier, Hobhouse had spoken of 'a violent attack on Ll.G. by K.'.[1] And, from one of Asquith's letters to Miss Stanley it is clear that the occasion to which Hobhouse was referring was an outburst by Kitchener against Lloyd George for having disclosed manpower figures to the Treasury Munitions Committee.[2] Lord Emmott, writing retrospectively a few weeks after the coalition was formed, stated that the cabinet dispute in April had been part of 'one of the wretched intrigues of Winston against K.'.[3] But Emmott, like Hobhouse, was guessing at the existence of an intrigue of which he had no proof.

Hobhouse did furbish his conspiracy charge with one piece of evidence in relaying his suspicions to Jack Pease. 'It appears', Pease recorded, 'that Balfour had had frequent meetings with Lloyd George at Montagu's house—a Labour M.P. told him, in passing down that St, one or other were constantly going out or going in.'[4]

Apparently, it did not occur to Hobhouse or his informant that the three men might have been consulting on matters of public business, or that they might have been innocently taking a meal together. Until February, Montagu had been Lloyd George's junior minister at the Treasury. All three men were members of the Munitions of War Committee and were naturally in close

[1] Hobhouse to Buxton, 30 April 1915, Buxton MSS.
[2] Asquith to Venetia Stanley, 16 April 1915, Montagu MSS.
[3] Emmott's Diary, 13 June 1915 Emmott MSS. 'K can tell nothing to anybody' Emmott wrote. 'He is never frank & tells lies if he does not want to tell at all.'
[4] Pease's Diary, (?26) June 1915, Gainford MSS.

consultation on munitions as well as other official subjects. If they had something to hide, it was hardly likely that they would have consorted so openly. Montagu's house at 24 Queen Anne's Gate was just about the most conspicuous venue for a conspiratorial gathering that could possibly have been selected. Sir George Riddell lived at 20 Queen Anne's Gate, H. M. Hyndman at 9, St Loe Strachey at 14, Lord Fisher at 16, Haldane at 28, Asquith's brother-in-law, Lord Glenconner, at 34, and another intimate of the Asquith family, Harold Baker, at 42. To add a further hazard, Montagu at this time was sharing his house with the Prime Minister's private secretary and Violet Asquith's suitor, Maurice Bonham Carter.[1]

Of course, there could have been a conspiracy at 24 Queen Anne's Gate. But Hobhouse's case is unconvincing. So flimsy is the evidence, so naive its presentation, that the historian can have little confidence in his competence as a political detective.

[1] Violet Bonham Carter, op. cit., pp. 381–2.

4 Treachery ?

The particular charge against Churchill was that he 'unquestionably inspired' Repington's attack on Kitchener in *The Times*.
'Winston', says Dr Koss, 'sought to wield the editorial columns
of *The Times* as a weapon against his political superiors.'[1] What is
the evidence? The Irish Nationalist, John Dillon, wrote to the
Chief Secretary for Ireland on May 15:

> The attack in yesterday's *Times* on the Govt and the state-
> ment of its Military Correspondent on which the attack is
> based is an unparalleled and amazing piece of blackguardism
> and treachery. How I should like to know did the Censors
> pass this atrocious statement? It looks to outsiders as if there
> were some extraordinary treachery going on in military circles
> or in the party itself.
> ... It is enough to bring down a Government—and its pub-
> lication *must* have had that object in view.[2]

Treachery perhaps. Lord Northcliffe had written to Sir John
French on May 1, reminding him that:

> A short and very vigorous statement from you to a private
> correspondent (the usual way of making things public in
> England) would, I believe, render the Government's posi-
> tion impossible, and enable you to secure the publication of
> that which would tell people here the truth and thus bring
> public pressure upon the Government to stop men and

[1] Koss, op. cit., pp. 265, 264.
[2] Dillon to Augustine Birrell, 15 May 1915, Birrell MSS, (Liverpool), 10.3.8; see
also General Sir Henry Rawlinson to Lord Derby, 23 May 1915, Derby MSS.

246

munitions pouring away to the Dardanelles as they are at present.[1]

But was Churchill implicated in this approach or in the actions of French and Repington? Although Northcliffe's motive was partly to direct British resources to the western front, the First Lord might have shared with him a common interest in under-mining Kitchener. Hobhouse believed Churchill to be guilty of collusion in France. How could Hobhouse have discovered in-criminating evidence? He cited no source for his charge. He gave no hint that he might have had a source. He could have picked up some local gossip in Paris on the week-end, May 8–9. However, the way in which he told the story to Buxton suggests that Hob-house's belief in a Churchill–Repington conspiracy was a simple deduction from the supposition that the two men were in the same place at the same time. Hobhouse does not seem to have grasped that the overwhelming preference of both French and Repington for concentrating British strength in France made them most improbable allies for a Dardanelles-oriented Churchill.

The fact that the First Lord of the Admiralty had paid a call on the Commander-in-Chief of the B.E.F. was no secret. What was not generally known was that Churchill had gone to France to join in the delicate talks between the French and Italians over post-war Italian bases on the Dalmatian coast.[2] He called at G.H.Q. after the negotiations were finished. Travelling under the name of Spencer, and staying at the Ritz, Churchill made only a per-functory effort to remain incognito.[3] His visit was actually the occasion of a parliamentary question.[4] Churchill was a frequent visitor to the front. His 'outings', as Fisher called them, had al-ready been the cause of some dispute. Kitchener's confidant, Lord Esher, wrote in his journal on May 14: 'Churchill's visits to General Headquarters are a deep-seated cause of trouble.'[5] In the

---

[1] Reginald Pound and Geoffrey Harmsworth, *Northcliffe*, p. 475.

[2] Winston S. Churchill, *The World Crisis, 1915*, pp. 331–2.

[3] Bertie's Diary, 6 May 1915. Lady Algernon Gordon Lennox (ed.), op. cit., vol. I, p. 159.

[4] Lord Robert Cecil asked what duties the First Lord was carrying out at the front. Asquith, with more truth than loyalty, replied that Churchill had no government business to perform. Honourable members were heard to say: 'Joy ride!' (71 *H.C. Deb.*, 5s, cols 1655–6, 12 May 1915.)

[5] Esher's Journal, 14 May 1915. Oliver, Viscount Esher (ed.), *Journals and Letters of Reginald, Viscount Esher*, vol. III, p. 233.

middle of December 1914, Asquith had advised Churchill: 'I do not think you ought to go again to French without first consulting Kitchener & finding that he approves.' Churchill replied that he had always followed the procedure which the Prime Minister was now recommending.[1] Asquith was not satisfied. After a talk with Kitchener he wrote: 'These meetings have in K's opinion already produced profound friction between French & himself & between French's staff & his staff, which it is most desirable to avoid.'[2]

What neither Asquith nor Kitchener knew—although they may have suspected—was how frequently and candidly Churchill and French were in communication both by letter and through inter-mediaries like Churchill's cousin, Freddie Guest. Complaints about Churchill's influence over French were already being heard at London luncheon parties at the beginning of February.[3] But, if Churchill had wished to feed information to Repington, there were very much easier ways of doing it than through a meeting at G.H.Q. in France. What is more, anyone wanting to leak damaging facts to the press was hardly likely to do it in France. Dispatches from the front were subject to a two-tier censorship. Articles written in England could be published uncensored. Who would take a double risk of interference when uncensored publication could be guaranteed at home? In fact, Repington's dispatch slipped through both the War Office and the Press Bureau by an astonishing sequence of misapprehensions which Churchill could neither have engineered nor foreseen.[4]

Nevertheless, other sources can be produced which appear at first sight to corroborate Hobhouse's information. Five such sources are known. First, reporting a conversation with Reginald

<hr />

[1] Asquith to Churchill, with Churchill's reply in red ink, 17 December 1914, Asquith MSS, vol. 13, f. 236.

[2] Asquith to Churchill, 18 December 1914 (copy), Asquith MSS, vol. 13, f. 237.

[3] Lady Carson's Diary, 7 February 1915, Carson MSS, D1507/6/1.

[4] For the War Office side of the story, see Major-General Sir C. E. Callwell, *Experiences of a Dug-Out, 1914–1918*, pp. 323–4. 'As it came from St Omer,' Sir Edward Cook of the Press Bureau concluded, 'Brade and Callwell were doubtless confused.' (Cook's Diary, 18 May 1915, Cook MSS.) Both Sir Reginald Brade, Secretary at the War Office, and Callwell were loyal to Kitchener, and Callwell was counted on by Lord Fisher as an ally over the Dardanelles. (Fisher to Sir John Jellicoe, 3 June 1915. Marder (ed.), op. cit., vol. III, p. 254.) See also Hankey's Diary, 20 March 1915 (Hankey, op. cit., vol. II, p. 300).

McKenna, Arnold Bennett wrote in his diary: 'Churchill with French at same time as Repington. Rep's article arranged.'[1] It will be noticed that Bennett did not say that Repington and Churchill *met* at French's headquarters, merely that they were there at the same time. Nor did Bennett say *by whom* Repington's article was arranged. It is, in fact, quite possible that Repington and Churchill met in France; but there is no proof that they did so. Even if Reginald McKenna had explicitly stated that there was a meeting, and that the Repington article was arranged in concert with Churchill, McKenna's own fierce jealousy of, and hostility towards, Churchill would cast immediate doubts on the value of his testimony. (On May 12, McKenna had 'promised to stick to Fisher through thick and thin' against Churchill.) Further it would have to be asked, what was McKenna's source?[2]

Then, we find Margot Asquith writing to Lord Haldane: 'Our wonderful Cabinet, [has been] smashed! ... Practically by the man whom I always said *would* smash it—Winston.'[3] However, this remark cannot be construed as proof that the Premier's wife subscribed to the conspiracy theory. The reference is not to a conspiracy—which, for once, had no place in Margot's mind— but to the obvious cause of the smash, Churchill's inability to work with the old man whom he had insisted on bringing back to the Admiralty. Had Mrs Asquith really believed that Churchill had intrigued against her husband, she was indiscreet enough to have said so. Yet none of her known effusions of this period so much as hints at a Churchill intrigue.

In correspondence with St Loe Strachey she expressed the opinion that, but for her husband's firmness, 'Ll.G, Winston & others wd long ago have made mischief as you know.' But, so far from castigating these two, she went on to say: 'Ll.G. has come grandly out of all this he has the *sweetest* nature in the *world*.'[4] At a time when she was also writing: 'England has never been so *contemptible* as it is now!' this was hardly the language which she

---

[1] Arnold Bennett's Journal, 21 May 1915. Newman Flower (ed.), *The Journal of Arnold Bennett*, 2 vols (London, 1932), vol. 1, p. 133.

[2] Arnold Bennett also reported that, after dinner on May 21, 'Hobhouse...came in to learn from McKenna his fate, who, however, couldn't tell him.' (Newman Flower [ed.], loc. cit.)

[3] Margot Asquith to Haldane, 18 May 1915, Haldane MSS, 5911, f. 40.

[4] Margot Asquith to J. St Loe Strachey, 26 May 1915, Strachey MSS.

would have used to describe someone she suspected of treachery.[1] As for Churchill, when his own fortunes had slumped, Margot wrote to him not as an enemy but as a stricken friend:

> You have always been very kind to me & I cannot help feeling sympathy with you just now. I am very loyal to my friends & never forget anything any one has ever done for me. Will you come & see me? Can you come at 15 to 6 today. This has been an agonizing week. The saddest from a political point of view in my career & in H's also. H is a man who looks on life not only with understanding but with emotion wh is rare.[2]

Balfour, too, was counted at this time as a friend of the Prime Minister. Margot hoped to enlist his services to muzzle North-cliffe, for whom her most venomous outbursts were reserved.[3]

A third corroborative source for the conspiracy theory is a letter from the editor of *The Morning Post* to the editor of *The National Review*. 'According to H. A. Gwynne,' Dr Koss writes, 'Churchill and Lloyd George had hoped to work with Andrew Bonar Law ... and had settled for Balfour only because "A.B.L. did not like the thing from the beginning and would have nothing to do with it." '[4] By 'the thing' Dr Koss wishes us to believe that Gwynne—an enemy of Churchill whose attacks included private letters to the Prime Minister as well as press criticism—was referring to a conspiracy against Asquith. Yet, a little later in his article, the same passage is made to refer to coalition overtures.[5] An examination of the letter reveals that its subject was indeed coalition not conspiracy. Gwynne's story was that 'Lloyd George and Churchill have for the last four months been making suggestions and proposals which have been sedulously carried to our side by F.E. [Smith].'[6] The aim of these overtures was co-operation

---

[1] Margot Asquith to Strachey, 24 May 1915, Strachey MSS.

[2] Margot Asquith to Churchill, 27 May 1915, Churchill MSS. 'H' stood for Henry, Asquith's second name, which Margot preferred to his first name, Herbert.

[3] Lady Cynthia Asquith's Diary, 21–22 May 1915. Lady Cynthia Asquith, *Diaries, 1914–1918*, with a Foreword by L. P. Hartley (London, 1968), pp. 25–6.

[4] Koss, op. cit., p. 267, paraphrasing and quoting from Gwynne to Maxse, 17 May 1915, Maxse MSS.

[5] Koss, op. cit., p. 269.

[6] There is nothing in Gwynne's letter to confirm Dr Koss's statement that Gwynne had 'obtained his information' from F. E. Smith (ibid., p. 267).

between Liberals and Conservatives. No phrase or nuance in Gwynne's letter implies anything more clandestine.

There were, however, some people who did believe that something discreditable had been going on. Alexander MacCallum Scott testified in 1916 that:

A section of Liberals who bitterly resented the formation of the Coalition, and who suspected Churchill of having conspired to bring it about, organised a movement against him, and bombarded the Prime Minister and the Chief Whip with letters threatening to oppose the Coalition if he were included in it.[1]

Churchill's 'rumoured leanings towards a coalition government' had been the talk of the clubs for some months, a Liberal sympathizer told him.[2] Lunching at the Reform Club on May 21, Lord Beauchamp learned from Stanley Buckmaster, the Solicitor-General, and Cecil Harmsworth, Under Secretary at the Home Office, that 'the feeling in the Liberal Party against Churchill was very bitter in degree and increasing in extent'.[3]

Beauchamp passed on this information in a letter to Loulou Harcourt. In the same letter he added another item of news which he could be sure would concern Harcourt. Lord Emmott had written to the Prime Minister the previous evening 'on the rumour that Churchill was to go to the Colonial Office protesting against the idea with much warmth'. On Monday, May 17, Christopher Addison found that: 'the Lobby and Smoke Room of the House were in the usual tumult, all gossip and rumour. The Smoke Room is the most neurotic place I know anywhere.'[4] In the next few days, incipient neuroses were aggravated by skilful manipulation. The movement of which MacCallum Scott wrote was inspired by Walter Runciman's parliamentary private secretary, W.M.R. Pringle. Pringle's campaign was carried all the way to Asquith in a letter of remonstrance:

A number of your supporters have been driven to the conclusion that the present crisis has been brought about by the

[1] A. MacCallum Scott, *Winston Churchill in Peace and War*, p. 148.
[2] Cecil Beck to Churchill, 26 May 1915, Churchill MSS.
[3] B[eauchamp?] to Harcourt, 21 May 1915, Harcourt MSS, Box 28.
[4] Addison's Diary, 17 May 1915. Addison, op. cit., vol. i, p. 79.

actions of Mr Churchill. I do not only refer to his differences with Lord Fisher but we believe that he was privy to the intrigue which resulted in the Repington disclosures.[1]

Not resting on this, Pringle sought to induce others to follow his example. MacCallum Scott's diary for May 21 records: 'Pringle writes asking me to tell Gulland & write to the Prime Minister, as he has done, that if Churchill is a member of the coalition ministry I cannot support it.'[2]

As far as MacCallum Scott knew, Churchill was guilty of nothing to deserve such a protest:

> I certainly have not the knowledge of Churchill's alleged offence, to enable me to denounce him. Pringle may have knowledge through Runciman but he has not shared the knowledge with me. I know of no case against Churchill save what is based on the merest gossip & surmise.

MacCallum Scott was a close student of Churchill's career. He had written the first Churchill biography in 1905, and was shortly to write another. A professional journalist who had been in the House of Commons for five years, he had enough political intelligence, as well as respect for Churchill, to treat Westminster *canards* with more detachment than some of his fellow M.P.s. 'People get mesmerised', he reflected, 'by rumour & get quite angry if one suggests a doubt or a desire to await for official confirmation.'[3]

It surprised MacCallum Scott that experienced men gave credence to unsubstantiated tales. The King, dependent on second-hand gossip, also thought that Churchill had been intriguing against Kitchener.[4] Who had put the idea into his head is a mystery, as too are the motives of Pringle. There were plenty of politicians who had old scores to settle with Churchill—'this brilliant unreliable Churchill who has been a guest in our party for eight & a half years' as Walter Runciman had not long ago

---

[1] Pringle to Asquith, 20 May 1915, Asquith MSS, vol. 27, ff. 178–9; Koss, op. cit., p. 275.

[2] MacCallum Scott's Diary, 21 May 1915, MacCallum Scott MSS.

[3] MacCallum Scott's Diary, 24 May 1915, MacCallum Scott MSS.

[4] King George V to Queen Mary, 19 May 1915, Royal Archives, G.V. cc 4/132, quoted in Koss, op. cit., p. 275.

described[1] him. But why the parliamentary correspondents of *The Daily News* and *The Times* were also spreading unfounded speculations is not clear. A. P. Nicholson and Gordon Robbins were 'the authors of most of the rumours' which MacCallum Scott overheard.[2] And Robbins, whose primary allegiance was to Printing House Square, was unlikely to be attacking Churchill if Northcliffe were conspiring with the First Lord. On May 18, *The Times* advocated the replacement of Churchill by Fisher, and accused the First Lord of 'overriding his expert advisers to a degree which might at any time endanger the national safety'. Somewhat friendlier remarks might reasonably have been expected from a newspaper controlled by a co-conspirator. To Churchill, the victim of 'much unfair and ill-informed public attack' by the Northcliffe press, they came as no surprise.[3]

If there had been decades of uncertainty or fierce controversy over the origins of Repington's famous dispatch it would be easy to understand a historian's enthusiasm about Hobhouse's story. However, the frank accounts of both Repington and French — though they do not settle every question — have long provided a satisfactory explanation.[4] We know that Repington acted first on his own initiative; and that French then aided him, and took further independent action to influence Lloyd George and leading Conservatives.[5]

Neither French nor Repington mentioned Churchill in their detailed narratives on May 1915. Of course, it is legitimate to object that great care might have been taken to keep Churchill's name out of the story. All the conspirators — Lloyd George and Balfour, in particular — might have concealed their roles and

[1] Runciman to Trevelyan, 4 January 1914, Trevelyan MSS.

[2] MacCallum Scott's Diary, 24 May 1915, MacCallum Scott MSS.

[3] Churchill to Northcliffe, 7 June 1916. *The History of The Times*, vol. iv, part 1, p. 287, fn. 2. The remark about unfair attacks referred to the years before 1916.

[4] Lieut.-Col. C. à Court Repington, *The First World War, 1914-1918*, vol. i, pp. 34-41; Field-Marshal Viscount French of Ypres, *1914* (London, 1919), pp. 356-61.

[5] French's plight was genuinely felt. He had been forced to ask his subordinates to exercise restraint in the expenditure of artillery ammunition. (Haig's Diary, 10 May 1915, Haig MSS. This entry is omitted from Mr Blake's published edition of the Haig Papers.) French's emissaries were dispatched to Lloyd George, Balfour, and Bonar Law, but also to Asquith and Kitchener. (French's Diary, 12 May 1915. Major the Hon. Gerald French [ed.], *Some War Diaries, Addresses, and Correspondence of Field-Marshal Rt. Hon. Earl of Ypres* [London, 1937], p. 199.)

destroyed the relevant documents, making, as Dr Koss puts it, 'a conscientious effort to leave behind ... little evidence of their motives and actions'.[1] Moreover, Churchill might well have been tempted to stir up controversy over the munitions issue, and even to instigate an assault on Kitchener. Not only munitions, but a host of lesser irritations had diminished the Secretary of State's reputation and influence. The wife of his own Under Secretary was bearing doleful tidings of muddle at the War Office to leaders of the Conservative opposition.[2] And Asquith himself was, it turned out, quick to try to avail himself of an opportunity to quietly replace Kitchener.[3] Had it not been that Northcliffe provoked a public outcry in Kitchener's favour by launching a ferocious onslaught on him in the *Daily Mail*—against the wishes of Repington, who wanted no further publicity—Kitchener might have been ceremoniously detached from executive office.[4]

But, however plausible a conspiracy against Kitchener may seem, it is a very different thing from a conspiracy to overthrow the government. The charge has been made that 'Churchill in 1915 did not hesitate to sacrifice the Liberal Party on the altar of national victory'.[5] 'The rebels', it is alleged, 'turned against Kitchener, presumably hoping to bring down Asquith and Grey by discrediting an equally prominent and far more vulnerable member of the government.'[6] What could Churchill have hoped to gain?

There were rumours that the prize was direction of the war effort, perhaps even the premiership itself.

[1] Koss, op. cit., p. 257.
[2] Mrs Jack Tennant tried to arrange a meeting with Austen Chamberlain after talking to Lord Milner and Edith Lyttelton. (Edith Lyttelton to Austen Chamberlain, 17 May 1915, Austen Chamberlain MSS, 13/3/57; see also Cook's Diary, 18 May 1915, Cook MSS.)
[3] Churchill, *The World Crisis, 1915*, pp. 366, 370-1, 374.
[4] Reginald Pound and Geoffrey Harmsworth, op. cit., pp. 746-7.
[5] Koss, op. cit., p. 266.
[6] Ibid., p. 262.

5 'Real Events, not dirty little incidents'[1]

It must be concluded that the credibility of the Churchill–Lloyd George–Balfour conspiracy thesis is shaken by an examination of its sources. It is further weakened by the testimony of the major characters in the story. In essentials, the accounts left by Asquith, Lloyd George, and Churchill are all consistent.[2] Inexplicably, Dr Koss refers to none of these accounts. He believes that 'it is futile to look for pertinent information ... among the private papers of the leading contenders in the struggle ... for these individuals were determined to hide the facts of the matter not only from posterity but from their own colleagues and supporters.'[3] It follows, presumably, that the published memoirs of these men—'the platitudes provided by the participants in the crisis' as Dr Koss describes them[4]—are unworthy of even a casual glance. But, if attention is paid to the contributions of contemporaries, additional stumbling-blocks to accepting a conspiracy thesis will be found.

Readers of Churchill's *The World Crisis*, for example, will be aware that Churchill wrote of how he had opposed the idea of making a coalition under duress. The First Lord wished to defer reconstruction until he had reconstituted his Board of Admiralty and weathered the disturbance caused by Fisher's resignation and 'trial of strength'.[5]

[1] Birrell to Churchill, 24 May 1915, Churchill MSS.
[2] Lloyd George's account is in his *War Memoirs*, vol. I, ch. VIII.
[3] Koss, op. cit., p. 261.   [4] Ibid., p. 257.
[5] 'If matters are pushed to a conclusion,' one senior naval officer believed, 'Churchill will have to go.' The phrase, 'trial of strength', and this assessment of Churchill's chances are from Rear-Admiral A. L. Duff's Diary, 20 May 1915, Duff MSS. See also Arthur J. Marder, *From the Dreadnought to Scapa Flow*; The Royal Navy in the Fisher Era, 1904–1919; vol. II, The War Years: To the Eve of Jutland (London, 1965), ch. XI; and Admiral Sir William James, *The Eyes of the Navy*: A Biographical Study of Admiral Sir Reginald Hall (London, 1956), pp. 83 6.

Churchill thought that Lloyd George had demanded a coalition and that he had 'informed the Prime Minister that he would resign unless such a Government were formed at once'.[1] For this belief there is no corroborative evidence. While Lloyd George might have been prepared to threaten resignation in order to influence Asquith, there is no reason to suppose that Asquith needed convincing. What was the Premier's choice? Churchill believed that Asquith should have 'laid the broad outlines of his case, both naval and military, before both Houses of Parliament in Secret Session', and thus fought off the Tory challenge.[2] On May 17, Churchill prepared a formidable speech—the draft of which is preserved in the Churchill papers—in defence not only of his own policy, but of the whole Asquith administration. Though self-preservation was naturally his dominant concern, his speech included eulogies of the government that were not to be expected on the lips of a treacherous colleague manœuvring to hasten his chief's downfall.

In his *Memories and Reflections*, Asquith explained why he disagreed with Churchill's 'hypothetical solutions and retrospective short cuts'.[3] To have attempted to negotiate a coalition in the lingering atmosphere of a contentious debate would have gravely jeopardized what was already a hazardous experiment in political co-operation. Nowhere in Asquith's published works or private correspondence and conversation does any glimmer of an indication emerge that he attributed the May 1915 crisis to a Churchill intrigue. Odd as this may have seemed to anyone who shared the suspicions of Hobhouse and Pringle, it would surely have been stranger if the Prime Minister had mistrusted Churchill. Had not Churchill offered to resign on the afternoon of May 16?[4]

When Churchill put his office at Asquith's disposal, none of the objects which suspicious critics might have ascribed to him had been achieved. Kitchener seemed safe; Asquith seemed safe; and the government seemed safe. Would a man bent on the overthrow of the Prime Minister and the Secretary of State for War, or eager to participate in the creation of a coalition government,

---

[1] Churchill, *The World Crisis, 1915*, p. 365.
[2] Ibid., p. 373.
[3] Asquith, *Memories and Reflections*, vol. II, pp. 104–5.
[4] Churchill, *The World Crisis, 1915*, p. 364.

have placed himself at the mercy of the most powerful of his intended victims before there was any sign that the authority of his enemies had been undermined? So suicidal a gamble would not have recommended itself even to a politician of Churchill's comparative simplicity.

For Asquith, the problem of reconciling Churchill the resigner with Churchill the plotter did not arise. The Prime Minister had no reason to be suspicious of Churchill. Why then did Asquith decide in favour of coalition? In answer to this question, Charles Hobhouse's letter reveals an entirely new causal agent. According to Hobhouse, 'A.J.B.[alfour] put a pistol at P.M.'s head threatening debates and disclosures at W.O. and Admiralty.' But there is a discrepancy between this imaginative allegation and the story, based on the testimony of all the principal figures, that has until now never been disputed.

The well-established fact is that Bonar Law and Lloyd George confronted Asquith. There was no pistol and no Balfour. Balfour was ignorant of the proceedings in Downing Street until 11.00 a.m. on May 17.[1] He had spent the early part of the morning at the Admiralty where he learned from Churchill that Fisher had resigned and that Sir Arthur Wilson had been designated to succeed him. Realizing that Fisher's resignation would disturb the Tories, Balfour set out, according to Churchill, to prepare his 'Unionist friends ... and steady their opinion'.[2]

If there was no pistol, why did Asquith agree to coalition? The Prime Minister, says Dr Koss, 'seized Fisher's fortuitous resignation as a pretext for decisions which were in any event forthcoming'.[3] What were these decisions? They are not obvious. Asquith, it might be argued, first thought of coalition as a way of divesting himself of Kitchener. That Asquith saw coalition as an excellent opportunity to be rid of his Secretary of State for War is beyond dispute. But this benefit was not the motive for the change.

Alternatively, it might be that the Prime Minister's decision for coalition was not taken to avoid external pressure 'but to

---

[1] Blanche E. C. Dugdale, *Arthur James Balfour*, vol. II, p. 102; Lady Cynthia Asquith's Diary, 19 May 1915. Lady Cynthia Asquith, op. cit., p. 24.

[2] Churchill, *The World Crisis, 1915*, p. 365.

[3] Koss, op. cit., p. 260.

R

avert pressures from within the government that had taken him completely by surprise'.[1] What, then, were these pressures and by what unsuspected agency were they applied? The final novelty of the conspiracy theory is simple to deduce. In Dr Koss's view, Asquith consented to coalition because he had realized that Churchill was conspiring against him! The Prime Minister proposed to throw Churchill out under the cover of a necessary reshaping of the government. As Dr Koss put it: 'From the moment that the culprit became known, he was determined to rid himself of Churchill. But how? A general reconstruction promised an easy way out.'[2] With this extraordinary conclusion, the conspiracy theory is complete. Or almost complete. Two little puzzles remain to be eliminated. Why were Churchill's fellow-conspirators not brought to book as well? Because, we are told, they were too powerful. Why, if they were so powerful, could they only manage to ensure that Churchill remained in the humiliating sinecure of the Duchy of Lancaster? Because, we are told, 'of the fact that the intriguers dissolved their alliance as soon as they had achieved their primary object, the disruption of the *ancien regime*'.[3]

This remarkable thesis has the additional advantage of explaining away the awkward absence of evidence for the continuation of a Lloyd George–Churchill–Balfour alliance after May 17. But the facts are inconveniently different.

If there ever was an alliance linking Lloyd George, Balfour, and Churchill, it is bizarre to contend that it ended on May 17 because its 'primary object' had been achieved. Dr Koss seems unable to make up his mind what his conspirators were really up to. First, it is the overthrow of Asquith and Grey. Next it is the removal of Kitchener (an objective held in common, though evidently unconsciously, with Asquith). Then it is the overthrow of the Prime Minister again. Finally, it becomes nothing more than 'the disruption of the *ancien regime*' —a disruption that apparently was deemed satisfactory although it left Grey, Kitchener, and Asquith secure at their posts.[4] Was it merely coalition that the intriguers wanted after all?

[1] Koss, op. cit, p. 266.
[2] Ibid., p. 275. Dr Koss appears to have partially retracted this argument in his book on *Lord Haldane*, pp. 198–9.
[3] Koss, op. cit., p. 273.
[4] Ibid., pp. 262, 273, and *passim*.

On the intentions of Lloyd George and Balfour, Dr Koss gives us little guidance. He refers to a letter from Balfour to Lord Robert Cecil on May 17 which is supposed to show Balfour at the moment of triumph in the act of betraying his ally, Lloyd George. The letter is interesting:

My dear Bob,

On reflexion I am convinced that you had better say nothing to Ll.G. He might regard the whole scheme as an intrigue. This would be grossly unjust: but it would also be disastrous. It would lower the whole moral level of the reconstructed Government. In *any* case do not assume that I could take any part. I know more of the inside workings of the existing machine than you do—and unpleasant though my present work is, it may well be the most useful that I can do.

Yrs. aff.

A.J.B.[1]

Obscure as is the meaning of Balfour's remarks, they lend little weight to the view that he was engaged in a double-cross. Nor does Fisher's belief—which Dr Koss does not challenge— that Balfour's intervention saved Churchill from relegation to the back benches. Dr Koss does not endeavour to square this view with his picture of the elderly Conservative statesman 'playing both ends against the middle' and then playing 'the middle against both ends'.[2] In fact, Fisher's obsession that Balfour was Churchill's saviour was not only improbable, but, later, explicitly contradicted by Asquith's private secretary.[3]

Asquith never believed that his First Lord and Chancellor of the Exchequer had intrigued against him in May 1915. How could he have reconciled such a belief with the diametrically conflicting advice which he received from his two lieutenants? How could he have known of such a conspiracy at all? Even Dr Koss admits

[1] Balfour to Lord Robert Cecil, 17 May 1915, Cecil of Chelwood MSS (Add. MS. 51071, ff. 33–4).
[2] Koss, op. cit., p. 273.
[3] Sir Maurice Bonham Carter to Arthur J. Marder, 29 October 1954. Marder (ed.), op. cit., vol. III, p. 244, fn. 1. Fisher mentioned his idea that Balfour had saved Churchill in three letters to Sir John Jellicoe, and letters to Bonar Law, McKenna, Lady Fisher, and Archibald Hurd. Within three weeks, however, Fisher had overcome his feelings and was offering himself to Balfour for re-employment (Marder [ed.], op. cit., vol. III, pp. 244–5, 249, 252, 279, 254).

that 'Churchill's machinations seem to have gone virtually un-detected by contemporaries'.[1] There is a simple answer. Asquith, like most of his contemporaries, did not suspect a palace intrigue because it had not happened. The Prime Minister did not even suspect until later the collusion which had occurred between Repington and French. When he read French's book *1914* on its appearance after the war, Asquith professed shock and dismay. Perhaps he had known all along about French's actions and chose only then to pose as the injured innocent. But it is asking too much of posterity's credulity to suggest that he carried unspoken to the grave the conviction that Churchill, Lloyd George, and Balfour had plotted against him.

[1] Koss, op. cit., p. 266.

6 The Great Underlying Conflict

In the letter calling for the resignation of his Liberal colleagues, and in his published memoirs, Asquith stressed his own responsibility for making the coalition. 'I have for some time past', he wrote to his ministers, 'come, with increasing conviction, to the conclusion that the continued prosecution of the War requires what is called a "broad-based" Government.'[1] This conviction, Asquith later suggested, was not the result of any communication from opposition leaders or of representations from his own colleagues.[2] There is no reason to doubt the essential truth of this. What Asquith really meant was that he had, in his own mind, accepted the impossibility of going on alone, if the government should be seriously challenged. This did not, of course, mean that he would not have preferred to go on alone. But as soon as it was plain that Bonar Law and Lloyd George were agreed on coalition, and that their assessment of the situation was the correct one, he made no difficulty.

It might have appeared on the surface to have been a hasty decision. 'What I never foresaw', the Premier's wife admitted, 'was that H wd take such a quick decision.'[3] Certainly the reactions of his colleagues and supporters indicated that to them the move was a surprise. But the only justified surprise was in the timing not in the substance of the decision itself. There was no chance to make preliminary soundings, leaks, and hints. Everyone was caught off guard. On Saturday, May 15, Asquith attended Geoffrey Howard's wedding. The following day Churchill had to follow his chief into the country to confer on the replacement of

---

[1] Asquith to the cabinet, 17 May 1915. Asquith, *Memories and Reflections*, vol. II, p. 95.
[2] Ibid., p. 97.
[3] Margot Asquith to Haldane, 18 May 1915, Haldane MSS, 5911, f. 39.

Fisher. No sense of urgency interrupted the Prime Minister's routine.

But the very speed of Asquith's decision on May 17 is the strongest evidence that he had long realized its inevitability. Had he not already been clear about the appropriate action for the circumstances, Asquith could easily have played for time; instead he consulted no one, and, as Crewe put it, 'with no preliminary discussion with one of us, even the most intimate and influential (in which he was absolutely right) he decided on reconstruction'.[1]

Candid disclosures in the recent biography of Asquith by Roy Jenkins, and in the late Lady Asquith's study of Churchill, have thrown fresh and significant illumination on Asquith's behaviour during the weeks immediately preceding and following the decision to coalesce.[2] We now know that two days before Lord Fisher walked out of the Admiralty, Asquith had received a stunning personal blow. Venetia Stanley, whose mainly epistolary friendship had sustained and comforted him, and nourished his ego, throughout the war, had decided to marry Edwin Montagu. The letters which Asquith wrote to Miss Stanley after she told him that she had at last accepted one of Montagu's proposals, leave no doubt that the loss of her companionship was deeply wounding. At the same time, there is no reason to suppose that this personal shock had a vital influence on the decision for coalition.[3] What it did affect was the way in which Asquith managed the consequential arrangements. In learning how deeply Asquith felt this altered relationship, we can see subsequent events in an extra dimension. We can, for example, appreciate more fully the state of mind of the Prime Minister whose actions in wartime were to be described by Churchill as those of 'a stern, ambitious, intellectually proud man fighting his way with all necessary ruthlessness'.[4] Churchill, humiliatingly relegated to the Duchy of Lancaster, was bitter. 'Asquith', he wrote some years later:

did not hesitate to break his Cabinet up, demand the resignations of all Ministers, end the political lives of half his col-

[1] Crewe to Hardinge, (?) 1915. James Pope-Hennessy, *Lord Crewe*, pp. 148-9.

[2] Roy Jenkins, op. cit., ch. XXII; Violet Bonham Carter, op. cit., ch. XXIV.

[3] Cynthia Asquith, the Prime Minister's daughter-in-law, thought otherwise. See her diary, 12 June 1915. Lady Cynthia Asquith, op. cit., p. 42.

[4] Winston S. Churchill, *Great Contemporaries*, p. 146.

leagues, throw Haldane to the wolves, leave me to bear the
burden of the Dardanelles, and sail on victoriously at the
head of a Coalition Government ... These were the convulsive
struggles of a man of action and of ambition at death-grips
with events.[1]

What we must now add is that these convulsive struggles were
those of a man enduring a private torment. He was feeling, perhaps for the first time, all of his sixty-four years; and was compelled to put to the test, at the least opportune moment, the
unaided strength of his own character. 'Forced by circumstances
to the most intolerable task that could ever be laid on man.'[2] Thus
Asquith portrayed himself on May 21. Even for a Prime Minister
compelled 'to sacrifice old & tried & dear friends, and to seem to
welcome into the intimacy of the political household strange,
alien, hitherto hostile figures', the lament seems disproportion-
ately melancholy.[3] Yet this self-pitying tone was not reserved for
appeals to Miss Stanley. Political associates, too, were subject to
uncharacteristic pleas for sympathy. Hard as it was to dismiss
Haldane—as the baying Tory rank-and-file demanded—it was not
the loss of this or any other old friend but of one very young one
which shattered the Prime Minister's placidity and reserve. 'At
last', one observer noted, 'the poor darling really looks tired and
worried, and his bridge—always bad—was an eloquent barom-
eter.'[4]

To Asquith, in May 1915, a coalition government had two
advantages. It preserved national unity; and it preserved him.
The job of reconstructing the government required, as Asquith
was remorsefully aware, some energetic butchery. And temporarily lacking the steady hand which expert butchery demands,
the Prime Minister constructed a coalition device which was
only a flustered evasion of the problem of organization for
war.

[1] Ibid., p. 148. See also Venetia Stanley to Churchill, (?22) May 1915, Churchill
MSS: 'I feel I was last night grossly disloyal to the P.M. I am sure that you are
doing him a very great injustice when you think that he's sacrificed you, even temporarily ... through lack of courage, or friendship, or loyalty.'
[2] Asquith to Venetia Stanley, 21 May 1915, Montagu MSS.
[3] Ibid.
[4] Lady Cynthia Asquith's Diary, 20 May 1915. Lady Cynthia Asquith, op. cit.,
p. 25, reporting Lady Essex's observations of the Prime Minister on May 19.

In a famous lecture, Mr A. J. P. Taylor has said that 'the great underlying conflict' in British war-time politics 'was between freedom and organisation. Could the war be conducted by "liberal" methods—that is, by voluntary recruiting and by *laissez-faire* economics? Or must there be compulsory military service, control of profits, and direction of labour and industry'.[1] Seeking 'to impose the charm of order upon the chaos of historical fact', Professor Alfred Gollin has elaborated on Mr Taylor's thesis both in his book on Lord Milner and in a subsequent essay.[2]

Professor Gollin's view is that freedom versus control was the master issue in May 1915. 'It dominated the minds of Asquith, Lloyd George and Bonar Law. It was the basic cause of their actions at that time.'[3] Enough has already been said to show that the participants thought rather differently about their actions. It may be added that the problems which were pressing for solution in May 1915 did not in themselves have much relation to the broad issue of the proper sphere of government action. On May 13, for example, Maurice Hankey learned with relief that the government had decided at last to return to the policy of interning enemy aliens. Still under discussion was whether or not the British should respond to German gas attacks with the same methods. Lloyd George, who was himself beginning to receive news of the demoralizing effects of gas warfare, was primarily concerned about the organization of munitions supply. The government had already taken wide powers to control war production. Moreover, if further measures to extend the central authority had been desired, coalition was by no means the only vehicle for achieving them. The Prime Minister, if he wished to stave off military conscription and industrial compulsion, had no need of coalition so long as Lord Kitchener retained his public magnetism and his conviction that it was for the politicians in the government to decide on such matters of fundamental policy. Nor had the Foreign Secretary anything to gain from coalition. At the same time as his Liberal colleagues were negotiating with

---

[1] A. J. P. Taylor, *Politics in Wartime*, p. 21.

[2] A. M. Gollin, *Proconsul in Politics*, ch. XI; and 'The Unmaking of a Prime Minister', *Spectator*, No. 7144, p. 586, 28 May 1965. The phrase quoted is from the article in *Spectator*.

[3] A. M. Gollin to the Editor, *Spectator*, No. 7146, 11 June 1965, p. 753.

the Conservatives he was arranging to offer to lift the blockade on food entering Germany in return for an end to the German submarine campaign against merchant ships and the termination of gas warfare. While the Tories might have been persuaded to accept such an agreement, it was more likely to secure the assent of Liberal ministers conscious of the need to placate their non-conformist and humanitarian supporters.

Although he may have had some sympathy with the appeals of Lord Milner and others for national service, Bonar Law's primary aims in May 1915 were to avoid an open attack on the Liberals by the angry Tory backbenchers and to side-step the disregard of his authority which a parliamentary controversy might have entailed. Unity, of party and nation, was his paramount objective. For this reason, he did not want to break the electoral truce and revert to the party warfare that might follow from a Conservative victory at the polls.[1]

The conflicts of which the political leaders were most conscious when they agreed to coalition were not the underlying ones. There were few crestfallen defenders of freedom in the Liberal section of the new government, and few excited compulsionists in the Conservative group. At a meeting of the shadow cabinet on the day that Repington's dispatch was published, Lords Selborne and Curzon and Lord Robert Cecil had persuaded their colleagues that the time had come to encourage the government to make preparations in case industrial and military compulsion should become necessary. It was then resolved that the Prime Minister should be advised that he could count on opposition support if and when compulsion was required. But the matter was not assumed to be one on which government and opposition would inevitably be in conflict. Neither was it asserted that compulsion was being dangerously delayed.[2]

In the House of Commons, Liberal voices too, were heard on May 19 taking up the cause of national service which hitherto had been anathema in the Liberal ranks. 'I am one of those

[1] A. M. Gollin to the Editor, *Spectator*, No. 7150, 9 July 1965, p. 39; see also John Redmond's Memorandum, 15 March 1916, reporting a conversation with Bonar Law (Denis Gwynn, *The Life of John Redmond*, pp. 467–8).

[2] For Austen Chamberlain's notes of the proceedings of the shadow cabinet meeting on 14 May 1915, see Austen Chamberlain MSS, 2/2/25, and Sir Charles Petrie, Bt, *The Life and Letters of the Right Hon. Sir Austen Chamberlain*, vol. II, p. 20.

people', the former junior minister Ellis Griffith announced, 'who, after nine months of war, do not much care to see recruiting advertisements.' Universal service, said Griffith, was justified because it ensured equality of service.[1] Sir Ivor Herbert proposed that: 'We should practically register every man in this country with regard to his fitness for service in the field, and with regard also especially to those occupations in which he may be most valuably employed.'[2] And Cathcart Wason, the elderly member for Orkney and Shetland, bewailed the scandal of loafers and shirkers ignoring their duty.[3]

MacCallum Scott, in his customary scrupulous way, set out reasons for a more cautious approach:

If the coalition proposes conscription the best line is to insist:
(1) on a general election before it is carried out. Mad folly to attempt conscription unless we are convinced the country is with us.
(2) It ought to be compulsory training only. No compulsion for foreign service yet:
(3) One or two days drill a week might enable industry to be carried on.
(4) Conscription should be adopted only after it has been shown that the voluntary method has failed.
(5) Our real task while bearing a certain share in the fighting is (1) to provide munitions (2) to provide money.[4]

Cabinet disputes in future months would centre around the question of what Britain's real task was. Never did the controversy become simply a struggle between defenders of freedom and proponents of more organization. Nor, by May 1915, had the preliminary skirmishings begun. It was the political crisis itself which precipitated discussion of conscription. Even then, uppermost in the minds of Liberal and Tory leaders were the

[1] 71 H.C. Deb., 5s, cols 2414-17, 19 May 1915; see also the fragmentary notes for Griffith's speech in the Griffith MSS, 132.

[2] 71 H.C. Deb., 5s, col. 2396 and cols 2393-2402 passim, 19 May 1915. Herbert was Lord-Lieutenant of Monmouthshire and a retired major-general.

[3] 71 H.C. Deb., 5s, cols 2408-10, 19 May 1915. Wason entered Parliament as a Liberal Unionist but joined the Liberal Party in 1902.

[4] MacCallum Scott's Diary, 22 May 1915, MacCallum Scott MSS.

problems of munitions supply, strategy, and leadership at the War Office.

Between Asquith, Lloyd George, and Bonar Law there were no differences on the need for intervention in the production of armaments or on the desirability of excluding Kitchener from this area of War Office responsibility. On strategy, even Lord Milner, the most influential of the compulsionists, recognized that settling the conflicting claims of the Flanders and Dardanelles campaigns 'may very well be the vital issue, & turning point of the whole struggle'.[1]

Both Asquith and Bonar Law spoke of the delicate Italian situation as one which made imperative the avoidance of dissension at Westminster.[2] But there was one issue, of overriding and ominous importance, on which the party leaders diverged. Who should lead the nation? When Bonar Law sought out Lloyd George on May 17 he came with more than an offer of coalition. A new Prime Minister was also wanted. The Conservative leader had three suggestions: Balfour, Grey, or Lloyd George. The Liberals, as Lloyd George pointed out, would certainly revolt at the prospect of a Conservative premier. Grey's eyesight and growing passivity made him less attractive than his chief. As for Lloyd George himself, he declined at once to accept the invitation. To Sir George Riddell he said on May 23 that he could not set himself up as a rival to Asquith who had treated him so well. To Bonar Law, he admitted that he was unwilling to expose himself to the jealousy and criticism that would follow any move of his to grasp the premiership.[3] To Frances Stevenson, he confided that, above all, he was deeply moved by the fact that he had been asked to accept the premiership. But he did not 'for one moment regret having refused it'.[4]

Asquith had no inkling that Bonar Law, Balfour, and other Tory leaders contemplated a change in the occupancy of 10 Downing Street. Lloyd George said that he did not mention the

---

[1] Milner to Austen Chamberlain, 17 May 1915, Austen Chamberlain MSS, 13/3/71.

[2] Asquith to the cabinet, 17 May 1915; Bonar Law to Asquith, 17 May 1915. Asquith, *Memories and Reflections*, vol. II, pp. 95–6.

[3] Riddell's Diary, 23 May 1915. *Lord Riddell's War Diary*, p. 94; Chamberlain's Memorandum, 17 May 1915, Austen Chamberlain MSS, 2/2/25.

[4] Frances Stevenson's Diary, 18 May 1915, Lloyd George MSS.

idea to the Prime Minister because he thought it might unnerve Asquith in his negotiations with the Conservatives.[1] A more likely explanation is that he knew how quickly Asquith would dismiss a suggestion to stand aside in favour of a Foreign Secretary who was almost blind, or a Conservative who had been driven out of the leadership of his own party. Lloyd George, being the only credible alternative, would stand revealed as a colleague disloyally thrusting himself forward in collusion with the Tories.

Oblivious to these calculations, Asquith also allowed no hint to pass his lips that coalition meant any change of policy.[2] Professor Gollin has argued that posts in the new ministry were allotted deliberately to balance two factions: the voluntarists and the compulsionists. Juggling men as a substitute for decision-making smacks of authentic Asquithianism. But the lines of fracture on the basic dilemmas were by no means clear enough in May 1915 for Asquith to have been able to distribute seals with the fine precision with which Professor Gollin credits him.[3] As it happened, on manpower questions, Walter Long's compulsionist tendencies at the Local Government Board, were counterbalanced in the following months by Walter Runciman at the Board of Trade and John Simon at the Home Office.[4] The pliable Balfour made no trouble at the Admiralty. Grey at the Foreign Office, and McKenna at the Treasury, were admirably placed to withstand pressure from the Conservative leaders, especially as Austen Chamberlain and Bonar Law were kept busy with the peripheral problems of India and the Colonies. But the wedding of offices to men was mainly designed to achieve a simple imbalance of power. The strength of parties not factions was Asquith's first

[1] Riddell's Diary, 23 May 1915. *Lord Riddell's War Diary*, p. 94.

[2] In *Memories and Reflections* (vol. II, p. 100) Asquith wrote: 'I let it be publicly understood from the first—lest there should be any suspicion that there was to be a new departure in policy—that three of the principal offices would remain unchanged: those of Prime Minister, of Foreign Secretary, and of Secretary of State for War.' The columns of Hansard, however, record mention only of the Prime Minister, and Foreign Secretary. (71 *H.C. Deb.*, 5s, col. 2392, 19 May 1915.)

[3] A. M. Gollin, *Proconsul in Politics*, pp. 260–4.

[4] Very soon Runciman and Simon 'concerted measures to confound the conscriptionists'. (Runciman to Hilda Runciman, 25 August 1915, Runciman MSS.) Their measures were not confined to cabinet wrangling. Pressure in the lobby and popular agitation were encouraged. (Pringle to Runciman, 27 August 1915, Runciman MSS.)

consideration. What is more, his choice was far from unfettered. Ambitions, unspoken but unchallengeable claims, and the immediate Tory proscriptions, limited the scope for a selection designed to produce a deadlock on future policy.[1] As John Gulland told McKinnon Wood, the Secretary of State for Scotland, after a long talk with Asquith on May 22: 'There are endless difficulties about the Coalition, & very little is settled. It is a superhuman task to fit everyone into places.'[2]

[1] See the discussion of 'A Delightful Conundrum', on pp. 277–82, for the key moves in the distribution of offices.
[2] Gulland to McKinnon Wood, 22 May 1915, McKinnon Wood MSS.

7 Reactions

The coalition was not welcomed with an outburst of rejoicing. Radical Liberals and the more vehement Tories were equally gloomy, though for different reasons. The fears of the radicals were well expressed by Francis Hirst:

> I think the time has come to act without delay in the matter of conscription. I fear that nearly all the Liberal journalists and newspaper proprietors can easily be got at and persuaded. The Liberal imperialists and the Tory imperialists together are quite capable of working up a panic and rushing the country into military slavery. I had a long talk yesterday with Lord Morley about it. He says that John Burns predicts a revolution in the north.[1]

From the point of view of F. S. Oliver, on the other hand, the initial fault of the coalition was that it actually seemed to delay the coming of 'military slavery'. Oliver's best-selling polemic, *Ordeal by Battle*, contrasted the new government with its predecessor:

> Its opinions were more numerous, its delays were even longer, its vacillation was more marked, its disagreements caused greater scandal. The old vat had been half-emptied of its former contents and filled up with new wine; but it was the same vat, and the predominating flavour remained the same. The same Prime Minister, pre-eminent and adroit in discussion, controlled its deliberations; and it continued to deliberate when the need was for action.[2]

[1] Hirst to Sir John Brunner, 31 May 1915, Brunner MSS. Hirst was soliciting funds for the production of an anti-conscription pamphlet.
[2] F. S. Oliver, *Ordeal by Battle* (London, 1916, abridged edition), p. Ii. The book had been reprinted twice within a month of publication by Macmillan in June 1915, and there had been a second edition in July 1915.

Oliver's judgment was undisguisedly partisan. Nevertheless, the sales of *Ordeal by Battle* showed that his view was popular. Oliver, and other associates of Milner, saw the formation of the coalition as a glowing opportunity for the introduction of national service as a condition of Conservative co-operation. Milner and his acolytes were tireless in attempting to convert potential allies. Austen Chamberlain was a regular target. On May 21, Chamberlain received a twelve-page exhortation in Milner's hand recommending a drastic policy, the virtual commandeering of the whole nation. A change of persons without a new spirit, Milner argued, would be useless:

> If the new Govt, like the old, begins by hesitating & drifting & toying with half-measures, it will not restore confidence, the unrest will continue, there will & must be a fresh agitation in the Press—with the lamentable result that the Govt, as before, will never take a lead, but always appear to have every strong step they take forced upon them from outside.[1]

Milner's criticisms and prophecies, irrespective of their validity, undermined confidence in the new combination. But an unenthusiastic reception from Milner was predictable, and less damaging to the Prime Minister than the wounded vanities of his ex-ministers—those who were unceremoniously drained out of Oliver's old vat. Haldane, Samuel, Montagu, Pease, Emmott, Lucas, Hobhouse, and Beauchamp, all had to go.[2] Most of them went gracefully, if reluctantly.

Only Haldane and Churchill were axed at the specific insistence of the Tories. Both had good reason to feel badly treated. Churchill, 'worn out and harassed', exclaimed to Sir George Riddell on May 20: 'I am the victim of a political intrigue. I am finished!'[3] The following day he wrote to Asquith, offering to accept 'any office—the lowest if it is of use'.[4] For Haldane, not

---

[1] Milner to Chamberlain, 21 May 1915, Austen Chamberlain MSS, 13/3/73. Four days earlier, a twenty-page letter from Milner had concluded: 'If ministers can't be compelled to do the right thing about national service, stale-mate is the *best* result we can hope for.' Austen Chamberlain MSS, 13/3/71.

[2] Subordinate posts in the government were found for nearly all of them, though Lucas happily seized the chance to venture out on active service. (Lucas to Runciman, 30 May 1915, Runciman MSS.)

[3] Riddell's Diary, 20 May 1915. *Lord Riddell's War Diary*, p. 89.

[4] Churchill to Asquith, 21 May 1915 (Marder, *From the Dreadnought to Scapa Flow*

even the lowest office was available. 'We have to search our memory in vain for an attack on a public man which has been more ungenerous, more ungrateful, and more unfounded,' *The Westminster Gazette* had written early in January 1915.[1] Kitchener, 'much disgusted' as he told Grey, authorized the release of information which would refute allegations that Haldane had been responsible for pre-war reductions in the nation's armed forces, guns, and ammunition reserves.[2] But the attacks were relentless;[3] and the Conservative leaders supinely followed where their most fanatical supporters led.

Too anguished and ashamed, perhaps, to find words for the occasion, Asquith let Haldane go without any expression of apology or regret. Haldane had offered to stand aside to make a place for Sir Edward Carson, but the new Lord Chancellor was a Liberal—the former Solicitor-General, Stanley Buckmaster —not a Conservative.[4] Haldane, though deeply hurt, accepted his dismissal without rancour. 'As to myself,' he wrote to Simon, 'I was not under the slightest illusion. If a Govt was to be formed which was to have undivided public opinion behind it, I could not be there.'[5]

Most of the other banished members of the ministry had no cause to complain of victimization. They could, and did, complain of the manner in which they were dispatched. Aggrieved more than anyone else was Hobhouse. Six months after the event, he wrote to Buxton: 'I do not see how it could be possible to sit in Cabinet comfortably with a Chief who would throw one over at a moment's notice.'[6]

No matter how annoyed they were at the abrupt demand for

---

vol. II, p. 288). The typed draft of this letter in the Churchill MSS is more abject still: 'I will accept any office—the lowest if you like—that you care to offer me.'

[1] *The Westminster Gazette*, 8 January 1915.

[2] Kitchener to Grey, 18 January 1915, Grey MSS, FO 800/102.

[3] 'I hope that the really admirable work of the *Daily Express* will be *daily* continued,' wrote Lord Milner's future wife to one of the editors who had attacked Haldane. (Lady Edward Cecil to R. D. Blumenfeld, 18 March 1915, Blumenfeld MSS.) Dr Koss's *Lord Haldane*, includes a useful discussion of the press campaigns against the Lord Chancellor.

[4] The best discussion of this episode is in R. F. V. Heuston, *Lives of the Lord Chancellors*, p. 224; see also Roy Jenkins, op. cit., pp. 361–2.

[5] Haldane to Simon, 26 May 1915, Simon MSS.

[6] Hobhouse to Buxton, 1 December 1915, Buxton MSS.

their resignations, the Liberal ministers made little protest. Most of them probably would have said, though perhaps not meant, what Herbert Samuel said to Asquith on May 26: that the Prime Minister had 'the most invidious & difficult task that had ever fallen to the lot of any Prime Minister' and that no one should add to his burdens by refusing to co-operate.[1] Such urbanity could not be expected from all quarters.[2] And, when Liberal loyalties were put to the test in the several political crises which preceded Asquith's resignation in December 1916, there was more than one occasion when disillusioned ex-colleagues focused parliamentary discontent rather than rallied support for their party leader.

Although senior colleagues were treated ineptly, they were at least taken partly into the Prime Minister's confidence in a memorandum which he sent to explain why he had decided on coalition. For the parliamentary Liberal Party, however, no conciliatory explanation was at first offered. There was, therefore, widespread shock and exasperation at the announcement of coalition. Lord Beaverbrook, characteristically, devoted only two sentences to this aspect of the story. 'The Liberal rank and file were annoyed by what seemed a kind of inexplicable overthrow. Old friends had to be excluded from office to make room for the newcomers—a painful business.'[3]

It was so painful a business that there was nearly a backbench revolt led by W. M. R. Pringle, Richard Holt, and the usually faithful Sir Thomas Whittaker. Not all the party was in a rebellious mood. Three Liberals had actually spoken in favour of coalition in the House of Commons on May 17. When secret negotiations for coalition had already been in motion for about

---

[1] Memorandum by Samuel, 26 May 1915, Samuel MSS, A/48/7.

[2] Further ripples of disappointment and reproach may be traced in Hobhouse to Runciman, 28 May 1915, Runciman MSS; Riddell's Diary, 19 June 1915 (*Lord Riddell's War Diary*, p. 105); John Bowle, *Viscount Samuel*, p. 125; Sir Almeric Fitzroy's Diary, 20 and 26 May 1915. Fitzroy, *Memoirs*, vol. II, pp. 594–5); Montagu to Venetia Stanley, (?) May 1915 (S. D. Waley, *Edwin Montagu: A Memoir and an Account of his Visits to India* [London, 1964], p. 71); Pease's statement, 3 June 1915 (72 *H.C. Deb.*, 5s, cols 7–8); Emmott's Diary, 13 June 1915, Emmott MSS. Roy Jenkins (op. cit., pp. 340–1) prints a class list of cabinet ministers drawn up by Asquith a few months before the formation of the coalition. There is a marked correlation between rank in the class list and survival in the ministry.

[3] Beaverbrook, op. cit., p. 127.

twelve hours, the colourful M.P. for Pontefract, Handel Booth, rose to rebuke one of his fellow Liberals:

> To say that there is an overwhelming opinion in this House against a Government which is above party, and in favour of the Government sitting on these benches, shows an un-familiarity with the opinions of Members of this House which astonishes me. I ventured to put a question to the Prime Minister some days ago, and since then a very large number of Members have made it their duty to speak to me privately and give me their views. I could astonish my hon. friend with regard to the views held by many of his own friends who sit near him. My opinion is ... that a united Ministry—call it what you will—is coming, and will come before very long. I have not often taken upon myself the role of a prophet, but I venture to say that the position will compel the formation of a Government which represents the House more fully than the present one.[1]

Booth needed no great foresight to see that trouble was loom-ing over the government's attempt to hinder discussion of the rumoured shortages of munitions. A Conservative, Sir Richard Cooper, had proclaimed minutes earlier that it was intolerable for the House to be muzzled. Sir Henry Dalziel, the Liberal proprietor of *Reynolds' News*, had urged reorganization of the War Office and 'a Government of national representatives'.[2] A number of Liberal M.P.s as well as members of other parties were chafing at the use of the party truce to stifle independent criticism.[3] Thus the Prime Minister's announcement of coalition, exactly a week after he had solemnly assured the House that a coalition govern-ment was 'not in contemplation', was sure to be received with mixed feelings.

On May 19, Asquith faced a gathering of Liberal rebels in a committee room of the House. His audience had just heard the news of planned reconstruction in 'black and angry gloom'.[4] They were indignant because the Irish and Labour leaders had

---

[1] 71 *H.C. Deb.*, 5s, col. 2107.

[2] 71 *H.C. Deb.*, 5s, cols 2103–5.

[3] See, for example, the debates on the Immature Spirits (Restriction) Bill, 17–18 May 1915.

[4] Violet Asquith's Diary, (?19) May 1915. Violet Bonham Carter, op. cit., p. 402.

been approached first. Some whispered that Churchill was to blame; others declaimed against Kitchener. Many looked with repulsion to the prospect of submitting to a coalition yoke.[1]

A crucial confrontation could not be avoided. The best account of this important meeting was written by MacCallum Scott:

> Asquith announced today that the Government was under reconstruction—personal and political. Pringle and Hogge and I put down an amendment to reduce the Whitsuntide adjournment from 3 weeks to 1 week. Afterwards we attended a scratch party meeting with Whittaker in the chair. Whittaker spoke very strongly against a coalition. Then Pringle announced an amendment and moved that the meeting support it. Holt supported. Leif Jones and Russell Rea and Murray MacDonald opposed. They all took the party line that the Prime Minister owed some explanation to his party—ought to take his party into his confidence. They wanted to have it out with him but they could not attack the coalition in the House—it had gone too far for that, and they strongly deprecated Pringle's motion as a vote of no confidence. Just then Asquith was fetched by Gulland who had heard how things were shaping. Asquith spoke with deep feeling—his voice husky and his face twitching. He looked old and worried. He flung himself on our mercy. Within a week a wholly new situation had been revealed to him. There had been unexpected disclosures which had taken them wholly by surprise. He could not reveal the truth to us yet without imperilling national safety.
>
> But the situation was of the gravest kind. Coalition became inevitable. He had no desire to retain office—he would not do it without our confidence. He was ready to resign tonight. It was not pleasant to go into harness with men who were the bitter enemies of everything he held dearest in public life—still less to part even temporarily from old friends and colleagues. He asked for our confidence—he would not let us down. He appealed to us not to have any discussion in the House, at the present stage. It would be disastrous. He could but suggest, he feared he was saying too much, that the

[1] Ibid., p. 404; Addison's Diary, 19 May 1915. Addison, op. cit., vol. I, p. 80.

intervention of neutrals hung in the balance and it was only by their intervention that the war could be brought to a successful conclusion. The meeting gave him an overpowering ovation.[1]

'Some of the members were moved even to tears, as was the P.M. himself,' Christopher Addison was informed.[2] We may surmise that a tear or two reached Asquith's cheeks for old and valued friends and fellow-workers. And some too, perhaps, for Venetia Stanley.

The Prime Minister's impromptu performance disarmed opposition but did not eliminate the disgruntlement in the Liberal ranks. Following the emotional applause came the candid confessions to friends and diaries. Richard Holt recorded: 'Liberal opinion is dissatisfied and many Liberal members ... are vexed and suspicious. The P.M. ... alleged foreign affairs of an unrevealable character as his reason—in a speech impressive but not ultimately convincing.'[3] Pondering over the same events, Christopher Addison concluded that some of his party chiefs were inclined to count upon infinite docility from their followers. 'It is well that they should be disillusioned.'[4] There was, however, only the palest flicker of revolt. After Asquith made his plea, and was hustled out of the room by the whips, he was chased by Pringle and MacCallum Scott. He granted their request that the new government would meet Parliament as soon as possible. They asked for no more.[5]

[1] MacCallum Scott's Diary, 19 May 1915, MacCallum Scott MSS.
[2] Addison's Diary, 19 May 1915. Addison, op. cit., vol. 1, p. 80.
[3] Holt's Diary, 30 May 1915, Holt MSS.
[4] Addison's Diary, 19 May 1915, loc. cit.
[5] MacCallum Scott's Diary, 19 May 1915, MacCallum Scott MSS.

8 A Delightful Conundrum

'Political leaders', wrote the Liberal backbencher, Walter Roch, in commenting on Asquith's appeal to his party in May 1915, 'live for the most part on, and by, the faith of the more simple-minded of their supporters.'[1] Because of the success of his appeal to the Liberal rank and file, Asquith was not quickly disillusioned. In a letter addressed to the Chief Whip, but intended for circulation to the parliamentary Liberal Party, the Prime Minister admitted that:

It is natural that such a sudden and fundamental upheaval of our traditional practice should create astonishment, and even arouse misgiving, among a large number of those upon whose loyal devotion and strenuous efforts I, like my predecessors in the leadership of the Liberal Party for generations past, have always relied ... [2]

Explaining that only a 'clear and urgent case of national necessity' justified the new departure, he declined to elaborate. 'I cannot in the public interest enter into any details, and must ask my friends to rely for the moment on my judgment.' From the astonishment and misgiving of his devoted followers, the Prime Minister tried to extract not merely goodwill but personal trust and obedience. At the same time he was brazen enough to plead difficulties with his own party as a bargaining counter in the negotiations with the Tories over the distribution of offices:

On the morning of Tuesday, May 25, I commissioned Ll. George to see B. Law and to point out:

(1) The resentment of our party at the exclusion of Haldane.

[1] Walter Roch, *Life of David Lloyd George: Mr Lloyd George and the War* (London, n.d., ?1919), p. 129. Roch's book was issued as vol. IV of Herbert du Parcq's *Life of David Lloyd George*. 3 vols and 1 vol. of speeches (London, 1912–13).
[2] Asquith to Gulland, 28 May 1915 (printed copy), Runciman MSS.

(2) Their resentment at the inclusion of Carson [as Attorney-General].

(3) The impossibility from a party point of view of both Admiralty and War Office being in Tory hands.

This was intended to prevent B. Law taking the office of either Munitions or the Exr.[1]

Asquith had little confidence in Bonar Law's capacity for high office. But was Lloyd George's mission intended to do no more than ensure that the Tory leader was not given a post to which he was unequal? If Bonar Law had been generally recognized as one of the most outstanding administrators alive, would it have saved him from Lloyd George's blandishments? An important letter from Lord Crewe to Lloyd George on May 24 furnishes some clues to the motives of the Liberal leaders:

I have been pondering over the delightful conundrum that has been set us to solve; and the following occurs to me: assume for the moment that the Opposition will not agree, (a) to your undertaking munitions, with Asquith taking charge of the Exchequer, or (b) to your remaining at the Exchequer, with Runciman undertaking munitions.

I think they may be stiff about this with some colour of reason; because besides the S/S for War, the Ministers directly dealing with the conduct of the main war are (1) the Prime Minister, (2) the Chancellor of the Exchequer, (3) the First Lord, (4) the Home Secretary, (5) the President of the B. of Trade.

The S/S for India and the Colonies have no real authority in it. Personally I have had some, from my long experience on the Defence Committee; but the Indian troops in Europe & Egypt have been handed entirely over to the War Office, so in ordinary circumstances the India Office would have not more to do with the war than the Post Office has.

Therefore our plan would place only one Unionist Minister

---

[1] Asquith's Note, 26 May 1915, Asquith MSS, vol. 27, ff. 216–17. (Roy Jenkins, op. cit., pp. 368–9; Robert Blake, *The Unknown Prime Minister*, p. 251; and, without the explanatory sentence, in Spender and Asquith, *Life of Lord Oxford and Asquith*, vol. ii, p. 171.) In referring to the War Office, Asquith probably had in mind the proposed Ministry of Munitions which was intended to perform what had been part of the War Office's function.

in the inner circle, and him [Balfour] not one of their inner circle as it now exists.

So that I should like to know what you think of a possible expedient which has occurred to me. Like you, I regard it as imperative for different reasons that both the Exchequer and Munitions should not fall into Opposition hands. Then let you take Munitions, and let McKenna come to the Exchequer. And let them have the Home Secretaryship, thus securing three S/S out of five.[1]

Crewe's letter leaves no doubt that Asquith's aim, shared and promoted by Crewe and Lloyd George, was to rigidly circumscribe the influence of his new partners. Bonar Law's supposed inadequacy was doubtless one reason for this determination. But the objection was not just to Bonar Law as an individual but to any Conservative. In fact, the scheme devised by the three Liberals was extraordinary in its boldness and in its impetuous disregard of obvious perils. Asquith accepted without demur the dismissal of Churchill from the Admiralty as one of Bonar Law's conditions for coalition. Haldane was also scheduled for sacrifice, albeit he was the 'victim to cruel and absolutely groundless accusations'.[2] But the Premier did not confine his ruthlessness to dealings with his own colleagues. To ensure that he and the remaining Liberals retained maximum power, he adopted and operated the substance of Crewe's solution to the 'conundrum'.

When it is understood that Crewe's solution was only second-best, then the true audacity of Asquith's conduct becomes apparent. How had Asquith originally intended to dispose of the principal offices? The essential move, the basis of the whole arrangement, was to have been the expulsion of Kitchener from the War Office. Kitchener's place was to be filled by Lloyd George. Who was to go to the Exchequer? Before he had time to master this part of the puzzle, Asquith was forced to meet Bonar Law. Having thought of no suitable alternative position for the Tory leader, and no plausible reason for excluding him from the Exchequer, Asquith was obliged to offer him the post. To

[1] Crewe to Lloyd George, 24 May 1915, Lloyd George MSS, C/4/1/22.

[2] Memorandum by Lord Stamfordham, 25 May 1915. Royal Archives, GV K/700, paraphrasing Asquith's statement at a meeting at 10 Downing Street before lunch.

have suggested at the outset of negotiations that Balfour alone among the Tories would be given one of the major ministries (the Admiralty) would have killed coalition before it was born.

Bonar Law was content to accept this distribution of the top places. Whether or not Asquith genuinely intended that Bonar Law should have the Exchequer it is impossible to say. Having been rushed into a cabinet-making exercise it is hardly surprising that Asquith was soon looking for a way of withdrawing the offer of the second post in the ministry to the Conservative leader. Why should Bonar Law not be Chancellor? We know that Lloyd George was briefed to say that the Liberals would not accept a Tariff Reformer at the Exchequer. Since this argument could also be used to block Austen Chamberlain, the last Conservative Chancellor, it served a desirable dual purpose. By eliminating the likely Conservatives on the basis of the same disability, Asquith had no need to fall back on his feeling that Bonar Law was particularly unfitted for the task. However, it was one thing to find a justification for keeping Bonar Law out of the Exchequer. It was quite another to fill the Exchequer with a Liberal without at the same time opening a new vacancy to which Bonar Law would have a strong claim.

The situation was further complicated by an unforeseen obstacle: Kitchener's unshakeable grip on the War Office. If Lloyd George had gone to the War Office, it might have proved possible to employ the 'no Tariff Reformer' argument to get another Liberal into the Treasury, especially if Asquith had sweetened the Conservatives by offering them the Home Office and the leadership of the House of Lords as well as the India and Colonial Offices. But Kitchener's removal, the prerequisite, was not easy to effect.

His fame having been magnified by a government publicity campaign of unprecedented intensity and duration, the Secretary of State could not be discarded with impunity. A reputation built over forty years and trumpeted to every literate household in the land was more than adequate protection against a Liberal premier's disfavour. If Kitchener were to vacate the War Office, some new and prestigious employment had to be found for him. Make him Generalissimo of the Home Forces, suggested Sir Ivor Herbert in the House of Commons on May 19.[1] Asquith's own thought was

[1] 71 H.C. Deb., 5s, cols 2400-1. Lord Esher had suggested on May 14 that

similar. But Kitchener's relations with French, strained as they were while he held a political appointment, would not have survived his resumption of military seniority over the Commander-in-Chief. The King advised him to stay at the War Office.[1] Maurice Hankey busied himself with retailing stories of his indispensability.[2] And the Prime Minister, flinching from dismissal, confirmed Kitchener in his post, adding the Order of the Garter as a mark of royal favour. With Haldane (solaced with the Order of Merit) gone, Kitchener remained with Churchill as a scapegoat in reserve for future emergencies.

Because Kitchener was immovable, it was imperative that the supply of munitions should be taken out of his control. The King himself, although standing by Kitchener, expressed the hope that the Secretary of State would be relieved of all responsibility for the supply of munitions.[3] To make this possible, the creation of a separate Ministry of Munitions was the logical step. It might have seemed equally logical that, if Bonar Law could not have the Exchequer because he was a Tariff Reformer, he ought to become the new Minister of Munitions. With Grey remaining at the Foreign Office, no other position in the first rank was available. Of course, Asquith would have preferred a man of proven ability for the vital munitions undertaking. But the leader of the Conservatives in the House of Commons—even if he was 'an untried horse' with no previous cabinet experience[4] could hardly be rejected on the grounds of unsuitability. A publicly defensible cause for disqualification had to be produced. As Crewe's letter shows, it was not enough merely to be able to say again that the mass of Liberals would protest. The argument about the likelihood of Liberal opposition to the appointment had to be combined with the production of an alternative candidate with impeccable qualifications. Thus, as Asquith (recorded, Lloyd

---

Kitchener should be both C.-in-C. Imperial Forces of the Crown at home and overseas, and Secretary of State, an idea that Kitchener put aside a week later, having no desire 'for any increase of authority or any enhancement of position'. (Esher's Journal, 17 19, 21 May 1915. *Journal and Letters of Reginald, Viscount Esher*, vol. III, pp. 236–41.)

[1] Philip Magnus, *Kitchener*, p. 325.

[2] Hankey's Diary, 19 May 1915. Hankey MSS, op. cit., vol. II, p. 316.

[3] Memorandum by Stamfordham, 22 May 1915, Royal Archives, GV K/770.

[4] Stamfordham to the King, 19 May 1915, Royal Archives, GV K/770, reporting Asquith's opinion.

George was instructed to persuade Bonar Law that it would be intolerable for Liberals if Kitchener, Balfour, and Bonar Law himself ran the three departments most concerned with directing the war. And, to this argument, Lloyd George added the presence of a uniquely qualified substitute Minister of Munitions—himself.

Crewe assumed, and Lloyd George and Asquith agreed, that the Tories would not accept Bonar Law's exclusion from Munitions if the job went to a Liberal other than Lloyd George. Runciman, for example, would not do. 'Both sides thought the Country would not regard him as of sufficient standing tho' he is an able man of business.'[1] On the other hand, the 'no Tariff Reformer' argument was so strong that Lloyd George could be safely shifted from the Exchequer and his place be taken by McKenna. Thus the conundrum was solved. Lloyd George became the first Minister of Munitions. And Bonar Law, ignoring the advice of his Conservative friends, took the Colonial Office, a post held by Joseph Chamberlain in the last Conservative administration, but a poor base from which to direct the Conservative forces in a national war government.[2]

[1] Memorandum by Stamfordham, 25 May 1915, Royal Archives, GV K/770.
[2] Asquith's attempts to juggle men and offices can be partly reconstructed from the notes in the Asquith MSS, vol. 27, ff. 196–213.

Part IV Prologue

1 The Gamble

Coalition was both a solution and an experiment. 'It's not very funny,' wrote Margot Asquith:

> & it is not a source of strength *really* as History has proved time after time. All I can say [is] H has done what he thought right. *It's a great gamble.* I wish with all my heart and soul it had not come about.
>
> I don't mind betting that B. Law & Curzon will never play fair.
>
> Austin [*sic*] is straight so is Walter but they are stupid. B.L. is slim & simple. Curzon an egotist & nearly equal to Winston—less dangerous however as he is more common-place.[1]

Asquith had succeeded, by a hastily improvised shuffle of personalities, in effecting 'a monstrous inequality in the distribution of power'.[2] Into his ministry came the leaders of the Conservative party—the slim, the simple, and the stupid—and a small contingent of Labour representatives, all in subordinate posts. Only the Irish Nationalists stood aloof, and they promised cordial support from outside.[3] Yet, according to Lord Beaverbrook, from the very moment at which Asquith and his principal Liberal colleagues set on foot their scheme to depreciate the status of their new partners, especially Bonar Law, the first coalition was doomed.[4]

Few historians would endorse so fatalistic a judgment without

[1] Margot Asquith to Strachey, 24 May 1915, Strachey MSS.
[2] Lord Beaverbrook, *Politicians and the War*, p. 131.
[3] Stephen Gwynn, *John Redmond's Last Years* (London, 1919), pp. 192-3; Denis Gwynn, *The Life of John Redmond*, ch. XII.
[4] Lord Beaverbrook, op. cit., p. 133.

qualification. Nevertheless, the student of these events will search in vain for evidence of contentment at the creation of the national government. 'I feel *no* confidence in the future,' Augustine Birrell confided to John Redmond. 'Thank God I have already missed *two* Cabinets. When George IV first saw his future wife he called for a brandy!'[1] Walter Runciman was no more hopeful. 'It is a queer unpalatable prospect for those of us who remain in this mixed company. At the worst it cannot last long.'[2]

For the Conservatives, Curzon entered with trepidation the 'long expected and (by me) much dreaded Coalition'.[3] Walter Long hated the idea of coalition and thought it was unnecessary. 'I loathe the very idea of our good fellows sitting with these double-dyed traitors; but of course I shall support our leaders and the Government.'[4] As Austen Chamberlain advised Bonar Law, if the government asked for help they had no option but to give it:

> God knows each one of us would willingly avoid the fearful responsibility; but the responsibility of refusing is even greater than that of accepting, and in fact we have no choice ... We cannot shirk this job because we don't like it or because we think the risks to ourselves too great. You and I have been absolutely agreed about our attitude all through, and, as I told you, I am wholly with you now.[5]

Radical Liberals, already disillusioned by a leadership which had taken the country into war and begun to infringe the rights of neutrals and curtail the freedom of industry and private citizens at home, found in the coalition confirmation of their gloomy forebodings about the future of the Liberal Party. 'This

---

[1] Birrell to Redmond, 29 May 1915. Denis Gwynn, op. cit., p. 427.

[2] Runciman to Samuel, 26 May 1915, Samuel MSS, A/48/6. See also Harcourt to Lord Novar, 7 June 1915, Novar MSS, MS 696/1330.

[3] Curzon to Lord Lamington, 18 May 1915. Earl of Ronaldshay, *The Life of Lord Curzon: being the authorized Biography of George Nathaniel, Marquess Curzon of Kedleston, K.G.*, 3 vols (London and New York, n.d. [1927–1928]), vol. III, p. 125. Lord Lamington was a former Conservative M.P. and Governor of Bombay, 1903–7.

[4] Long to Carson, 25 May 1915. Ian Colvin, *The Life of Lord Carson*, 3 vols (vol. I by Edward Marjoribanks) (London, 1932–6), vol. III, pp. 50–1.

[5] Chamberlain to Bonar Law, 17 May 1915. Sir Charles Petrie, Bt, *The Life and Letters of the Rt Hon. Sir Austen Chamberlain*, vol. II, pp. 23–4.

is the end of the Liberal Party,' Charles Trevelyan predicted, 'now all Liberalism will be abandoned and we shall live under conscription and martial law.'[1] The inclusion of Sir Edward Carson as Attorney-General, particularly when there were no Nationalists in the ministry, was an offence to Liberals as well as to Irish members. 'It is', wrote MacCallum Scott, 'like calling in a burglar to guard the house against rioters.'[2] To Ramsay MacDonald, continued reflection on the coalition only made him like it the less. 'I think it is heartbreaking', he confessed to Charles Trevelyan, 'that the Labour Party could have been so misled by personal vanity & self-seeking.'[3] Brooding in Lossiemouth, MacDonald came to the conclusion that, although the coalition was not popular, people at least wanted to try it.

MacDonald's assessment of public opinion was sound. The spirit of patriotic acquiescence was the major element in the national mood upon which the Prime Minister's gamble rested. However much Asquith, or anyone else, disliked the cessation of party government, nobody could offer a more attractive alternative than coalition. And, if the party leaders were prepared to attempt a temporary and limited fusion for the safety of the nation, then an inescapable obligation devolved on lesser men to strive to make it work.

In reserving all but one of the senior posts in the reconstructed ministry for Liberals, and especially in putting McKenna at the Treasury and leaving Runciman at the Board of Trade, Asquith fostered the belief that a united government could be created without the 'sacrifice or compromise in any quarter of settled convictions and principles'.[4] Even the Home Office went not to a Tory, as Lord Crewe had suggested, but to Sir John Simon. Those of Asquith's Liberal colleagues who were curious about 'what demands were made or assurances given on *policy*' were partly mollified by the Prime Minister's declarations.[5] But, the more remote that Liberals were from his personal entourage, the less they were convinced by Asquith's implied guarantees of

[1] Trevelyan to Mary Trevelyan, 21 May 1915, Trevelyan MSS.
[2] MacCallum Scott's Diary, 24 May 1915, MacCallum Scott MSS.
[3] MacDonald to Trevelyan, 28 May 1915, Trevelyan MSS.
[4] Asquith, *Memories and Reflections*, vol. ii, p. 104.
[5] Runciman to McKenna, 19 May 1915, McKenna MSS. Stephen McKenna, *Reginald McKenna*, p. 223.

voluntarism and free trade. 'Nothing', wrote Charles Hobhouse to Walter Runciman, 'will persuade me that this is not the end of the Liberal Party as we have known it: and that you and others will not find yourselves responsible for measures you disapprove, but cannot in the supposed "national" interest reject.'[1]

The backbench diarists, Richard Holt and Alexander Mac-Callum Scott, were also pessimistic. MacCallum Scott feared that the next general election might come when a national Liberal Party machine was no longer able to support candidates against a coalition with 'unlimited funds at its disposal'. It followed, he thought, that critics of the coalition, if they wished to retain their seats, would be well advised to keep in close touch with their constituencies. 'They may have to rely on their own personal reputation & influence among the electors. They ought to be busy educating the public.'[2] MacCallum Scott was soon turning to concerted activity in the House of Commons with W. M. R. Pringle, J. M. Hogge, and a handful of like-minded critics.[3] The basis of their attitude was acceptance of coalition for the purpose of carrying on the war. 'Let us criticise the government only where we think its policy or administration are not calculated to lead to the speedy end of the war.'[4]

Richard Holt, too, participated in 'consultations between independent Liberal members'.[5] By the middle of June, Holt thought that the government and the House of Commons were settling into a new routine: 'the latter to watch the former rather in an anxious & puzzled frame of mind'.[6] Holt was associated with a small group—originally called 'the seven wise men'—organized by Sir Charles Nicholson. Its members were Holt, J. W. Wilson, Russell Rea, Sir Thomas Whittaker, Leif Jones, Murray Macdonald, James Falconer, Sir Frederick Cawley, and

[1] Hobhouse to Runciman, 28 May 1915, Runciman MSS.
[2] MacCallum Scott's Diary, 23 May 1915, MacCallum Scott MSS.
[3] Pringle, Hogge, and MacCallum Scott dined with Sydney Arnold, Sir Arthur Marshall, and J. W. Pratt at the Grand Hotel Grillroom on June 2. They agreed to form a group, work together, and consult regularly. Arthur Sherwell, Harry Watt, and C. T. Needham were invited to join, additional new members being restricted to those unanimously approved by the group. (MacCallum Scott's Diary, 2 June 1915, MacCallum Scott MSS.)
[4] MacCallum Scott's Diary, 25 May 1915, MacCallum Scott MSS.
[5] Holt's Diary, 6 June 1915, Holt MSS.
[6] Holt's Diary, 20 June 1915, Holt MSS.

Sir William Middlebrook. Their common aim was 'giving the Government a Liberal pull whenever possible'.[1]

The obvious discontent on the Liberal benches encouraged the leaders of the Union of Democratic Control to hope that numbers of government supporters might be ready to listen to the tocsin of dissent. 'At first I was inclined to think', Arthur Ponsonby wrote to Charles Trevelyan:

> that so far as you, MacDonald & I were concerned there was no real change as it was not the *conduct* of the war but the *origins* & the *settlement* about which we would want to express ourselves. But I am not quite sure this is the case because we have new elements to deal with.
>
> (1) The imminence of Conscription.
>
> (2) The declared view of members of the new Government as to our aims in the war. Bonar Law, Austen Chamberlain, Curzon & perhaps Milner all having declared in one way or another that we should only stop when we get to Berlin.
>
> (3) Churchill's monstrous betrayal of his trust in keeping the Cabinet in the dark about the Dardanelles (hotly resented by many Liberals as the chief cause of the breakdown).
>
> (4) The necessity of getting a declaration of policy from the new Government.
>
> (5) All viewed in the light of the casualties which are said now to average 2,500 a day.
>
> (6) Bearing in mind that attack on this new Coalition will not be resented but welcomed by many Liberals, if it is judicious & can be shown to be really patriotic.
>
> Should we therefore continue to remain silent?[2]

Ponsonby's thesis was that 'bewildered members released completely for the first time from party allegiance will welcome a lead'. And Trevelyan believed that only patriotism prevented seething unrest erupting from the febrile parliamentary equilibrium.[3]

In so tense and unpredictable a situation, it is hardly likely

---

[1] Ibid.

[2] Ponsonby to Trevelyan, 22 May 1915, Trevelyan MSS. Milner did not, in fact, become a member of the government.

[3] Ibid.; Trevelyan to Mary Trevelyan, 4 June 1915, Trevelyan MSS.

that the Prime Minister should have felt 'serene and confident in his own powers', the master of his own destiny.[1] On the other hand, it is misleading to speak of 'Asquith's surrender' or to regard the making of the coalition as 'a triumph in party warfare for the Conservatives'.[2]

According to Professor Wilson, Bonar Law's coalition overture on May 17 'marked the point at which a series of attacks on ministers culminated in an attack on the ministry as such'.[3] And Mr A. J. P. Taylor has written of 'Law and Lloyd George dictating action to Asquith'.[4] But there were deeper forces at work. If coalition was a defeat for the Premier, it was a defeat for Lloyd George and Bonar Law as well. With Tory backbenchers in the Unionist Business Committee, Irish Nationalists, and even some Labour members beginning to unite in what Mr Taylor calls 'a common discontent', the union negotiated by the party leaders was indeed a coalition of 'the front benches against the back'.[5] Professor Hewins of the Unionist Business Committee, instigators of the parliamentary rebellion over shells, had complained that 'B.L. and Co. have always—up to the last moment deprecated and discouraged strong action.'[6] Coalition was an assertion by the leaders of both major parties that they, not their followers, would dictate the course of events. None of the three creators of the national government wanted to depart from accustomed political arrangements. In doing so, they recognized a joint interest in national unity and personal survival which, while it lasted, was to be the unifying inspiration of their partnership.

Much that was clear to the perceptive few in May 1915 had only slight impression on the minds engaged in olympian compromise. The need for shells nobody could ignore. Strategic options, west and east, were also obvious and controversial.

---

[1] This is the view of A. M. Gollin, *Proconsul in Politics*, p. 255 and ch. XI. Gollin adduces the testimony of Lord Beaverbrook (op. cit., p. 145) in support of his belief that Asquith was 'a man convinced of his own power' in May 1915. However, the passage cited refers to the 'summer months' of 1915 and not to the period when the coalition was being formed.

[2] Trevor Wilson, *The Downfall of the Liberal Party*, pp. 49, 53.

[3] Ibid., p. 56.

[4] A. J. P. Taylor, *English History, 1914-1945*, p. 30, fn. 2.

[5] Ibid., pp. 31–2.

[6] Hewins's Diary, 20 May 1915. W. A. S. Hewins, *The Apologia of an Imperialist*, vol. II, p. 32.

Among Liberals, C. P. Scott was ready to inveigh against drift, and hanker vaguely after 'a courageous initiative and an organising mind'.[1] Augustine Birrell, more sharply, wished for a governing instrument truly fashioned for war:

> As for the twopenny-halfpenny Coalition ... I can take no interest in it. A *Big-Swollen*-Loose-fibred affair with a lot of *unwarlike* commonplace fellows from all quarters. Why should the country have any more confidence in it than its predecessors? My opinion, had it been asked, would have been in favour of a *War Council* of Eight (4 from each side) to meet *daily* for *War* purposes only, to leave the *Cabinet* alone to manage its several *departments* as before & meet once a month.[2]

But advocacy of the unworkable by the ineffectual was not enough. Nor was the oracular rumination of Lord Esher, who discerned that 'the real flaw is in the want of unity of command'. What purpose would be achieved by calling, as Esher did, for 'one brain and a single responsibility' to take great decisions?[3] Asquith might agree, but retort that fit as he no doubt was to supply the mental power and assume the responsibility, there were proper constitutional barriers to dictatorship. Asking the Tories would be still more futile. Their demand was not for Napoleonic rule — who among them could they trust to be paramount? — but for seats in council, voices in debate.

Marginal improvements there could be. Maurice Hankey, as secretary to the war council, knew as well as anyone the defects of Asquith's administration. 'There is literally no one in this country', Hankey wrote in a minute for the Prime Minister on May 17, 'who knows, or has access to, all the information, naval, military and political on which future plans must be based.'[4] On May 21 he persuaded Asquith to insist on receiving all naval and military operational telegrams and letters in addition to the regular batches from the Foreign Office. Hankey himself was to be

---

[1] Scott to J. L. Garvin, 18 May 1915. J. L. Hammond, *C. P. Scott*, p. 187.

[2] Birrell to Churchill, 24 May 1915, Churchill MSS.

[3] Esher to Lionel Brett, 12 May 1915. *Journals and Letters of Reginald, Viscount Esher*, vol. III, p. 232.

[4] Hankey's Diary, 21 May 1915. Hankey, *The Supreme Command*, vol. I, p. 326.

the link between Asquith, the War Office, and the Admiralty.[1] Through Hankey's busy liaison, and digestion of the daily record of his ministers' actions, the premier would 'get a much closer grip on the war'.[2]

Instinct apparently satisfied Asquith that, with the formal machinery of opposition dismantled, the coalition would for some months enjoy immunity from attacks by fragmentary combinations in the House of Commons. The mutterings of agitated Liberals could even be an advantage to a Prime Minister under pressure to make concessions to his Conservative colleagues. Whether or not John Gulland's intelligence work uncovered the activities of Sir Charles Nicholson's 'seven wise men' or the group led by Pringle and Hogge, so long as the principles of these groups remained traditionally Liberal Asquith had little to fear. By June 1915, Liberals were very far from having crystallized into rigid factions. Attitudes to the war and to its conduct were confused. In the Union of Democratic Control, it is true, there were more certainties than doubts. But other men sought in informal collaboration little more than the pooling of information and the clarification of issues. Their associates were often those with whom they had worked in other causes—for temperance, perhaps, or Scottish interests—and who shared as yet half-intimated fears rather than defined objectives.

Within six months, Sir Frederick Cawley was no longer interpreting the Liberal creed in the stubbornly cautious manner to which Richard Holt clung. 'A more vigorous prosecution of the war', became Cawley's touchstone, the Liberal War Committee— a new group of some forty determined backbenchers—his vehicle. From the Pringle–Hogge circle, J. W. Pratt left to become joint secretary of the new group; and MacCallum Scott also gradually detached himself from his old Scottish allies and moved into the company of Cawley, Sir Henry Dalziel, Sir Arthur Markham, and the other moving spirits in the Liberal War Committee.[3]

But this was in the future. In May, what most Liberals wanted was a sense of participation in the direction of the nation's war

[1] Hankey's Diary, 21 May 1915. Ibid., p. 317.
[2] Hankey's Diary, 15 May 1915. Ibid., p. 315.
[3] MacCallum Scott's Diary is the best source for the history of the Liberal War Committee. There is a brief autobiographical note by Lord Cawley in the Cawley MSS. The files of Dalziel's newspaper, *Reynolds' News*, should also be consulted.

effort. Lord Murray of Elibank believed that the Prime Minister should call his supporters to a party meeting and 'make use of that wonderful personal magnetism, which I used to find so effective when I was in a difficulty, namely, the personal touch and hold that the P.M. has over his own people when they are brought together.'[1]

John Gulland was unconvinced, probably less because he doubted the efficacy of the Asquithian magic than because he could think of nothing which might be said that had not already been said when Asquith appealed for loyalty on May 19.[2] Presumably, Asquith too saw no point in another meeting. Unhappy after 'the most hellish fortnight of his life', he was not likely to be disposed towards further consumption of humble pie on a public platform.[3] That, at least, he could be spared.

The Prime Minister's Liberal followers had to be content with a circular letter from their leader, dated May 28, which asked much and explained nothing. Gulland's contribution was a covering note in a style of risible piety:

In view of the national circumstances, I am sure that every Liberal will appreciate the difficult position in which the Prime Minister has been placed, and will rally to his support. The Liberal Party well knows how he had given himself wholeheartedly and successfully to the Liberal cause.[4]

[1] Murray of Elibank to Gulland, 14 June 1915 (copy), Murray of Elibank MSS vol. III, f. 167.
[2] Trevor Wilson, op. cit., pp. 60–1.
[3] Birrell to Redmond, 29 May 1915. Denis Gwynn, op. cit., p. 426. Birrell was reporting on Asquith's feelings.
[4] Gulland's circular letter, 28 May 1915, Norman MSS.

2 A Lightning Streak of Nobility

Asquith's decision for coalition coincided with an intimate shock. Filial affection from an unsuspecting daughter softened the blow.[1] Political comfort had to come from elsewhere. To whom did the Prime Minister turn? Lord Crewe, as usual, gave what Asquith called 'wise counsel, and your loyal and unselfish help'.[2]

But it was Lloyd George whose agreement to organize the supply of munitions was the keystone of reconstruction. 'I doubt whether there will be much competition to undertake that responsibility,' Professor Hewins wrote. 'I think the man who does so is going to certain death and some dishonour with the present generation.'[3] Yet Lloyd George vacated the second post in the ministry to take up the challenge. And, at Asquith's behest, he carried out the unpleasant task of persuading Bonar Law not to insist on securing the high office to which he was entitled. A few hours after his interview with Bonar Law, Lloyd George received a letter so unusual in tone that he printed it in facsimile in his *War Memoirs* twenty years later:

Tuesday, May 25, 1915   10 Downing Street,
                                              Whitehall. S.W.

My dear Lloyd George,

I cannot let this troubled & tumultuous chapter in our history close without trying to let you know what an incalculable help & support I have found in you all through. I shall never forget your devotion, your unselfishness, your powers of resource, what is (after all) the best of all things your self-forgetfulness.

These are the rare things that make the drudgery and

[1] Violet Bonham Carter, *Winston Churchill as I Knew Him*, pp. 384–5.
[2] Asquith to Crewe, (?) May 1915. James Pope-Hennessy, op. cit., p. 149.
[3] Hewins's Diary, 20 May 1915. Hewins, op. cit., vol. II, p. 33.

squalor of politics, with its constant revelation of the large,
part played by petty & personal motives, endurable, and
give to its drabness a lightning streak of nobility.
I thank you with all my heart
     Always yours affectionately

H. H. ASQUITH[1]

Here was gratitude. And something more, a barely disguised
appeal for continued help. Losing Venetia Stanley and gaining
a new government, Asquith tacitly acknowledged that he was
entering into a new stage in his long relationship with his senior
Liberal colleague. Out of emotional distress and political reverse
there had come an unexpected personal dependence. Where once
the Chancellor's flamboyance had required Asquith's calming influence, now it was the premier who looked to Lloyd George for
sustenance through the turbulent times which he divined ahead.

It had not been easy for Lloyd George to go to Munitions.
'I remain in the Exchequer,' he told his brother on May 17. The
next day he affirmed that he could 'retain my present office if I
want to'.[2] However, it already had been provisionally decided
that he was to replace Kitchener at the War Office. 'You have the
courage', St Loe Strachey wrote, 'to tell people home truths and
to make them do disagreeable things.'[3] Lloyd George had already
warned the war council on May 14 of the danger of going on
from day to day at the Dardanelles 'merely drifting'. Reports were
beginning to reach him of the drastic decline in British morale
because of German gas attacks.[4] And, as the war had continued
he had taken an increasing interest in the non-financial aspects of
war policy. Concerned as he had become with strategy and the
supply of munitions as well as army and civilian morale, tenure
at the War Office would give him commanding authority in
formulating and applying new solutions.

We have seen that Asquith finally kept Kitchener at his post.

[1] Lloyd George, *War Memoirs*, vol. 1, facsimile letter between pp. 234-5. There are
several errors of transcription where the letter is quoted on pp. 239-40.

[2] Lloyd George to William George, 17 and 18 May 1915. William George, *My
Brother and I*, p. 251; Frances Stevenson's Diary, 18-19 May 1915, Lloyd George
MSS.

[3] Strachey to Lloyd George, 21 May 1915, Lloyd George MSS, C/11/3/80.

[4] Robert Donald to Lloyd George, 6 May 1915, enclosing 'a poignant appeal sent
to me by a colonel commanding troops at the front', Lloyd George MSS, C/4/8/10.

It should also be observed that Lloyd George made scarcely any effort on his own behalf to capture the War Office. It was almost as if, foreseeing imminent conflict over military and industrial compulsion, he prudently avoided thrusting himself into the centre of the controversy. Munitions was another matter, the issue of the moment, on which men of all parties had agreed that action was overdue. 'A Cabinet Committee cannot have executive power,' Lloyd George reminded the Prime Minister on May 19, 'it can only advise and recommend. It is for the department to act.'[1] Nevertheless, he was not eager to grasp the responsibility. Asquith offered a tempting package: the Chancellor could stay at the Treasury—where there was comparatively little business after the recent Budget—and organize munitions from there. 'In three months', as the Prime Minister explained hopefully to the King, 'Mr Lloyd George ought to have the whole matter systematized and on a proper working basis after which there would not be enough work for one Minister.'[2]

The Conservatives, understandably, would have nothing of such a proposal.[3] Nor was Lloyd George's 'brilliant inspiration' that Asquith might himself mind the Exchequer while Lloyd George created the new department treated with much gravity, notwithstanding the Prime Minister's enthusiastic endorsement of this proposed revival of Pitt's dual position during the Napoleonic Wars.[4]

For Lloyd George to leave the Treasury for Munitions would be a bad bargain. But it was the only way to stop Bonar Law from achieving his legitimate ambition for one of the major posts. Asquith was equal to the problem. With the formal announcement of the detailed disposition of places in the government, there came an important footnote:

The Prime Minister has decided that a new Department shall be created, to be called the Ministry of Munitions, charged

[1] Lloyd George to Asquith, 19 May 1915. Lloyd George, op. cit., vol. 1, p. 204.
[2] Stamfordham's Memorandum, 22 May 1915, Royal Archives, GV K/770.
[3] Lord Beaverbrook thought, at the time, that Lloyd George was trying unreasonably to block Bonar Law's path for his own selfish ends rather than at Asquith's request. (Lord Beaverbrook, 'The Politics of the War', May 1917, galley proof, first draft for *Politicians and the War*, Book 1, Lloyd George MSS, F/4/5/8.)
[4] Frances Stevenson's Diary, 24 May 1915, Lloyd George MSS.

with organizing the supply of munitions of war. Mr Lloyd George has undertaken the formation and temporary direction of this department, and during his tenure of office as Minister of Munitions, will vacate the Office of Chancellor of the Exchequer.[1]

Walking in the garden of his home at Walton Heath, Lloyd George informed Sir George Riddell that he had to do it. 'They all wanted me to, and the King was anxious that I should. It will be a temporary arrangement only. I shall go back to the Treasury and shall retain my house at Downing Street, which I shall probably use as the offices of my department.'[2]

Clearly implied in this private conversation and in the official press statement was the understanding that whoever went to the Exchequer remained there only at Lloyd George's pleasure. As Lord Crewe had pointed out on May 24:

> If later on Munitions cease to be absorbing, and Treasury matters become so, with a fresh Budget impending, you could either shift places, or you could work jointly [with Reginald McKenna] at financial measures; so that you would still exercise a great deal of control over them, in a manner which would prevent anything being proposed of which you do not approve.[3]

The public humiliation of McKenna which this arrangement entailed breathed dangerous life into an enmity but recently buried. Had McKenna been a junior minister who could be expected to be grateful for such lofty elevation on any terms, then Lloyd George's security would have been cheaply bought. But McKenna was not a young suppliant. He was a rival of long standing. His previous record and status entitled him to almost any post in the Prime Minister's gift: holding the Exchequer as a seat-warmer for Lloyd George could not fail to be a deeply distasteful duty. It might have been argued that McKenna's continuing unpopularity over the aliens question made him lucky to survive the upheaval at all. Conservative hostility made it difficult for him to make conditions. Nevertheless, Asquith had

[1] Asquith, *Memories and Reflections*, vol. II, p. 104.
[2] Riddell's Diary, 26 May 1915. *Lord Riddell's War Diary*, p. 96.
[3] Crewe to Lloyd George, 24 May 1915, Lloyd George MSS, C/4/1/22.

intended to let him stay at the Home Office which would have been a mark of confidence and esteem. On the tentative list of ministers prepared for the King on May 22, McKenna was allocated to the Home Office.[1] The move to the Exchequer as a stand-in was, in the circumstances, a slight that could not quickly be forgotten. Against Lloyd George, McKenna was to have in the months ahead a festering grievance, augmenting the distrust and rivalry which had never been a secret.[2]

Lloyd George, so far as he made any calculation, seems to have thought McKenna's embitterment a price worth paying for insurance against boredom or failure to master the problems of munitions supply. That the insurance was even believed to be necessary was testimony to the trepidation with which the Chancellor relinquished the massive authority of the Treasury. 'Whatever I had done directly or indirectly to hasten or assist in the creation of this [Munitions] department ... the last thing I desired was to have to assume control of it.'[3] It was 'a horrible job' to begin.[4] And the future, Lloyd George later wrote, was 'a wilderness of risks with no oasis in sight'.[5]

Historians have delivered a different verdict about Lloyd George in May 1915. Most of them have pictured not a hesitant man, uncertain about his own political safety, but a decisive manipulator of men and events. Dr Guinn writes that 'by threatening further exposure of the delays and obstructions in munitions supply, [he] was able to procure the formation of a Ministry of Munitions with himself at the head'.[6] Dr Gollin portrays 'tremendous and fearful energy' only to be kept in check by denying both Lloyd George and the Tories any control over the departments traditionally dealing with industry and manpower.[7] Mr A. J. P. Taylor, as we have already seen, is 'not sure that Lloyd

---

[1] Stamfordham's Memorandum, 22 May 1915, Royal Archives, GV K/770.

[2] Lord Beaverbrook (op. cit., p. 143) wrote that 'Lloyd George and McKenna had agreed amicably enough to part Bonar Law's ministerial heritage among them.' But later events soon exposed the tension which McKenna's dutiful acquiescence and his wife's effusive gratitude concealed in May 1915. (See Pamela McKenna to Asquith, 26 May 1915, Asquith MSS, Vol. 27, f. 220.)

[3] Lloyd George, op. cit., vol. I, p. 237.

[4] Lloyd George to Asquith, 28 May 1915, Asquith MSS, vol. XVII, f. 225.

[5] Lloyd George, op. cit., vol. I, p. 238.

[6] Paul Guinn, op. cit., p. 83.

[7] A. M. Gollin, op. cit., p. 263.

George played so passive a part. Perhaps he pushed Law forward.'[1] But it is Professor Trevor Wilson who supplies the most
formidable catalogue of Lloyd George's assertive sins: 'blatant
disloyalty to his colleagues, open intriguing for office, and a ready
acceptance of compulsion and Conservative allies.'[2] According
to Professor Wilson, Lloyd George was 'mobile in his party
allegiance if it meant furthering [his political career]'. And, 'the
war having placed Lloyd George in a position to displace Asquith,
he did not scruple to seize this opportunity for his advancement'.
Finally, Professor Wilson contends:

> Lloyd George's great abilities in war, far from helping the
> Liberal government, contributed to its fall. He was so de-
> tached from most of his colleagues that his achievements did
> not redound to their credit but rather high-lighted their
> shortcomings, thus enhancing the case for a new govern-
> ment in which his talents would be better supported.[3]

The deductive gymnastics of this last paragraph are not persuasive. However much Lloyd George's talents were admired—as
they were, though not without misgiving, by Professor Hewins,
for instance—there is no evidence to link such approbation with
the causes of the government's fall.[4] What of the other charges?
Blatant disloyalty to colleagues? Which ones? Masterman, for
whom he had run the risk of offending his Welsh supporters?
McKenna, whose Welsh Church policy he had defended against
the attacks of the Welsh Parliamentary party? Or Kitchener, who
had frustrated every independent initiative in the field of munitions? Nowhere does Professor Wilson provide cases or evidence,
though over shells, and Lloyd George's relations with Northcliffe in the week after coalition had been agreed, there is at least
a hint of collusion.[5]
If the charge be that Lloyd George's actions on May 17 and
the subsequent days were obviously disloyal to Asquith, then

---

[1] A. J. P. Taylor, *English History, 1914–1945*, p. 30, fn. 2.
[2] Trevor Wilson, op. cit., p. 41.   [3] Ibid., pp. 52, 45, 52.
[4] 'If Lloyd George were a big man he would make the move,' Professor Hewins
wrote in March 1915 with reference to industrial organization and manpower. 'He
would take the bulk of our party with him, not to speak of his own, and the others
would not dare to do anything. But I doubt Lloyd George is man enough to do it.'
(Hewins's Diary, 19 March 1915. Hewins, op. cit., vol. II, p. 21.)
[5] Lord Beaverbrook, op. cit., p. 88.

Asquith's own letter of May 25 is more than sufficient answer. 'Ll. G', testified Mrs Asquith on May 26, 'has come grandly out of all this he has the *sweetest* nature in the world'.[1] As for the allegation that Lloyd George dedicated his abilities not to strengthening the Liberal government 'but to further[ing] the formation of a coalition in which he would have the Conservatives as allies', there is not the slightest proof that he was more enthusiastic for coalition in 1914 or 1915 than Asquith, Grey, or Crewe. Indeed, in an unpublished memorandum preserved in the Royal Archives, Lord Stamfordham revealed the complete equanimity with which Lloyd George faced the prospect of the breakdown of coalition negotiations:

> In the end [at a meeting on May 24] Mr B. Law said that if the P. Minister could not agree to his terms, it might be better to give up altogether the Coalition Government. Mr Lloyd George did not seem to regard this alternative with much alarm and had even thought of some other arrangement by which the Prime Minister might bring into the Government some non-party Peers e.g. Lords Revelstoke, Sydenham, Esher—Mr Duke M.P. as one opposed to a Coalition etc.[2]

The persistent accusation that Lloyd George, having once proposed a national government as the way out of a critical situation in 1910, always thereafter had only 'a tenuous association with the Liberal Party' has never been supported by credible evidence. Professor Wilson offers the proposition that 'one sign of the instability of his party allegiance was his craving for a coalition'.[3] But the best that he can produce to convince us of this 'craving' is a further undocumented assertion that Lloyd George encouraged Conservatives to attack his own government, a guess by the *New Statesman* on May 22 that he favoured coalition, and the fact that 'a number of his supporters were publicly agitating for it'.[4]

[1] Margot Asquith to Strachey, 27 May 1915, Strachey MSS; see also Margot Asquith to Lloyd George, 17 May 1915, Lloyd George MSS (Family).
[2] Stamfordham's Memorandum, 25 May 1915, Royal Archives, GV K/770; Trevor Wilson, op. cit., p. 52.
[3] Trevor Wilson, op. cit., p. 52.
[4] Ibid., p. 53. Of the two 'supporters' agitating for coalition, Handel Booth had never enjoyed Lloyd George's confidence; and Sir Henry Dalziel speaking on May 17, had probably learnt that coalition had already been accepted in principle.

In fact, Lloyd George perceived no greater advantage for himself in a coalition than in a party government. Nor, if the record be examined, does he appear to have been a proponent of conscription in the period up to May 1915. On at least one occasion when the subject had been raised in cabinet, he argued in favour of continuing the voluntary system. On 25 August 1914, according to Lord Emmott, 'Winston wasted our time most atrociously today in pressing on our notice a premature scheme of conscription. He was both stupid and boring. Asquith contemptuous at first, but did not bear him down.'[1]

Asquith's contempt extended to omitting any mention of the discussion on Churchill's proposal in the cabinet letter to the King.[2] But Jack Pease kept a private note, summarizing the proceedings:

> Churchill haranged [sic] us for half an hour on the necessity of compulsory service. Pointing out the importance of young unmarried men going to the front rather than the Territorial, a married man who had trained with a limited obligation, & now his patriotism was exploited by being pressed into going abroad & almost compelled to agree to do so, whilst others were loafing & cheering & doing nothing for their country etc. etc. etc.
>
> We all sat and listened, much bored. The P.M. took it with impatience—the matter he said was not urgent. George said we need not be in a panic—the people would not listen to such proposals. The P.M. asked how many of our own men in the H of C would now assent, such a proposal would divide the country from one end to the other ... K said it might come to this later on. He made no appeal for compulsion yet, he had got his 120,000 men & recruiting was still going on although he had only asked for 100,000—he could not arm more before April.[3]

At this early stage, Lloyd George's attitude in cabinet was indistinguishable from that of Asquith. But from mid-November

[1] Emmott's Diary, 25 August 1914, Emmott MSS.

[2] Asquith to the King, 25 August 1914 (Cab. 41/35/36). Venetia Stanley was informed that Churchill had indulged in 'a long and rhetorical diatribe' on compulsory service. (Asquith to Venetia Stanley, 26 August 1914, Montagu MSS.)

[3] Pease's Diary, 25 August 1914, Gainford MSS.

onwards he had faced and accepted the possibility that compulsion might become necessary. He had, since September, been in communication with St Loe Strachey who had persuaded him that the best way to avoid conscription would be to register compulsorily all men of military age liable to service and to allocate shire and city quotas as targets for local recruiting authorities. When Lloyd George put the quota scheme before Kitchener, the Secretary of State said:

> 'You know what lies behind that?' Lloyd George said, 'I know very well.' Kitchener said, 'You know that means that every district that does not contribute its quota is liable to Conscription.' Lloyd George said, 'I know that very well.' Kitchener said, 'Then I can have no objection.'[1]

The scheme did not obtain cabinet sanction. Nor does any official record of it seem to survive. But the correspondence of St Loe Strachey with Robertson Nicoll and Charles Masterman leaves little doubt about what Lloyd George had in mind.[2]

Although he had recognized that the failure of the voluntary system would necessitate conscription, it does not follow that Lloyd George wanted the voluntary system to fail. Anyone who has read his speeches between September 1914 and May 1915 cannot fail to be struck by the powerful pleas which he made again and again for recruits to come forward in such numbers as would make conscription irrelevant.

In the Queen's Hall speech on September 19, commenting on reports of German outrages, he said: 'If you turn two millions of men forced, conscripted, and compelled and driven into the field, you will certainly get among them a certain number of men who will do things that the nation itself will be ashamed of.'[3]

At Cardiff, on September 29, he told the assembled Welshmen: 'All we are asking is to escape conscription. We are not liable to the military tyranny that dominates the Continent. We have the

[1] Robertson Nicoll to Strachey, 11 November 1914, Strachey MSS, reporting a conversation with Lloyd George.

[2] See Strachey to Robertson Nicoll, 13 November 1914 (copy), Robertson Nicoll to Strachey, 18 November 1914; Strachey to Major-General John Adye, 30 November 1914, to Masterman, 25 August and 16 October 1914, and to Lieutenant-General Sir H. C. Sclater, 8 December 1914 (copies), Strachey MSS.

[3] Lloyd George, *Through Terror to Triumph*, p. 5.

protection of the seas ... a volunteer army of 250,000 is just as good as a forced army of 250,000 ...'[1]

And, after his speech at the City Temple on November 10, *The Times* reported:

> In a passage which was evidently interpreted by the meeting as significant of the Chancellor of the Exchequer's own views on the subject of conscription, he laid emphasis on the fact that we had raised hundreds and thousands of men who had 'volunteered'. It was the greatest Volunteer Army that the world had ever seen.[2]

A series of pronouncements of this kind cannot be reconciled with the idea that Lloyd George readily accepted compulsion. It is true that in March 1915 he joined Kitchener in arguing for compulsory powers to control workers in munitions factories. But on that occasion he was supported by McKenna whose credentials as a last-ditch opponent of compulsion have never been queried.[3] Moreover, in negotiating the Treasury Agreements a few days later Lloyd George personally committed himself to a voluntary and co-operative basis for industrial relations that had hardly anything in common with the coercive regulations which Kitchener and Churchill had wished. And in the same month, in an interview published in *Pearson's Magazine*, he again emphasized the efficacy and democratic nature of voluntary recruiting.

Treacherous colleague, intriguer, ardent compulsionist and coalitionist, Lloyd George was none of these in the first nine months of the war. He had struggled to find a role in the unaccustomed environment of war politics. 'It is a great wrench', he told Free Churchmen, 'for most of us who have during the whole of our lives been fighting against militarism to be driven by irresistible force of conscience to support a war.'[4] In the teeth of tremendous doubt and danger he had learned a new rhetoric and a new resolve. The war had to be won. Whether conscience dictated that Belgium be defended or simply that Britain be

---

[1] *South Wales Daily News*, 30 September 1914.

[2] *The Times*, 11 November 1914.

[3] Pease's Diary, 4 March 1915, Gainford MSS; Emmott's Diary, 7 March 1915, Emmott MSS.

[4] *The Times*, 11 November 1914.

preserved, the conclusion was the same. 'Mere optimistic bluff is not going to float us through this hurricane,' he warned the Prime Minister.[1]

In May 1915, the conflict had merely begun. The nation was discovering the cost of continental war. Politicans had seized upon coalition as the vessel to ride out the storm. Who would command? 'People say', wrote Lord Esher to his son Maurice on 16 June 1915, 'that Lloyd George will oust Asquith. It is possible. He has the ear of the groundlings and the Tories have taken him to their bosom as I always knew they would.' The Tories were ready for a new leader. What of the Liberals? 'It isn't Munitions alone that you will have before long to organise, I expect,' wrote C. P. Scott to Lloyd George on May 24, 'but the nation for war.'[2] Other Liberal eyes were starting to look in the same direction.[3] And in their gaze they found a compelling but enigmatic personality. He knew that within him were the energy and persuasive powers that could gear the nation for victory. But years as chief lieutenant had welded dependence to ambition. Whatever deficiencies war had revealed in the Prime Minister's capacity, his magisterial authority outweighed Lloyd George's brilliant flair. How could the Asquithian magic be challenged? Compounded of 'incomparable intellect', 'probity of mind', 'precision of speech', and 'freedom from all paltry motives', Asquith stood as yet beyond the reach of those who sought his place.[4] Why, indeed, should Lloyd George wish to topple the man with whom he had worked so long in harmony? Edwin Montagu was convinced a year before that Lloyd George's loyalty was irreproachable. 'To work with him', Montagu had written to Asquith:

is a revelation of rare and marvellous qualities of enthusiasm, of courage, and of industry, and also of directed ambition. I used to think he was out for popularity: that is quite untrue. He will do nothing for popularity which he believes to

[1] Lloyd George to Asquith, 18 February 1915. Beaverbrook, op. cit., p. 81.

[2] Scott to Lloyd George, 24 May 1915. J. L. Hammond, op. cit., p. 188.

[3] Even J. M. Hogge, before striking out on an independent course, extended a feeler in Lloyd George's direction. (Hogge to Lloyd George, 27 May 1915, Lloyd George MSS, D/20/1/1.)

[4] The phrases are all from A. G. Gardiner's sketch in *The Pillars of Society*, (London, 1916, Popular Edition), pp. 81–7. The book was first published in 1913.

be unsound ... I believe him to be perfectly honest when he says, as he frequently does, that he never wishes to be Prime Minister. He wants to control the machine, and the policy of the machine, but he recognizes his own limitations. He has a reverence and a loyalty for you, and if the Party would let him, I think they would find genuinely that he would rather serve under almost anybody, provided he could be secured in the second place.[1]

Three months of peace, and nine of war, had only confirmed Montagu's judgment. But coalition brought a new world. And, in its challenges and opportunities, with victory the only measure of success, all loyalties would be on trial.

[1] Montagu to Asquith, 27 May 1914 (copy), Montagu MSS.

Appendix: Military Planning before the Outbreak of War

Four recently completed studies have examined aspects of British strategic planning before August 1914.[1] It is clear from these and earlier works that the policy of the War Office remained essentially unchanged from March 1911 onwards.

General Henry Wilson, as Director of Military Operations, assumed that the Germans would only attack France through Belgium, and that the right wing of a German attack would not be extended beyond the line of the Meuse and the Sambre. However as Dr Summerton shows, although Wilson 'did not abandon the view that the Germans would not cross the Meuse, he never completely satisfied himself that they would not'.[2]

In May 1914, despite an adverse report from the invasion subcommittee of the Committee of Imperial Defence, General Robertson (Director of Military Training), General Douglas (Chief of the Imperial General Staff) and General Wilson persuaded Asquith to accept the plans which the War Office had made to dispatch the bulk of the expeditionary force if war should come. 'I spoke openly about it all,' Wilson wrote in his diary, 'with the result that Asquith settled to allow my present arrangements to stand, viz. 5 Divisions to go at once and the 4th Div to hold back for the moment. This is *good*.'

The two documents from which extracts are printed in this appendix demonstrate the continuity of British military thinking between 1911 and 1914. Henry Wilson's 'Appreciation of the

[1] Samuel R. Williamson Jr, *The Politics of Grand Strategy* (Harvard, 1970); Nicholas J. d'Ombrain, 'The Military Departments and the Committee of Imperial Defence 1902–1914' (unpublished Oxford University D.Phil. thesis, 1968); Howard R. Moon, ' The Invasion of the United Kingdom: Public Controversy and Official Planning 1888–1918' (unpublished London University Ph.D. thesis, 1968); Neil W. Summerton, 'The Development of British Military Planning for a War against Germany, 1904–1914' (unpublished London University Ph.D. thesis, 1970).

[2] Summerton, op. cit., p. 392.

Political and Military Situation in Europe' was written in September 1911. Wilson wanted the memorandum to be sent to the Foreign Office and to the members of the C.I.D. Sir William Nicholson, the C.I.G.S. at the time, did not circulate the paper. Sir John French, Nicholson's successor, submitted it to Lord Haldane, the Secretary of State for War, in April 1912. Haldane did not circulate it. Nor did Jack Seely, who succeeded Haldane, although it was twice placed before him by French. On 27 January 1913, Seely instructed his private secretary to put the document 'in a safe place for future reference'. Seely's copy, with some corrections added by Wilson in October 1912, is the source of the passages quoted below. Another copy may be seen in the Public Record Office (W.O. 106/47/E 2.26).

The second document, by Major A. H. Ollivant, appears to be the only piece of evidence in existence which illustrates the precise thinking of the responsible military authorities in the week before war was declared in 1914. Major Ollivant, a General Staff officer, had been attached to the Admiralty War Staff, at the request of the First Lord of the Admiralty, since 1913. This 'very gifted officer', as Winston Churchill later described him, prepared (apparently from some lecture notes) 'A Short Survey of the Present Military Situation in Europe' on 1 August 1914. The paper was sent, on Churchill's suggestion, to Lloyd George. Ollivant presented a simple exposition of the views of Henry Wilson, whom he had consulted before dispatching the document. It is notable that in this time of crisis, Ollivant re-asserted that the British expeditionary force could be a decisive element in the 'first big collisions'—a view which Churchill had challenged in 1911 and on which Wilson had wavered in October 1912. Ollivant's paper is in the Lloyd George MSS (C/16/1/14).

* * *

APPRECIATION OF THE POLITICAL AND MILITARY
SITUATION IN EUROPE

1. A war between France and Germany would affect all the Great Powers of Europe, and possibly terminate the existence of some of the smaller Powers.

2. It is therefore necessary to pass in general review the Euro-

pean situation of today before dealing in detail with the military problem which such a war will raise.

3. The Triple Alliance, the terms of which have never been made public, will probably be found to contain provisions which will bring Austria into line with Germany, if the latter declares war on France, and which will ensure assistance from, or at least a benign neutrality on the part of, Italy. No other State is concerned in this Alliance.

4. The Dual Alliance and the *Entente Cordiale* may have the effect of putting France, Russia, and England into the field in opposition to the signatories of the Triple Alliance.

5. Therefore, in the event of a war between Germany and France, it is not only possible but probable that Austria and Italy, on the one side, and Russia and England, on the other, may be forced to take up arms.

6. But this is not all. It is certain that many of the smaller States will find it necessary either to maintain their neutrality by force of arms, or to take sides with the principal actors ...

12. Last, and perhaps most important, of the smaller States comes Belgium. Unfortunately for Belgium her territory lies directly between Berlin and Paris, and this thoroughly inconvenient position is made worse by the system of French fortifications from Verdun to Belfort, which forbid 110 miles out of the total of 150 miles of the French and German frontier to the advance of Germany armies. The consequence is that the unguarded 90 miles of Belgian-German frontier has become the natural line of deployment of the greater mass of the German forces. It is true that the great Powers (Prussia being one of them) have guaranteed the neutrality of Belgium. Germany has already, to all practical purposes, violated this guarantee by her economic and administrative absorption of the Duchy of Luxembourg, and it has come to be considered as natural, if not justifiable, that Southern Belgium should be the theatre of the first great clash of arms between two at least and possibly three of the Powers who guaranteed the neutrality of that very country. What is the Belgian attitude of mind in regard to this extraordinary state of affairs?

Until within quite recent years Belgium, like some other countries, turned a blind eye to Germany's future plans, and, by pretending to ignore the growing German menace on her eastern frontier, she hoped to obviate it. The time for this pretence is now past, and Belgium, knowing the blow that is impending, knowing that some of the guarantors of her territory may possibly secure her ultimate independence but cannot prevent the violation of her country by Germans, appears to be disposed to take what she thinks is her safest course, and seems to contemplate the curious procedure of treating that part of her country (about one-third) which lies south of the Sambre and Meuse as being in a different category to that part which lies to the north of those rivers. In other words, it seems to be likely that the Belgians will not treat a German advance across her country as a violation of her territory, so long as such an advance is restricted to the country south of the Sambre and Meuse. It need scarcely be stated that the Treaty guaranteeing the neutrality of Belgium did not differentiate between different parts of the same country. It would appear, therefore, that under the Treaty of 1839, both France and England would not only have the right, but be under the obligation, to move into Belgium and expel German troops from Belgian soil.

The wholly untenable theory that there is some difference between Belgium south of the Sambre and Meuse, and Belgium north of these rivers, has a very grave bearing, if allowed to continue, on the military problem with which I will presently deal.

What is the feeling of Belgium as regards a French and German war?

The Belgians, like the inhabitants of every other country, would only like a war if they were certain of gaining some advantage by it. How do they stand in regard to this particular war?

They know well, no one better, that if Germany is successful their independence is gravely threatened. It is for this reason that they catch at the last straw of hope and imagine, or pretend to imagine, that by allowing Germany to violate one-third of their territory they may gain the good graces of the German Empire, and thus save the independence of the remaining two-thirds.

Nothing but fear of the power of Germany, and the full knowledge of their own military incompetence, and of the doubt, which is very present to their mind, of the action which England will take, makes the Belgians pursue their present cowardly, but easily understood, line of action.

It cannot be doubted for one moment that if Germany succeeds in this war, the independence of Belgium is not worth a year's purchase. On the other hand, it is equally well known that if France, England, and Russia are victorious, the independence of Belgium will become more secure, and will be more effectively guaranteed than it has been any time since the German armies crossed the Rhine in 1870.

On which side then does Belgium self-interest lie? The answer is clear. It lies on the side of France, England, and Russia. Perhaps it is not past the powers of diplomacy to bring this home to the Belgian Government, and get them to combine with those Powers against German aggression? The advantage of such a line of action, from a military point of view, is of great, almost of vital, importance, as will be seen later on.

13. The foregoing very brief review of the present international political situation has been necessary as a prelude to a military appreciation of the European situation as it now exists.

14. In a *mémoire* drawn up in 1860 on a hypothetical war between Prussia and Austria, Marshal von Moltke wrote as follows:

> The result which we require to enable us to form a judgment of the initial military situation can be reached only along the slippery but inevitable path of political speculation.

And von Moltke's dictum of fifty years ago is as true today as it was then.

15. The mobile military forces of the interested European Powers may be taken in round numbers, to be as follows:

	Divisions.
Triple Alliance—	
Germany	121
Austria	61
Italy	36
Triple *Entente*—	
France	75
Russia (including Russia in the Middle and Far East) ..	78
England	6
Neutral or semi-neutral States—	
Turkey (including Turkey in Asia)	67*
Bulgaria	13½
Roumania	10

Servia	..	..	..	..	..	..	8
Norway	..	..	..	..	..	..	3
Sweden	..	..	..	..	..	..	5
Denmark ..	..	..	..	..	..	..	4
Holland	..	..	..	..	..	..	4
Belgium ..	..	..	..	..	..	..	4
Switzerland	..	..	..	..	..	..	8

* Calculated on the numerical basis of an average Continental Division. Of the total number of Divisions shown, not more than 46 would be available for field armies, and they would take a considerable time to concentrate at any given points.

16. Of these Neutral or Semi-Neutral States, it will be sufficient for our present purpose if we cut out the forces of Norway and Sweden as having only an indirect bearing on the problem, and if we contain the forces of Turkey and the Balkans by a sufficient number of Russian and Austrian troops, in Europe and in Asia.

Switzerland may be considered as capable of preserving her own neutrality and of not wishing to join either side in the war.

There remain Denmark, Holland, and Belgium. None of these three States are in a position to enforce the neutrality of their frontiers and territory, and therefore they are in quite a different condition from Switzerland or the other Neutral or Semi-Neutral States to which reference has been made.

They would appear to be very liable to persuasion, or open to threat, either on the one side or on the other, and ... their action in the war will be governed mainly by the opinions they have formed during peace as to which belligerent is the stronger, the readier, and the more determined to win. In a word, these three countries are sitting on the fence, knowing on which side their interests lie, but afraid to move because of their present fear of Germany.

They are therefore excellent subjects for diplomatic pressure in the time of peace.

17. It will be possible now to make a forecast of the initial disposition of troops on the various frontiers of Europe, and to indicate the strong and weak points in the opposing forces.

18. To take the Triple Alliance first: —

(a.) Of the 121 Divisions which Germany disposes of, 27 are placed facing Russia, 10 are allotted to the coast defence of both the North Sea and the Baltic, and 84 are destined for the Western frontier. This distribution is made on the assumption that Austria will be ready to assist Germany by mobilising her Army and by threatening, if not by positively invading, Poland; that Italy will mobilise and contain a certain number of French troops; and that Denmark, Holland, and Belgium will remain neutral. If any of these five States were not to carry out the role that has been allotted to them, or if they were to become actively hostile, then further detachments from the main Armies would be necessary, and the forces which Germany and France could place at the decisive point on their frontiers would be correspondingly decreased or increased.

(*b*.) Of the 61 Divisions which Austria possesses, 30 Divisions are put facing Russia, 12 Divisions are put on the River Isonzo and 3 Divisions in the Austrian Tyrol facing Italy, 6 Divisions are put as against Servia, and 10 Divisions are held back in central reserve.

(*c*.) The Italian 36 Divisions have been distributed as follows: 12 Divisions in North-Western Italy, in the Turin–Alessandria country, threatening France, supported by 6 Divisions in the area Milan–Piacenza partly to reinforce the Turin Army and partly to watch the Swiss frontier; 9 Divisions in the Verona–Venetia area watching the Austrian frontier; and 9 Divisions in the Peninsula as central reserve and for coast defence.

19. The troops of the Dual Alliance and *Entente* are disposed of as follows:—

(*a*.) France has 75 Divisions. Of these 9 have been put facing the Italian frontier, and 66 are available against Germany, the Spanish frontier being watched by Territorials, and the French fleet in the Mediterranean and the British fleet in northern seas making the defence of the French coast-line, outside fortresses, unnecessary.

(*b*.) Of Russia's 78 Divisions, 40 Divisions have been allotted to Poland, 4 Divisions to face Roumania, 7 Divisions in the Caucasus, 7 Divisions in Finland and for coast defence, 13 Divisions in Asia, and 7 Divisions as central reserve and for internal troubles.

(*c*.) England possesses 6 mobile Divisions available at the outset of war, and within three or four months she might add 4, 5, or 6 more Divisions of regulars from the Mediterranean, South Africa, and India. The action of England's troops in this war will be dealt with later, the assumption being made that the whole of her 6 Divisions will be available at once.

20. We are now in a position to see how the forces of France and Germany will stand along their common frontier at the opening of the war.

France can place 66 Divisions as against Germany's 84 Divisions. To the 66 French Divisions must be added the 6 English Divisions, making a total of 72 against Germany's 84 Divisions.

But there are still some other factors in this problem.

What of Denmark's 4 Divisions, of Holland's 4 Divisions, of Belgium's 4 Divisions, totalling 12 Divisions? ... I would like to repeat here the importance of gaining their support in the time of peace and active co-operation in the time of war. An exception to this might perhaps be made in the case of Holland, and we might be content if she maintained a strict neutrality for the opening weeks of the war and joined us in active operations later on.

The geographical position of these three States (all based on the sea) makes their position and action of greater importance than the mere weight of their armies might at first sight lead one to suppose.

23.

(1.) The effective neutrality of Belgium means that German and French troops would be confined, in crossing the frontier, to the 150 miles between the Duchy of Luxembourg and Switzerland. This restriction would tell much more heavily against Germany than against France, because, owing to the French system of fortifications, there is scarcely 40 miles of the 150 miles which is not barred by fortresses or other works to a German advance, and in the event of Belgium being able to retain her neutrality the opening months of the war might be spent in siege operations which financial considerations would probably render impossible. In addition to this, a neutral Belgium would deny her territorial waters to both belligerents.

The neutrality of Belgium is so obviously in favour of France, that she may be relied on not to be the first to violate Belgian soil. But as I have already pointed out in paragraph 12, there does not appear to be the remotest chance of Germany agreeing to such a neutrality.

I have alluded to the danger that Belgium may allow German troops to cross her southern territories (under verbal protest of course) and confine her energies and defence to the neutrality of her northern provinces. This would be a violation of the 1839 Treaty, and it should be made clear to Belgium at once that the signatory Powers of France and England would not tolerate such a procedure. Belgium may think that following a course such as I have just described, she may be spared the horrors of war in the major portion of her country and succeed in preserving her independence after the war was over. To allow German troops to pass through Southern Belgium and to forbid French and English troops to enter Northern Belgium, would be to give Germany preferential treatment, and Belgium should be told that such a course would be treated as a hostile act, that she would be liable to such action on land as France and England thought fit to carry out and that Antwerp and all the Belgian ports would be at once blockaded.

There can be no half measures as regards the neutrality of Belgium. Either she is completely neutral—and if her frontiers are crossed by German troops she must call on France and England to repel such an invasion—or she is friendly to Germany or hostile to Germany.

(2.) A Belgium friendly to Germany would mean an addition of four divisions to the German Army, a friendly country from which to operate against France, secure bases in the fortresses of Liège and Namur, and the enormous assistance of the Belgian railway system. It would, on the other hand, mean that the Scheldt and the other Belgian ports would be closed. A Belgium friendly to Germany would be of incalculable advantage to that country, and would add in equal degree to the difficulties of the French and English Armies.

(3.) A Belgium hostile to Germany would mean that all Belgium north of the Sambre and Meuse would be kept open to her friends and closed to the Germans. The line of the Sambre and Meuse would be secured by the fortresses of Maubeuge, Namur, and Liège, and the country to the north would form a secure and friendly base from which to conduct hostile operations on the flank or rear of the invading German forces. A Belgium friendly to the cause of England and France would add greatly to the powers of those countries both offensively and defensively, both from the geographical position of the country and the fortresses and troops (200,000 in all) which would come into play. Finally, the Belgian ports—possibly even Antwerp—would be open to our war-ships and our commerce.

24. The case of Denmark is comparatively simple. The geographical position of Denmark, both from the point of view of land operations and of sea operations, and the fact that, so long as England maintains command of the sea, she can always be reinforced from without, makes her action in the war more important than her insignificant land and sea forces might lead one to suppose ... nothing further need be said here except that a Denmark actively hostile to Germany would add in some degree to Germany's difficulties.

25. Before summing up the conclusions which this paper leads to, I will discuss in the briefest manner possible the probable line of advance which German troops will take when marching through Belgium.

The Rivers Sambre and Meuse cut Belgium horizontally into two unequal parts, about two-thirds of the country lying to the North and one-third lying to the South. The line of these rivers has been greatly strengthened by the fortresses of Maubeuge, Namur, and Liège, and the strong fort of Huy, all placed astride of the rivers. Immediately to the East of Liège the Meuse passes into Dutch territory. It follows that Germany will enter Belgium on the South of Liège, unless she also intends to violate Dutch territory. A German advance is therefore confined to the South of the Sambre and Meuse unless the fortresses of Liège and Namur are taken, and later on Maubeuge would have to be taken or masked. But the three fortresses named cannot be taken either by a *coup de main* or by assault if they are properly garrisoned; they will require siege operations before they can be reduced. This will be a slow and costly procedure quite foreign to German methods of war which are essentially brusque and forceful.

It seems certain, therefore, that unless Germany is prepared to violate Dutch neutrality, or unless Belgium, through cowardice or neglect, allows the fortresses of Liège and Namur to fall into German hands, the advance of the German armies will be confined to the country South of the Meuse.

The importance, under these circumstances, of a Belgium friendly to France and England can scarcely be overrated.

A German advance through the country South of the Sambre and Meuse would be open to sudden and vicious flank attacks the whole way from the German frontier to the French frontier. The enemy, using the river line to conceal his movements, and secure behind the line of fortresses, could attack either from the fortresses themselves, all of which stand astride the rivers, or in the gaps between the fortresses. The Germans would be obliged to do one of three things; they would have to violate Dutch territory and thus turn the Meuse defence which would then have to be masked; or they would have to attack across the Meuse and lay siege to the fortresses; or they would have to protect their forward movement by a force sufficiently large and mobile to mask three fortresses and repel the sudden and surprise attacks of the Belgian and possibly English armies. It is difficult to say which of these three courses would be the least disadvantageous to the Germans. They would all be exceedingly awkward; for by violating Dutch territory they would add to the number of their enemies and would find that Amsterdam and Rotterdam would be immediately blockaded; on the other hand, by attacking across the Meuse and laying siege to the fortresses they would have to deflect a large force to the North which would give France a great opportunity; and lastly, if the Germans decided to continue the great movement to the West and turned up a sufficient force to mask three fortresses and to ward off the surprise attacks of the Belgian and English armies they would find themselves in inferior numbers at the decisive point, *i.e.*, at the point where the German and French Armies met for a decision.

The value to France and England of the neutrality of Holland and of the active assistance of Belgium, in the case where Germany has already violated her southern territory, is now apparent.

26. In this paper it has been taken for granted that the English Fleets hold the North Sea, and that therefore the passage of troops from England to France is always both practicable and safe. The proposal to reinforce the Expeditionary Force by troops from the Mediterranean, Egypt, South Africa, India, and the Dominions, raises rather a larger and more complicated question. It is realised that for all practical and immediate purposes, we

have now lost temporary and local command of distant seas, but in the war under consideration the only dangerous sea, other than the North Sea, would appear to be the Mediterranean, and it ought to be possible for the English squadron, assisted by the French Fleets, to ensure safe transit for our transports across that sea. Otherwise it will be difficult, if not impossible, to relieve any of the Mediterranean garrisons, or to bring our Indian reinforcements through the Suez Canal.

27. It is important to realise that the time of year and the weather may have some effect on the course of the campaign. There is no time of the year when the movement of troops in large bodies is seriously interfered with in Eastern France, Western Germany, Belgium, or Holland. The months of August and September are hot, and, as a rule, dry, and there might be some inconvenience as to water, but nothing serious. The months of January and February are cold, but except for a few days at a time, there is not sufficient snow to interfere with military operations.

But on Germany's Eastern frontier, in Poland, and in the Austrian Carpathians, the case is different. Russians would be greatly impeded in military movements between the months of March and August, for the melting snows in the spring, and the heat and heavy rains in the summer, make all movements, except those on good roads, very difficult.

On the other hand, the period favourable to Russian offence would be from September to the middle of February; also at this season of the year the Baltic becomes frozen over.

All the Great Continental Powers take in their recruits in the autumn and early winter, so their Armies stand alike in this respect.

The crops on the French and German frontier are gathered by the end of August, or the middle of September.

The spring and summer would find Russia and Austria somewhat crippled in regard to movements of large bodies of troops, and would therefore probably be a favourable moment for German aggression, but, on the other hand, the sea conditions and long days of summer would be favourable to our fleets, and the months of August, September, and October would in many respects suit the Germans better, in so far as their Western frontier is concerned, and as the crops would have been gathered, the effect of a blockade would not be so instantly felt.

It is difficult, then, to lay down that Germany would force on a campaign at one time of the year rather than at another. No time is impossible, and the balance of advantages of one period over another does not seem to be very great.

28. To sum up: —

(1.) To take the political side first: —

We may ignore the action of Spain and Portugal. Switzerland desires, and is able to enforce, her neutrality. We may hope to confine the action of the various Balkan States and of Turkey within the limits of their encircling frontiers by watching them with Austrian and Russian troops; and we may for the moment, though probably not for long, remain easy as regards a Turkish movement against Egypt. Norway and Sweden, from the purely military point of view, need not cause apprehension. There remain the three Powers of the Triple Alliance, the three Powers of the Triple *Entente*, and the three smaller Powers of Denmark, Holland, and Belgium, whose geographical position and political and military action will have a direct effect on the course of the war.

Of the Triple Alliance Powers we have taken Germany to be the aggressor ... the action of Austria in this particular war would probably be more passive than active, and ... Germany and Austria would only hope to gain a very moderate amount of assistance from Italy; in fact, it would not be surprising to find Italy neutral.

On the side of the Triple *Entente* we would find all three Powers — France, Russia, and England — in close agreement and in cordial co-operation.

... Denmark has much more to gain if the present power of Germany was reduced, and therefore her friendship and assistance might be gained for the *Entente*.

The position of Holland is much more difficult to diagnose ... Holland's one desire is to keep neutral during the war and remain neutral after the war, and when the pros and cons of such a line of action are carefully weighed it would appear that this course would be agreeable both to Germany and to France and England — at all events during the opening weeks of the war. Later on it might be found advisable for England and France to force Holland to take sides, for in the event of initial German successes it might be found imperative to close the mouth of the Rhine, and in the case of French and English successes it would not be difficult to gain Holland as an ally, and make use of Dutch territory as a base for further operations in Germany itself.

Last comes the case of Belgium. In paragraphs 12 and 23 the various courses open to Belgium and the effect of each on the course of the war were fully discussed. It only remains to say that the part that Belgium will play should be clearly ascertained beforehand, and every effort should be made to gain her active assistance and to make her stand by the Treaty of 1839.

(2.) To take the military side of the problem: —

... There only remains for consideration the action of the British force of six Divisions, and the possibility of its further reinforcement.

The old maxim that the best way to win campaigns is to have decisive numbers at the decisive place at the decisive time holds good to-day as it has done since time immemorial. Applying this maxim to the case of this war we must first fix the decisive place and time, and then produce and apply the decisive numbers.

All secondary operations such as the landing of troops on the coast of Germany, or the seizure of islands off that coast, or attempts made against outlying German possessions, or even the reinforcement of Mediterranean, Egyptian, or other garrisons, must be absolutely put aside until the conditions of the maxim quoted above are first fulfilled.

Where is the decisive place and what is the decisive time?

An exhaustive and detailed examination of this question made last year has led to the conclusion that the decisive place will be either in or somewhere in the neighbourhood of, the Ardennes, and that the decisive time will be between the fifteenth and twentieth day after mobilisation has been ordered.

Can our six Divisions be at that place and at that time, and, if so, will they fulfil the third condition and constitute decisive numbers?

The answer to all three questions is in the affirmative.

Our six Divisions *can* be at the decisive place at the decisive time, provided proper arrangements are previously made, and provided our policy and strategy move hand in hand they *will* make the numbers decisive.*

* This paper was written in September 1911 since when the position of affairs on the Continent has altered considerably, and it can no longer be claimed that our 6 Divisions will make the numbers decisive. H.W.17.10.12.

It may not be out of place to mention here the possibility of Germany endeavouring to prevent our six Divisions, or some of them, from crossing to the Continent in time to be present at the decisive action, by organising and dispatching a small expeditionary force, with a view to effecting a landing somewhere on the coast of England, and in the hopes that such action would compel the British Government to delay or cancel their previous arrangements. This paper is not the place in which to consider the possibility of such an enterprise being crowned with success, but it may be well to point out that, provided proper arrangements are made for the interception and the reception of such an attack, and provided the Government of the day are not turned from the true course of strategy, the larger the force thus detached by the Germans from the decisive point the better it would be for France and ourselves; and it must be remembered that owing to our great naval superiority and the consequent immunity from attack when crossing to France which our troops thus enjoy, it will at any time be as easy to move troops back to England as it was originally easy to move them into France. In fact, from a military point of view, England and the Continent become one theatre of war.

The policy advocated is this: —

(a.) A closer union with France and Russia;

(b.) A rapprochement with Italy;

(c.) An understanding with Denmark, Holland, and Belgium on the lines of the self-interest of those countries, and on the basis already indicated.

The strategy advocated is as follows: —

(a.) The absolute safety of the United Kingdom to be guaranteed by Naval superiority, and by Military Forces, other than the troops of the Expeditionary Force;

(b.) The perfecting, in every detail, of the arrrangements for making the Expeditionary Force ready for despatch abroad at a moment's notice, and for making good the wastage of war;

(c.) The despatch of the Expeditionary Force to the decisive place at the decisive time;

(d.) The completion of all plans for reinforcing the Expeditionary Force by troops from Home, from the Mediterranean, Egypt, South Africa, India, and the Dominions.

September 20, 1911.

A SHORT SURVEY OF THE PRESENT MILITARY SITUATION
IN EUROPE

... I will ask you to regard the situation, as all such situations should be regarded, from the point of view of the adversary, in this case Germany.

Germany occupies a central position in Europe; on her West and East are enemies, France and Russia. To the South are allies, Italy and Austria. To the North is a possible enemy, England.

Let us estimate their capacity for mischief or help from the point of view of Germany.

The forces available are the following: —

Total Divisions	Country	Strength in Divisions	Ready for action in
181	Germany	119 in all, viz:	
		55 First line,	10 to 14 days
		64 Reserve	?
	Austria	62 in all, viz:	
		49 First line	10 to 17 days
		13 Reserve	?
182	France	75 in all, viz:	
		41 First line (at home)	10 to 14 days
		3 First line (Algiers etc.)	
		31 Reserve	?
	*Russia	87 in all (in Europe) viz:	
		55 First line	14 to 42 days
		32 Reserve	?
	Servia	20 in all, viz:	
		10 First line	11 days
		10 Reserve	?
	Italy	36 in all, viz:	
		25 First line	14 to 21 days
		11 Reserve	
	Great Britain	6	12 to 14 days
	Montenegro	4	7 days

* Russia would probably have 20 divisions available on the 14th day; another 20 on the 20th day. The other 15 divisions might be up in another fortnight. Russia has further some 20 divisions in Asia possibly available in 6 weeks or two months.

x

Austria is a staunch ally, Italy is a lukewarm ally. France is a bitter foe, Russia a less bitter foe, England a much less bitter foe.

England and France are quick moving enemies. Russia is a cumbrous and slow moving enemy.

The allied Powers, Italy and Austria, are intermediate in speed, between France and Germany.

The German plan of operations is clearly deducible. The German forces must crush France with as strong and swift a succession of blows as possible before Russia can assist her, leave some Reserve troops to hold her, and then turn Eastwards with their main forces to defeat, detach, or frighten away Russia, with the assistance of Austria.

Again the importance of the time factor forces itself on our notice. France must not only be defeated, but defeated within a certain short limited time; if not, if Russia has time to develop her strength, Germany may be taken between the hammer and the anvil. The maximum possible of German strength must be exerted on the Western frontier as early as possible.

Faced with this situation the allotment of German forces (119 divisions) at the beginning of war may be roughly estimated as follows: —

(a) For the offensive stroke against France in the Western theatre, some 84 divisions.

(b) For the temporary defence against Russia in the Eastern theatre, 27 divisions.

(c) To guard the North coast and watch Denmark, 8 divisions.

2. (b) The situation in the Western theatre preliminary to the great and decisive collisions may now be examined in slightly more detail. Leaving necessarily out of account the numerous factors, political, geographical, etc., which complicate the problem, and confining ourselves to the major factor, man power available, the following picture is presented: —

(i) German army. Some 84 divisions, detrained and marshalled on an area behind the line Cologne–Strasburg. Ready for a concentric advance directly Westwards into France and Southwestward through Belgium into France, against the main French armies.

(ii) French army. Some 66, or if the neutrality of Italy be assured, 72 divisions, detrained and marshalled an area behind the line Sedan, Nancy, Epinal, ready to oppose the German movements and if possible strike and defeat in succession their Westward and Southwestward advances.

If Italy should be hostile, France would have to retain 6 divisions on her South Eastern (Italian frontier), a very difficult mountainous terrain, charged with the duty of checking and delaying the Italian advance, which is expected to be somewhat slow, dilatory and difficult.

(iii) Italian army (if used). Of somewhat inferior fighting material. 36 divisions. Detrained and marshalled in the area behind the line Ivrea–Turin–Savona. Ready to advance and force their way through the difficult Alpine defiles into France.

We see therefore that in the event of Italy remaining neutral the French main armies in N.E. France may have to fight Germany with a numerical inferiority of some 9 to 12 divisions; an inferiority which might well be decisive of the whole campaign in the Western theatre.

How can France redress this inferiority? If the action of Russia cannot be speeded up, there are two ways only: —

(i) She may be reinforced, directly in France, or indirectly in Belgium, by a British army of from 4 to 6 divisions.

(ii) She may be reinforced by 3 divisions of her own troops from Algiers via Marseilles.

Both of these reinforcements come, if they come at all, by sea. The question of ensuring, or of preventing their arrival is a naval question.

The German view is that the first big collisions in Alsace Lorraine are of paramount and determining importance. Whether or not we accept this view in its entirety, it is a view by which German action will be dictated, and that action cannot but react on our strategy. It is sufficient for us to know that on the continent enormous importance is attached, by France to ensuring, by Germany to preventing, the arrival of these reinforcements. These considerations must primarily influence the naval strategy of both parties. It would appear therefore that until this first great land decision has been reached, naval strategy will be largely complementary to military strategy, and the safe conduct of these reinforcements will constitute one of the most important duties of the naval forces of the Entente.

(b) The Eastern theatre may now be briefly considered ...

The chief object of Germany and Austria in this theatre will be to gain time, to hold back the forces of Slavdom until France has been crushed, and the main German forces can return and throw their weight into the scale.

It is of vital importance to France, that the Russian forces should go right in at the earliest possible moment. A threatened seizure of Berlin would force the Germans to detach to meet it and relax their pressure in the Western theatre.

The possibility of Russia so doing is adversely affected by two main considerations: —

(1) The unavoidable slowness of her mobilisation and concentration.

(2) Geographical considerations and the strategic conditions to which these give rise.

With regard to (1), the disadvantages under which Russia labours have already been indicated. The great spaces, the undeveloped state of roads, telegraphs and postal facilities, the paucity of railways, make rapid mobilisation impossible. Slow mobilisation as has been shown involves concentration at a considerable distance behind the frontier, and further postpones the moment of decisive contact with the enemy.

Thus we see that on the 14th day Russia has only 20 divisions available for action against Germany, and these at some days march from the frontier. It is not until the 20th day that another 20 divisions become available, by which time a decision will probably have been reached in the Western theatre.

These hindrances to rapid action on the part of Russia are much intensified by the geographical features of the theatre of war. The salient position of Poland, jutting out between hostile German territory on the North and hostile Austrian territory on the South is unfavourable for an offensive movement on Berlin. The line of communications is within easy distance of forces striking from flank positions either to the North or to the South of it. To contain or to defeat such forces is a necessary preliminary to any serious advance Westward against the German capital. German East Prussia is a highly defensible country, full of lakes and bogs and suitable for delaying action by a German detachment thrown out from the main German force behind the strongly fortified line of the Vistula from Thorn to Dantzig. The district round the strong fortress of Thorn affords an ideal flank position, from which blows could be struck Southwards at the communications of a Russian force advancing Westwards via Kutnow and Posen. Should the Russians choose a more Southerly route via Glogau or Breslau, their communications can be similarly struck in the flank by the Austrian force acting from Galicia. To wheel a large army at right angles to meet such an attack is a slow and difficult operation. The Great Polesian marsh (or Pripet Swamp) extending N.E. from the N.E. corner of Austria, prevents close co-operation between the Russian army acting in Poland and that (probably the Kiev army) acting Westwards against the N.E. frontier of Austria in the direction of Brody.

Given unlimited time, Russia could no doubt bring up her Asiatic armies and organise her reserve divisions; she might then be able to crush the Austro-German forces by sheer weight of numbers. In the problem under consideration time is of the essence and it appears little likely that the action of Russia can be sufficiently rapid to influence effectually the course of events in the Western theatre.

A subsidiary point of interest is the great importance of the attitude of Bulgaria and Roumania, especially of the latter. Should her weight be thrown into the scale at an early date on the side of Slavdom, a redistribution of the Austrian forces would be necessary; the Austrian forces in Galicia available for a Northward movement against Russia would be largely diminished, and the task of Russia correspondingly facilitated. Even this, however, would hardly enable the Russian forces to act with the necessary rapidity.

More detailed investigation of the conditions and probable course of events in this theatre tends only to throw into greater relief the impotence of Russia to affect the course of events in the all important Western theatre in the earlier stages of the war.

Summary

The views that have been here expressed are German views. It is the firm belief of the military thinkers of the nation, a nation in which military thought is organised with a laborious thoroughness and consistency all its own, that the decisive point of the forthcoming struggle of the nations lies on the battlefields of

Eastern France. That all available means will be co-ordinated, all secondary objects ruthlessly subordinated, and tremendous sacrifices unhesitatingly accepted, in order to obtain the maximum numerical superiority at that point of decision, is not for one moment doubtful to those who have studied the military mentality and methods of Germany.

How does British action appear from the German point of view? What influence can Britain exert during the first and most important phase of the struggle? How can the German navy be best used, not necessarily with the primary object of an isolated, even if successful, combat with the British fleet, but from that of the great general object which has been indicated? What are the best methods Germany can employ for preventing the arrival of British military reinforcements, consistent with the deployment of the maximum German forces in the Western theatre? These, and many other such questions must have an intimate bearing on British naval strategy. Seen from the standpoint of our adversary, many matters, invasions, attacks on ports, and bases, defence of commerce, etc., appear in a different perspective to that in which they are often regarded. Germany's chief object, as far as this country is concerned, lies in preventing the arrival of the British expeditionary army. Its absence from the battlefield will exercise an influence out of all proportion to its numerical strength. The initial deployment, that most delicate and important of all operations of war, will on the French side be dislocated; and that, at a moment when there is little or no time to improvise fresh arrangements. That the effect on the 'moral' of the French army will be great is not doubtful to those who have studied the military history of France. 'Nous sommes trahis' are three ominous words, which have been the precursors of most French disasters. There is reason to suppose that the presence or absence of the British army will determine the action of the Belgian army. It will very probably decide the fate of France.

A. H. Ollivant

Major Gen. Staff

Aug. 1 1914

Bibliography

Most of the published works upon which this book is based are well-known and readily accessible. But a large number of private archives — some of them never before studied by scholars — have also been examined in the course of my research. The following list includes all of the major collections of official and personal papers which I have been able to consult.

The Royal Archives	the correspondence of His Majesty King George V, at Windsor Castle, examined by the gracious permission of Her Majesty the Queen.
Cabinet Papers Papers of the War Council Papers of the Dardanelles Committee Papers of the War Committee Foreign Office Papers	in the Public Record Office.
F. D. Acland MSS	the papers of Sir Francis and Lady Acland, in the possession of their son, Sir Richard Acland, Bt.
Asquith MSS	the papers of the first Earl of Oxford and Asquith, in the Bodleian Library, Oxford, examined by courtesy of the Hon. Mark Bonham Carter.
Balfour MSS	the papers of the first Earl of Balfour, in the British Museum; references to folio numbers in this collection are provisional.

Balfour MSS (Whittingehame)	additional papers of the first Earl of Balfour, in the possession of his nephew, the third Earl of Balfour.
Beauchamp MSS	a collection of press-cuttings, photographs, and printed ephemera, relating to the career of the seventh Earl Beauchamp, in the possession of his son, the eighth Earl Beauchamp.
Augustine Birrell MSS	a collection of letters and official papers on Irish affairs in the Bodleian Library, examined by kind permission of Mr J. C. Medley.
Augustine Birrell MSS (Liverpool)	a small collection of letters presented by Sir Charles Tennyson, Birrell's stepson.
J. Brunner MSS	the papers of Sir John Brunner Bt, in the possession of his grandson, Sir Felix Brunner Bt.
John Burns MSS	in the British Museum.
Nuxton MSS	the papers of the first and last Earl Buxton, in the possession of his granddaughter, Mrs Elizabeth Clay.
Carson MSS	the papers of the first and last Baron Carson, in the Public Record Office of Northern Ireland.
Cawley MSS	a small collection of papers and press cuttings relating to the career of the first Baron Cawley, in the possession of his grandson, the third Baron Cawley.
Cecil of Chelwood MSS	the papers of Lord Robert Cecil, first and last Viscount Cecil of Chelwood, in the British Museum; references to folio numbers in this collection are provisional.
Austen Chamberlain MSS	the papers of Sir Austen Chamberlain, in the Library, University of Birmingham.
Winston S. Churchill MSS	the papers of Sir Winston Churchill, consulted by permission of the late Hon. Randolph S. Churchill, Mr Martin Gilbert, and the Chartwell Trustees.
E. T. Cook MSS	the diaries and correspondence of Sir Edward Cook, in the possession of his nephew, Mr Douglas Duff.

Craigmyl MSS — the papers of Thomas and Alexander Shaw, first and second Barons Craigmyle, in the possession of the third Baron Craigmyle.

Crewe MSS — the papers of the first and last Marquess of Crewe, in the Cambridge University Library.

Derby MSS — the papers of the seventeenth Earl of Derby.

A. L. Duff MSS — the Grand Fleet diary of Rear-Admiral Sir Alexander Duff, kindly lent to me by his widow, Lady Duff; the bulk of the Duff papers have been deposited in the National Maritime Museum.

Elibank MSS — the papers of A. C. Murray, third Viscount Elibank, in the National Library of Scotland.

Murray of Elibank MSS — the papers of Alexander Murray, Master of Elibank, and first and last Baron Murray of Elibank, in the National Library, Nuffield College, Oxford.

Gainford MSS — the papers of J. A. Pease, first Baron Gainford, in the Library, Nuffield College, Oxford.

Grey MSS — the papers of the first and last Viscount Grey of Fallodon; an incomplete collection, mainly of official correspondence and memoranda, in the Public Record Office.

Ellis Griffith MSS — in the National Library of Wales.

J. W. Gulland MSS — a collection of letters from J. W. Gulland to his wife, and letters of condolence on Gulland's death; in the possession of his nephew, Mr J. Gulland Osborne.

Haig MSS — the diaries and papers of Field-Marshal Earl Haig of Bemersyde, in the National Library of Scotland; the diary was consulted by kind permission of the second Earl Haig.

Haldane MSS — the papers of the first and last Viscount Haldane, in the National Library of Scotland.

Harcourt MSS — the papers, mainly official correspondence and memoranda, of the first Viscount Harcourt, in the possession of his son, the second Viscount Harcourt.

Hardinge MSS — the papers of the first Baron Hardinge of Penshurst, in the Cambridge University Library.

T. E. Harvey MSS — in the Friends' Library, consulted by permission of Harvey's biographer, Mr Edward Milligan.

Richard Holt MSS — diaries and a small file of correspondence with the Hexham Liberal association, formerly in the possession of Holt's daughter, Miss Anne Holt, now at the Liverpool City Library.

P. Illingworth MSS — a selection of letters and a collection of press cuttings and printed ephemera, in the possession of Illingworth's son, Mr Henry Illingworth.

E. T. John MSS — in the National Library of Wales.

Kitchener MSS — the papers of the first Earl Kitchener of Khartoum in the Public Record Office.

Lansdowne MSS — the papers of the fifth Marquess of Lansdowne, in the possession of his grandson, the eighth Marquess of Lansdowne.

A. Bonar Law MSS — in the Beaverbrook Library.

Lennoxlove MSS — correspondence from the papers of Admiral of the Fleet, Lord Fisher of Kilverstone, in the papers of the fourteenth Duke of Hamilton; transcripts examined by courtesy of the late Hon. Randolph S. Churchill.

J. H. Lewis MSS — in the National Library of Wales.

Lloyd George MSS — the papers of the first Earl Lloyd-George of Dwyfor, in the Beaverbrook Library.

Alexander MacCallum Scott MSS — diaries in the possession of his son, Mr. J. H. MacCallum Scott.

Reginald McKenna MSS — in the Library, Churchill College, Cambridge.

Manchester Guardian MSS — a collection of office correspondence, supplementing the C. P. Scott collection in the British Museum, in the Manchester offices of *The Guardian*, examined by courtesy of the newspaper's historian, Mr David Ayerst.

Leo Maxse MSS — in the West Sussex Record Office.

Milner MSS — the papers of the first and last Viscount Milner, in the Bodleian Library, Oxford.

Montagu MSS — the papers of Edwin and Venetia Montagu in the possession of their daughter, Mrs Judy Gendel.

Mottistone MSS — the papers of J. E. B. Seely, first Baron Mottistone in the Library, Nuffield College, Oxford.

Northcliffe MSS — transcripts and microfilm of the papers of the first and last Viscount Northcliffe, in the possession of his biographer, Sir Geoffrey Harmsworth Bt; the Northcliffe collection has been deposited in the British Museum but is at present closed to scholars.

Henry Norman MSS — the papers of Sir Henry Norman Bt, in the possession of his daughter, Lady Burke.

Novar MSS — the official correspondence as Governor-General of Australia, 1914–20, of Ronald Munro Ferguson, first and last Viscount Novar, in the National Library of Australia.

Oxford and Asquith MSS — the 1914–15 diary and some correspondence of Margot, first Countess of Oxford and Asquith.

Parliamentary Recruiting Committee MSS — minute books, in the British Museum.

Ponsonby MSS — the papers of the first Baron Ponsonby, in the possession of his son the second Baron Ponsony.

Rawlinson MSS — the diaries of the first and last Baron Rawlinson of Trent, in the Library, Churchill College, Cambridge.

Runciman MSS — the papers of the first Viscount Runciman, formerly in the possession of his son, the Hon. Sir Steven Runciman, and now deposited in the Library, University of Newcastle-upon-Tyne.

Samuel MSS	the papers of the first Viscount Samuel, in the House of Lords Record Office.
C. P. Scott MSS	a collection of letters, and memoranda in diary form, in the British Museum; the the rest of Scott's correspondence is in the *Manchester Guardian* MSS.
Simon MSS	the papers of the first Viscount Simon, in the possession of his son, the second Viscount Simon.
J. A. Spender MSS	in the British Museum.
Stansgate MSS	the surviving correspondence, press cuttings, and autobiographical notes of William Wedgwood Benn, first Viscount Stansgate, in the possession of his widow, Lady Stansgate.
J. St Loe Strachey MSS	in the Beaverbrook Library, formerly in the offices of *The Spectator*.
H. A. Taylor MSS	transcript of his interview with J. Ramsay MacDonald, and press cuttings relating to the publication of Mr Taylor's biographies of Robert Donald and Lord Brentford.
Charles Trevelyan MSS	the correspondence and diaries of Sir Charles and Lady Trevelyan, in the Library, University of Newcastle-upon-Tyne.
Harry Verney MSS	the papers of Sir Harry Verney Bt, in his own possession.
Henry Wilson MSS	the diaries of Field-Marshal Sir Henry Wilson Bt, in the possession of his nephew, Major Cyril Wilson.
T. McKinnon Wood MSS	a box of letters in the possession of his daughter-in-law, Mrs H. McKinnon Wood.

I have also examined the papers of Robert Donald, Lord Gladstone, Sir Donald Maclean, Lord Merrivale, and Lord Templewood, and a selection of correspondence from Lord Noel-Buxton's papers; these collections have yielded little evidence directly relevant to this study. Lord Long's papers at the Wiltshire County Record Office contain nothing of importance for the period 1914–15.

The papers of Lord Addison, Lord Birkenhead, Lord Curzon, Lord Esher, Lord Hankey, Geoffrey Howard, Lord Lloyd, Lord Lucas, C. F. G. Masterman, Lord Reading, Lord Riddell, and Lord Selborne were closed to scholars while this book was in preparation.

I have been unable to examine the papers of Lord Morley and Francis Hirst which are in the custody of Mr A. F. Thompson of Wadham College, Oxford; but Mr Thompson assures me that they contain nothing which is directly relevant to this book. Nor have I seen the papers of Lord Buckmaster or John Redmond. The papers of Sir Charles Hobhouse and Colonel Repington cannot be traced.

Mr A. J. P. Taylor has kindly allowed me to quote from the Frances Stevenson Diary, an edition of which he is preparing for publication by Hutchinson under the title *Lloyd George*: A Diary by Frances Stevenson.

Index

Gardiner, Alfred G., Liberal journalist, 18, 34
Garvin, J. L., editor of *The Observer*, 108 n, 228, 240, 244; on Lloyd George, 223
George V, King, 26, 31, 74, 81, 86, 87, 98, 100, 114, 252, 296, 298, 301; takes pledge of abstinence during war, 211, 213–14; advises Kitchener to stay at War Office, 281; and separate Ministry of Munitions, 281, 297
George, William, 61, 295 and n
Germany: declaration of war on Russia, 92; ultimatum to Belgium, 101; Britain's ultimatum to her, 101
Gladstone, Viscount, 156 n
Gladstone, W. E., 16, 98, 115
Glenconner, Lord, 245
Globe, The, 124
Gollin, Professor Alfred M., 290 n, 298; on issue of freedom versus control, 264, 268
Gooch, G. P., 60
Goschen, Sir Edward, British Ambassador in Berlin, 81, 82
Gosling, Harry, 181
Grey, Sir Edward, Bt, Foreign Secretary, 16–17, 35, 39, 41, 49, 55, 58, 59, 65–7, 75, 77, 79, 84–95, 98, 108, 109 n, 111 n, 112–15, 127, 136, 139, 160, 174, 185, 193, 240, 242, 244, 254, 258, 264–5, 272, 300; Liberal Foreign Affairs Group urge neutrality on him, 35–8; and Britain's obligation to France, 44–5, 51–2; his policy, 50–3; lack of candour about pre-war policy, 51; and Cabinet 'anti-war group', 52–3; rejects German bid for British neutrality, 81–2; warning to German Ambassador on neutrality of Belgium, 92; and decisive Cabinet of Aug. 2, 92–5; speech in Commons (Aug. 3), 42 n, 43–8, 123; and Belgian resistance, 99–100; issues ultimatum to Germany, 101; tribute to Lloyd George, 105–6; on resignations of Burns and Morley, 58 n
and dispatch of B.E.F., 121; attacked by Ramsay MacDonald, 125; relations with Opposition, 158; 162; wartime strains and failing eyesight, 165–6, 228, 234; desire for

voluntary agreement with workers, 207; alleged attempt to dislodge him, 227–8; as possible Prime Minister, 267–8; remains at Foreign Office in coalition, 268, 281
Griffith, Ellis, Liberal M.P., 223 n, 266
Guest, F. E. ('Freddie'), Liberal M.P., 132, 133, 248
Guinn, Dr Paul, 298
Gulland, John W., Liberal Chief Whip, 131–4, 204, 251, 252, 269, 275, 277, 292, 293; and the drink problem, 211, 214
Gwynne, H. A., editor of *The Morning Post*, 221; letter on coalition (May 1915), 250

HAIG, FIELD-MARSHAL SIR DOUGLAS, 101 n
Haldane, Viscount: Lord Chancellor, 17, 59, 77–9, 101 n, 112 n, 136, 152, 160, 174, 241, 245, 249, 307; and British intervention (1914), 55, 83, 84; on German mode of attack on France, 71–2; and use of expeditionary force, 88 and n, 89 n, 90; and measures to avert financial panic, 91; and dispatch of B.E.F., 121; relations with Opposition, 158; on compulsory military service, 222; campaign of vilification against him, 234, 272; dismissed by Asquith, 222, 263, 271–2, 277, 279, 281; receives Order of Merit, 281
Hamilton, Duchess of, 237
Hammond, J. Lawrence, 65
Hankey, Lt.-Col. (retd) Maurice, 14, 154, 160, 172 n, 186, 189, 196 n, 234, 281; and preparations for war, 80; and internment of aliens, 143–5, 264; proposes burning and blighting of German crops, 188; proposals for improved administration, 291–2
Harcourt, Lewis ('Loulou'): Colonial Secretary, 17, 92, 136, 172, 251; and British intervention (1914), 54, 56, 60, 66, 71, 82–3, 95, 97, 103, 112–14, 116; and measures to avert financial panic, 91; remonstrates with Grey over 'Triple Entente', 112–13; ill-health and wartime strains, 165–7
Hardinge of Penshurst, Lord, 114